UNDAUNTED

Life's Toughest Battles Are Not Always Fought In A War Zone

[Signed: BUD/S CLASS #215 EXCELSIOR!]

Christopher Mark Heben
with Dustin S. Klein

Undaunted: life's toughest battles are not always fought in a war zone © 2015 Christopher Mark Heben

All rights are reserved.

No part of this publication may be reproduced, distributed or transmitted in any form or by any means, including photocopying, recording or other digital or mechanical methods, without the prior written permission of the author, except in the cases of fair use as permitted by U.S. and international copyright laws.

For permission requests, please submit in writing to the publisher at the address below:

Published by:
SEAL Team Consulting
3960 Medina Rd
Fairlawn, OH 44333

Cover design: Chris Heben and Randy Wood
Interior: Randy Wood

Printed in the United States of America

ISBN: 978-0-9966090-0-5

Library of Congress Control Number: 2015913303

DEDICATION

This book is dedicated to my amazing son Mason: May he be bigger, faster, stronger, smarter, and more successful than I will ever be, and may his life story eclipse any bedtime story he has ever read or ever been told.

I'd also like to thank my spirited and stellar lady: She is my rudder, my compass and my North Star.

Lastly, this book could not be possible without all the amazing and dedicated Patriots that I have gone into harms way with and the support personnel who keep all the wheels turning while we're doing it.

God Bless America!

—C.M.H

To Laura, Sam, Cole and Mollie.

With love, DSK

ACKNOWLEDGEMENTS

I ran a Patriotic quote contest for my fans and followers, wherein, if one lucky individual came up with an original patriotic quote that I liked, I would publish it in my book. Well, after sorting through well over a thousand entries, I was able to narrow them down to four winners. Most were not original quotes, but I was still very moved and inspired by everything I read. The lucky four are published below.

Congratulations to these Super Patriots:

Courage is moving towards danger when there is an avenue of escape. True patriotism requires such courage

—Bradley Mead

A person should not be judged by what they have, but what they have given.

—Neil Hoskins

May we think of freedom not as the right to do as we please, but as the opportunity to do what's right.

—Hosea Herman

There is no service too small, too minor to make it unimportant.

For each act of service, each sacrifice made in the spirit of liberty honors those who came before in a way that gratitude cannot.

—Helen Walters

CONTENTS

Dedication 5
Acknowledgements 6
Chapter 1 9
Chapter 2 23
Chapter 3 39
Chapter 4 53
Chapter 5 77
Chapter 6 89
Chapter 7 107
Chapter 8 125
Chapter 9 143
Chapter 10 159
Chapter 11 179
Chapter 12 195
Chapter 13 219
Chapter 14 239
Chapter 15 261
Chapter 16 273
Chapter 17 295
Chapter 18 313
Chapter 19 323
Chapter 20 341
Chapter 21 367
About the Authors 377

CHAPTER 1

"I'VE NEVER BOUGHT INTO THE BANALITY OF BLACK AND WHITE... RATHER, I CHOOSE TO LIVE MY LIFE IN THE GRAY, MASHING THE PERSONAL WITH THE PROFESSIONAL AND DEFINING MYSELF BY WHAT I LOVE, NOT SIMPLY BY WHAT I DO...MY WORK IS MY PASSION AND MY LIFE IS MY WORK. IN THIS WAY, I AVOID PARALYZING FEAR AND AM CONTINUOUSLY ABLE TO PUSH PAST MY COMFORT ZONES. THUS, I HAVE REMAINED UNDAUNTED."

—CHRISTOPHER MARK HEBEN

My buddy Dan Kohlstrohm dropped me off at the Ouagadougou airport. Only a week previously, I had surgically removed his left testicle after he sustained a sexual intercourse-related trauma to that area. But more on that story later. That was just one of the many unexpected events that peppered my most recent 60-day rotation as the Director of Medical Operations and Mission Planning for the United States, Joint Special Operations Aviation Detachment (JSOAD) in North Africa. As a former U.S. Navy SEAL, I was now a sub-contractor for Blackwater Worldwide on this combined Department of Defense/State Department mission, and we operated out of a safe house in Ouagadougou, Burkina Faso, a small, landlocked West African nation that is one of the least developed countries in the world.

Working for Blackwater certainly provided its share of moments—from defending and evacuating embassies under attack to scraping friendlies off the ground after being blown up by land mines—but nothing had ever prepared me for the welcome I was about to receive back in the United States.

I was exhausted and finally heading back home to re-group for the next month before I had to man up and do it all over again. This had been my schedule for the last year or so—launching from our safe house in Ouagadougou, Burkina Faso to operate in more than a dozen different cleptocratic African nations. Nations with names like Mali, Morocco, the Central African Republic, Benin, Ghana, Guinea, Nigeria, Niger, Chad, and a few others I can't mention due to still-classified directives. We were there to lay down the initial groundwork, leg work and, if necessary, the smack down for USSOCOM's AQIM initiative: al-Qaeda in the Islamic Maghreb. The pace was hectic, the pay was good, but the price could be very high. I was ready to go home.

Between sitting in terminals and the time spent in-flight, the total transit time from Ouagadougou to my home in Cleveland, Ohio, would take roughly 22 hours and include stops in Paris, France, and Atlanta, Georgia. I didn't know it at the time, but this particular trip was going to take about 1,368 hours to complete—give or take a dozen hours or so. It was March 18, 2008, and it was the last day of my so-called-normal life—or at least as normal as your life can be when you're a former U.S. Navy SEAL and still an active member of the Special Ops community as a private military contractor (PMC) for the 'evil empire' known as Blackwater. Yes that was my normal: We kicked a metric-shit-ton of ass around the globe, and we didn't care what anyone thought about it.

The day started out as any other when I was on this particular assignment. I was leaving Ouagadougou, the capital of Burkina Faso, located 12 degrees north of the equator. Even at 9 a.m., the temperature quickly reaches a semi-steamy 90 degrees Fahrenheit. Thanks to Dan and my wardrobe sharing, I had only one suitcase, but was happy to have a porter haul it to the check-in area for me. Hell, Blackwater was paying me $11,000 every two weeks, so I figured I could afford the luxury. Besides, at least the porter, a kid named Salaam, wasn't perched on the side of a road holding an empty tomato can, reciting *Al-Fatiha* from the *Qur'an* and begging me for my money.

In truth, this 'beggars' money is really a misnomer. Every dime collected goes straight to the local *Madrasa*, where it is used to promote the jingoistic teachings of Islam through the two basic courses of study, known as *Hifz*, the memorization of the Qur'an to produce a *Hafiz*, and *Alim*, which leads the student to become an accepted scholar in the community. The Muslims have been very successful in fostering their religion worldwide because, unlike the U.S., they don't separate Church from State. Religion is law in Muslim nations and law is religion. If you ask me, Islam is a political movement disguised as a religion. Period.

Islam was taking big chunks of real estate in Africa, and this is what we were sent there to mitigate. To the new guys rotating in, my message was clear: Don't give money to the tomato-can crew! If you do, you are essentially contributing to your own demise. I always told my men: Don't feel sorry for these kids, even for a nanosecond, for they were born into this filth. It's not like their families lost millions on Wall Street and they were then forced, overnight, to beg on the streets in order to survive.

I liked Ouagadougou, or 'Ouga' as we all called it. Ouga gained its independence from France in 1960 and today remains heavily French influenced. There was always someplace deliciously cultured and captivating from a culinary standpoint to make it interesting to grab some eats and have a few drinks. Besides, there was never a shortage of Peace Corps gals wandering around. We dudes in the 'War Corps' called them *targets of opportunity*. In fact, for two groups who had diametrically opposed missions, we sure got along just fine. I always enjoyed singing a few songs for any number of them at the local piano bar. This particular skill set made for many a sexual slam dunk on the Dark Continent. Hell, I'm a frogman, and we are known for embracing and living out many mantras, but the one we favor the most is 'Drink, fight, fuck!' On any given day in Ouga, and Africa in general, all of these were a possibility.

In typical NGO fashion, the Peace Corps higher-ups lived in opulence and worked in an ivory tower while the worker bees slugged it out in squalor. Yet, there never seemed to be a shortage of the 'bees' the world over. Reputedly, the Peace Corps was a major role player historically in the gathering of intelligence for use by the U.S. government. Judging by what I saw during my time in the Special Ops community, I'm pretty damn sure this isn't the case anymore.

Burkina Faso has an interesting history. As with most African countries north of the equator, it was a French colony and then protectorate. Most everyone who lives there speaks proper French. This was very helpful in order for me to expedite my grasp of the beautiful French language. And of course, spending time with that wonderful French lady, Catherine, from the French embassy, and her two amazing daughters, didn't hurt things either. They were great people, and I still speak with them today.

I'm always amazed when I hear my fellow Americans proclaim that the French are cowards or the French are snobbish, especially when they've never even met one. My experiences with the French have always been very favorable. They are passionate people who crave culture and truly enjoy one another to the fullest. Their love of art is eclipsed only by their passion for life. Their lust for wine is only eclipsed by their passion for cigarettes and, thankfully, their consumption of the former makes up nicely for their inhalation of latter. It's almost like having two addictions that are mutually beneficial, but take either one of them away and you run the risk of an early demise.

But I digress: After more than 60 days of 24/7 operations, more than 150 flight hours, two critical injury rescue missions, one U.S. Embassy evacuation, and a slew of other JSOAD missions of general ass-kickery, it was time to rotate home. I was always sad to leave Africa, no matter what happened there. The place has a way of growing on you like a creeping vine or, better yet, a fungal infection. It just hits you one day and you realize that the people and the province have incorporated themselves into the fabric of your being. Not a bad thing, but this time I was more than ready to go home. Besides, I thought, I would be back before I knew it. I always was.

The flight from Ouga to Paris was uneventful and, as always, I enjoyed flirting with the professional Air France flight attendants. Yes, I even batted my eyes as I conversed with the male version of that variety, as they were only too willing to get me another glass of red wine if and when I asked. Yes, I was bilingual, but I can assure you that linguistics was as far as my duality ever went. You see, as a Navy SEAL, we are taught to manipulate our environment in order to achieve victory. I was doing just that—one Beaujolais at a time!

After landing in Paris and un-ass'ing the plane at Charles de Gaulle Airport, I ravenously attacked a major amount of food at a buffet-style establishment in the concourse. And, since I had been to France more than a dozen times, I didn't feel the need to venture out of the airport—despite the fact that I had over three hours to kill before my flight departed to Atlanta. I will say that the French are in no way anywhere close to offering the grandiose gluttony and palatial palatine products found at buffets in the United States, but all that meant was that I had to take a few more trips to feel stateside satiated. I did just that, then sat for two hours sipping espresso and people watching as I let the bolus of food in my belly do its thing.

By now I was refreshed and I actually looked forward to getting back on a plane. I was going to be seeing my son when I landed, and that always made me smile! During the last flight I was seated next to a very large African woman who had given me her permission to use her jumbo-sized shoulder, and arm area, as a comfy pillow, and catch a few Zs. The woman had explained to me that she had dual citizenship in Burkina Faso and France, and she was extremely wealthy. This had explained her state of corpulence, as most Burkinabes were built like Flo Jo. She was built more like Oprah, circa 1992, plus 100 or so extra pounds. Comfy and nice, she never said anything about the puddle of drool I left on her arm. Maybe she didn't see it or feel it. Maybe the speed at which I fell asleep caused her to have pity on me. Either way, never look a gift horse in the mouth, especially when it's a Clydesdale. In all seriousness, I was quite thankful for this wonderful lady's whopping anatomy for providing me with a plenteous pillow. I fell asleep quicker than a narcoleptic on NyQuil and slept better than a coma patient.

My upcoming leg back to the U.S. would be a breeze—flying First Class always was. Besides, I had a foolproof over-the-counter (OTC) pharmaceutical plan to make the time pass: 1) Pop a Celebrex to combat one form of inflammation. 2) Pop an 800-mg Ibuprofen to combat another. 3) Pop an aspirin to keep the blood thin. 4) Dissolve half an Ambien under my tongue to get immediate R.E.M. sleep and help hit the reset button on the last two months of life. 5) Lastly, instruct the flight attendants to leave me the hell alone.

Once I was settled in, I promptly laid the seat flat, initiated the plan, and racked out for the next six hours of the 10-hour flight. It's what I always did. And it's a damn good thing I did, because when we landed at Hartsfield-Jackson International Airport in Atlanta, things went to shit PDQ—pretty damn quick!

I waited patiently in line with other travelers who had disembarked the plane, and then handed my passport to a U.S. Department of Homeland Security, Immigration and Customs Enforcement agent.

He looked at my passport and then looked up at me.

The gentleman eyeballed me like this for a few moments to compare the photo in his hand with the man who stood in front of him. They didn't exactly match. At this time, I was probably 225 pounds of sheer muscle, with long shoulder-length hair, crowbar facial hair, and a deep, dark 'Afri-tan.' I didn't exactly look like a Middle Eastern terrorist, but I certainly didn't look like a Midwesterner from Ohio, or the clean-cut, clean-shaven guy on my passport photo.

After another long moment, the agent decided I was indeed me and he swiped my passport. And that's when it made a noise that I'd never heard before.

"BEEEEEEEEEP!"

Automatically, my internal alarms started ringing.

The agent nervously looked up. "Sir, are you in any kind of legal trouble right now?" he frantically asked.

I hesitated for a moment and then replied, "I'm in the middle of an ongoing case. Why?"

"There's a bench warrant out for your arrest," he said. "I'm going to have to get the Port Authority guys here to take you into custody."

I noticed a couple of large security guys approaching immigration, quickly, and taking up positions around me.

Despite this, I remained calm. I was in the middle of an airport in the United States of America. This was no time to go Jason Bourne on anyone. Besides, this had to be a mistake.

"Really?" I asked.

"Yes, sir. You're going to need to go with these two gentlemen. Now."

All of my training and experience had taught me that right now cooperation was the best option: Find out what was going on and deal with it head on. Make no sudden moves. Do nothing to give these guys a reason to hurt themselves on your body.

"OK then gentleman," I said. "Let's bounce. Let's do this."

As we walked to the Port Authority office a realization swept over me. The judge in my pending court case had taken action against me. My attorney, who knew when I was arriving back in the U.S., hadn't done a thing to give me a heads up about what was transpiring.

I followed the officers into their office. Slowly. So as to not give them any reason to make a move against me. Ever since 9/11, our country has been on hyper-alert in the airports. And rightly so, so indeed, cooperation was the surest way to get through this quickly—or so I thought.

Once inside the office I politely, but assertively, asked what the hell was going on.

"Mr. Heben, Judge Vincent Culotta from Lake County, Ohio, issued a bench warrant for your arrest," one of the officers explained. "You're to be taken into custody and are scheduled to be extradited from Atlanta back to Lake County, Ohio, via the U.S. Marshals Service."

I shook my head. Of course the shit-bag judge ordered a bench warrant for me. Of course he contracted with the U.S. Marshals Service. Of course I am to be taken into custody. That asshole had it out for me from the get-go. Apparently, being public enemy number one is all it's cracked up to be!

In actuality, it shouldn't have gone down this way. It really shouldn't have. I had made a dumb mistake a year earlier by writing three forged prescriptions for two buddies of mine for Class III anabolic steroids. I was lead to believe that they both had a medical issue that warranted such prescribing. Regardless, I probably would have done it anyway because they were men that I respected. To be clear: I was not selling or trafficking drugs, nor am I a drug addict. I don't even use drugs. I had tried to do two friends a favor and it ended up costing me everything— including my voluntary and immediate surrender of my physician assistant medical license. Again, no good deed goes unpunished. While

UNDAUNTED

my case was being adjudicated I was allowed to travel back and forth to Africa for Blackwater to earn a living. I was a former U.S. Navy SEAL and I never back down from a fight, and I was certainly not a flight risk. Less than 24-hours ago I had a top-secret security clearance and the ability to be armed to the teeth. But now, here I was, in custody. It's ironic how quickly things can change.

I should have seen this coming. On the day I left for this most recent rotation, my attorney had called in a panic. It was a cold February day and I was standing in line at the Akron-Canton Airport waiting to board my plane. My bags were in the belly of the plane and I knew I shouldn't have answered the phone. But it was my attorney, and I was sure it was something important about my case.

"Chris, the prosecutor just called me," he explained. "He doesn't want you to leave the country. He wants you to appear in court tomorrow."

"I'm boarding a plane right now. What am I supposed to do? I've got a multi-million dollar government operation contingent upon my presence. They're expecting me there. I have to go."

"Chris," he said. "Don't do it. The prosecutor was adamant. He wants you to appear in court tomorrow."

I was annoyed. These guys had given me permission to travel. They knew I was working for Blackwater, which was being contracted by the Central Intelligence Agency of the United States of America and the Joint Special Operations Command to support and conduct clandestine special operations missions in Africa. It wasn't like I was taking a vacation. And it wasn't as if I could, or would, call Blackwater from the airport and say, 'Hey, I can't make it there. You're screwed.' I had an obligation and I was going to fulfill it. That's what Navy SEALs are trained to do—follow through, no matter what. Once we have our mission, we're undaunted.

"You're my attorney," I said, in an aggravated-but-calm tone. "You need to handle it. You have my address at the safe house where I'm going to be in Burkina Faso. Give that information to the court and let them know I'll be back in the U.S. in a couple months. Get an extension. I'm doing work for our government. It shouldn't be that hard. If they want to roll up on me there, tell them to roll hard and to bring a lot of guns."

I was pissed! They had over a month to let me know they wanted me to appear for something. They knew my schedule. And now that I was in H-Hour, they could kiss my ass.

And so I hung up, boarded my plane, and headed off to Africa.

Here it was, 60-days later, and apparently my attorney had failed to do his job. Not only should I have never been required to be in court within 12 hours, but there never should have been a warrant issued for my arrest. There's a fine line, in every profession, between being non-partisan, proficient and professional, and being a pussy. The court was not being the former, and my attorney was being the latter!

"OK, officers. Is there anything I can do about this? I'm sure this is all just a big misunderstanding that can be cleared up with a couple phone calls," I casually asked. But I could feel my blood starting to boil.

The men looked at each other. One nodded. "Sure. You can try to call your attorney. He can call the judge and see if he'll rescind the bench warrant. If that happens, we can let you go. Hell, call anyone you think can help you."

Then the officers paused for a moment. The other one cleared his throat and said, "Look, we looked at your record. You're like an American Hero. If we don't handcuff you, you won't try to kill us, right?"

"Guys," I said, "you're doing your job. I'm just trying to do mine. I understand the predicament you are in and I appreciate that you understand mine. Thank you for the opportunity to pick up this fumble and advance the ball if possible."

They put me in a room and I began making phone calls. First, I called my ex-wife, Michelle, who is the mother of my son, Mason. The two of them were supposed to meet me at the airport in Cleveland in a couple hours. Clearly, that was no longer going to happen. Michelle knew nothing about my legal troubles. I hadn't told her. I figured I would get through it, end up on probation, and life would go back to normal. Now I knew that wasn't going to happen and I would need to come clean with her.

After several failed attempts to reach my ex-wife I finally left a message: "Tried to call you," I said. "Some stuff to tell you. Not going to make it to the airport, so no need for you and Mason to pick me up." I really needed to hear her voice at that moment and the fact that I didn't was almost worse than being a sick child and wanting your mother. If anyone would understand, it would be Michelle. She is an amazing woman and a wonderful mother and a good friend still to this day.

Having failed in the previous comms mission, I then called my attorney.

"I told you not to leave the country," he said.

Great advice in hindsight, but not very helpful right now. I wanted to reach through the phone, throttle him, and then choke slam the shit out of him for doing absolutely nothing in the last 60 days to help me.

"Get me out of this," I said. "Call the judge and the prosecutor. Didn't you get in touch with them months ago and let them know what was going on?"

"Yes, but they were adamant about you appearing in court and not leaving the country. The judge sees what you did as direct defiant action against him."

"Well, it would have been nice for you to warn me what was going on. I would have never re-entered the U.S. this way. Now, I'm in custody in the Atlanta airport."

"He's not going to do anything," my attorney said. "You snubbed your nose at him. But I'll make some calls."

"I get it," I said. "He's pissed off. But I can be in front of him tomorrow morning with you there. If he wants to slam me in jail then, fine. He could have his chance in 12 hours. Just get me the ability to get on a plane back home."

"I'll try," he said in a tone that indicated he was already defeated. I held little hope.

Unfortunately, as I suspected, my attorney's attempts were unsuccessful. He tried to reach the judge, the bailiff, the prosecutor, anybody and everybody who could help rescind the bench warrant and get me home. But my fate was sealed. I firmly believe they were instructed to be incommunicado with anyone from my camp. Made sense: I kicked Culotta in the balls, flipped him off, and snubbed my nose at him and his court when I got on that plane in February. He had many weeks to figure out his revenge, he enacted it, and now he was surely going to enjoy it. Me? Not so much. Not cool, but I did get it. And, I got it.

The officers in Atlanta, on the other hand, were pretty cool. They let me put my luggage on the plane to Cleveland and arrange for my uncle Tom to pick it up for me from Cleveland Hopkins International Airport. In the meantime, two Fulton County Sheriff deputies were dispatched to pick me up from the airport and take me to jail.

When they arrived, they had a different appearance and a different demeanor than the Port Authority officers. They were 20-years older, 40-pounds heavier, and looked like they beat their wives for fun. Right away they handcuffed me.

"Could you guys at least put a jacket over the cuffs so I'm not walking in public in an airport with handcuffs?" I asked. The only way it could have been worse is if I'd had one of those Hannibal Lector masks on and was being wheeled away on a dolly!

But they weren't having any of that. I was a 'tough guy' and I looked like a tough guy, and anytime a cop can put handcuffs on someone and take them on a perp walk in public, they're going to relish the opportunity. Not being one to let them down, I played it up and actually levied some menacing scowls on some people. I was always taught to be in the moment, and that was the only way I could think of to stay amused with my current predicament and with these two big badges.

The deputies shoved me into a car and drove me to Fulton County Jail, where I was painstakingly processed and dumped into an overcrowded holding tank for the next 18 hours.

It was a dirty, nasty and stinky place. Designed to hold about 10 people, there were 25 of us in it that day. By now, I was noticeably pissed off and aggravated. Sure, I brought some of this on myself, but there had to have been something my attorney could have done to have prevented this from ever happening.

Although I certainly didn't need it, my gruff appearance and please-come-fuck-with-me attitude, provided a built-in safety zone around me in the tank. I had spent a lot of time in Africa at the safe house working out, doing MMA, kettle bells, riding bikes and hitting the weights. When you're not involved in a direct operation there's enough down time to keep in shape—great shape. To say I was cut would have been an understatement. So, between my SEAL swagger, long hair, crow bar facial hair and dark tan, nobody wanted to be anywhere near me. In fact, they all pretty much just looked at me and said to themselves, "Nope. I'm not going there." Lastly, and I did not know it at the time, there was an international heroin trafficker that was taken into custody the night before. I would later learn that a lot of the inmates thought I was him because we looked very similar. In fact, so much so, I was approached over a dozen times by inmates offering me their work services upon their release. So, it is true that the U.S. prison system is a great networking establishment for societal ne'er-do-wells. Yet, we continue to build more. Very interesting.

Finally, after nearly 18 hours in the tank, I was taken to the pod in the jail where I would spend the next two weeks waiting for the U.S. Marshals to pick me up. It was here that I was able to make my first real phone call.

With a lump in my throat, I called Michelle and told her what was going on. I asked her not to tell Mason any of the details. Needless to say, it didn't make for a very good conversation, but I was comforted by the fact that she was now in the know and that she would not be worried about my whereabouts. I couldn't even begin to let my brain engage on the subject of how crushed my 5-year-old son would be when he learned he would not be seeing me anytime soon. Apparently, he was marking the days off on his calendar. Little did I know that this would be the very same technique I would use during my nearly 60 days under the auspices of the U.S. Marshal's extradition service. Beyond that, it was also this phone call that was the tipping point with respect to Michelle and I ever getting back together.

But all this was a temporary respite to what had been a long, unexpected journey. Such is the life of those of us who work in the Special Ops community. We don't have the luxury of living lives that are black and white. Instead, for us everything becomes a shade of gray, and we learn how to navigate through it. You either become undaunted in everything you do or you die trying. Me? I've always preferred life. And that's the key to my story—always find a way to not just survive, but to dominate!

CHAPTER 2

> "WHEN THINGS ARE SHITTY, TAKE COMFORT IN KNOWING IT CAN ALWAYS GET SHITTIER. WHEN IT CAN'T GET ANY SHITTIER, TAKE SOLACE IN THE FACT THAT THINGS CAN ONLY IMPROVE. REMEMBER, ADVERSITY IS A FACT OF LIFE. IT CAN'T BE CONTROLLED. BUT WHAT WE CAN CONTROL IS HOW WE REACT TO IT. I CHOOSE TO KICK ASS EVERY DAY. AND I CHALLENGE YOU TO DO THE SAME!"
>
> —CHRISTOPHER MARK HEBEN

Navy SEAL training is about as brutal a process as any human being can withstand—physically and mentally—but it's what should be expected at what I call our nation's 'Captain America Factory.' Those of us who survive the experience earn the honor and distinction of being counted among an elite group. In fact, since President John F. Kennedy initiated the SEAL Teams in January 1962, less than 17,000 U.S. Navy SEALs have ever been created. I say 'created' because, in essence, one is re-born and re-made during the course of the SEAL forging process known as Basic Underwater Demolition/SEAL training (BUD/S). Navy SEALs are some of the most resilient and resourceful warriors in the world. We are inserted into the worst possible environments and situations, and must be prepared for whatever happens, no matter how unexpected. The trials and tribulations faced during training are necessary to forge minds and bodies of steel.

A few lessons from my SEAL training stand out more than others, but one of the most important ones that I carried out with me into the field was one I learned from sports and then re-learned at Navy Boot Camp before BUD/S: You take care of your team—no matter what. My Recruit Division Commanders; BMC Charles Plyler and OS1 Tom Trevino,

UNDAUNTED

hammered the importance of teamwork into me and my shipmates during Basic Training at NTC Great Lakes Chicago. Both of these men made it very clear to us all, from the get-go, that without teamwork, battles could never be won. The concept of teamwork was further instilled, distilled and quantified during BUD/S training in Coronado, San Diego. Here, my classmates and I were taught that each of us had to be individually squared away so that we could deliver the best possible package of ourselves to our team. This is an important distinction. If you're not squared away personally, you won't be able to offer your best. And if you fall short, your team will suffer. God help your team if you make them suffer because of your lack of preparation. "Are you physically and mentally prepared for war today? If not, you should be!" Signs like this are carved in wood and can be found hanging everywhere at BUD/S, and, as I would later find out; in the SEAL Team areas.

Another lesson that stuck with me is that small unit integrity is critical. Trust is non-negotiable. If you can't trust your teammate, and he can't trust you, you're both destined to fail. Your life and his life depends on this mutual integrity.

So in March 2008, when my friend Dan arrived at the airport in Ouagadougou in very bad shape, I didn't hesitate to turn to my training to rectify the situation. Dan didn't hesitate to put his trust in me and ultimately, it was our mutual trust that saved his life.

At the time, I was Director of Medical Operations and Mission Planning for the Joint Special Operations Aviation Detachment (JSOAD), AQIM Mission in North Africa, which meant I handled all medical operations for the team and was Blackwater's most competent medical authority on the continent. I also handled logistical planning for our group, which quickly became another one of my specialties. During kinetic operations, I was the guy charged with developing the plan.

One of our safe houses was in Burkina Faso, tucked away in the city of Ouagadougou, or Ouga (*wa-ga*), as we called it. The safe house was nice and comfortable. To go along with a very generous kill zone—and the fact that our nearest neighbor was a large prison with a massive compound—we had individual rooms, a swimming pool, a weight room and satellite internet and TV. The individual rooms and the satellite internet sure came in handy for surfing porn, or so I was told. It also made keeping in touch with friends and family back at home a whole lot easier. The U.S. government, and U.S. Special Operations Command in particular, realized that a happy and connected soldier was a hardened and effective one. Blackwater made sure to adhere to these self-evident truths.

Until now, the current deployment had been only mildly challenging. We assisted in the evacuation of the U.S. Embassy in Chad, after Sudanese and Chadian rebels stormed the city and began shooting up everything in sight. Additionally, we managed to scrape two injured Malian soldiers off the desert floor and take them to a higher echelon of care. Land Cruiser versus land mine never works out to well for the vehicle's occupants. Other than that, I'd had a pretty uneventful deployment and was anticipating my usual three-to-seven-day turnover period, where I could sit with my replacement Dan, compare notes, and get a little R&R. The overlap was designed to create a smooth hand over and to ensure the mission's goals would continue without interruption.

I was looking forward to Dan's arrival. With all the legal trouble I was facing before I left, spending some time hanging with him before I went back would be awesome. We'd set aside a full week—we would complete the hand over; then have some fun around town. What could go wrong?

At 0600 hours local time, Dan's plane arrived in Ouagadougou. He suspected something was physically wrong with him as he was getting ready to head to the airport. Shortly after leaving home, he had tremendous groin and testicular pain, but he pushed through it. After he was airborne, that strange pain in his groin and testes got gradually worse. Yet, even he wasn't aware of the extent of the injury with which he was traveling: Over the course of his 24-hour transit from Bradley International Airport to Ouagadougou, Dan's scrotum had enlarged to more than the size of a grapefruit. Not even his first-class seat afforded him any comfort. Dan was certainly not free to roam about the cabin.

I arrived at the airport around the same time Dan texted me, "Meet me outside the baggage claim area."

UNDAUNTED

As I pulled up to the curb I promptly spotted him and it was obvious that something was wrong. Dan looked stressed and was walking toward the car like an 80-year old with a broken hip. Like Moses parting the Red Sea, the Burkinabes that witnessed the scene got out of his way as he dragged himself toward my vehicle.

I got out to help and, as I got closer, immediately recognized further signs of distress: Yes, Dan was ashen white, but he was also shaking and sweating. It was obvious he was in extreme pain. The early onset of shock was in full effect.

"What the fuck is going on, bro?" I asked.

"Fuck me...just help me get in the car and I'll give you the 411," he muttered. "I'll explain everything."

Dan put his arm around me. I got him down the steps, and then eased him into the car. He slumped back against the side of the door as we pulled out of the airport; then unbuckled the belt on his pants and popped open the button and unzipped the zipper.

"Hold on a second!" I half chuckled in protest. "I haven't seen you in two months, but this isn't what I had in mind for a reunion." You see, in the Spec Ops community, there is always an undertone of feigned homosexuality. It's not that we are haters of that lifestyle, but only that we are so close to one another that we have to laugh about the fact that 99 percent of us aren't gay. More on this later. But at that point in time, I knew Dan wasn't even remotely in a joking mood.

"This is what the fuck is happening...." Dan said, and then pulled down his pants. I nearly leapt out of the driver's seat with shock at what he showed me: His nut sack was enormous, engorged with blood, it was the size of a grapefruit; a red, purple, black and blue grapefruit.

"Holy shit! How in the holy fuck did that happen?"

"Exactly! Sex with Tiffany."

Apparently, in their zest to maximize the last few hours of time together before his 90-day deployment to relieve me, Dan and his pretty-but-very-thin (read: bony) wife decided to spend a few hours having extremely vigorous sex. According to Dan, in the process of their aggressive coupling, he and Tiffany's bodies repeatedly and forcefully collided to the point of causing him significant vascular damage to the vessels located in his left inguinal region, as well as in the scrotum. These collective insults caused blood to seep into the inguinal canal as well as inside the cavity surrounding and containing Dan's left testicle. It was a significant and painful injury. While Dan traveled, a steady flow of blood pulsed into his scrotum with every heartbeat. He was hurting, and the situation was getting more serious by the minute. Our normal, relaxed, meet-and-greet, and have a local beer near the airport, quickly turned into a hurried car ride back to the medical bay at the safe house as I listened to him talk about the nuances of acquiring the injury. What would have been a normal conversation about his sexual exploits, turned into a story that made my groin area hurt!

By the time we arrived, another half-hour had passed. Little did either of us know at that time that we were quite literally racing against the clock to save Dan's anatomy and quite possibly, save his life.

Special Operations Forces (SOF) medics are taught to constantly ask themselves, "How would I diagnose and treat this patient if they were my teammate, wife, child or parent, and I was alone, with no assistance, evacuation or consultation, in an isolated environment, armed only with the most basic of medical tools?"

As a SOF medic and physician assistant/surgeon assistant with a Master's degree, I know that answering this question often means breaking with the conservative paradigms of medicine. But those are the risks you have to take when you're out in the field and, especially when, you are the only person who stands between your buddy's life and certain death.

Over the years, I've come to recognize that the tenets of the SOF medical mission are a radical departure from those found in any U.S. medical facility. Daily, we SOF medics practice medicine in some of the most abhorrent conditions on earth, and we do it very well. Essentially, I believe the SOF medic has the following uber-medical mission: To provide immediate care with insubstantial resources in Spartan, hostile, demanding, and hermitic environments, caring for the patient for up to 72 hours until they can be delivered to a higher echelon of care.

My current experience with Dan fit this aforementioned mission homogeneously. My actions and reasoning for what happened next, and how I saved Dan's life, may be viewed as outrageous, inappropriate, and possibly even bordering on malpractice for those who work in traditional, conservative, hospital-based medical settings. However, you don't have to be someone who has struggled with life-and-death decisions in the austere environment of a SOF medic to truly appreciate the need for the actions I took. And, quite frankly, I really didn't and still don't, give a shit, what anyone else thinks. As a trained Navy SEAL Corpsman, and Physician Assistant, my only concern at the time was my teammate's safety.

As a SOF medic and Physician Assistant, I learned about orthopedics, bullet wounds, avulsions, concussions, general field trauma, and even some Veterinary care, but up until this moment I had never messed medically (or in any other fashion!) with somebody's scrotum. Immediately upon returning to the safe house and entering the small medical bay that doubled as my sleeping quarters, I thought that I would first take a shot at a conservative approach to treatment—for at least a few hours. I wanted to get Dan's legs up in the air ('toes above the nose') and start some anti-inflammatory drugs into his system to see if I could reduce the swelling and return some of the blood flow to systemic circulation and away from his injured area.

My approach included elevation, scrotal support, non-steroidal anti-inflammatory medication, icing, and pain control. By now, Dan was exhausted. The combination of the worsening medical condition and his lengthy travels had completely wiped him out. I gave him some Ambien to help him sleep while I treated him. At the very least, I figured my solution would buy some time for me to figure out my next move. I also informed my boss, Dave D., the Deputy Chief of Station, of the situation and my plans. Although I was carrying some small hope for a miracle cure, I was merely enacting a conservative plan in order to extend the ever-shrinking timeline before Dan's injury could possibly became fatal.

It was brutally hot that day—110 degrees—but despite the Sub-Saharan temperature, Dan was 'snowed and on ice' and 'chillin' a few feet away from me as I picked up my Africa cell phone and placed a call to the nurse at the U.S. Embassy in Ouagadougou. By now, more than six hours had passed since I began conservative treatment and it was clear what I was doing wasn't working. Dan may have been resting comfortably, but we had a big problem on our hands and more drastic measures were needed. Dan's scrotum had enlarged, by my estimation, about another 10 percent. His pain level was also increasing. I re-administered pain medication at Hour 4 instead of Hour 6 in order to knock it back down. If you don't stay ahead of the pain game, things get real ugly, real fast. If it weren't for the fact that Dan was a hardened former Green Beret, the situation would already been pretty damn ugly. He sucked it up until he reached me, and I will never forget that fact.

I asked the nurse if she had a number to a local urologist, and to my dismay, she said she had spoken with him earlier in the week and that he would be in France and not returning until Sunday afternoon or evening. Unfortunately, it was early afternoon on a Friday, about 1300 hours local time, and I needed a different plan.

To say the Internet is a wonderful thing is an understatement, especially in somewhere as desolate as Africa, and even more so when the satellite antenna and the satellite that delivers it to you are both actually functioning. On this day it was smooth sailing, or should I say smooth 'surfing', and I was able to visit a few medical reference sites in order to self-educate myself on Dan's specific trauma.

After reading a *Journal of Urology* article, I discovered that I should be using ultrasound to determine the true extent of his injury and administer the proper treatment. I had poked around Dan's scrotum about as much as he or I was comfortable with and was convinced I had stabilized him as much as possible. But I still wasn't sure of the full extent of his injury. Things were getting worse for him and tense for me. I quickly got back on the phone with the embassy nurse to discuss next steps.

By some divine blessing, Ouagadougou is home to the only ultrasound unit for about 250 square miles. It turns out they deliver a lot of babies. The unit was housed in a nearby obstetrics clinic and, luckily, the ultrasound tech was on duty. But I needed to hurry. The tech said he was only going to stay for another 20 minutes—even though we had an emergency situation—and unfortunately, the clinic was a 25-minute drive in good traffic. This was Ouagadougou, and the words 'good' and 'traffic' never went together. Ever. But I was undaunted, as always. Dan was a member of my team, and he needed help.

After breaking all the traffic laws the country had, I managed to make it to the clinic in just under 20 minutes. I justified my maniacal driving as being a medical emergency. And, aren't the traffic lights and signs in Africa merely just suggestions anyway? After more than a year on this continent, that was my takeaway—or at least my justification *de jour*.

I maneuvered Dan into the clinic. After the tech put his eyes back in his head and recovered from the sight of Dan's monstrous man bag, he fired up the ultrasound and proceeded to show me what I needed to see. None of it was good. In a nutshell, no pun intended, I saw the textbook words for Dan's injury right before my eyes in black and white: A "heterogeneous echo pattern of the testicular parenchyma with a loss of contour definition."

To add insult to injury, the tech also noted that the pocket of blood that had swelled due to the injury was now approximately 10 cm, and Dan's left testicle was unsalvageable. Luckily, the way the scrotum is designed there are two halves that are walled off from each other. It's the body's way of keeping them segregated. In Dan's case, it meant he wasn't going to lose both of them, if I could act quickly enough.

Our next course of action became clear: Decompress Dan. That meant, opening him up and getting the blood out of there. His pain had escalated and had become agonizing. Dan was barely holding himself together. That was saying a lot, as he was normally immune to pain. We had to move fast. I promptly gave him another round of pain medication and tried not to look as freaked out as I felt. Surgery was inevitable, and I needed further help to make sure I did the job correctly. I was going to have to learn how to become a battlefield urologist immediately, and the Internet seemed as good a place as any to get my training. It was 1430 hours local time, and the clock was still ticking against the two of us.

As SEALs, we have a saying: "We're experts at becoming experts." People think such a statement is conceited and cocky, but that couldn't be further from the truth. To us, that expression simply means that if we need to know everything there is to know about a certain subject by tomorrow morning, we are going to do everything we possibly can in order to make that happen. Anything. This is exactly what I did, except I didn't have a night to do it—I had about an hour.

I hit the Internet and perused several websites belonging to prestigious medical training institutions that shall remain nameless. On more than one occasion I was required to log in with a fictitious name and portray myself as a medical student who was currently attending that institution. Navy SEALs are taught not to let anything get in their way—especially when lives are at stake—so after about an hour and a half of reading and re-reading everything I could find on treatment, I was confident I knew what needed to be done. I was right when I initially thought about decompression. Dan needed me to immediately open his scrotum to drain out the old blood. Then he needed an orchiectomy. In other words, after relieving pressure, his testicle had to be removed. It wasn't what I wanted to do but it's what had to be done. I summoned the personal testicular fortitude necessary to perform the procedure and started preparations.

Next, I informed my boss Dave D. that I was going to use his office as a surgical suite. He didn't offer much push back. Dave even volunteered to be my 'first assist' on the case... that is, until I informed him that it would be his job to manually retract the penis in order to keep it out of the surgical field. As suspected, he promptly resigned from his self-appointed position and decided to be the DJ for the event. It was 1600 hours local time and we were closing in on the final steps. I hoped I was a better surgeon than he was a DJ, or else it was going to be a very long day.

Feeling increasingly anxious and insanely nervous about the impending surgical undertaking, I needed to lay it all on the line for Dan. First, I did not give him the next dose of pain medication. It was imperative to explain the risks and complications of the procedure. This was one surgery where there was no reversal or correction possible. Once I removed his testicle that was it. I also needed to let him know that he would soon be receiving much more effective pain medication, and I did not need any synergistic complications from that.

UNDAUNTED

I also thoroughly explained the other risks to Dan: Anesthesia issues, bleeding, infection (this is Africa), wound infection (again, this is Africa!), dehiscence (wound ruptures), pain, scarring, failure of the procedure (I'm an orthopedics and emergency room guy!), potential injury to other surrounding structures (yes, penile injury could happen; I did mention I specialized in orthopedics, not urological surgery), various blot clots, heart failure, stroke, prolonged wound drainage, injury to various groin-related nerves, and of course....death. There was always death.

Dan took it about as well as a man in his situation could take it. He was, after all, a U.S. Army (18 Delta) Special Operations Medical Sergeant. So, not only was he familiar with the risks, he immediately and robustly accepted them. Additionally, he told me that he had undergone a vasectomy five years earlier and that I was "not to worry about cutting anything that looked important!" That gave me at least a modicum of comfort. It was 1700 hours local time and we were, I believed, ready to proceed past the point of no return.

DJ, could I get some music please?!

Because I had to convert an administrative office into a makeshift surgical suite I did not have all the fancy fenestrated surgical drapes, a Mayo stand or even the standard complement of surgical instruments one would expect to be on said Mayo stand in your average hospital or surgery center. This was, after all, a nondescript safe house in the middle of Ouagadougou, the capital city of Burkina Faso on the continent of Africa. In short, I did what I could with what I had. That's what I do.

The conference table was repurposed as an operating table. Betadine was all I had to clean and prep the surgical site. Chux pads, and some surgical towels and a few simple instruments scavenged from some sterile suture kits, rounded out the whole affair. My boss's desk served as the Mayo stand and I used a Princeton Tec, tactical headlamp, as a surgical headlamp. One of the pilots stationed at our safe house who flew the CASA C-212 turboprop-powered medium transport aircraft, offered to scrub in as a surgical instrument tech. Another agreed to record the event on Dan's camera via pictures and HD video. Who wouldn't want to have stills and a HD video of something like this? Especially, God forbid, if something went drastically wrong.

In a near state of nerve-induced hyperthermia, as well as an impending state of hyperhidrosis, I orally administered Dan a benzodiazepine and then had the 'DJ' press play on my iPod—we needed theme music. I prophylactically administered Dan intravenous antibiotics while the sounds of country music filtered through the air. After about 15 minutes, I gave him a combination of morphine and ketamine to serve as the general anesthesia. Then we placed Dan in the supine position and prepped and draped him for surgery. Without another willing assistant, I taped Dan's penis to his abdomen and subsequently injected his scrotum with Marcaine and lidocaine with epinephrine to minimize the pain and control the bleeding.

Then I went to work.

After opening up Dan's scrotum via a postero-lateral incision, I was able to remove copious amounts of dark red blood 'pudding' and what was left of Dan's testicle. I poked around and did my best to ensure nothing else was wrong inside, then set out to stop the internal bleeding. Unfortunately, we were working under battlefield conditions so I could only address what was overtly visible. Patiently, I waited and searched for all things that would and could bleed. I even attended to the vasculature that entered the scrotum through the inguinal canal because I needed to preemptively address the fact there was a 75-percent chance of re-bleed after surgical closure. So yes, I had that shit-factor going for me!

Once I was convinced I was done, I installed a Penrose drain, closed Dan up and allowed myself to take a few deep breaths. It could have been a lot worse. Now there was nothing else to do but see how he felt once he woke up, so I decided to let him naturally awaken upon withdrawal from anesthesia and, without complications, transferred him to his bunk room, which had been transformed into a makeshift recovery room.

Dan was in stable condition. I, too, was in stable condition, and I sat on the floor next to his bed. I would be spending the night there in order to monitor him in my makeshift PACU. It was 1930 hours local time on Friday—just another not-so-normal day in the life of a former Navy SEAL turned private military contractor guy. Good times.

About an hour later, Dan was awake and coherent—not bad for a guy who only a few hours ago looked like he was beating on death's door. I was still sweating, but was pleased so far with the results.

"How did it go?" Dan asked.

I smiled. "To my knowledge, about as good as it could have gone—considering what we were dealing with and who was dealing with it! It's definitely a fucking resume builder, but, hopefully, I won't ever have to do this again."

We both shared a quiet laugh, a few minutes of pleasantries and promptly concocted a few potential alibis that we might have to use later. Then both Dan and I fell asleep.

Four-hours later, when I woke up, I gently nudged Dan awake and reassessed his condition. His scrotum appeared to have increased in size by about 1 cm while we were asleep. I tried not to look too concerned. There was no reason to add to Dan's angst. Besides, this wasn't my specialty. A little swelling might have been normal. I gingerly propped Dan's feet up higher on some pillows and re-applied some ice and administered more anti-inflammatories. I had a brief *déjà vu* moment and then reassured myself that everything was OK. Dan was sleeping peacefully again and I had initiated another round of early-stage, conservative, post-surgical care. In essence, I was still well within the best practices of SOF medicine. I then went to my room and got some quality sleep for another two hours.

I awoke to the sounds of concern. One of the pilots was standing by my bed, a grim look on his face.

"Dan's in pain. He's asking for you."

My heart sank. Immediately, I knew this was not going to be good. I composed myself and walked into Dan's room. He had the same look of concern on his face that the pilot had.

"I think I need more surgery," Dan said. "This doesn't look or feel good."

Dan lifted the blanket. I didn't like what I saw. His scrotum was significantly larger than it had been four-hours earlier. Though nowhere near the pre-surgical size or condition, he had good reason to be concerned and I needed to get back in there and see if I could figure out what was wrong. Clearly, there were further bleeding complications that weren't visible or that I couldn't identify the first time around. My lack of experience here was about to bite us both in the ass!

"You're right," I told Dan. "Let me see what we can do."

It was 1030 hours on Saturday morning and the time had come for Plan B. I like to say that there will always be someone who will take a ride with you in the limo. But what you want is the person who will walk with you, hand-in-hand, down that road when the limo breaks down. Today, that was me.

After re-prepping the surgical suite, it took about another hour to develop a plan of action that would be less invasive than the first surgery. Things aren't always better the second time around, especially when you have no past experience with the kind of events that occurred during the first go-round. Besides, I didn't think it was wise to subject Dan to more polypharmacy this close to the first surgical procedure and, in fact, his pain level was currently being managed despite the ever increasing size of his scrotum.

My best guess about the problem was that there must be a slow bleeder in there somewhere, most likely close to where I had stopped the initial internal bleeding. I decided to re-administer a low dose of morphine, inject another mixture of local anesthesia, irrigate heavily, remove and place another makeshift Penrose drain (made from IV tubing) into the previous incision. I tied off the drain and packed it in gauze. Everything went well. The drain seemed to be just what was needed to stabilize Dan's situation until the embassy urologist returned from France. In the meantime, Dan could rest in relative comfort.

I called the embassy nurse again and asked if she could reach the urologist and try to expedite his return. She said she would call me back if there was any change in his schedule. There was nothing more that could be done for Dan so I decided to turn my attention to other duties, including making a CASA 212 run to Mali in order to re-supply some ODA (Operational Detachment Alpha) bubbas who were experiencing a car issue in the Sahel. On the way, I inventoried the medical supplies and equipment on the CASA and managed to get three hours of flight time in the cockpit. It had been a very interesting and fulfilling 36 hours, but my trip home soon was looking better and better.

At 0615 hours on Sunday morning, I was awakened by a call from the embassy nurse. In excited fashion she explained that she had just got off the phone with the urologist and that he was on his way to the local hospital to prepare for surgery on Dan. We should get there ASAP.

I woke Dan and shuttled him into the car. We reached the hospital in 15 minutes. After briefing the French-educated and French-trained Burkinabe urologist, Dr. M., on what I had done for Dan, I was asked to join the doctor in surgery. We scrubbed in while Dan was prepped for surgery. Then we went back to work.

Dr. M. was impressed with my handiwork and said I had made the right decision on both surgical occasions.

"The IV tubing was a brilliant substitute for a Penrose," he said. "It's a good thing you attempted to explore for the source of the re-bleed. The damage to your friend was more extensive than you were able to see."

After performing a second surgery and cleaning up another vascular issue, the doctor closed Dan up.

"That should do it," he said. "Nice work on stabilizing him. If you hadn't done what you did, the situation could have really become much worse. Dan might have died from any number of things, including sepsis." Sepsis is a blood infection.

I was glad it was over, but happy to have been able to aid my brother. Like any SOF medic, I refused to quit. I am my brother's keeper. And so I spent the next five days 'nursing' Dan back to health, along with our teammates at the safe house.

The remainder of Dan's 90-day deployment went by without another medical hitch. He went on to tragically lose his life two-years later during a deployment to Afghanistan. But in between we would often talk about that fateful day in Africa when two SOF medics reached an even deeper level of understanding and appreciation for the art and the discipline and the passion that is SOF medicine.

Over the years, I've come to learn that amidst men of valor and honor, the moments proceeding uncommon acts are extremely forthright and exceptionally forthcoming. It is under the auspices of these undertakings that certain immutable bonds are formed. Bonds that, when decisively applied and tactically tested, have commonly led to the liberation of lands and the deposition of despots. I am honored to be counted amongst such men. Dan was one of them, too, and it was an honor to have known him and to have served with him in the capacities that I did.

Once I was sure Dan was OK for duty, I packed my stuff and headed home to the States. Little did I know what awaited me in Atlanta.

CHAPTER 3

> "Yeah, life can be hard.
> Suck it up and stop complaining."
>
> —Christopher Mark Heben

The journey to become a Navy SEAL is different for each of us, but there are a few common traits among my brothers and me. As SEALs, we must be strong of mind and body; and we must think quickly on our feet to see the world around us a few moves ahead of everyone else. All of us are shaped by a myriad of experiences—whether a singular, life-changing moment, as in the loss of a loved one, or in my case a lifetime of overcoming challenges. Sometimes, it takes a battle to discover what you truly believe in. If it's not worth fighting for, run from it, because it's certainly not worth having in your life.

My journey began the day I was born, even if I didn't know it until I was in my late 20s. I am the second oldest of 12 children. My mom birthed nine boys and three girls. People don't believe me when I tell them this, but the girls of the clan were, and still are, the best athletes in our family. If women could enter U.S. Special Forces training, my sisters would probably be the first ones to sign up. Growing up, my father was an attorney who owned a law practice, a title company, a mortgage company and a real estate company. He also owned rental properties and an apartment complex in East Cleveland, Ohio.

East Cleveland, as its name might imply, is the first suburb on the eastern outskirts of the city of Cleveland. My father's apartment complex, Nelacrest Garden Apartments, was comprised primarily of Section 8 housing units.

When I say my "father," I really mean my stepfather. My biological father and my mother divorced when I was young. I grew up with my mom, my grandma, and my grandfather. We lived on the west side of Cleveland until I was about four-years old. That's when my mother met and married my stepfather, Ed Heben. But it wasn't until I was 17 that he officially adopted my older brother, Jon, and me. Heben became our official last name, too. Up until then, and unbeknownst to me, I had been writing Heben from the time I could write my name and legally, I should not have been. Ed was—and still is—a very demanding man. On more than several occasions, we butted heads, and as I got older and into my teens, these confrontations often turned physical. He didn't physically abuse me, but constantly challenged me physically. Ed was rough, demanding and had a 'do as I say, not as I do' attitude. Like other kids who didn't know they had a choice, I accepted many unwarranted punishments. Admittedly, some of those I fully deserved. When the tangles began, I didn't always fight back, but when I did, I had the feeling he enjoyed it. Sometimes, I did too, and over time this yo-yo process of push-me-pull-you caused rage to slowly simmer inside me.

When we were old enough, my father put my brothers and me to work at his apartment buildings. I cut the grass, pulled weeds, dug tunnels for pipes, taped and painted walls, and refurbished the apartments after tenants moved out. My father's philosophy was simple: When you have teenage boys, you have an unlimited supply of slave labor. Ed took full advantage of a full brood of kids. When I wasn't working at his apartments, Ed put me to work at home and other business locations he owned.

Traveling to the apartment buildings in East Cleveland was often a challenge. Ed didn't drive us there to do the work. He was too busy running his law firm and other businesses and playing in AAU basketball leagues to bother with it. Instead, the majority of the time I relied on public transportation—Cleveland's Regional Transit Authority (RTA), a comprehensive bus and above-ground rapid transit or train system that connects the east and west sides of Cleveland. First, I had a 3-mile walk to the station. Then, the closest RTA stop to the apartment buildings was at Windermere Road, another 3-mile walk. So, after un-assing the train, I had to walk that 3-mile stretch from the RTA stop, through the city of East Cleveland, to reach Nelacrest Gardens. East Cleveland is—and was—a very rough city. With a 99.9 percent black population—the bulk of whom have incomes well below the national poverty line—it is also the most financially destitute and politically bankrupt city in Ohio. Being white, young, and alone, was neither advantageous nor conducive to survival there. And, as luck would have it, my walk to Nelacrest Gardens sent me straight through the heart of the roughest part of East Cleveland. As a result, I was always harassed, nearly robbed and sometimes assaulted, on a weekly basis. In some ways it was fun, and in other ways it was frightening.

When I was about 14-years old, I finally had enough. The rage within me that was simmering for years finally boiled to the surface. It had manifested itself several times during scrapes my brother and I got into from time to time but it had never been truly realized. Once, when we still lived in Cleveland Heights, some 16-year-old kid tried to steal my boom box. You remember those things! Well, I went after him and kicked him in the back, knocking him to the ground. The radio fell to the ground, too, hit pretty hard and broke, so the next logical move to me at the time was pushing his face into it after he was down. Made perfect sense to me at the time. On this particular hot summer day, however, I was walking from the RTA stop toward the apartment buildings when an older teenage thug, probably 18- or 19-years old, approached me with a menacing look. He stepped into my path and blocked me from walking any further.

"Nice watch," he said, and then he punched me in the face, outmuscled me and wrestled the watch off my wrist.

The thug punched me again; then shoved me to the ground, and turned and walked away. I was 5'7" and roughly 130 pounds at the time; he must have been at least 6-feet tall and about 175 pounds. He used a combination of surprise, size, force, and violence of action—principles

I would later learn to use as a SEAL. Yes, I was learning without even knowing it, but sometimes life lessons are painful. Well, at least the ones that mean anything are!

That was it, I thought to myself. Enough was enough. I stood up and for about five minutes, I watched the thug walk down the street and duck into a green-paneled RTA booth that served as a bus stop. For a few moments I just stood there, staring at his two feet as he sat on the bench inside. His first mistake was fucking with me. Sitting down at that bus stop was his second. I was furious and felt like a huge pussy, and that rage soared to a whole new level. I kept replaying what had just happened over and over in my brain. It ran like an unsavory YouTube video stuck on repeat. In that moment, the whole idea of me 'letting' him take my watch and walk away really pissed me off. The moving target was now stationary, and that's when I decided to move.

I formed a plan, gathered myself, and moved out. Calmly and quietly, and trying not to look like I was up to something, I crept over to the RTA booth and positioned myself just around the corner from the opening of the small overhang building—at a location where I could lean in, hook my arm around and reach the guy. I don't know why I cared if I looked like I was up to something because nobody gave a shit that I was just robbed.

I took a few deep breaths and steadied myself. What I had in mind could potentially have very negative, physical consequences for me if it didn't work, but I didn't care. Even at that age, I was not a toe-touch kind of person. I was an all-in guy, another quality that I would benefit from later in life.

Channeling all the rage that was within me, I swung my fist around the corner of the little building as hard and as fast as I could. My head followed, and I was able to identify my target to make a last-second trajectory adjustment for accuracy.

There was a loud thump and an "Umph!"

Pay dirt! My fist landed squarely in the middle of his face.

With continued momentum I leapt into the RTA booth and pounced on the dude. Rage had taken over, and I let loose with my fists, pummeling him over and over in the face and body, his head pounding against the back of the shack. I continued my assault until the thug laid semi-conscious on the cement. Then, just as quickly as it had begun, the battle was over. I reached into the thug's pockets and poked around until I found my watch. Then I removed it, strapped it back on my wrist and stood up. I stood over the thug for another moment or two and admired my handiwork before continuing on my way, this time running, toward my father's apartment buildings to get to work.

The next day, when I got off the train, the thug was there, waiting for me. Only he wasn't alone. He brought a buddy.

The two men watched me get off the train, menacing smiles on their faces. Once the train pulled away and I was alone, they came at me. I was ready. I had no choice but to be ready.

There was no way I was going to take shit from these guys. Sure, there were two of them, but somehow I knew how to take the rage and anger and use it to my advantage. I had been getting roughed up at home, and in that moment I told myself, "I'll be damned if I'm going to get beat up on my way to work for my family, even if my family included the guy who I was sometimes fighting with!" It was again perfect logic.

As I approached, I noticed the low-hanging support tubes for the canopy that covered the train platform and identified one I could use to my advantage. I took a few more steps toward the thugs and launched myself off the ground at an angle, grabbing a metal bar and using it to swing toward one of my potential assailants, like a LeBron James-ninja gymnast. I used my abs and thighs to add more kinetic energy to the mix, and under the force of that momentum struck the closest kid—the new thug—with both my feet in his face. He was out cold before his limp body hit the ground.

The dude from the day before promptly turned and ran. I never saw him again. I guess he figured out that the guy he brought to help just got his ass beat, and he wasn't about to be pummeled a second time. Thankfully for all of us, I never saw either of them again.

Looking back, I should have recognized what had been happening to me. Those scrapes my brothers and I had gotten into years earlier when we lived in Cleveland Heights were portents of things to come. One such incident specifically sticks out in my mind—another day when

UNDAUNTED

I was walking down the street near my house in Cleveland Heights carrying a boom box radio. Yes, I had a thing about boom boxes.

This was the 1980s, long before the invention of the iPod, and boom boxes were the thing. Being an avid break-dancer and an appreciator of all things hip-hop, Motown, and R&B, of course I had a kickass one. Well, low and behold, some punk 16-year-old kid jumped out from behind a van, punched me in the head and stole my radio. I was in 6th grade, scrawny, and often the target of opportunity for many a more physically mature lad. But what I lacked in size I often made up for in ferocity. Late bloomers have to face the facts, and I often had the facts punched or ground into my face.

I picked myself off the ground but was a bit too woozy to give chase. However, I saw where the kid went and tracked him back to his house.

When I arrived, I stayed out of sight. He was sitting in a chair on his porch listening to my boom box. That was pretty damn cocky, and didn't sit well with me. I quietly approached the house, making sure not to be seen by staying in the bushes. Then I hopped over the porch, blindsided the kid with a forearm to the face and proceeded to stomp him into the porch. While he was writhing in pain, I grabbed my radio and left.

My point is, I didn't always have the immediate balls to abort a situation right away—especially when it was going awry—but I learned that if I let it go, it didn't sit well with me and I was compelled to make it right. Ever since those days with the thefts of my watch and the two boom boxes, I have effectively used anger and rage as tools. It's akin to what SEAL training teaches you—when you're cold, wet, hungry, tired, miserable, pissed off, angry and hurt, channel it. Take it out on your adversary or apply it to the present situation in a manner that is of benefit, not a disadvantage. A lot of that carries through to the rest of my life. We are all created with different types of awesome; it's up to us to decide how much of it the world gets to see.

Cleveland, Ohio was my home growing up—the city that infamously had a river catch fire in June 1969. Though this was not the first time it blazed, the event was featured in Time magazine, which made it all the more prolific. In fact, it was the last time the Cuyahoga River went up in flames.

The name Cuyahoga, in Native American speak, means "crooked river." This name, while describing its many twists and turns, also serves as a metaphor for many a political and financial undertaking here: Twisted. If you recall or care to research it, only recently, the city and many of its surrounding counties were caught up in an FBI dragnet of corruption. And that doesn't even take into account the U.S. Department of Justice's assessment in late 2014 that the Cleveland Police Department had engaged in way too many incidences of use of excessive force—primarily against blacks.

Let me be clear: I respect all police, and I could never do what they do. They have one of the toughest jobs on the planet. And, as a SEAL, we began most workdays with the prior knowledge that it was our job to stop people from having birthdays. We weren't sent to build hearts and minds, only to rip them out. As a cop, if you take that attitude to the streets, you are in the wrong line of work. Never send a cop to do a SEAL's job and it definitely isn't a good idea to send a SEAL to do a cop's. Mutual respect, however, is important. Mad mutual respect.

Back to the water, however: The Cuyahoga River isn't just a geographical barrier, it also serves as a social-political dividing point. Even though its flames have been extinguished, there is—and probably always will be—a hot rivalry between the east and west sides of the city due to political, racial, and social issues. Thankfully, I have experienced life on both sides of its banks.

Initially a west-sider—born and initially raised on 103rd and Baltic—my family next moved to an apartment off Lorain Road in Fairview Park, then we moved to the east side of Cleveland in Cleveland Heights, near Severance Shopping Center, and finally as a teenager moving back to the west side. These experiences made me tougher than most kids my age, especially since circumstances forced me to stand up for myself and to learn how to adapt to uncomfortable situations. It helped that I was always a mischievous kind of go-getter who believed it was better to plead for forgiveness than ask for permission. That attitude has served me well. It has also bitten me in the ass more time than I have pages to write about!

My first retrievable memory of a holistic experience as a member of a community occurred in Cleveland Heights. The 'Heights' was a great place to grow up and, in fact, I credit it with helping me lay the initial groundwork for my ability to adapt and integrate into the many environments I would find myself thrown headfirst into as a SEAL and as a private military contractor.

The city is rich in racial, ethnic, and religious diversity. At one point in the early to mid-1980s, it was ranked as the most integrated and diverse neighborhood in America. Jews, from Orthodoxy to Reconstructionism, have a major presence there, as do blacks and whites of all Christian denominations, as well as Catholics too. I fall into the latter category. Our neighbors came from all of these classifications, along with mixed racial and mixed religious families. When I say I am not a racist, I truly mean it. In fact, I am an equal opportunity hater: I don't give a shit what you look like, what you wear, who or what you pray to, or what direction you're facing when you do it, you are an asshole until proven otherwise. You can quote me on that.

I attended Ruffing, a Montessori school, for about five years from the time I was seven-years old until I was 12. The Montessori Method was, at that time, a very cutting-edge educational concept that utilized an open, semi-structured, and oftentimes, self-taught/exploratory environment. It followed the concept of experiential learning and tactical approaches to the discovery of everything from music, literature and theater, to sports, math and science. I loved it, but I also learned how to be a devious slacker. It's easy to look like you are doing something when no one is hovering over you and telling you what to do. I say it today all the time: Walk around with a clipboard and look pissed, while writing things down, and no one will ever question you.

My first week at Ruffing was pretty rough. Born severely pigeon-toed, I was in constant need of corrective orthotics in order to help properly align my legs. From birth until about the age of four, I was in and out of plaster casts and leg bar devices. If you didn't know it, you'd have sworn I was a child that somehow missed his polio vaccination.

Despite this, I started walking at the age of seven months and was full on running by the time I was 9-months old. By the time I started a full day of classes, I was walking around in dynamic leg braces that went from my hips all the way down to an incorporated and custom-made pair of leather shoes. From an orthopedic standpoint, I was the Ohio version of Forrest Gump. As such, I was an easy target for teasing.

This was a big hurdle for a kid for overcome, but it never really held me back because I refused to allow it to! I played basketball and baseball and ran track—I was the fastest kid in the school. Later on, when I went to St. Louis Catholic grade school and eventually lost the braces, I was one of the fastest kids in the city of Cleveland, not to mention an insanely aggressive football player to boot. I never left the field for two championship seasons as a 7th and 8th grader.

At Ruffing, I told the kids I was special—that I was better than them—I had to, so I wouldn't get picked on. My line was that I had bionic legs, and I didn't take shit from anybody. Believe it to achieve it! Right? Even back then I was developing an undaunted mentality.

My brothers and I were always doing something rambunctious—especially Jon and Eddie. Jon was 13-months older than me; Eddie was three-years younger—he's deceased now. Though we could take the bus, the three of us would often opt to walk home from school whether the weather was good or bad. It was about a two-mile walk, and we would have to walk through Severance Shopping Center, a large indoor and strip-mall complex. Our game was which of us could steal the most stuff. It was a lot of fun, but sometime it got us into trouble; my poor mother.

Jon loved music, and he would try to steal as many 45s (45-rpm records) as he could carry. Eddie was a candy freak, and would stuff piles of it into his pockets. I was into weapons of war—even back then—and would steal pocket knives, 'Wrist Wrocket' slingshots, BB gun pistols, and the BBs for them.

Inevitably, once in a while one of us would get caught at the Gold Circle or whichever store was our target de jour, and our mother would be called to come get us. They never called the police on us, which was how it was back in the 1980s. Mom was great. She wouldn't tell our father—he would have seen it as yet another excuse to hammer us—but she would ground us in her own way.

Even before my hot button got closer to the surface, I stopped taking punishment from anyone. I became my brothers' protector. Sometimes during our walks—both home from school and around the neighborhood—we would run the gauntlet of people trying to hassle us. There were many of them.

I would act scared and pretend to run away. The bully would chase me, drawing him away from my brother or, if the bully had a friend with him, his buddy. I would let the unfortunate junior thug catch up with me, then turn and beat him up. I learned the art of how to divide and conquer at an early age, and while I didn't really know it was an actual tactic, it seemed like a good thing to do. Yes, I was laying groundwork for my future life.

My younger brother Eddie (my stepfather's first-born child), didn't know how to fight. He hadn't tapped into his inner warrior yet, so I had to assist him in potential fight situations. Hell, I wasn't going to let him get beat up, so if I could get one of the guys away from him and pound him into the ground, I could rush back and take out the other guy before he beat up my brother. Or, when the kid ran to assist his bully buddy, it was an even better outcome for me. Not for them! This happened quite a few times. Sometimes, the other would-be assailant and my brother would watch as I administered the distant bully beat down. Then the kid I left with my brother would scamper away as I ran back toward him. Even then, I was already thinking outside the box in combat situations. My brother would sometimes laugh—if he hadn't taken any licks in the interim—and together we would reminisce about it for days. Eventually, he found his inner warrior and we were able to both apply it to adverse situations.

We lived in this stimulating and diverse melting pot until I reached the age of 14. That time challenged and prepared me in a lot of ways: It taught me honor, courage and commitment, as well as how to defend myself and protect my brothers. In some weird early childhood and protective way, it taught me to cheat and steal—skills that have both served me well, as well as disserved me later on in life. It also was enough time living in a diverse city so that I was able to add many characters to my mental inventory of learning and mimicking voices, accents, dialects, physical behaviors and social customs—other skill sets that would come in handy in my not-so-distant future. The ability to blend in is very important as a covert/clandestine private military contractor. It's not always as critical for being a SEAL unless one is on special projects.

From Cleveland Heights we moved to the west side of Cleveland and to the polar opposite city of Lakewood, Ohio. Lakewood was, at that time, a white-washed community compared to the Heights. In fact, within a high school of 3,600 students, you could count on one hand the number of black students. The city grade schools were identical, if not worse. You can only imagine the look on my face when my mother dropped me off at St. Luke Catholic grade school for the first day of 8th grade and said to me, "You may have to start talking and behaving more like a 'white person' now. There are no black kids here."

Because I grew up in the diverse community, Motown and early rap influences were my sole musical existence. In Lakewood, I was in for a shock. I soon found out that this west side enclave and its children—my new peers—had never heard of LL Cool J, Al Green, The Ohio Players, Gino Vanelli, The Jackson Five, The Gap Band, the Dazz Band, or even George Clinton. Instead, I heard names like The Who, Jethro Tull, The Rolling Stones, Bruce Springsteen, and Led Zeppelin—all bands I would grow to appreciate in time. Again, I was becoming diversified.

By the time I entered Lakewood High School I had become a stellar athlete. One of quite a few; there was always a 'who's fastest' argument. It was a debate that I constantly had with Brian F. and Bill F., two of the other dudes that were in running for said title. I always had explosiveness, even when I wore the braces. I'm still a touch pigeon-toed today. If you look at kinesiologic studies, most explosive athletes (linear speed or the ability to jump vertically and horizontally) are pigeon-toed to a certain degree. It turns out that muscles and muscle fiber types are built a certain way for explosiveness. This gift of speed would not be so friendly to me in the future at BUD/S, but I'll get to that soon.

UNDAUNTED

Another strange phenomena I encountered, on the west side of Cleveland, was that a lot my peers seemed stuck in the late 1960s and 70s drug counterculture. For, along with a rabid appreciation for the music of this era, they also smoked pot, snorted coke, ate mushrooms, dropped acid, and drank a lot of beer and booze. It was as if they were locked in a time capsule. Obviously, not everyone I knew was moored as such, but I'd say around 65 percent of the kids in my social circles were part of it. The weekends were not so much about, "What are we doing?" as they were, "Where are we going to do it?"

Thankfully, I managed to avoid this whole scene. Well, not so much avoid it as opt not to heavily partake in it. I'm not saying I never indulged; it's just that after some less-than-agreeable early experiences with some of these substances, mostly alcohol, I learned that at a cellular level my body was not engineered to be anesthetized by drugs or alcohol. I've always believed the body is a temple. Why would you want yours to be the Temple of Doom? In fact, it goes further than that. I've learned that you don't just eat to satisfy your appetite. Rather, you eat to set yourself up for the future feast of a long and healthy life

Alcohol made me feel like shit for days. I realized this after the first time I got drunk during a wedding reception at a neighbor's house. I was 15-years old. Inside the span of five minutes, I slammed a rum and Coke, a cranberry and Absolute, and a Jell-O shot. In the 75 feet it took me to walk home, as I realized my faculties were crashing on me, I became nauseous enough to puke in the kitchen sink as soon as I stumbled in through the back door of the house. I spent that night on the couch because I couldn't get up the stairs to my bedroom in the attic. I also saw many of my friends from St. Luke grade school, who went on to attend private Catholic all-male high schools, struggle with alcohol abuse. I guess being cooped up with dudes all week made it hard for them to approach girls on the weekends. It also caused some major rivalries with another Catholic all-boys' high school close by, as well as with dudes who went to my public high school. Because my high school was co-ed, I never had issues with talking to girls. And because I had a pretty violent childhood, I never had a problem kicking anybody's ass. As a result, I didn't have to use alcohol as an enabling tool for those two endeavors. I simply did what I felt I needed to do in any given situation. The fact that I was sober made me a more effective pugilist and a more prolific paramour. Still to this day, I am a two-drink drunk, and I am OK with that.

Weed was everywhere when I was a teenager, but it made me feel dumb, slow, tired and hungry. Hell, I was proud of my smarts, was one of the most fleet-footed kids in the county (probably in the state), was never without energy, and was always hungry already. I tried it a few times and never went back to it. Acid was available too. It was an obnoxious 15 hours of Alice in Wonderland meets Fantasia meets Fear and Loathing in Las Vegas meets Apocalypse Now. None of that appealed to me. But, I never did mushrooms, and the fact that one of my favorite Cleveland Browns players, Don Johnson, died from a cocaine-induced heart attack kept me from going anywhere near that stuff as well.

Ironically, during my time overseas—both as a Navy SEAL and a private contractor with Blackwater—we came across a metric shit ton of drugs ranging from marijuana to heroin. Not coincidentally, I had long hair, a beard, and a very well-tanned or ruddy complexion that made me look like someone who operated outside the legal moors of society, i.e.; a drug dealer. But looks can be deceiving.

The bottom line is that my formative years prepared me for whatever curve balls life threw at me later. Those early lessons learned turned out to be pretty handy when I was in the Middle East, Africa, and even during my time in the tank in Fulton County, Georgia. It was a rough—but happy—childhood that instilled in me a few necessary skill sets and I gained knowledge that would later allow me to adapt to life in nearly any circumstance, so when I found myself a guest of the Atlanta and the Federal Prison systems, I was ready for whatever could possibly happen next.

CHAPTER 4

> "SOME PEOPLE CAN'T ACCEPT THEIR FAILURES AND FLAWS. THEY WORK VERY HARD TO HIDE THEM VIA LIES, ALIBIS, DECEIT AND CONTROL. EVENTUALLY, THAT HOUSE OF CARDS COLLAPSES UNDER THE WEIGHT OF ITS MANY ELABORATE AND ILL-CONSTRUCTED LAYERS. PERSONALLY, I BELIEVE FLAWS AND FAILURES ARE A GODSEND FOR THEY ARE OUR TRUEST STORIES...AND WHEN SHARED, THEY CAN BECOME BADGES OF HONOR, COURAGE AND HUMILITY. THEY ARE A TESTAMENT TO THE FALLIBILITY AND HUMANITY IN ALL OF US AND THEY CAN DEFINITELY SERVE TO BUILD TRUST AND TO INSPIRE!"
>
> —CHRISTOPHER MARK HEBEN

My post-SEAL Team troubles began in March 2007, when I was working as a Board Certified, Master's degreed, Physician Assistant (PA-C) with Dr. David V. Mungo at the Carnation Clinic, an orthopedic sports medicine practice in Alliance, Ohio. We had a pretty robust operation—our office hours were Monday, Wednesday and a half-day on Friday; Tuesday and Thursday were our surgery days. We did the surgical 'heavy lifting' on Tuesdays at Alliance Community Hospital; procedures such as total knee replacements and total hip replacements. Usually, we scheduled the more difficult or demanding cases for first thing in the day. Thursdays were reserved for smaller, less complicated or demanding procedures, such as carpal tunnel releases and minor arthroscopic procedures on shoulders and knees. Occasionally, we'd do some minor rotator cuff repairs and knee procedures. Dave and I developed a damn good system; we both scrubbed in on the first case, I closed up, he opened the next case, I would close up on that procedure, and so on it went until the last patient was finished. We could do almost 10 carpal tunnel procedures and be finished before noon. It was what I called NASCAR surgery. It was that efficient, and we were that good. For the first 18 months of the job, things were going well. Very well. In fact, we were dominating the orthopedic and sports medicine space in that neck of the woods.

Let me back up for a hot second to explain: Prior to my arrival at Carnation Clinic in August 2005, Dr. Mungo was seeing about 38 patients each day. He was usually done with the last patient at 5:15 p.m., and then finished with chart dictation by about 6:30 p.m. This was his reality every night he was in the office. In just a few months after my arrival, however, we were seeing 52 patients a day and were done and dictated by 5 p.m. A PA's job is to be an extension of the physician and allow him or her to apply more intense focus on the more critical cases while the lesser medical maladies are addressed by the PA. This concept was born out of returning combat medics from Vietnam and how crucial they were to aiding battlefield surgeons with critical patient care. This got the American Medical Association thinking. You see, in the mid-1960s, physicians saw an impending shortage of primary care MDs. To fix this critical finding, Dr. Eugene A. Stead Jr., an MD at Duke University Medical Center, in 1965 proposed and placed four men into what became the first class of PAs. He selected four Navy Hospital Corpsmen because they had received considerable medical training during their military service. Doctor Stead based the Duke curriculum for the PA program on the fast-track training doctors received during World War II. It was like condensing four years of medical school into 27 months: no summer breaks, very little time off for holidays, and four or more tests per week. It was a 100-plus-hour week every week. The first PA class graduated from the Duke University PA program on Oct. 6, 1967.

They say the hardest steel is forged in the hottest fires. PA school is a blast furnace. If you are attempting it, you better buckle down. Let me know if you need any inspiration as I have been known to guest lecture from time to time, and I know how to make any material very interesting.

In keeping with this right-hand-man (or woman) concept, and via my influence and implemented practices and procedures, I increased our patient load while I simultaneously decreased Dr. Mungo's workload. This, in turn, reduced Dr. Mungo's total time in the office. It also made his wife, Michelle, very happy. Additionally, our billable revenue increased by nearly $150,000 per month. Essentially, we both enjoyed working less time while making more money and helping more people. It was a win-win-win situation. What more could you ask for in a PA? What more could I have asked for in a job, virtually, right out of PA school?

I say virtually because I joined Carnation Clinic after first working at Fairview General Hospital. Fairview is part of the world-famous Cleveland Clinic Foundation health system. I spent three months as a PA/SA in general surgery. As a PA/SA student, it was my goal to work right out of the gate: I graduated from Cuyahoga Community College's combined Physician Assistant/Surgeon Assistant (PA/SA) program on a Friday and started working for the Cleveland Clinic the following Monday! Goal Achieved!

It was a great place to get experience in a very short amount of time. I was assigned to general surgery and would assist, on a daily basis, in surgeries ranging from tonsillectomies and circumcisions to total joint replacements and total hysterectomies, as well as everything in between. I can clearly remember the first case I scrubbed in on as a PA there: It was an open bowel procedure. The patient was draped and lying on her back. We were attending to the repair of her transverse colon in a procedure known as an end-to-end anastomosis. The entire abdominal contents were in clear view and it was very interesting. After we completed the procedure, we began to close the first layer of fascia. Everything was going smoothly until the doctor suddenly said to me, "OK, Chris, close up the rest of the surgical incision and tell me how you did it so I can enter it into the post-op note. I'll go get started on that now."

And just like that, she broke scrub and headed out into the hallway.

To say I was shocked would be a complete understatement. I must have looked like Bubba from Forrest Gump and as I stood there, mouth-breathing like Sponge Bob Squarepants on the deck of a boat. And if I didn't look like that, I sure felt like it because my brain was yelling a mixture of "Run Forrest, Run!" followed by, "There's the simple interrupted suture, the continuous suture, the vertical mattress suture, horizontal mattress suture, running subcuticular suture, the buried suture. And that's all I know about that." Interspersed between that madness, was the incessant laughing of Sponge Bob, "Aaahhhyayayaaeyeyey!" Talk about cartoon cogitation!

This went on for what seemed like minutes, but in reality was probably about five seconds. Thank God I had a surgical mask on and a double layer of a bandana and surgical head cover to block my gaping jaw and mop up the sweat that was forming all over my head. I soon snapped out of it and into SEAL 'suture sniper' mode, and in no time was soon bouncing out the door of that operating room with a different type of swagger. My SEAL swagger morphed into Surgical PA swagger, and it was a good blend.

Later that week, I had an equally poignant yet totally different experience: I was called into the head PA's office, wherein I was told to head over to Lakewood General Hospital to assist on a breast biopsy. Lakewood General Hospital was also a part of the Cleveland Clinic Foundation, or the 'Medical Mafia' as I like to call it. All in good fun, as it were, because the CCF is the most amazing medical institution on the planet and I am thankful that their roots are firmly planted in Cleveland. So I drove the approximately five miles from Fairview General Hospital to Lakewood General Hospital thinking to myself that I had not been inside Lakewood General since 1991, when I worked there. Back then I worked second shift (a 12-hour shift) in housekeeping, four days a week. My job was to clean: empty trash, mop, vacuum, dust and polish floors. Occasionally, I was needed in surgery to clean up the floors after really bloody operations. It was a great paying job, and I worked with some pretty funny characters. On this day, however, I would not be wearing dark blue Dickie's pants and a light blue Dickie's shirt, I would be wearing light green surgical scrubs.

Once this procedure was over and we were ready to close up the incision, lo and behold, the same 'You close this one up, Chris, while I go dictate the surgical note' scenario happened, again. This time, I felt no lack of confidence. Instead, there was a rush of emotions. The last time I was in that room was 1991, when I made $8 per hour to clean up a bloodbath from the floor: bloodstained towels and surgical buckets filled with blood drenched sponges and, throw-away, single-use tools.

Every time I was called in there to do that, I knew it was going to look like a scene from *Saw* meets *The Texas Chainsaw Massacre* meets *Friday the 13th*. Oh yes, there will be blood! Now it was different. It was 2005, there was a lot less blood, and I was now given the very precise task of closing the incision on the left breast of a 30-year old female patient.

I told the nurses what you just read, and they all stopped what they were doing and tilted their heads back and forth. Then the questions started: Did you work with Fred? How long were you here? Were you in school then? What shift did you work? All these rapid-fire questions came as I was striving to meticulously place sutures on this young woman's breast incision. I knew she would think about the person that gave her this scar, and I wanted her thoughts to be as minimal as possible. In short, I wanted to do the best job ever for this young gal.

I believe I did—despite the continued questions that seemed to go on and on. Then the door opened, and Fred appeared. He stood there looking at me with the same look I must have been giving him.

"Damn dude, you're still here?" I said, at almost the same time he said, "Damn duuuuude, you're back?"

Fred had this Al Jolson-like voice, big and booming, yet smooth and occasionally raspy. He was the Sydney Poitier of the Surgical Suite and everyone knew it. He had worked exclusively in surgical housekeeping for more than 30 years. I don't know who was more inspired: me of him or him of me. It was great to see him. After the case, we would grab lunch and catch up. I hope he is doing well today; we haven't spoken in years. Remember, everyone has a story and everyone's story deserves to be heard. It's the best way to honor a person's life!

My personal story at the Cleveland Clinic Foundation and Fairview General Hospital was relatively short-lived. Job retention required me to pass the Physician Assistant National Certification Exam—PANCE—and, despite graduating from the PA program with a 3.85 GPA, I didn't initially pass the PANCE. Worse, due to the Cleveland Clinic's stringent requirements, I wasn't able to keep working while I studied to retake it. Luckily, I had networked enough to learn there was a doctor in Alliance, Ohio, who was looking for a PA. In light of this, I called and secured

UNDAUNTED

an interview with Dr. David Victor Mungo the day before I left the Cleveland Clinic.

The two of us hit it off immediately. He offered me a job and I went to work with him within a few days. We became fast friends, a friendship that continues to this day. Yes, Dave and I have a lot in common: We are both athletes; we are both military buffs/enthusiasts; and we are five-months apart in age. His birthday is also the same day as my stepfather's—a fact I never held against him. Dave is a Civil War re-enactor and he does so while perched on top of a horse as a Union cavalry soldier. At first, he was a private, but now (I believe) he has achieved the rank of Lieutenant. He can often be overheard telling his patients: "I'm a surgeon to support my Civil War habit!" And that is no joke, as he just so happens to own an authentic, working, 1859 6-pound field artillery cannon.

Yes, everything was going very well until about March 2007. That's when I received a call from a friend and mentor, a non-practicing MD/PhD. I had taken a few amazing classes taught by him, had been to his house and met his family, and was also a student teacher for him at one of the university's I graduated from. He was an avid human performance and strength enthusiast as well as a very knowledgeable dude when it came to sports science and human nutrition. He was, by all accounts, a stand-up kind of guy. He still is to this day, but let me keep the momentum going here.

"Chris," he said. "I have a favor to ask."

"Anything," I replied. "Just let me know, what, where and when."

"I want to do some body re-composition. I'd like to gain 10 pounds of muscle and lose about 10 pounds of fat. You know, basically end up where I am currently on the scale, but with a different look in the mirror."

"Sure," I said. "How can I help? Do you want me to train you—work with you on a diet and exercise routine? Look into some supplements that may work for you?" He knew I had an extensive supplement and exercise background.

There was a brief pause on the other end of the line before he finally said, "Not exactly. Could you write me a couple of prescriptions, one of which would be for anabolic steroids? I'd like one for Deca Durabolin and another for Synthroid." Synthroid was a Thyroid medication and the Deca Durabolin was a Class Three Controlled Substance (CIII).

The request took me just a bit by surprise. But, at the same time, I didn't think he was planning to abuse the drugs and he certainly knew more than me about the potential side effects. I know this because he'd worked at a very prominent and well-known U.S. clinic in the field of neuromuscular rehabilitation and had also taught classes of this nature. Classes that I attended. He and I also co-wrote a chapter and sidebar pertaining to performance enhancement and blood-doping currently in use in a college textbook. In short, he was a brilliant guy, and if he wanted this steroid he had certainly done his homework and it was exactly what he needed.

My first thought was to track down Dr. Mungo, talk it over with him, and get his approval. That would have been the smart move. Instead, it became my first mistake. I thought about the request for a few moments and then replied, "Sure. I'm happy to help."

"Thanks," my friend said. "By the way, you know Todd, right?"

"Yes." Todd was a biochemist, and he worked in a lab that formulated sports supplements and workout formulas for most major companies in that space. He and I had met a few times over a period of two years.

"Todd's lost 25 pounds in the last year," my friend said. "I think he has an AIDS-like wasting syndrome. It's very concerning. He can't say anything at work because they'd fire him from the laboratory. He doesn't want anyone to think he has any health issues, so he's trying to find a way to treat his problem quietly. Can you help him out, too?"

I took a deep breath and exhaled.

"Yes," I said. "Let me do a little research on the problems he's having and get back to you with the right prescription plan for him."

That was my second mistake.

I hung up the phone and began my due diligence on Todd's condition. I approached this in the same way I would have for any patient and any medical procedure and found drug treatments that the major medical clinics in San Francisco were giving to AIDS patients to help them keep muscular composition and to avoid further wasting.

And then I made my third mistake: I used Dr. Mungo's prescription pad and wrote three prescriptions with two refills on each one, and gave them to my two friends.

I did this knowing that as of that March of 2007, the state of Ohio was still prohibiting Physician Assistants from bottom-lining (signing) on the prescriptions they wrote for patients, or having their own DEA number with which to do the same. Today, the laws are very different. In fact, the State Medical Board of Ohio changed the rules on PA prescribing in October 2007, allowing PAs to fully write prescriptions. A few months later, in February 2008, they also approved the formularies which defined PA prescription writing for everything BUT Schedule II controlled substances and a few additional and highly dangerous drugs. Shortly after that, the Drug Enforcement Administration (DEA) began issuing PAs DEA numbers so that they could write their own prescriptions without a physician's approval. Had the phone call with my friend been in March 2008, none of this would have happened. What I did then, which constituted and warranted three felony charges, would have been completely legal. But it wasn't. And the decision would come back to haunt me, changing the path my life would take.

All of this could have been avoided; I really have no one to blame but myself. I could have simply told my friend, "No." I could have said I'd talk to Dr. Mungo and see if he could help. Dave and I had a great relationship and he trusted my medical judgment. Had I gone to him first, my life wouldn't have been turned upside down. In fact, not only would he have said "No", but he probably would have smacked me upside the head and said, "Hell no, knucklehead!" which I would have deserved and could have definitely benefitted from.

Unfortunately, Todd, it turns out, was also a knucklehead. He decided he didn't want the prescription I had written for him. He wanted a different drug, the same drug I wrote for my other buddy. So, without calling me to discuss, he simply crossed out the drug name and wrote in another, and changed the prescribing orders. He also changed the number of refills by adding a "1" in front of the "2" and, thereby, making it a "12." Or so I was told, I never actually saw any of his handy work. I only know that when he submitted it to the pharmacy, the pharmacist immediately noticed the changes, which necessitated a call to Dr. Mungo's office, in an attempt for some clarification. This was logical and warranted, as he was the prescribing physician. Or so the pharmacist thought.

Once again, bad decisions and bad timing doomed me. When the pharmacist called Dave at the office, I was off in the hospital doing post-surgical rounding on our patients. Dave was, however, in his office. He answered the phone and listened attentively as the pharmacist explained the questionable prescription.

"No," Dave said. "That name doesn't sound familiar. I didn't write those prescriptions."

Had I been there I would have overhead the conversation. Things could have taken a different course. I would have gotten Dave's attention and said, "Press hold." That would have provided an opportunity to explain that I had written those for a good friend of mine who didn't go to his doctor, and his friend, whose health was failing him. I would have explained how I was trying to get them into a better medical position in life. Dave likely would have said, "OK. Don't do that again, Jackass." And that would have been it. He would have picked up the phone again and said, "Actually, my assistant just informed me that I signed about 25 prescriptions that day and those were among them. I just didn't recognize the names. Sorry about that."

But that's not what happened.

Instead, when Dave said he didn't write those prescriptions it triggered a report to the Drug Diversion Task Force of the DEA in Lake County, Ohio, where the pharmacy was located. Their subsequent investigation uncovered the other prescriptions I had written for my friend, and my fate was sealed.

A full-fledged investigation—followed by prosecution—could have been severely damaging to Dave's practice. I didn't want him to get into any trouble, so I drove myself up to the Lake County DEA's office, met with the investigating detective, Chris Begley, and basically told

UNDAUNTED

him everything. I then, voluntarily, rescinded my privileges at Carnation Clinic, Alliance Community Hospital and the local surgical center because I felt it was necessary to step entirely away from the situation. Dave had done nothing wrong, and an ongoing investigation would have caused him more angst and he didn't need any of this trouble. So, in essence, I stopped practicing medicine in the United States.

I later learned I could have kept practicing until the State Medical Board officially said they were yanking my license. Because my case didn't move into the courts until 2008 I could have actually practiced medicine for another year and a half in the U.S. But stepping away was in the best interest of everyone involved—especially me. I needed time for introspection and some heavy self-analysis; time to understand why I consciously made such a huge mistake.

Sure, I was used to living in the gray areas of life, but this was something else. Writing prescriptions for Schedule Class III steroids was considered felony forgery—a Felony 5, the lowest level of the felony charges in Ohio. I knew this. Each count carried a maximum of three years in prison and I would be charged with one count for each prescription I had written. That meant I was facing up to 12 years in jail.

I hired a law firm to represent me and I met with a court-appointed psychiatrist, who determined that I didn't have a problem with drugs or alcohol. However, the best outcome for my case was *treatment in lieu of conviction* (TIL)—my friend Bob and Tim each received TIL—so I would have had to lie and say I had an addictive personality, as well as come off to the court-appointed psychiatrist as such. The very thought of that left a bad taste in my mouth, and it was probably the only way I was going to avoid any jail time, but I decided I could not live with it.

I also began considering my next work options and decided to reach out to Blackwater and my old friend, Ray Horst. Ray was a former U.S. Army Special Forces 18 DELTA (Special Forces Medical Sergeant) who was now a recruiter and operator for Blackwater.

"Ray," I said, "I need a gig."

"I'm glad you called me, sir!" he said. "Brother, we're currently looking for a Director of Medical Operations in Africa for a Joint Special Operations Command Aviation Detachment gig. We do short take-off and landing transport and re-supply missions as well as low-level RECON and possible assault missions. We also do short medical transport for people who are wounded. When we're not doing medical transport and that other cool guy shit, we're transporting VIPs from one host country to the next. How does that sound?"

Without a millisecond of pondering, I said, "Sign me the fuck up."

It was as simple as that, and once again I was working for Blackwater. It was April 2007.

Around this time I was still trying to sort out why I did what I did. Why had I put a six-figure-a-year job in jeopardy and ruined things for two other guys—one of which I loved and one whom I didn't even know all that well? In hindsight, it's easy to see the warning signs. Over a two-year period, from 2005 to 2007, I lost one of my siblings—Edward Thomas Heben—to a heroin overdose, as well as a couple great friends who were SEAL buddies—including those who were killed in action during the ill-fated 2005 Operation Redwings, the Marcus Luttrell operation that became the basis for the book and the movie of the same title: *Lone Survivor*.

To be sure, I was still reeling from all of the losses—even if I refused to admit it. They hit me really hard. The combination of losing good friends who were SEALs in that operation and losing my brother to a heroin overdose put me in a state of denial—about a lot of things. Life seemed good because I enjoyed my job, but I was drinking between a pot-and-a-half to two pots of coffee a day just to feel normal enough to see patients, perform surgery, and be this magnanimous, loving, caring, compassionate and giving person that I am at my core. At the end of the day, I still had a job to do for Dr. Mungo, and I still had to be the best father that I could be to my son. But I was hurting pretty bad. I was also self-prescribing things to keep the stress hormone, cortisol, and the other inflammatory substances in my body at bay.

The reality was that I WAS going through a rough time. My divorce from Michelle in 2004 probably silently teed it all up. She had provided me with friendship and love, and a true sense of companionship and stability to my life that was no longer in place. And, in a lot of ways, writing those prescriptions helped me to justify what was happening in my life. In some twisted way, I thought if I could help two of my buddies feel better, then maybe I could feel better. But no good deed goes unpunished. And, to add insult to injury, in 2008, while the case was winding its way through the courts, I lost another brother—Mark Anthony Heben—to a methadone overdose after he was exposed to this substance as a clinical step-down from his heroin usage with my other, now-deceased, brother Eddie.

God, I miss my siblings, and I miss a lot of my SEAL brothers. You never know how death is going to affect you. Even if it doesn't seem to affect you first at all, it finds a way of creeping up on you before too long. However, mine didn't creep; it bum-rushed me from the side and hit me over the head with a lead pipe and knocked me off the tracks. It was like Godzilla rampaging my own personal Tokyo.

So I headed off to Burkina Faso in May 2007 to clear my brain and to get back to work.

Luckily, the Lake County Prosecutor's Office didn't object to me working overseas. They allowed me to retain my passport and didn't deem me to be a flight risk. It was a good thing. The Blackwater gig paid well—about $1,200 a day. I set my own schedule and did eight-week rotations. Then, I would get four weeks off. That meant that every two weeks I was working I would make about $17,000.00—nearly triple what I was making as a PA. This covered my $7,200-a-month in bills, including two mortgages, utilities, a credit card, a car, a truck, motorcycle, and, of course, my attorney bills. Sure, working for Blackwater involved a lot of travel and put me in situations where I could lose my life, but it was worth it. I have always been a Special Ops slanted-and-directed guy, and I'd spent three years out of the game. But now I was back in it, and I was ready for whatever the job would throw at me. Service to country doesn't always involve wearing a military uniform. Sometimes it involves not wearing a uniform and doing things in a low-profile fashion, and without the ancillary assets that Service men and woman enjoy: Air support, admin department, medical and life insurance, satellite communications, and hot chow. No matter. True patriots always find a way to act.

All of this became moot once I headed off to Africa in March 2008 and the judge issued the bench warrant for my arrest. Before I was even taken into custody in Atlanta, I was already considered a fugitive from justice. After my arrest, the long road through the American justice system—and that of rebuilding my life—had only just begun.

U.S. Marshals were supposed to pick me up from the Fulton County Jail and transfer me to a federal detention center, from which I would be extradited to Lake County, Ohio. Despite my best efforts I was unable to expedite things and get directly transferred back home to Ohio.

If any of you have never been arrested before, one of the first things that happens is you are processed into the system. This is also where I learned about the full extent of the charges against me and where I was asked to sign a form saying I consented to the fact there was a mandatory 14-day window of time during which the Marshals Service could come pick me up. Apparently, if they didn't arrive to get me by the end of the 14 days, I would be released. I signed the form and began my wait. Needless to say, what choice did I really have? I didn't put much faith in it, but it would be nice to walk out of that shit hole in 14 days a free man.

As it turned out, I spent the full 14 days in the Fulton County Jail—two full weeks—and right around Day 8 I decided to see what was going on.

My question was: How hard could it be to send a couple of Marshals to pick up a prisoner and transport him 30 miles to the nearest Federal Detention Center in Atlanta? I was sure that the Lake County judge, the asshole that issued the bench warrant and extradition orders for me, had also arranged to have them drag their feet. I figured he had already overstepped his authority and violated his state of impartiality by doing a few things like personally sending sheriffs to my house and issuing an APB for me at home. It only made sense that he would maximize his abilities to mess with me some more. In some ways, I admired his tenacity. In many ways, I felt sorry for his bald-headed, self-proclaimed intellectual, megalomaniacal state of being. But I digress. With this suspicion in mind, I called one of my buddies, a federal agent in Washington, D.C., and asked him to look into it. He explained that

UNDAUNTED

14 days was normal and there was nothing malicious at work with my case. Despite this, and not being one to rely on only one source for information (the U.S. Government taught me well), I also called my uncle, Steve, who used to be the Assistant U.S. Attorney in Cleveland (AUSA). He also did some back-door checking and confirmed there was no unofficial message traffic to the effect of "let that guy rot in jail as long as possible during his extradition." I was simply stuck in a wildly inefficient, if not broken, extradition system.

To be very fair, I'd been in trouble a few times before when I was younger. I have four misdemeanor charges on my record: 1) Aggravated menacing 2) Petty Theft 3) Telephone Harassment 4) Deception to Obtain a Dangerous Drug. To be fair: From age 16 to 24 I had some scrapes with the law. Some warranted, some unwarranted. Some I would do again and some I would approach differently. That's life. I believe that mistakes should be called experience. But, to be sure, I had never faced anything like this. I was so over my situation, but I recognized I would have to deal with it. After all, I truly put myself in this situation. Luckily, I was a guy not to be trifled with in jail. I entered that pod weighing 220 lbs. with long hair and a goatee. So, in my pod, everyone gave me space. A lot of it. They thought I was scary, and I was scary. I was so pissed off that I would have beat someone half to death as a form of exercise. If they sensed that, I sure as hell didn't do anything to discourage their thoughts. After all, it was the truth.

I also adapted to my situation. It was my job to be physically and mentally prepared for war every day, no matter what, no matter where. I knew that you never let your location interfere with your vocation, so I began a daily regimen. I worked out twice a day—doing pull-ups (in all forms) from the rafters and underneath the step, sets of hundreds of pushups (in all forms), arm-haulers, lunges, squats, Iron-Mike's, eight-count bodybuilders (basically, the real man's version of a burpee)—anything and everything I could do to keep in shape and maintain the razor-sharp edge I needed to have.

Inmates who were more relaxed, or intimidated by me, gave me extra food they didn't want to eat. I was informed that these were known as peace offerings. My presence in the Fulton County jail for

14 days disrupted the normal order of things—whatever alpha male there was during that time simply went away. It became obvious that whatever the pecking order had been prior to my arrival was gone, and my biggest fear was killing someone and incurring a federal case for murder before I even got transferred to the detention center. I prayed to God, daily, that nobody messed with me. Not only am I a trained killer, but I was also extremely pissed off and agitated. Thankfully, I am highly disciplined too.

As it turned out, I had a couple near-misses, but otherwise my two-week stay in Fulton County Jail was uneventful. One night, right before I was transferred to the detention facility, my cell mate worked up the nerve to ask me if I was a "straight-up killer."

"Word is you are," he said. "Chatter 'round here is you off-ed a bunch of people and that you are an international drug dealer."

I could have set him straight, but instead I just gave him a demonic grin, and shrugged. The chill that went up his spine and the look on his face was priceless.

Those two weeks in jail were more time of self-reflection. I kept replaying everything that had happened. The times when we are the most exposed, the times when we feel the stress of the extremes, the times when we believe we may never return, and the countless times we risk it all for others...well, as it turns out, these are the honest moments that allow our humanity to press through. And it is this very humanity that allows us to push on. This was one of those times, and it's an understatement to say I was pretty stressed and majorly exposed. Within a 24-hour period I went from having a top secret security clearance to being in handcuffs and being taken away in a sheriff's car to jail and dumped into a holding tank with 25 people that was only meant to hold 12 people. And now I was waiting to be transferred to a federal detention facility for God knows how long. The entire situation was initially embarrassing and humiliating and was now crossing into the realm of ridiculousness. I was getting frustrated and I needed to check myself before I further wrecked myself or, worse; somebody else.

No matter how many times I replayed the situation, I came to the same fucking conclusion—I essentially did this all to myself. My commitment to the mission—and to my buddies—outweighed any potential personal consequences. But that was the way I lived my life—putting others, the Team, before myself. It's what they drilled into our heads during training. And you learn how to deal with your current reality—what's put in front of you—with no questions asked and no regrets.

It took the full 14 days for anyone to come get me. When they did, it wasn't even real U.S. Marshals who showed up. Instead, it was a couple of corpulent contractors who appeared in the middle of the night to collect me. I was awakened around 2 a.m. and told to pack up my stuff. I didn't grab anything and whatever was left in my cell, my 'cellie' was more than welcome to have. I was then moved to another holding cell, where I was out-processed and shackled around my waist, at the wrists, and with a chain reaching down to my legs where I was also shackled at the ankles. If I would have had a face mask on, I would've been mistaken for Hannibal Lector. When the contractors finally arrived, they made me do the pirate-ship shuffle from the holding cell to a bus. Inside the bus, I was chained to the floor via the ankle chain. We traveled exactly 30 miles south, as I was able to do the easy, direction/time/speed/distance, calculations based on road signs, the speedometer and the clock. It's funny that they would let inmates even see these bits of information. Information is power, and you'd be surprised how many ways you could use location, direction, time and distance in a criminal transport situation. Hell, if I was going down for murder and looking at the death penalty, I'd definitely have some ways to put that information to use. Remember: Information is power and more on this later.

Onward and downward to the Robert A. Dayton Federal Detention Facility we drove, which, to my surprise, was my new home for the next month.

After I was strip-searched and in-processed, for the second time on this journey, the intake guard asked me about my ethnicity. I was so aggravated over my situation that I told her I was Hispanic. I still had the dark African tan (my 'Afritan'), long hair and a goatee, so she didn't even question it—despite my non-Hispanic name. It was another small victory, and these can keep you from going off the reservation. I wasn't close, but I didn't want to be either.

This little deception tactic got me a Hispanic roommate. His name was Pastor and he was from some austere mountainous region of Mexico. Pastor was about 5-foot nothing, weighed one hundred and nothing, and his grasp of English was identical: Nothing. It was a triple nothing that, indeed, was good for something. This was because I felt it was a good opportunity to practice and expand on my Spanglish. And, because he and I and a bunch of the other Hispanic guys were always chatting in and out of Spanish, the guards never questioned whether I was really Hispanic or not. As I said, this was one of my small victories every day. There would be more.

In federal prison, roughly 45 percent of the inmates are apprehended illegal aliens—most all are from Mexico. The system is clearly broken. When you get caught the first time, you get sent back for free. The second time you're caught, you receive a mandatory five-year sentence in federal prison. Usually, illegal aliens end up working in the U.S. for between five and seven years before they get caught. That's the monetary equivalent of over 20 years of working in Mexico. So these guys end up doing five years in jail and their families back home in Mexico have been sent a lot of money—which they can use some of to help keep their family member comfortable in prison for five years. All in all, it's a pretty good deal for the illegal aliens, who in reality, were just looking for solid employment. Well, at least the ones who were not there on drug-trafficking charges. We need to clamp down on the big businesses that employ them and use them like fodder. We have immigration laws for a reason. They should be strictly enforced. Hell, that's a topic for another book.

On the second day I was in the facility, my current status of staying out of any altercations ended. On this day, I woke up with my shoulder hurting from sleeping on the maxi-pad of a mattress I was given, and I wanted some Motrin. I got in line for the twice-daily medical cart. Another guy was in line in front of me, but he left to go get a drink of water. He didn't come back for a while, so naturally, I took his spot. When he finally returned, he wanted to get back in line in front of me.

I wasn't having any of that. He decided he wanted to fight me over it. While I could appreciate his moxie, I also knew that he was making a big mistake.

"You don't want to do this," I offered. I always give people a chance to avoid maiming themselves on my body.

He smirked and replied, "Motherfucker, you gonna regret this."

Ha-ha, I chuckled to myself and thought: I don't think so. Before I calmly said with a smirk, "I don't think so."

By now I was closing the gap and collision was imminent. I'm sure he thought we were going to have some chest bumping, shit talking, MMA weigh-in style, face-to-face shoving match. He tried to look menacing. But he soon found out that I'm not a guy who gets intimidated—I've faced death on more than one occasion. Nor am I a guy who enters a fight with a push. I believe in calmly taking direct and immediate action. And when I take it, you'd better not blink because I'm quicker than a long-tailed cat in a room full of rocking chairs. I was taught by my high school football coach, Pat Fahey, that speed kills. Not only on the highway, but on the gridiron as well, and it was fourth-and-goal, and I was going for it with brute strength and bad intentions.

Before the guy could even blink, I moved. I hit him with a quick rabbit punch to the Adam's apple and he lurched forward. He crumbled actually. This put him in perfect position to receive my knee to his face. He did so unwillingly but very acceptingly. I drove my knee up and into his chin, and this caused his head and his body to rocket backwards. Where the head goes, the body is soon to follow. He was unconscious before he hit the floor.

And then it was over—two swift moves, barely visible behind the line of inmates, barely audible above the TV and pod chatter, and with two or three inmates doing crunches nearby on the floor, none of the guards paid attention to another body there. And that was it.

Most of the other inmates saw what had happened. After that, everyone in the pod wanted to be my buddy, and there were no more incidents. I actually apologized to that guy a few days later and explained that I had been having a rough couple of weeks. As it turns out, he was in prison for gang and drug-related charges, was only 24-years old, and was looking at a very long time in a place like this. We ended up becoming pretty cordial for the remainder of my stay. If we hadn't, I would have gladly beat him down again.

Another guy I ended up spending a lot of time talking with was an attorney named Ted H. Ted had owned an import/export business in the Atlanta area. Apparently, he had been working with some folks in Afghanistan and Pakistan, so we spoke a lot about our time in that region of the world. He was serving a two-and-a-half to three-year sentence for supposed nefarious dealings with some of the imports he was involved with. In fact, he was close to the end of his sentence. Ted went to law school at Cornell, so he and I were able to have some conversations that were unlike many you would expect to have in a federal prison pod full of people who never earned a high school diploma or, for some, even a GED. Our conversations were yet another source for small victories for me there.

Another one was the med-cart gal that came by the cells every night at 10:30 p.m. in order to pass out medicine to the inmates who were on a regular schedule for them. The first night I heard her speaking, I could tell that she had a Haitian-French accent. When she came to our cell to deliver medicine to my cell mate, Pastor, he was asleep and I told her as such, en Français (in French)! After that, she and I would have many short conversations in French until the night I left. Again, little victories add up.

By now it had been over two weeks in captivity and I decided it was time to call Blackwater and explain my situation. Basically, tell them why I would not be back for my next rotation. I called Sheri, and my friend Ray.

"Don't count on me being back in Africa 30 days from now," I said.

I told them about the falsified prescriptions, my pending court case, and the recent sequence of events in my life that would keep me from returning. I think their first clue was the caller ID that stated the call was coming from a Federal Corrections Institution. I said I had no idea it would come to this because I had been allowed to come and go for a year.

Both Sheri and Ray understood.

"Let me know if something changes," Sheri said. "Nobody in the countries you're going to will care about any of this. There's no governing body for PAs in Africa, so even if you can't practice in the U.S., there's still a place for you here. Let me know when you're ready to return." Or some version that went a lot like that. Ray also said a version of the same, plus a few added expletives to flavor it all.

It was comforting to know neither of them looked at what I had done as a negative. Their attitude was different: You took action for two brothers and we get that. It wasn't as if I had been trafficking or selling drugs on the street. The gray zone is alive and well in the private military contracting business. And that is a very good thing. I would, most likely, be going back overseas.

Next, I had to deal with my family. I hadn't told anyone what was happening. Nobody knew any of this was going on except for Dr. Mungo and my attorney. I thought it would get resolved, but things were unraveling quickly and it was distressing to say the least. When things unravel like that, it's stressful. I was in a precarious situation that made me look deceitful. I was always a person people saw as disciplined. All of a sudden I'm in handcuffs and in jail and being extradited. It's drastically different from the image people had of me, and that wasn't a good thing. I had briefly explained my situation to my ex-wife Michelle when I was in Fulton County Jail, but now I had to tell it all to everyone. It wasn't pleasant, but there was some peace to it. The burden I had carried alone was going to be lifted.

Admittedly, I wasn't so much worried about what my family, as a whole, would think, other than the fact that my stepfather would look down on me. I was sure he was going to give me the hardest time; he likes to be the one to point out all your flaws and failures in an effort to help. It's really his attempt to seize control over you for whatever he needs to accomplish at the moment. If there is nothing that needs to be physically achieved, he will do it just to make himself feel better, more powerful, and more successful. Such is the way of a control-freak attorney—but it had reached a point where keeping it to myself was no longer feasible. Yes, telling Michelle was one thing, telling my mother was another and dropping it on my stepfather was going to be a different story altogether. Yet, this extradition, I felt, was going to be a long, drawn-out affair, and I needed all the support I could muster—especially, potential legal support—even if it came with a lot of other bullshit baggage.

When I told my stepfather, as expected, he wasn't very supportive. I explained I didn't think that my attorney was handling things properly—how could he have let this reach the point of a bench warrant? But my stepfather only offered his support to a certain point—as I've mentioned, he's never truly been my advocate. In fact, he thought I was getting exactly what I deserved and I was told by some family members, after the fact, that he stated I should receive a lengthy jail sentence to straighten me out and if he was the judge, I'd still be in jail. Now you see what I had to deal with as a kid in that house. To make matters worse, he would later make official documented statements to the State Medical Board that he believed I had a problem with drugs. What father would do that? Moving on...

My mother, other family members, and friends saw it differently. They rallied around me with their full support.

The whole time, the thing I was most upset about was not being able to see my son, Mason. My last communication with him was by satellite phone before I left Africa. He was six-years old and I couldn't very well tell him what had happened. He wouldn't have understood. But he did understand the letdown of my not showing up when I promised—and that hurt a lot.

I explained that it was going to be many, many days before we saw each other again. It didn't sit well with me, but he understood. He was still disappointed, I could hear it in his sweet little voice, but it was more earth-shattering for me—I had to think about that every day for the next two months. You see, his mother and he were supposed to pick me up at the airport in Cleveland after I arrived from Atlanta. My son had been marking the days off on his calendar and he was very excited to see me. When I was home for 30-day rotations, we spent every day together doing dude stuff: dirt bikes, hunting, fishing, swimming, shooting guns, riding on my Harley or in my 1972 Chevy C-20. We just engaged in total dad-son activities. Also, the older he got, the more that magical 'time-space-continuum' collapsed for him, and consequently, for me as well! A day was no longer a week was no longer a month was no longer a year. He realized the length of time I was away and it affected him for sure. And this greatly affected me. When people ask me what was the hardest thing about being deployed, I always tell them it's the family separation.

Finally, one night at 0230 hours and 30-days after I arrived, I heard the voice from the other side of my cell door tell me to "pack up your things, you're outta here." It wasn't the French voice I was used to, but it was still very pleasant to hear. And again, the pudgy contractor people from the U.S. Marshal Service showed back up to collect me. I was shackled again around the waist, wrists and ankles, loaded into a barred windowed, Blue Bird prison bus, and driven BACK to Hartsfield-Jackson Airport, which was where this road started about 45-days before. Still to this day, I hate that damn airport.

We pulled up to an unmarked 737 jet aircraft—a decrepit-looking white plane that served, quite literally, as Con Air. We were placed into alphabetical order and I was loaded onto Con Air and transported West where we stopped in Jackson, Mississippi and finally onto Oklahoma City, where I was delivered to Oklahoma City Federal Prison to face the next leg of my journey through the American federal prison system.

The plane taxis right up to a gangway and you enter the prison without ever touching dirt. I was strip-searched again and taken to a pod and assigned a cell with another cell mate. I didn't even make it 12 hours here without getting into a fight over, of all things, a seat at breakfast the next morning. Some dude insisted I was in his seat. I told him twice that I was not. After his buddies egged him on and he approached me a third time, I had about enough of him. I rocketed out of my seat and hit him square under his chin with the palm of my right hand. Palm strikes are crippling, and he did just that. But he couldn't go too far as my foot was planted on his foot at the same time. He fell flat on his side and I side-mounted him, placing my knee on his throat and both my thumbs in the corner of his eye sockets. He was dazed and shocked and so were many around us. Yelling, and looking around me, I asked: "Does any other motherfucker think that this is their seat!?"

All I got were open-mouthed stares followed by heads shaking 'no.' Next, I looked down at my choking victim and said to him, "I'm going to count from 1 from 5. When I get to 5 I will let you up. Your job is to get as far away from me as fast as possible." He indicated that he understood.

And so it went. I had an interesting conversation with an Aryan Brotherhood leader after that, but I told him I was leaving soon but also that I appreciated the offer to join. I understand that people join groups they wouldn't normally consider, when they are in such places. You can't watch your back 100 percent of the time. It's sad, but it's true. I think of some of the dudes I met in prison and I wonder what they must think when they see me on TV today. I hope they are all doing well.

I was out of that place and back on Con Air within seven days. I was flown to Kentucky, then onto Pittsburgh, where I was chained to the floor in another prison bus and taken to a Federal facility in Youngstown, Ohio. Twenty-four hours later I was finally back in Lake County, Ohio, waiting to go before the judge. It was another five days before that happened.

CHAPTER 5

"DON'T ACCEPT YOUR LOT IN LIFE AS IT CURRENTLY STANDS. ROGER UP AND ASSAULT IT HEAD ON. ALWAYS LOOK FOR A WAY TO DOMINATE, NOT JUST BECAUSE YOU CAN, BUT BECAUSE YOU WERE BORN FOR IT. SUCCESS IS IN YOUR DNA. A LOW BLOW IN LIFE WILL ROCK YOU FROM TIME TO TIME, BUT IN THE GRAND SCHEME OF THINGS IT WILL TAKE A HELL OF A LOT MORE THAN THAT TO KNOCK YOU DOWN AND TAKE YOU OUT! I REMEMBER WHAT MY FAVORITE MASTER CHIEF ALWAYS SAID: 'TRAMPLE THE WEAK, HURDLE THE DEAD!' AND ALWAYS, FOR YOUR FAMILY, FAITH, COMMUNITY, COUNTRY, AND FREEDOM: ONWARD AND UPWARD!"

—CHRISTOPHER MARK HEBEN

Show me a person who has lived a long and successful life without ever experiencing any adversity and I'll tell you that I'm looking at a person who never really lived at all. If there's one thing I've learned in my life it's that you must be resilient no matter what happens. If you cling to the essentials of who you are as a person and what you are at your core being, you can't go wrong. You can't quit. That's a very powerful thing. I try to convey this to anyone and everyone that asks me for advice.

Many people have a shitty upbringing or grow up in bad social or family situations. But inherently, intrinsically, most of us are truly resilient. Too many of us don't realize that.

Yet this is one of the basic skills the Navy expects for anyone who aspires to become a SEAL. At the onset, you're given a test that's like a modified version of an MMPI—the Minnesota Multiphasic Personality Inventory psychological test—wherein they ascertain just how resilient you are. Let's face it, you can't be in someone else's country at 0330 hours in the morning with bad intentions and not be resilient. You're out there trying to make a person, place or thing disappear, while other people are trying to prevent you from doing that. It's a very deadly cat-

and-mouse game. If you're not resilient, you're going to put everyone in danger; your entire team will be at risk. As SEALs, we can't have that. I take this same message to corporate America when I tell them how critical resiliency is in business.

SEALs rise to the occasion when the chips are down. We find ways to ante up and win the match. If you send 16 of us to do a job, you damn well better kill all 16 of us because we are all trained equally—and we are all deadly. Until there are none of us left, there's still a chance for mission completion. We're that resilient. It's our hallmark, and it's something that every person on this planet has within them—they just need to look deep enough inside to discover it. Those who cannot or will not, have no business in the SEAL teams, at the helm of a business, or in a lofty corporate position. Yes people are only as good as the person asking them the questions. I'd rather surround myself with those who ask the tough questions and already know the hard answers. These are your asskickers, your winners, and your survivors—those who are willing to do whatever it takes to come home or seal the deal. I am honored to be counted among such men.

I learned resiliency at an early age. When you have a childhood like mine, you either sack up or fold your tent and go home—there's no middle ground. My mother, Patricia Ann Holmes ('Pat' or 'Patty'), met my birth father, Caid McKinley, on a summer outing to Cedar Point when my father was working a summer job there. Caid was 17-years old; my mom was 15, but she confabulated and said she was 17 as well. It was love at first sight—or whatever constitutes love when you're a couple of teenagers. They hooked up, and my mother became pregnant with my brother Jon. Caid and Patty were soon married, but not too long after that he shipped off to Germany during the Vietnam War. He returned on extended leave for the birth of my brother. Then, 13-months later, I arrived on September 26, 1969. My father was back in Germany.

Caid was born and raised in Willard, Ohio. He had already joined the U.S. Army before he met my mother, so he was pre-committed to a post in Europe. He went off to war; my mother, brother and I, stayed with my grandparents at W. 103rd and Baltic Avenue on the near west side of Cleveland. During the war, Caid came home on leave a few times.

I don't remember ever meeting him on any of the leave visits after I was born. It didn't take too long before my grandmother became sick of the soldier who was never home for her daughter and her grandchildren, so she began hiding Caid's letters from my mother, meddling in the relationship, and eventually broke up the marriage. Caid and my mother were divorced when I was three-years old, and I never really had the chance to get to know him.

My mother and her family knew Edward J. Heben, Jr., from around the neighborhood. My grandparents liked him and his family—they felt he was from the "right side of the tracks." Ed's father was a dentist, and his wife had a PhD in Education. Ed was going to graduate from Kenyon College and was already accepted to law school. My grandmother wanted her daughter to be with someone like that, from a family like that, and, more important, someone who was home. She pushed to make the relationship happen, and the two were married in 1972. I was three-years old when Ed became my stepfather.

Growing up, my relationship with Ed was, at times, tumultuous. When I was a junior in high school, we'd fight at least once or twice a month—often punching and wrestling. When I was a senior, this rose to more than two or three times a week. Ed wanted me to do well, but only if I did it his way. We rarely saw eye-to-eye on anything. The day I turned 18, I walked into my high school principal's office and promptly told Mrs. B that I was emancipating myself. Also, I had already secured an apartment and proceeded to move out that day. Thankfully, this was in the first month of my senior year of high school.

I think Ed and I were always at odds because he was very controlling. To this day, that has never really changed. It only abated after I became a SEAL—but it took on new life shortly after the U.S. Marshal's Service delivered me to the Lake County Sheriff's Office to face the criminal charges for writing forged prescriptions.

The first time I ever truly met my father, Caid McKinley, was when I was 17-years old and a junior in high school. I was playing in a football game, and right before the game I was warming up when my brother came over to the fence at the edge of the field in order to get my attention.

"See that guy over there, next to Aunt Mary Jane?" he said, pointing at a guy I didn't recognize in the stands.

"Yeah. OK. What about him?"

"That's our dad." He said.

"Dude, thanks for dropping that bomb on me right now you jackass!"

With that, I stole one more look and tried my best to re-focus on the biggest game of the year. But, to say that I was shocked was an understatement. He could have told me that after the game—even made a personal introduction. Instead, my first recollection of my real father was visually seeing him sitting up in the stands at the 50-yard line from my vantage point down on the football field. I had known for more than five years that I'd had a different father than Ed—I found my birth certificate in my mother's room when I was in fifth grade. It read "Christopher Mark McKinley," and I had questioned my mother about it.

Ever since then, I had wondered about this man called Caid and what had happened between him and my mother. I just never thought my curiosity would be visualized during my warm up before a high school football game. In many ways, it taught me to always expect the unexpected and to perform in spite of it and the associated pressures. In life, there is always a lesson to be learned. There would be many more.

After the game, I introduced myself. We have stayed in contact ever since. In fact, I talk to Caid a lot, probably once a week or so. He still lives in Willard, Ohio. Caid retired from the U.S. Army as a Lt. Colonel, and today is a licensed attorney and real-estate broker. But what I find most intriguing is that he is a legit auctioneer. Maybe that's where I get my fast thinking and fast-talking abilities from.

The military has always been in my blood. My mother told me a little about Caid after I found my birth certificate. She explained he had served in the Army during the Vietnam War. I also learned that two of my grandfathers served—one in the Army; the other in the Navy; and that my great uncle Eddie Planta (on my mother's side) was a pilot in three different wars. My stepfather's father (my step-grandfather), the dentist, was the veteran who served in the Army. During the war, he was stationed in the Fiji Islands, and it was his job to relay Japanese ship movement to the U.S. military command centers via telegraph and teletype devices. He told me quite a few stories about his time overseas, and I became hooked on all things military.

I devoured everything I could find—reading voraciously about Vietnam, Korea, World War II and World War I. I became a military-history fanatic, and to this day, I can still tell you all about the German Tiger tank with its 88-millimeter gun, which was the largest tank-mounted gun in WWII. The armor plate on the German Tiger tank was so thick that the U.S. M4 Sherman's guns could not penetrate it. If you were unlucky enough to face this tank in war, and could not get a shot on it from behind, it was almost a certain death sentence if that 88mm fired on you..

Ed's father and my step-grandmother lived on W. 110th and Edgewater in a large English Tudor style house. The basement was very cool—it had what I called 'catacombs' or little dark rooms. I'm sure it was just my child brain that saw the room this way. But there was a room where the water heater tanks were, and that's where I found a box with pictures from World War II. I was either nine- or 10-years old when I ran across it. There were photos of Japanese tanks and destroyed Japanese tanks, and photos of dead Japanese soldiers with weapons in their hands. The photos were pretty gruesome, but in some macabre way, I was completely enthralled. I mean, these were real photos, taken by my grandfather, which had probably not been seen by anyone in a very long time. I felt like I had found a box of buried treasure and I set out to learn as much about the images in those pictures as possible.

In 1984, when the movie *Rambo* came out, I definitively decided right then and there, I wanted to be a Green Beret. I had already watched John Wayne in *The Green Berets* over a dozen times, but *Rambo* was truly great. I was completely infatuated with that movie. Operating under this enthusiasm, I squirreled away some money and bought a 12" Rambo knife from the back of a *Gung Ho* magazine—you know, the one with the 7" blade and serrated edge and the compass on top of the hollow handle that contained matches and trip wire. Here's a funny fact: A few years ago, my mother ran across an ID badge I made when I was in 8th grade. It read that I was a sniper in the U.S. Army with expert marksmen qualifications with pistol and rifle, as well as an expert in hand-to-hand combat. It also stated that I was a demolitions expert and free-fall master. It was my very own Army Green Beret US Military ID! LOL. Little did I know, but all of those qualifications would become truisms in the very near future, just under the auspices of a different branch of the DoD.

It helped that I had access to military magazines. My stepfather and mother owned a Natural and Gourmet food store called Doc Heben's Natural Food Market/Doc Heben's Nutrition Center. Across the street from it, there was an international bookstore that carried publications like *Soldier of Fortune* and *Gung Ho* magazine, among others. When I wasn't stocking shelves or waiting on customers at my family's health-food store, I was in the bookstore poring over the cool military magazines and adding more data to my cranial collection on war, weapons, and the importance of strengthening your mind and body for it. Yes, it seemed I was always importing data that would come in handy later.

The mind is the master and commander of your body. Anyone who tells you otherwise has probably never amounted to shit. Your body may be strong, but if you don't have a mind that's commanding that strength, you're essentially weak. The two are interrelated, and when you add a proper diet into the equation—what you put in your fuel tank—then you're really looking at the big picture. You could have a NASCAR engine under the hood. You could have all the complex computer control systems that are monitoring engine output and fuel output and precise internal combustion processes. That's great. But if you don't have the right fuel in the tank, it doesn't matter. You're not going anywhere far or doing it anytime soon. Those three things are critical—quality fuel, a powerful engine, and a robust neural capacity to oversee it. It's the triad of brain, body and diet. It's all connected, and it must be balanced.

I have taken this idea very seriously since I was a kid. My parents opened their Natural Food store in 1981, and I spent a lot of time there. I'm very thankful to have had that early access to things like vitamins, minerals, herbs and organics. And, because I was an athlete I knew that most of it worked. Today, when I don't work out for a couple days, I don't feel as if I'm running at peak capacity. I've also learned that the older you get, and if you've built a good foundation and structure on top of it, the less hardcore your workouts need to be. You just need to engage in some sort of kinetic activity and eat right. It's the type of thing I teach these days as part of my SEAL Team Challenge. I say: "Once you've built your dream house, there's no need to constantly tear it down and re-build it. All you have to do is the proper maintenance." The problem is that most people don't have the drive to build it in the first place. Most Americans are always playing catch up or pointing fingers with respect to their state of physical wellbeing. We all want it, we just don't want to work for it. This same attitude plays a big role in the constant, 90-percent attrition rate at SEAL training. But I never bought into that bullshit—you earn what you get and you get what you earn. Entitlement, quotas, and Affirmative Action are all bullshit, and they are destroying our nation!

This philosophy has followed me throughout my life—to the playing field, SEAL training, as well as overseas operations and assignments. I was 28-years old when I went through SEAL training, so it was even more important for me to be in great shape. If I had been 18-years old, I would have been able to muscle through the training with brute strength and ignorance. But when I was 18, I may not have had the mental acuity or fortitude to succeed. It was the combination of those things that helped me achieve what I did. And it was this same special combination that helped me remain undaunted throughout many extreme trials and taxing tribulations.

<<<>>>

My life truly changed after Atlanta and I became a convicted felon. My journey of recovery and rebuilding was possible only because I essentially spent my entire life preparing for it.

UNDAUNTED

I started playing organized sports when I was in fourth or fifth grade—by then I didn't wear the braces on my legs all the time. But those braces made me stronger—both physically and mentally, because they forced me to deal with an inordinate amount of B.S. Who wants to be on the playground with a leather belt around your waist that buckles in the front and has rubber-coated metal rods on each hip that travel down each leg attaching to specially made shoes? Physically, when the braces came off, I felt free, loose and lighter. So, in many ways, by wearing them I became even faster than I had been before. It's the classic Overload Principle—when you walk with weights and then take them off, you have that much more strength and speed. You feel untethered and immune to the laws of gravity. At least that's what I always told myself. Again, there's that brain-control component I've mentioned.

When I was 12, my stepfather took me to meet with a social worker at John Carroll University to assess why I couldn't sit still and why I was wired the way I was. I think the interview and assessment was just as much for his benefit as it was for mine. The social worker told us that I was the type of person who needed a constant physical and mental challenge. He stated that I needed a mind and body workout at least once every 48 hours or I was going to be miserable in life. As a result, sports became the best immediate outlet for my energy. It wasn't until a few years later that I would decide to incorporate the brain component of that formula.

I played football in junior high and high school as a tailback, middle linebacker, second-string quarterback and defensive back. My eighth grade team even won the city championship while only allowing six points to be scored on us all season. Personally, I set a league touchdown record on both defense and offense. Ah, the glory days.

At home, I still had my issues. Ed and I butted heads, but I always got along with my brothers and sisters. Every warrior has a nurturing side, too. You can't be all *yin*; you need an equal amount of *yang*. Being the second oldest of 12, I would often assist my mother around the house by changing my siblings' diapers, feeding them, and caring for them—I was a good big brother. I love the fact that I can pick up my sister, give her a hug, and then go outside and, if necessary, beat up the neighbor kid for pushing my brother around.

That strong sense of family was important growing up, but it was even more important after my arrest. When I got to Cleveland from Oklahoma, via Atlanta, everyone in my family knew what was going on. They were supportive in the way only family can be when your back is against the wall and the odds are stacked against you.

Despite our historic differences, my stepfather helped. He looked into my case and gave me advice on how to approach the charges. Between him and my uncle Steve I felt there were a couple knowledgeable advocates who had my back and were checking on things from a different angle than my attorney was.

I spent five days in Lake County Jail after the U.S. Marshal's Service delivered me from Oklahoma City to Youngstown to Lake County Jail. Then I bonded out for $100,000—at the time one of the largest bonds in that county's history. I relied upon my uncle Tom to spot me the $10,000 that was needed as 10 percent.

One of the things my stepfather found when he looked into the case was that the judge called the Lake County Sheriff's department and asked them to send deputies to my house to see if I really left the country or if I was just hiding out there. I don't hide and I don't play games. That asshole judge told me I could leave the country for work, then he attempted to pull the rug out from under me at the last minute. Screw him.

At that time, I had been living on 10 acres in Minerva, Ohio. Minerva is about one-and-a-half hours southeast of Cleveland, and remote enough to have been my own private Idaho. My house was about 1,000 yards off the road and buffered from it by a 50-foot, tree-covered, ravine. The property had formerly been an RV trailer park in the 1980s and early '90s called Sherwood Forest, and there were active 110-volt, 220-volt, and water hook-ups all around the property on the remnants of two pea-gravel roads. There was a main house, where I lived, and a detached guest house, where my uncle Tom lived.

Tom was a mechanic and loved classic cars. I had an eight-car garage on that property, and my uncle would pick up old cars and tinker with them. Tom is my mother's brother. He is nine-years older than me, so he was more like a big brother than an uncle. Tom was the youngest of my mother's siblings, so he lived with my mother and I at grandma's when I was younger. Needless to say, he and I had been tight my entire life.

Tom is a big man—about 6' 7"—and used to weigh more than 350 pounds. Most of my uncles and siblings are tall. In fact, I am one of the shortest males in the family at 6'0". Hell, my sister Sarah in 6'1½" tall! Tom was a big dude, even after he lost about 100 or so pounds, but the damage to his knees from carrying around all that weight was pretty much permanent and he had to undergo a few knee surgeries from Dr. Mungo in order to get around effectively. And he did. When I was overseas on missions for Blackwater, Tom kept my machines running by driving them around, my Harley, my truck and one of my cars—a black 5 Series BMW.

During what was to be my final Blackwater mission in Africa, Tom was out and about in the BMW when the Lake County Sheriff's department decided to check out my house in Minerva. At the same time, they put out an APB on my car to see if they could catch me driving around. A Stark County deputy sheriff saw Tom driving my car and called for back-up—I was, after all, apparently very, very dangerous. Public enemy *numero uno*! Three additional officers joined the pursuit and pulled Tom over.

The officers approached the car as if Tom was a terrorist, guns at the ready. Thinking they were looking for me, they were in fact doing a felony traffic stop. To my knowledge, I had not been convicted of anything, yet.

"Chris Heben!" they called out. "Put your hands up and slowly get out of the car!"

Uncle Tom put his hands up and methodically stretched his large frame out of my European super cruiser.

"I'm not Chris Heben," he said, and slowly turned around to face the officers.

A female Stark County deputy sheriff was standing in front of Tom, pointing her gun at him. "Don't take another step," she barked, her hands shaking like an alcoholic in need of a few drinks.

"I'm not Chris Heben," my uncle repeated. "He's in Africa." Then he stated, "Hey, shaky lady, get that gun out of my face. You look like a scared, chubby, little child, and you're making me uncomfortable."

Finally, the officers realized that Tom wasn't me and, dejectedly, they let him go. Tom would later go on to describe how humorous it was to watch these officers trembling as he got out of the car. To this day, I often apologize to him for having to go through that.

Because of the aggressive approach, my father concluded that the judge was biased. He overstepped his vow of impartiality when he directed the Sheriff's department to seek me out—he also believed that the bench warrant was issued because the judge thought I snubbed my nose at the court.

In reality, I was merely following through with my job commitment at Blackwater and going on a pre-arranged mission overseas. My father recommended that we submit a motion for recusal because the judge had seemingly lost his impartiality in the case. I considered my father's advice, but at the time was more concerned about how long it would take to get the case resolved. If a new judge was assigned to the case, what would then happen to me? Would I have to start the process over again? Would it be worse for me? Would I be stuck in jail longer? Nobody had an answer for these questions. I finally decided not to submit a motion for recusal and to take my chances with the asshole, overbearing judge. Now for the record, I am not anti-judge at all, I just hate the ass-hat judge that was assigned to my case. The shit-bag still sits on the bench today. Oh, and there's another one too. I'll get around to that douche bag soon.

I bonded out in May 2008. Nearly three months had passed before my day in court. On August 20, I appeared before the judge again, pled no contest as advised under a plea agreement, I was found guilty of three felony forgery counts and received a 90-day jail sentence. He gave me credit for the 57 days I had already served and then sentenced me to the Lake County Jail to serve out the remaining 33 days. I ended up serving 30—I signed up for the prison work program to sweep floors and do other odd jobs.

All in all, it ended up being pretty easy. While there, I worked out twice a day and thought about my future. The guards watched my intensity and even approached me to ask if I could give them exercise tips. And, because they knew I was a trained Navy SEAL and served in Blackwater, they asked about weapons training. That was pretty surreal.

I was finally released on September 20, 2008, and placed on probation. That meant I had to check in twice a month with, Tim L., my probation officer for the next two years. That, unfortunately, put a crimp in my plans to return to active duty with Blackwater and resume rotations in Africa. Flying back and forth twice a month became logistically impossible. It was only logistically impossible, but not technically impossible, for although the judge had my civilian passport in his possession, the dumbass didn't realize, know, or even think to ask for my official passport. For someone who fancies himself an intellectual, he sure is a pompous dumbass! But for him, it was mission accomplished. Let's golf clap for him now. Shall we?

My entire experience in the criminal justice system was bizarre. If you had told me a few years earlier that I would spend a full quarter of the year in 2008 in jail, I would have told you to put down the crack pipe! But that's what happened, and it turned my life upside down from that moment forward. Between voluntarily stepping away from my job as a PA and then logistically losing my opportunities with Blackwater, I estimate that I lost more than $1.2 million in unrealized income.

So once again, I found myself unemployed, with a mountain of debt, and few prospects to earn a living. After a quick assessment of my skills—I knew a lot about medicine—I sought out a way to put that knowledge to good use. Through a friend I found an opportunity to work for a medical device distributorship and sell spinal implants and spine-related, biomedical products. This led to me realize that I could start my own device distributorship. Thus began the next chapter of my life as an entrepreneur.

CHAPTER 6

"I'M NOT A BIG FAN OF LOOKING BACK, BUT EVERY NOW AND THEN IT'S NICE TO HAVE A QUICK LOOK AT WHERE YOU'VE BEEN IN ORDER TO REMIND YOURSELF OF WHERE YOU ARE AND WHERE YOU NEED TO BE."

ONWARD AND UPWARD!

–CHRISTOPHER MARK HEBEN

My road to becoming a Navy SEAL was a circuitous one. Most people join the Navy directly after high school—between the ages of 18- and 20-years old—but for me, that wasn't the case. I didn't join the Navy until I was 27-years old. Instead, in 1988 after graduating from high school I headed off to Bowling Green State University. I played football in high school, and despite not receiving a scholarship, I walked on at Bowling Green and made the team as a strong safety. Thirty of us tried to walk on; only two of us made it. I became one of the team's 12 defensive backs.

College was much different than high school—I majored in girls and screwing around. At one point, I was placed on academic probation because I had a 1.86 GPA. My fascination with all things military continued in college, and I took a few military science courses to satisfy my curiosity and bolster my GPA. Unfortunately, it didn't help enough. Despite eventually raising my GPA to a 2.75, I soon realized that I was blowing upwards of $10,000 a year for college and wasn't yet disciplined enough to commit fully to doing what it took to scholastically succeed. It didn't help that I wasn't starting for the football team either, which might have provided some of the structure I desperately needed. So, after my freshman year, I decided to leave BGSU and move back home to Cleveland.

Back home, I found an apartment and began working odd jobs to earn a meager living while I figured out what the hell I was going to do next. I worked at a bar called Shooter's in the Flats of Cleveland—a strip of bars and restaurants on both the East and West banks of the Cuyahoga River. With major bar-side boat docking, it was one of Cleveland's premier party places—especially for the rich and privileged. I was neither. I tried taking a few classes at Cuyahoga Community College to raise my GPA, thinking I would eventually go back to college full-time. But it was pretty clear that I didn't have any real future plans for it, and I slowly chipped away at life while waiting for something exciting, something better, to come my way.

After a series of fly-by-night bouncer and bar-back jobs at places with names like Fagans and Howl-At-The-Moon Saloon, I realized the life I was living had no meaning. And so I started the arduous task of buckling down. I enrolled at Cleveland State University and began taking courses—racking up more than 100 credits, close to the 128 or so I needed to complete my college degree. At Cleveland State I realized my affinity for water and learned I could hold my breath underwater for a long time.

I functioned well in the pool, and received my PADI SCUBA diving license from an amazing teacher named John Norris. John really pushed his students. He made them work to be even better than the PADI standard required. I took his class with a good high school buddy of mine, Scott Morris. Scott went on to become a Physician Assistant and, at the time of this writing, is still working as one. Scott is married to a wonderful woman named Eileen, and together they have twin boys.

Around the same time I was at CSU and SCUBA diving, I was going on hunting trips with several friends and their older brothers. That exposed me to hunting rifles, compound bows, and other guns, which re-fueled my long-standing interest in all-things military and weapons.

And, I also started dating Michelle. She and I had met, through her mother's introduction, in 1990, when she was in her sophomore year in high school. I had graduated two-years earlier, and chased her for four years after that. We went out a few times and then she went to college at Edinboro University of Pennsylvania. I visited her there to watch her play volleyball. And in 1993, we started dating seriously. But I was still seriously a knucklehead.

It's funny to think about those days, considering all that's happened since. I believe that the only time you should ever run into the person you were meant to be is when you bump into a mirror. It's never too late in life to make a change. Don't delay, and don't put it off until tomorrow. Most important, don't fail yourself. The problem with having no idea about what you want to do in life is that you get into trouble, or more accurately, trouble finds you.

Joining the military became my saving grace; I was pretty lost during the decade after high school. I got into trouble with the law—not nearly as bad as I did in 2008, but trouble nonetheless. First, I committed a misdemeanor for aggravated menacing. Some kid who lived next to two of my female cousins was verbally and sexually harassing them. This wasn't going to fly. I showed up at his house and warned him to leave the girls alone. Then I caught up with him at a football game and told him to stop or he would suffer the consequences.

This guy didn't listen. He continued harassing them, and I was true to my word.

One day, I was at North Shore Gym in Lakewood when I saw him and a couple of his friends pull up in a car. I stopped working out and quickly headed outside to confront him—which in retrospect was a mistake.

I reached their car just as they were parking it. The guy was sitting in the driver's seat with his window down.

He didn't see me, and before he could react I reached in. As I grabbed him by the neck with my left hand, I shouted, "I told you to leave my cousins alone!"

Then, I punched him in the face several times with my right hand.

While he was reeling I grabbed him by the scruff of his neck, dragged him out the window into the parking lot and proceeded to give him some more.

UNDAUNTED

At the time, I was probably about 238 pounds; he was maybe 165. It wasn't anything close to a fair fight, but I was passed the point of being fair. I asked the others if they wanted to help, but his friends in the car wanted no part of me and didn't even get out to help. They just watched.

After I pounded him again, I just left him lying there.

"This is your last warning," I said. "Leave my cousins the fuck alone. Next time you won't be able to walk away."

He ended up filing assault charges against me. They were lowered to menacing.

That was my second conviction. The first was a petty theft charge from a few years earlier. I had gone to visit my brother, who at the time was working at a restaurant called Pacers, and to fill out a job application. When we walked out, I held the door open for him. Unfortunately, I wasn't aware that my brother had stuffed a half slab of ribs into his bag about four hours earlier—but his employer was. We were both charged with petty theft. I looked at the police report from the incident, wherein it states, "Not enough evidence to support any charge against Christopher Heben." Yet somehow I was still charged and found guilty after I entered a no-contest plea. Such is the case when your family consists of nine boys and each of them has been in some sort of police trouble. It doesn't help when the city's lawgiver, Judge P. Carroll, has a hard-on for every one of them. He is the textbook example of when a Napoleonic complex meets Judge Dread. Not to mention the fact that my stepfather had one of his young attorneys on the case. He must not have read the "Not enough evidence" part in the two-page police report.

My next misdemeanor was for telephone harassment. I was working at bar in Westlake, Ohio, when, after it closed, the manager and part-owner was holding $500 that I was owed. This same person just so happened to be an attractive blonde. She and I had been friendly, so I had her phone number. Needless to say, I called her to get my money. She refused, and I must have called her once or twice a week for several weeks. Then, after a night out drinking with some buddies, things got ugly over the phone during that weekly call. It was right around the time the O.J. Simpson case was in the news, so there was a lot of sensitivity to attractive blondes being aggressed upon by men. My less-than-choice verbiage on the phone to her earned me the third misdemeanor charge.

Finally, a friend of a friend asked me to pick up a prescription for his father. He was running late from work and knew I lived on the next street over from the pharmacy. Prescription in hand (for Vicodin ES), I went to the pharmacy. They didn't give it to me because I was not a blood relative. I simply left without a fuss, but the damage was done. Apparently, my buddy and his crew had been forging and filling out these scripts for many months for Vicodin ES and other pain killers. I was the one who was finally nabbed for it, and I was charged with attempted processing of a drug document. It was eventually lowered to 'Deception to Obtain a Dangerous Drug' and earned me misdemeanor No. 4.

I was in my early 20s and still hadn't found my true calling in life, but I kept hearing the call of the wild and I was only getting myself into more and more trouble because of it. Tragically, that friend for whom I attempted to do the favor soon would lose his life in a motorcycle crash. The bottom line: I needed a break in this town.

My stepfather came to my rescue—one of the few times in my life he did—and offered me a legit job. It helped get me out of the bar scene and enabled me to start cleaning up my life. I would handle the signing of closing papers for his title company—yet another venture he dabbled in as an attorney—and serve as his courier, taking the documents to people for final signature. While working for my dad I took a hard look at what I was doing with my life. I wasn't happy with what I saw.

About a year later, I left my stepfather for a higher-paying job at a mortgage brokerage firm. It was a mundane job working with mundane people—we took phone calls, prequalified borrowers, and managed closing paperwork. I wore a suit and tie every damn day. It was stable, but it was routine, and I thoroughly hated routine. There was no excitement, no passion, and no challenge. I felt like a glorified used-car salesman that prayed on non-educated customers or who took advantage of people who were in a bad spot with their home.

UNDAUNTED

Some of the things we did were scandalous, and it's easy to see how the mortgage industry and real-estate business, in general, ended up in the shitter about a decade later. It was clear that this was not what I wanted out of life but it was what I needed to experience. It was the fall of 1996 and I was about to be 27 years old. I was floundering, flailing, and failing.

I'm a firm believer that the key to achieving anything lies in taking that critical first step. On your life's journey, this is the only time you should ever look down. Your life is up to you. If you want it to mean something, go make it what you want it to be.

So that's what I did—take that first step. At the time, I was in phenomenal physical shape: I was 6'0", weighed 218 pounds, and had 4-percent body fat. I know that because that year, I competed in three bodybuilding shows as a light heavyweight, finishing second in each of them. I managed my diet and watched what I ate very closely—which meant lots of protein bars and shakes, and raw and natural foods. Basically, I was making all of my own meals as well as spending about two-and-a-half to three hours each day at the gym—working out, lifting weights, hitting the Stairmaster or the stationary bike, and dutifully sculpting my body. And as a result, I was totally pumped and completely shredded.

One day, I decided I needed to get the hell out of the office and clear my mind. I left the building, walked around the corner to a coffee shop, and grabbed a cup of Cleveland Crud. While I was standing in line I also decided I was going to break from my diet and eat a pastry. So after snagging a cup and a chocolate chip croissant, I found an open table and sat down. To be certain, I have a weakness for damn near all things chocolate and don't care who knows it. Little did I know then, but I would soon be traveling the world and would get the distinct pleasure of being able to sample some pretty amazing cocoa concoctions everywhere I went. In fact, I made it a point to do so.

As fate would have it, there was a magazine rack a few feet from my table, inundated with old and new publications that patrons could pick up and read while they sipped away at their coffee and gnawed on their grub. The front and center magazine was a year-old issue of

Popular Mechanics, and it caught my attention. I picked it up and stared at it. On the cover was a Navy SEAL coming out of the water in full combat dive kit with a Drager LAR 5 re-breathing device on his chest and clutching a kickass looking H&K MP5 Submachine gun. The headline read:

> "Special Weapons and Tactics of the Navy SEALs:
> How This Elite U.S. Commando Strike Force Meets
> Threats Around The World."

He was menacing looking, and I must have sat there for five minutes like some brain-dead mouth breather as I studied every detail of every centimeter of that photo.

The SEAL operator dude looked totally bad-ass! By then I was a certified SCUBA diver and I knew a bit about what gear the guy was wearing. Well, a small bit of it anyway, but I truly had no knowledge of the Dräger LAR 5 whatsoever. It was like I had found the Holy Grail of ass-kickery, and I planned on inhaling every word a few times over. I flipped through the magazine and thought it was pretty damn awesome, so I decided I had to take it with me. I finished my coffee and pastry, rolled up the magazine, stuffed it in my inside jacket pocket, and headed back to the office. I didn't feel too bad about it, as the true owner's name had been cut away from the corner, so I assumed it was a donated magazine anyway. I was merely re-donating it to a more worthy cause: Me! And, even more important, that of helping me to un-fuck my life.

That afternoon, I didn't do shit at my desk. I pulled out the magazine and read the article again. Then I read it twice more when I got home. There was something about the Navy SEALs that simply and purely fascinated me. I guess it all made sense in hindsight: I loved water, I enjoyed guns, and I loved the military. These guys got to be the ultimate bad-asses in every environment where one could fight a war. Forget about being a Green Beret. I needed to be a SEAL.

Later that evening I read the damn thing yet again—probably reading the story and looking at the photos another two or three times. By now I was completely engrossed, enthralled, and infatuated. I needed to find out more about these guys and what they did. This was in the early days of the Internet, right after Al Gore invented it, so I researched everything I could find there—which wasn't much. I went to the library and found a couple books that had been written about—and by—SEALs—including Orr Kelly's book; *Brave Men, Dark Waters: The Untold Story of the Navy SEALs*. I checked these out, as well as a pile of books on Vietnam that were written by men who served. I read all these books voraciously—some of them twice—and concluded that this was, without a doubt, what I wanted to do: I was going to become a Navy SEAL.

About a week and half later, I told my then-girlfriend Michelle, that I was going to enlist in the Navy. I also informed her that I was going to become a Naval Commando. We were driving back from Blacksburg, Virginia, after visiting her cousin at Virginia Tech.

"I'm going to become a SEAL," I told her.

"OK," she said, calmly. Michelle wasn't one to get easily worked up. She was a very smart and motivated gal and also an amazing college athlete. In short, nothing phased her—especially when it concerned me. Plus, I didn't think she believed me, but I believed me. I'd decided that whether Michelle supported it or not, this was what I was going to do with my life. Nothing was going to stop me. As it turned out, Michelle was very supportive—which she has always been. Even after our divorce in 2004, we remain good friends. By and large, and until only recently, I felt that divorcing her was probably the biggest mistake of my life.

At the time, in 1996, I was living with a roommate named Tim M. Tim thought, as most of my dude friends did, that it was a joke when I told him I was going to become a SEAL. I was making pretty damn good money at that time and I was a very congenial and easy going guy, when I wasn't pulling people out of car windows or cussing them out on the phone.

"You're too nice of a guy," he said. "You'll never make it." In fact, this was the mantra from most of my buddies, but most of them never admitted it to me until after I had, indeed, made it. Tim was the only one who had the balls to tell me what everyone else wouldn't.

Well, Tim was wrong. As were the rest of my buddies who jumped to the same initial conclusion. No worries, he and I are still close friends today. Tim has two children, including a son who is the same age as my son. The two of them play sports together. In fact, I'm still friends with all the buddies I had at that time and we all have a laugh at where I have come today from that time period in my life. It just goes to show you what true passion, desire and maximum effort will get you; it'll get you whatever the hell you want, good or bad. Show me someone who gives 99 percent and I'll show you a failure.

I learned during my rather limited Internet research, that there were certain vision requirements to become a Navy SEAL. You must have 20/30 vision in one eye and no worse than 20/40 in the other. I had 20/400 vision in each eye and I wore soft contact lenses. To say I was visually challenged was an understatement, because I was nearly fucking blind! But otherwise, I was in great shape and I wanted it more than I wanted oxygen, so I knew that if I could just pass the eye test I would succeed.

I did more Internet research and found a doctor named Dr. Darrell White, a prominent eye surgeon. Dr. White initially started an ophthalmology practice near me and would eventually go on to found SkyVision Centers in Westlake, Ohio. But early on, he was pioneering LASIK eye surgery and was also teaching it to other U.S. eye surgeons. To put it another way, LASIK wasn't approved by the FDA until 1999. Those early trials were, according to Dr. White, designed for people who had 20/600 vision or worse. In essence, you had to be legally blind in order to qualify for the procedure. But, and there's always a but, after meeting with Dr. White and explaining why I wanted it, he agreed to do the procedure. He said he expected the surgery to be FDA-approved soon and also to be performed on persons with lesser cases of myopia. That would be me. He also said he believed in what I wanted to do and he liked that he could be the one to help me to dramatically change my life. The only way any of that would happen is if I had my vision surgically corrected by him. Additionally, he satisfied his medical check boxes by making me a longitudinal study for the procedure. About the only thing he didn't do for me was to give me a price break. Instead, I had to pay the full price of $5,000. Graciously, however, I was allowed to be on a payment plan of $183.00 a month. I didn't hesitate for a second as I signed all the papers and scheduled the first surgery.

Dr. White warned me that if he did the surgery I would need to claim it never happened. I knew I would need to lie on my enlistment medical application and say my eyes were perfect. Further, he explained that if anyone—a Navy Ophthalmologist or any other doctor—conducted a slit lamp examination of my eyes, they might see the corneal scars. My story would need to be as such: I was punched in one eye and took a snowball to the other...or some shit like that. I told him that I was on board because if the Navy ever found out, at the very least they would bounce me out of the Navy. At the very most, I'd be breaking rocks at Leavenworth while wearing safety goggles to protect my perfectly corrected vision. Never mention the fact that if he screwed up, I would be legally blind. Oh, and let's not forget about the fact that nobody, not even Dr. White himself, knew how the eyes would hold up to the differing atmospheric pressures of SCUBA diving and skydiving after the procedure. I guess this is where the whole 'longitudinal study' came into the picture. I was going to be a guinea pig for him and, eventually, for ophthalmologists everywhere, but I would be a SEAL guinea pig, and that was all that mattered.

In hindsight, it's pretty fortuitous that Dr. White was very much on board with my quest to become a SEAL because today he's one of only a handful of eye surgeons approved to operate on people in U.S. Special Operations Command: all U.S. Special Forces—guys in Army Delta Force, Green Berets, and of course my fellow U.S. Navy SEALs. In many ways, I look at our link-up as an event that altered both of our lives for the better. You just can't make that shit up!

Dr. White did my left eye, or non-dominant eye, first. He wanted to see how it would respond from a healing standpoint as well as from a vision-correction standpoint. The technology for LASIK was not nearly as advanced as it is today. Most of the procedure was done by hand before the laser was finally used on the inner surface of the cornea. It felt like I had been scratched by a cat across my eyeball and then punched in the eye by Mike Tyson. It was painful, and the fact that the eye is so close to the brain meant the pain didn't have too far to travel to make a point. It was short-lived, however, as the eye enjoys a rich blood supply and heals quickly. In a matter of just 10 days, my vision went from 20/400 to 20/15. The surgery on my dominant right eye, my sniper eye, as I like to say, resulted in a more aggressive surgery and an even better end result: 20/12 vision.

Dr. White said he could not have been happier with the results. I concurred! A few weeks later, and once I felt mentally ready, I walked into the U.S. Navy's recruiting office in Lakewood, Ohio, ready as hell to accelerate my life.

I was intercepted at the front door by an Army recruiter. It was like he was manning his post all day and I was the first target of opportunity he had. He was like the prototypical used-car salesman and extended his hand before my eyes could even adjust to the overhead fluorescent lighting. After I gathered myself, I promptly asked him to direct me to a Navy recruiter, after which he gave me the 'are you fucking serious' look. He then, reluctantly, and with a finger point reminiscent of the ghost of Christmas Past, directed me to the desk of Randy Brogden, an AO-1 (Aviation Ordinance Man, 1st Class), who was the head Navy recruiter that manned the Lakewood office.

Not knowing jack shit about Navy rank or how to address anyone in a Navy uniform, I sad "Hi, my name is Chris Heben," as I started sitting down across the desk from Randy. "And I came here because I want to be a U.S. Navy SEAL."

Randy chuckled. "Do you know how many people come in here and say that, Chris?"

I smiled.

"Probably a lot," I confidently replied.

"Yes," Randy said. "And do you know how many of those people actually become Navy SEALs, Chris?"

"Not too many, in fact, only about 10 percent," I responded.

"Correct."

I nodded.

"Well, I'm going to be a Navy SEAL. What do we need to do to make that happen today, Randy?"

UNDAUNTED

Randy paused and took a long, hard look at me. He pursed his lips and nodded, slowly.

"OK, Chris. Let's discuss that. When guys come in here and say that, I take a pretty hard look at them. Most of them have no chance to become a SEAL, much less even succeed in the Navy. People look at the former as a crazy fantasy and the latter as a way of running away, as an escape. But you know what, Chris? I don't think you're delusional and I only think you're running out of time. I think you may just have a chance and the cutoff age before I need to get your ass an age waiver is 28. And I don't want to work that hard, so here's what you'll need to do."

And with that, Randy took my overtly displayed passion seriously and got cranking on my packet, which was encouraging. He explained I would need to take an Armed Forces Vocational Aptitude Battery test (ASVAB). Then I would then need to qualify in certain line scores, or scores in certain critical areas of assessment, those being: verbal reasoning, math concepts, reading comprehension, and mechanical concepts. There were minimum scores for each area, and if you didn't meet the minimums, you were disqualified from even pursuing a SEAL contract. It was that simple: If you didn't have the brains, they could care less about the brawn. More wars have been fought and won on the cerebral capacity used in combat as compared to the magnitude of muscle.

He then showed me a video about the SEALs. It was totally awesome, and if I hadn't already been hooked, that would have certainly sealed (no pun intended) the deal.

I took the ASVAB and qualified.

"OK," Randy said. "On paper, you're good to go. If you really want to do this, you'll need to get medically certified first."

He looked me up and down. I was about 220 pounds of solid muscle and in the best shape of my life.

"You're 26 and an ass hair away from 27 (I was about to turn 27 in a few weeks). Most of our recruits are quite a few years younger than you. In fact, they are about eight- to nine-years younger. But you look to be in peak physical shape," he said. Then he went on to tell me, "If you pass the physical exam and an eye test, you'll be well on your way."

Randy gave me a preliminary physical, which I passed, and asked me to a fill out a medical history report. I blazed through the medical history pretty quickly, as I had NEVER had any surgical procedure whatsoever, let alone any experimental non-FDA approved ones! What type of fool would do that? He then sent the full physical questionnaire, as well as my entire personnel report, to the Cleveland Military Entrance and Processing Station (MEPS)—the United States Military's equivalent of first base in baseball. Swinging the bat took place at the recruiting station. Now I was on first. Acceptance and boot camp would be second base. BUD/S would be third base, and getting my Trident would be crossing home plate with the winning run. One bite at a time, however, that's how you eat an elephant. And this one was massive. Time for processing.

A few days later, Randy contacted me. He was excited. He told me MEPS had accepted my prescreening report and that I was scheduled for a full physical there. Of course I scheduled this next step with him, met with him and together we went to MEPS in downtown Cleveland. That morning, I took each of the exams, passing them all with flying colors. No one even examined my eyes. Well, not that I can recall at that point in time. They would do so later, in boot camp.

Now, there WAS the tiny little matter of my criminal record—I had those four pesky misdemeanors in my recent past—and I had to explain all of them, in full detail, to a U.S. Navy Captain from Washington, D.C., over the phone.

After patiently listening and making only a few small comments, the captain said, "OK, son. So you want to be a SEAL, right?"

"Yessir!" I exclaimed, in my best Rambo voice I could muster.

He then proceeded to say, "Well, the SEALs aren't supposed to be choir boys." Then, after an uncomfortably long pause, "Consider yourself accepted, son."

Fuckin'-a-double clutch! I was in.

The good captain wrote a brief letter that was promptly faxed in to MEPS and added to my file. That single document was the icing on the cake that allowed me to join the Navy. I promptly signed a Dive Fair Corpsman contract and took an oath to protect and serve my country.

UNDAUNTED

This was October 1996, only one week after I turned 27-years old. I was excited to get the process rolling. So much so, that I asked for the earliest ship-out date. They told me to report to the airport the Friday after Thanksgiving. It couldn't come fast enough. I wasn't running from anything, I was running toward something; my dream of becoming one of the world's most deadly and capable Commandos, a U.S. Navy SEAL!

After Thanksgiving, on November 27, 1996, my girlfriend Michele and I drove to Cleveland Hopkins Airport and met up with a handful of other new recruits from Cleveland who were also heading off to boot camp. For the next eight weeks, I was headed to Recruit Training Command, Great Lakes (RTC), just outside of Chicago, Illinois. December and January would be very cold there, but I didn't care. I had a bigger mission to accomplish and this destination was only a very small part of it. Necessary, but small.

I said my good-byes to Michelle and tried to remain stoic and calm as I did so, but deep inside I was battling conflicting emotions. Michelle and I had been together as a couple for a solid four years, and before that, I had chased her for nearly four years. So it was hard for me to self-eject from that comfort but I was also very excited to begin my journey. She and I were solid, and our families were very supportive of each other and our relationship. I already knew we would somehow survive this experience, but I also knew it would not be easy for either one of us. Nothing good comes without taking a chance or without paying a price, and I was about to lay myself open to both of those true-isms. I and about 10 others, all boarded the plane and left for our new life at the RTC. I was almost officially in the U.S. Navy now, and life was about to become very, very interesting. Onward and Upward!

Everything in my life converged in that single moment when I picked up that *Popular Mechanics* magazine and then walked into that recruiter's office. My buddy and business partner, Mike Lemire, found a copy of that *Popular Mechanics* issue a few years ago and sent it to me. It's still near and dear to my heart. The bottom line is that I was fed up with mediocrity. From an employee standpoint as well as from a patron position, I was done with the whole bullshit bar scene. There was a big world out there and I had never seen it. Up until that moment I had been a typical American male in his mid-'20s: I was working out every day (OK, maybe not so typical) and chasing girls and money. But I finally saw the writing on the wall that things were not going to end well if this kept up much longer. And, I had several things in my favor—a razor-sharp mind, fit body, good diet, and the discipline to synergistically apply it all to a single goal. These prepared me for boot camp and, eventually, Basic Underwater Demolition/SEAL (BUD/S) Training. I took huge leaps of faith when I quit my job, underwent unapproved eye surgery, walked into that recruiting office, and shipped off to boot camp and BUD/S. I made a pretty similar leap of faith when I decided to become an entrepreneur in 2008.

<<<>>>

At the time, I was on probation. My case had been adjudicated in August, and I was trying to figure out what to do next. I had a friend, Mike R., who owned a spinal implant device company. Mike was trying to get some penetration in the Alliance/Canton area for his spinal products—screws, rods and biologics. I contacted him, interviewed, and was hired to market and sell these products for his company. I worked with Mike for about three months, and then I had one of those light-bulb moments when I decided I could do this on my own. I founded two medical device distributorships, Trident Medical, LLC and Spine Align, LLC. One was designed to handle government-funded health insurance and the other would deal with traditional HMOs. I elected to keep the money separate because of the strict requirements the government placed on programs they had their hands in. It made the accounting and paperwork that much easier and any potential government investigation that much easier to deal with. I heard of many such audits and investigations and I would be damned if it was going to happen to me. I already went through enough shit at that point!

Within a few months, my businesses took off and I was soon making around $15,000 a month. In fact, because of this, I knew I needed some help to keep up with the growth and any legal issues that may arise with vendors, etc., and I knew that my stepfather's companies had existing framework for bookkeeping and accounting. I spoke with him about

UNDAUNTED

it all and, seeing the potential for gain, he promptly offered to let me tap into his systems if he came on board as a partner, as well as my attorney. All of this, on retainer, of course, and to the tune of roughly $5,000 per month. Reluctantly, I agreed, and he started to handle all of those aspects of the business. Business was good and I realized I couldn't be everywhere at once, so also I brought two of my brothers into the company to help market the products to many other physicians as well as to help support them in the operating rooms during surgery. I paid them both a monthly draw and a car allowance, which cut into my take home pay, but they are family, we were profitable, and things were going well, very well.

The two businesses thrived for over a year. Then my stepfather, who was also my business partner, and who initially usurped 49 percent of the company, started to become very aggressive. I had given him power-of-attorney to handle paperwork, legal issues and the like, but I never fully realized that what I had turned over to him, allowed him to do many other things. Worse, the amount of money I was drawing from the company to pay my bills—including past attorney fees—was suddenly cut even further as my stepfather decided to pay himself more of a salary from the company and further regulate how much money was being taken out of the company and by whom.

He also started dictating the rules of our daily operations—along with fighting with our suppliers and customers about every line—and dime—in our agreements. This wasn't sitting well with me, but what power did I really have at that time? I was a convicted felon on probation and I was dealing with government-funded insurance programs. Beyond all that, we were partners and I had given him power-of-attorney to make those contractual decisions. My options were pretty limited.

Finally, things came to a screaming head when my father tried to muscle our largest client—a neurosurgeon—into an exclusive, five-year agreement that would have precluded him from using any other products beyond the lines we currently carried or would be carrying, based upon his possible recommendations. Basically, if he wanted it and we couldn't get it, he would have to use something else we had until we could get it or we could find something he approved of as an alternative.

The doctor outright refused.

I didn't blame him. I still don't. Patient care is paramount to everything else, and a physician needs to be able to make choices on a case-by-case basis.

My stepfather wouldn't budge. No surprise there!

Unwilling to deal at all, they both continued to hold their ground and things turned nasty. I was so pissed. I found myself frequently giving them both a piece of my mind. After it was clear we could not find a middle ground, the neurosurgeon walked away and we lost him as a client, along with 60 percent of our revenue that promptly went right out the door with him. For a couple of accomplished and educated men, they sure were pretty fucking stupid. In fact, I have found this to be the case with a lot of doctors and lawyers I have come across (save for a very select few): They know a lot about a little bit and very little to nothing about a lot of everything else, including, and especially business. Yet, that doesn't stop them from being some of the most vociferous individuals about almost anything. How do you know when a surgeon is in the room? Easy: HE'LL TELL YA! I love putting these guys in their place whenever it is truly warranted. Otherwise, I try to avoid them all at all costs. Of course this is gross generalization, but you all know what I'm trying to say: A surgeon, a SEAL and a lawyer walk into a bar...LOL!

<<<>>>

Getting back to the story: With respect to the businesses, from there, things went south pretty quickly.

Erroneously, my stepfather thought we could pick up other clients to replace the loss, but that didn't happen fast enough to keep the doors open. Just as quickly as we had burst onto the scene, my companies were on their way out of business—and my livelihood was going to go right along with them. In 2010, we were forced to close the doors of the company.

I have never truly forgiven my stepfather for what he did. What parent (step or otherwise) would do that do his kid? He already had a good business going that he fully owned—making several hundred thousand dollars per year. He was, in fact, a well-established attorney. Why he had to muscle his way into my company and then cause our downfall is beyond me. Luckily, as always, I remained undaunted. I had my military and medical expertise to fall back on, so I founded a new company—without my stepfather—called Medical Security International (MSI): A medical and security concierge service, as well as a tactical training organization for police officers, security officers and emergency-response teams in the United States, the Middle East and Africa. Once again, I was forced to adapt to changing circumstances, and my life went in a new direction. Either you become what is or you will surely become what isn't!

CHAPTER 7

"FOOLS CREATE THEIR OWN PRISONS. THEY KNIFE THEIR OWN PEOPLE IN THE BACK AND IN THE HEART. BUT EVENTUALLY, THEY REAP WHAT THEY SOW. THE WISE TAKE A KNIFE, CUT THE HEART STRINGS, AND BACK AWAY, THUS LIBERATING THEMSELVES FROM THE FOOLS. LIFE IS TOO SHORT TO BE ANYONE'S FOOL. WHAT ARE YOU WAITING FOR? CUT THE CORD TODAY!"

—CHRISTOPHER MARK HEBEN

When I left Cleveland, Ohio to begin Navy boot camp I essentially cut the cord that tethered me to my former life. Save for my wonderfully understanding girlfriend, I left behind all the bullshit that had been holding me back since I'd graduated from high school, and I did it to embark upon something new, something I felt in my heart I was meant to do. I was going to become a United States Navy SEAL and I was going to serve my country. Nothing would stop me from reaching my goal.

This isn't to say that my time at the Navy's Recruit Training Command (RTC Great Lakes) nor SEAL Training in BUD/S was easy. It sure as hell wasn't. As a matter of fact, it was one of the most challenging, most demanding, and most physically and mentally arduous periods of my entire life—but perhaps the most fun! In life there will always be obstacles to climb. Some are more difficult than others, and of those, some must be approached alone. Only you can decide whether or not you will ever see the other side. It's up to you to make it happen. Boot camp, and BUD/S more so than boot, were two such obstacles I faced, and even though the Navy hammers into your brain the concept of teamwork, you are essentially alone during all aspects of your training.

UNDAUNTED

I say this only because no one else is going to do it for you. You have to take the shit that you want, and the way you take it is to earn. I hear it all the time with respect to work and school work. The classic "I got an A" or "I got a promotion" then "He/she gave me a C/D/F" or "They gave the position to someone else!" This is bullshit. People only want to own up to something when it is good. In that regard, today's youth have mostly lost an edge. They believe they are entitled to many things they never earned—so much so, that I made sure my son knew all about merit and earning what you get. At the age of 7, I told him that if he ever came home carrying a 4th place trophy, I would make him smash it on the ground in front of me. The same went for a participation certificate or other such award because those things are complete and utter bullshit. No one should ever be given anything just for showing up, other than the chance to do your best and to succeed because of that effort.

Meritorious achievement and solitary personal victories suited me just fine, allowing me to play to my strengths. I've always been a fighter and a dreamer. I choose not to live under the microscope of scorn nor beneath the umbrella of cynicism that some would hold over my head. As I reflect upon my life so far, I've come to realize that others did not work to achieve my successes nor were they the cause of my epic failures—and of both there have been many. Despite these, I have learned to take pride in ownership of it all—the good and the bad. It is in this spirit of self-awareness, growth, and personal understanding that I constantly press on—forward—not on the narrow route lit by a candle held by another, but rather, on a path widely illuminated by the glow from the flames of the fire that burns inside of me. I challenge you to look inside yourself and ask the same question I constantly ask myself: What will you fight for today? As they say, if you don't stand for something, you will fall for anything.

I challenge you to take a hard look at your life. What do you dream of doing? What path will you take? What's holding you back? It is always far better to try something new and fail than to spend a thousand tomorrows wondering what could have been. Ignite your torch and move out! Onward and Upward! That's what I always say, good or bad, easy or hard, and even right or wrong, it's what I've always chosen to do. In fact, if I were to call AAA and order a TripTik of my life, it would take you down almost every pot-holed path and roadway there ever was. But along the way there would be some torches to help you avoid some of those potholes.

I am most proud of my failures because without them, I would never know how sweet the taste of victory and success truly are. Because of my failures, as a result of the hard times, and the many moments I have spent outside of my comfort zone, every good moment is a thousand times more satisfying! In many ways, you should welcome and expect the bad times. In fact, show me someone who has never experienced failure and I will tell you that I am looking upon a person who has never really lived at all. Blaze your own path through life and never regret it.

Joining the Navy as a 27-year old was the way I ignited my life's torch. At the time, I was making about $65,000 a year, which was more than enough to cover my $383 lease payment on my 1996 Jeep Grand Cherokee, rent, food, fun money and some credit card bills. Also, it was not too bad a sum for a 26-year-old dude in Cleveland. Yet, I was not satisfied, I gave up that income to willingly assume eight-plus months of physical and mental hardships, many of which were much more intense than anything I'd previously faced. This was beyond taking a simple leap of faith; it was voluntarily entering a war that pitted a system designed to ferret out the weak against my ability to rise to the challenge and persevere. To be certain, this wasn't high school or even college football two-a-days, this was for real and this was exactly my kind of challenge. Exactly what I was looking for!

At 27, I was one of the oldest recruits in my boot camp division. I think there was another dude who may have been 32. They placed us into buildings they called 'ships' and we were then further classified into divisions. Most of the other guys were between 18- and 20-years old and had no life experiences other than high school—fresh meat, so to speak. I was still a piece of meat, but I wasn't so damn fresh. After arrival, we did what every other recruit does: Met our fellow recruits, got our heads shaved, received uniforms, ship and bunk assignments, and then launched, head first into basic training. I saw some guys crying when they were getting their heads shaved. Really? That was fucking

UNDAUNTED

annoying. After all, it's just hair and everyone knows it has to happen. I always wondered how the crying game guys fared in boot. From what I understand, some kids never stop crying and are sent home, and others end up swinging from a bathroom stall with their belt around their neck. Sad, but true.

Since I was a bit older—and because at 218 pounds I looked mean as hell with my newly shaved head—the powers-that-be named me a Recruit Petty Officer in Charge (RPOC). Basically, I was the head recruit in charge of the other 129 recruits in my ship and did the brain component for our Assistant Recruit Petty Officer (AROC), Seaman Recruit (SR) Owens. I barked out the marching orders and commands anytime we went somewhere on base—the learning center, chow hall, exercise facility, pool, fire and flood control trainer, etc. I did this in-between, over, and around SR Owens calling the marching cadences. It was fun, and I also ran more aspects of the division with respect to the other recruits, as far as verbally keeping them in line during our eight weeks of boot camp. When I could not reach another recruit nicely, I would summon the help of SR Lumpkin. Lumpkin was given the title of Master at Arms (MA). He was my enforcer; we played good cop, bad cop. I was most always the good guy.

At one point along the way, Owens contracted laryngitis and was out of cadence-calling commission for three weeks. He was from Florida, and we were in Chicago during the middle of winter, so he wasn't used to that type of cold. On some days, it was 10 degrees below zero when we trained outside. On colder days, we were ordered to stay inside our ship.

While Owens recovered, I called out the marching orders and kept the cadence. I was definitely up to the task. My whole life, I had been fooling around with singing and creating voices, so while I called out the commands and cadence, I decided to also have some fun. As I've mentioned, in addition to country music, I love Motown, Hip Hop and R&B. I channeled that soulfulness and transformed the marches into a quasi-gospel revival-James Brown-Al Green-Garth Brooks-concert event while we marched. As it happened, this was a big hit—both with my fellow recruits and amongst many who saw and heard us in action.

It definitely had a very positive effect on the other recruits in my group, as well as the other recruit divisions—especially the female divisions who halted and hushed themselves in order to observe me leading the way. Later on at boot camp graduation, a few of these females approach me and said, "We just loved listening to your division march. We actually stopped doing what we were doing when you guys came by, so we could simply watch, but mostly just listen." So I ended up singing this hodge-podge of melodic sounds that, apparently, stopped people in their tracks.

My division, Division 130, became a Hall of Fame Division, earning the highest honor a division of recruits can receive. The designation is based on such things as march-offs, where they measure everyone's ability to march on command in a crisp unison formation as well as our group's written and verbal test scores. You're also measured on the physical scores you receive during the many, simulated emergency-aboard-ship challenges faced. Somewhere at the command center in Chicago is a plaque that lists Division 130, our graduation year of 1996, and my name on it. To this day I'm still very proud we were able to accomplish this as a group.

Boot camp is pretty much what you think it would be. In between a whole lot of yelling and screaming and physical activity, that isn't really physical, you learn some useful Navy things: Rate, which is a Navy job. Your rate might be a Quarter Master (QM), a Yeoman (YN), Radio Man (RM) or a Personnel man (PN). You learn rank, what each branch of the U.S. military calls the others' equivalent for pay and other privileges, and you learn recognition. Recognition is the practice of understanding all the other military branches' uniforms so you're able to recognize them on sight, and know what each person deserves in the way of a military salute and other respectful military greetings. You're taught things like: What a Corporal in the Army or a Lieutenant in the Air Force looks like and what they do. You learn the difference between an Army Lieutenant and a Navy Lieutenant. This may all sound pretty mundane but it's actually very important that you're able to recognize people by their uniforms, and be able to do it at a distance—they take it very personally when you call a lieutenant, who's an officer, a chief, who's

UNDAUNTED

an enlisted guy. Both wear khaki uniforms, but there are differences in the insignias they have on their lapels and differences with respect to what they do and how they are addressed. You learn to make sure you give the people the proper respect and never, ever, want to call a chief "Sir," because he doesn't really warrant a "Sir." You call him "Chief." But a lieutenant warrants the title "Sir." If you don't call a lieutenant "Sir," he's going to get pissed. These are subtle things, but in the military, they're important. In fact, in my work today, I am still required to utilize all these skills. And remember, you don't have to respect the person wearing them, but you always respect the uniform!

You're also taught U.S. Navy and U.S. military history, how to function on a ship or a boat or a sub, and how to fight fires and do other damage control on these structures. Lastly, utilizing the proper paperwork is another very important lesson. And here you learn how to properly fill out all sorts of requisition forms and other official Navy documents. There truly is a form for just about everything, each with its unique set of numbers to go with it.

One of the drawbacks I discovered from being the ARPOC was that by the time I ended up marching everyone into the chow hall I became the last guy who got to sit down and eat. Consequently, I had the least amount of time to get my fill. This became annoying very quickly because I was trying to become a SEAL and one of the things I knew was critical to my success was proper nutrition. Less time to eat meant less time to ensure I was getting the right calories and nutrients. Needless to say, I decided to take action. I started sneaking food out of the mess hall whenever I could, stuffing it in my pockets and carrying it off to eat later. Most people didn't care, but there were a few who didn't like the fact that while they were hungry later in the day, I always seemed to have a snack in my pockets. On one occasion, I was anonymously turned in to our superiors and forced to face the music.

Our chief was a guy named Charles Plyler. Chief Plyler was an E7, a Chief Boatswain Mate (BMC). Chief Boatswain Mate Plyler was a career Navy guy. He was just a bit under 6-feet tall and at 170 pounds was built like a high-tension wire. He was all skin and muscle and bone. He wore a pair of Coke-bottle, Navy-issue glasses. He looked like a cross between one of the Village People and a really pissed off Henry Rollins, rolled into one person. To my amusement, he called everyone "Chuck." It was funny because he would call out, "Hey! You fuckin' Chucks better get movin'." Or, when he didn't know what you were doing or why you were doing something, other than it wasn't what you should be doing according to him, he'd scream; "WHAT THE FUCK CHUCK??" His philosophy was simple: His name was Charles and he was going to treat all of us the same way he treated himself, ergo his nickname for everyone: "Chuck." Right below BMC Plyler was Tom Trevino. Trevino was an E6, an Aviation Ordinance, 1st Class Petty Officer (AO1), and he talked with a deep Texas twang. I think he was from San Antonio. He always had this wicked gleam in his eye like he was plotting your destruction. In fact, he was. He usually had Chief Plyler implement his sinister plans. It was a good old game of good cop, bad cop, and these dudes were pretty damn good.

After I was anonymously turned in, the two of them confronted me in the division barracks (our ship), where we lived. But not until they had had a little bit of fun: Chief Plyler grabbed my trench coat and found two bananas and about six Smucker's peanut butter single packs in each of the pockets. In front of everyone else, and unbeknownst to me at that time, he took the coat off the hook, laid it on the floor and jumped up and down on it, smashing all the bananas and peanut butter together in both of my pockets. Then he called me into the office to have me answer for what I had done.

"Heben!" he yelled, pointing to my trench coat, "What the fuck is this, Chuck?!"

"I've been sneaking food out of the galleys," I replied. "I need to eat more."

I thought it was the right answer. When you're wrong, say you're wrong. I'd rather face the quick consequences rather than get caught in a lie.

"Wrong answer, Chuck," he said. "So here's what we're going to do about it, and I'm doing this for your own good. You're going to remediation PT tomorrow at 0500 hours."

Remediation physical training (PT) was what the Navy called its most hard-core physical training. Hell yes! Instead of being upset, I was suddenly excited. I had been getting up at 0230 each morning and sneaking into the bathroom to do circuit sets of sit-ups, push-ups on the floor, and pull-ups. I had been using the middle support bar in the bathroom stalls as a pull-up bar. Any extra workouts I could get in were epic!

"Aye, aye, Chief!" I replied. "0500 hours."

It was like my own little slice of heaven, and I felt refreshed while everyone else in remediation was tired and worn out. Because of this, I re-approached Chief Plyler.

"Chief, I've got a deal for you," I said. "I love that Remedial PT. I don't feel like getting in trouble every time I want to go, so could you let me go to that another two days each week voluntarily?"

"Son," he said. "I've been here for three years and ain't nobody ever asked me to do that kind of shit on purpose."

Then he looked me square in the eye and continued, "Do you think I want you to get in trouble on purpose and sabotage me and our chance to be a Hall of Fame Division, Son?"

"No, Chief."

"So here's what I'm going to do. I will let you spend the next three weeks going to PT as extra training." At week five, much like an older parent, BMC Plyer had actually mellowed a little bit.

"Thank you, Chief!"

"Get out of my sight, Chuck!" he said through lips that were trying not to smile. BMC Plyler had been hard on me since day one, but I knew he was only doing it to test my resolve and to make me tougher for BUD/S. He would often make me crawl across the ship deck on my belly using only my hands and barking like a Pinniped while all the other recruits watched. He would make me do this back and forth until I was covered in my own sweat. Never once did I quit. In fact, he told me one day that I was a "wannabe." To which I promptly answered, "At least I'm a wannabe something!" This was followed by more beatings. The lesson: If you're going to be stupid, you had better be hard. I would hear this all through BUD/S as well.

Remedial PT was nothing like the SEAL PT, but it was something. Plus, it allowed me another two days during the week when I could get out on my own and away from the ship. Combined with my stolen night sessions in the bathroom, I was able to recover from the first two weeks of not working out and get back into shape.

It's important that I explain a little about the SEAL screening test: This happy little event takes place on the first day of the second week of basic training (2-1 day). This is the first day anyone is eligible to take the test. I took it on my 2-1 day, as you may have expected. That day, 125 of us showed up for the test.

The test began with a 500-meter swim. We had to complete it in less than 12 minutes and 30 seconds; I finished at 12 minutes and 20 seconds, barely meeting the requirement. Then, I could only use side stroke and breast stroke as choices of swim technique. I chose the side stroke. Nowadays, you learn the stroke we use at BUD/S, the combat recovery stroke, and can take the screening test utilizing this style. It is, basically, a non-stop sideways flutter kick with one arm pulling water toward the other arm that is pulling it all behind you. Or, you can opt to simply utilize a sculling movement with the downside arm. Whatever variation you chose, it is much faster. But damn, I missed failing the swim by a paltry 10 seconds. I had been practicing this test for two months, but I guess the water there was slower...LOL.

In actuality, I was nervous and because of this, I found it hard to breath. No oxygen equals no energy. I later learned to control my anxiety, fear, heart rate, respiratory rate, and exertion rate; more on that later. One of the dudes completed the swim in nine minutes that day—and I'll explain more about him later as well.

After the swim, you were required to do as many push-ups as you could in two minutes. As you might imagine, your arms are fairly smoked after 500 meters of swimming your ass off and utilizing a completely inefficient swim stroke. The minimum amount of pushups needed to pass is 50; I did 110. Next, we did two minutes of sit-ups. Again, after 500 meters of swimming, your hip flexors are spent but you still need to do 50 of these as well. I did 100. Following sit-ups were the pull-ups. By this time, you're arms are telling you a different story than your brain is

UNDAUNTED

telling you, which is never good. Needless to say, I needed a minimum of 8 (it's 10 now) and I was able to crank out 18. You NEVER want to do the bare minimum or you will not fare well with the instructors when you get out to BUD/S, or, I should say, *if* you make it. They might just decide to label you a turd and flush you out of the program at the very beginning. That happened to a lot of the guys that day. Many of them, however, did it to themselves.

Last, and certainly nowhere near the least, is the mile-and-a-half run. The run had to be completed in less than 10 1/2 minutes. After the swim, the push-ups, pull-ups and sit-ups—which are all done on the pool deck with no rest in between—you are pretty damn tired. Nonetheless, whoever is still left is ushered right back into the lockers to change. We were required to get dressed in under two minutes and head out to the indoor gym/drill hall/track area. Big, clunking, steel-toed, boon-docker boots and heavy, ill-fitting, canvass blue-jean dungarees, and a white t-shirt were our running uniform for this event. We looked like an Amish version of Frankenstein! It's no wonder Frankenstein had to ambush all his victims, because he couldn't run for shit in that get up. The entire test was one physical challenge after another, plus a wardrobe challenge, with no time to rest and no time to recover in between. Without a doubt, after my shitty swim time, I was so worried about failing the run that I actually finished it in nine minutes and 20 seconds. I was be able to pull this pace out of my ass whenever I absolutely had to all through BUD/S. I still can!

Here's a crazy fact: Of the 125 people who took the SEAL screening test that morning, only four of us passed it—me, Michael Branch, Travis Lively and George Hunt. As fate would have it, all four of us eventually made it through BUD/S and became official U.S. Navy SEALs.

Mike was 5'6" and solid muscle. Before joining the Navy, he was a California Highway Patrol Officer, a CHiPs guy. He was insanely unique in that he was the one guy among us all who had a confirmed kill BEFORE he ever became a SEAL. Apparently, Mike had responded to a domestic dispute call in the line of duty as a CHP Officer. It was to a house right off the highway. He pulled up and a man came out brandishing a weapon at him. Mike had to shoot the dude center mass in his chest, killing him on the spot. He realized then that his talents would be better served in the SEAL Teams than amongst the general public. Even stranger than that was the fact that Mike and I would wind up being swim buddies all through BUD/S. You see, he was the dude that smoked the swim with a nine-minute time while I nearly drowned in the 12 minutes, 20 seconds it took for me to complete it. But perhaps most bizarre is that he and I ended up becoming one of the top two swimming pairs at BUD/S. Technique, mindset, teamwork and athleticism often collide to form awesome. Mike and I did just that.

George Hunt was a very disciplined and God-fearing dude. He was the son of a Baptist preacher from Georgia but he was built like Kermit the Frog. Accordingly, he ran and swam very well. Travis...well, Travis was a wrecking ball of a man with a mile-wide smile and shiny round head. He hailed from Massachusetts. Travis, like me, ran distances like a Mac truck, sprinted like an elk and sank like a rock in the pool. He became one of my best friends and was the best man at my wedding. Travis and I later travel to Kenya to film a TV show called *Ivory Wars*; and we have both been heavily featured on the Discovery Channel as well as many other TV networks.

For the remainder of boot camp we spent two days a week in specialized BUD/S, 'Diver Motivator' pre-training, and we spent additional time at the pool doing swim workouts and extensive PT. The SEALs who were on duty ran those exercise programs. I remember two of them well—Brad Danse and Johnny Dual. They were members of SEAL Team Eight and had spent time overseas in the first Gulf War, as well as Bosnia-Herzegovina. The program was run by Master Chief Rick Kaiser. This tough SOB was involved in the Mogadishu conflict with Task Force Ranger. That entire operation was the basis for the movie *Black Hawk Down*. Master Chief Kaiser ran a tight-but-cool ship. Those guys who trained us were true bad asses, and I thought it was awesome.

By now, Chief Plyler had taken a liking to me. He would come up and give me a hard time, saying things like, "Son, I didn't think you were going to pass that SEAL test. So even though part of your ass now officially belongs to Navy Special Warfare, most of it still belongs to me." But, the proud gleam in his eyes was hard not to notice. Hell, I was proud too.

Later, after I had graduated SEAL training, was assigned to SEAL Team Eight, had my Trident pinned on my chest and had done several cool schools and an overseas deployment, I came back to visit Chief Plyler. He was still at RTC Great Lakes.

I walked in on him, unannounced, and presented myself.

"Petty Officer Heben," he barked upon seeing me. "Holy fuck, son! You son of a bitch! I always knew you'd make it, son. Show me those shiny assed medals and that rack of ribbons."

Then he poked at my chest and smiled. "I guess that extra PT really did help!"

Everything that happening to the other recruits and me in Chicago was a test. They tested you every day—physically and mentally. The drop-out rate for Navy boot camp is 10 percent. But Chicago was only the initial gauntlet you had to run. It paled in comparison to what was waiting for me when I went to San Diego and entered BUD/S at the Naval Special Warfare Training Center. At BUD/S, the dropout rate is close to 90 percent!

During boot camp, I realized I could put up with a lot of physical and mental discomfort—much more than other people. Even though I was named the recruit-in-charge of the other recruits, I was going through the same thing they were. But I had to do a little more—I was the shoulder for the young kid from Kansas or Oklahoma to cry on when he thought he couldn't take another day. I was the one who kept the two kids from Flint, Michigan—one black, one white—from beating the shit out of each other. I may have been in the same initial crucible as the other recruits, but I had to manage the psychodynamics, tics, tendencies and psycho-social issues of them all. In a lot of ways, it was Boot Camp 1.5 for me.

It was actually a kickass break to be officially assigned to Navy Special Warfare and get a workout in at 0530 hours several days a week. Not only did it prepare me for what was coming with BUD/S, it also allowed me to further hone my body and be in the best possible physical shape I could muster before I hit the door in Coronado, San Diego.

Boot camp—and later BUD/S—changed me in a lot of ways; some subtle and others not-so-subtle. I found out I could do a hell of a lot more than I ever thought I could. And I found out I could continue to set the bar higher—and reach it. I had always been one of those people who said, "Do whatever you need to do to get the job done." After my training I was able to live that motto.

I learned chance favors the prepared mind. Athletic abilities help you succeed only so far, but if you have the proper training and volition those things are the ones that help you get through when you need something more.

Many things about boot camp were frustrating. One was not being able to see Michelle for eight weeks. Thankfully, my position as ARPOC provided not just extra responsibility but some leeway when I was left in charge on a Saturday or Sunday. So, at about week 4, when the real Navy guys would get some weekend time off from us and be back at home, I would be required to march my fellow recruits to the chow hall and back to the barracks, after which I would promptly do an about face and march my own ass to the base medical center. The medical center was, for the most part, closed on the weekends. Except for the emergency intake area on the first floor, the whole building was a ghost town. Here, I would find some empty doctor's office—belonging to a lieutenant, commander, or a captain—and proceed to take up camp. I would basically sit there and place a phone call to Michelle and talk to her for about an hour or so. Yes, I called my mom too!

Not only did this provide some comfort, it also provided unintended positive consequences—something I like to call leverage. The RDCs used a lot of psychological warfare during training in order to keep us all in line. One of these was with the art of holding phone calls over our heads like they were golden tickets. If you got out of line you might lose your phone time. We only got phone time once every three weeks, so everyone looked forward to it like a kid at Christmas.

Since I was sneaking phone calls with Michelle every weekend, as well as one of two days a week after SEAL PT, I suddenly had a special bargaining chip I could use—not so much for me with RDCs Plyer and Trevino, but on behalf of my fellow recruits. For example, Chief Plyler would often take some kid's phone privileges away from him for doing something stupid and we would all watch as the dude would have a melt-down. I would suddenly step in and save the day:

"Chief Plyler, I would be happy to give my phone call time to Seaman Recruit 'Jones' I don't have anyone to call and he needs it more than I do."

Chief Plyler would turn to Jones while pointing to me and say, "Now that's leadership, Chuck! Maybe you, Chuck, could learn something from Seaman Recruit Chuck Heben."

Jones would be excited and grateful. All the other guys in my group would see it and that provided me with even more juice and respect, especially when the regular Navy guys weren't around to be in charge. It allowed me to take this stressful boot camp situation that was designed to push you, break you, and rebuild you, and suddenly, in those brief moments, transform it into something even more special, something human. And it was those small acts of humanity, I believe, that served as a tool to foster even more teamwork!

Doing this taught me a few valuable lessons I applied when I became a SEAL, and then even later as a private military contractor: Get the job done right, keep your troops motivated and earn their respect, and then they'll trust you to help keep them alive in a place where everyone is trying to kill you. And lastly, if you aint cheatin', you aint tryin'!

Boot camp was definitely something not everyone could handle. Fights constantly broke out. There was a lot of crying, bullying and meltdowns. Despite this, I saw it as nothing more than a necessary-but-petty torment, interspersed with a Navy history lesson, in order to check the box so that I could move on to what really mattered to me, BUD/S—SEAL training.

To say that my initial Navy training changed me would be an understatement. I learned more about teamwork than I ever had before—even more than when I played team sports in high school and college. This was a different type of teamwork, one where your life was on the line instead of just a win. I learned how to survive and thrive under a more powerful microscope—one with greater scrutiny and one with more dire consequences at stake. I also learned a greater appreciation for my country and the military. This country has a proud history—and its military has a pretty amazing past. We produce people who keep us free. Wearing the uniform changes you as well. You learn how to hold the line and work in foreign countries.

Even to this day, I think about the guys I went through boot camp with and see how they changed from the day I met them to the day they graduated. Those who made it realized they were part of something bigger than themselves. We worked together to be part of that Hall of Fame Division, which gave us all a sense of pride and accomplishment. And it was this *esprit de corps* that carried over into our time in the Navy, no matter what job we did.

One thing Navy training did not teach me—especially boot camp—was how to die in combat. We don't learn how to fail! But I was definitely aware that it was a potential consequence of going to war. We learned that through the history we studied—cataclysmic battles like Khe Sanh, Tet Offensive, Battle of Huế, Inchon and the Chosen River, Midway and Guadalcanal, Iwo Jima and the Battle of the Bulge. We're taught that no matter what happens, you man your post until the ship goes down. Then, make sure you work to ensure maximum survivors. You are never out of the fight and you never abandon the team. That's a valuable lesson anyone can apply in life—whether it's personal, family, sports or business. That type of intestinal fortitude is imperative to survival and to success.

Once I completed boot camp and passed all the required pre-BUD/S medical and psychological screenings, the Navy activated what's called my 'Dive Fare Corpsman Contract', which meant that instead of heading across the street from the Recruit Training Center to the Navy Training Center (where you learn your Navy job for the next six to 10 weeks), I went straight from boot camp to BUD/S training. Remember, I asked for the 'quickest route to BUD/S', and this was it. After I completed BUD/S training—no sure thing—I would report to Fort Benning, Georgia for three weeks of static line, Jump School training. After Jump School,

I would be sent directly to SEAL Team Eight, where I would work to perfect my job: U.S. Navy SEAL.

<<<>>>

Being both a SEAL and a Navy Corpsman (Medic) gave me the expertise needed to change careers in the spring of 2009, when I founded a company called Medical Security International or MSI. My partner was a fallen-from-grace ER physician named Matt. Dr. Matt had written himself some prescriptions for painkillers and sleeping aids while he was on the emergency room team at the local hospital Trauma Center, and was then dealing with a suspended medical license. He and I shared a similar blip on the EKG strip of our lives. A wrinkle in the fabric of time that, if pressed under enough heat, and after much self-realization and reputation restoration, would eventually go away.

MSI's motto was "Protect the Protectors; Save Lives". Our original business model was products, gear, training and consulting. We taught badge-wearing first responders (police officers and SWAT cops) how to effect survival in deadly force encounters from a tactical and medical standpoint until they could be delivered to a higher echelon of care. Matt and I made a good splash. We probably trained 50 percent of the SWAT Police in the Northern part of Ohio—from Madison to Bay Village and from Cleveland to Columbus. Things were going well and we started making decent money. We made a lot of local media appearances and were even featured in a national magazine, called *SWAT*. One of our big successes was doing regular consulting and field work for the Cleveland Clinic—in 2012 we went to Abu Dhabi to conduct a threat assessment for the 4,000,000-square-foot medical facility the Clinic built there: The largest cantilevered structure in the world.

But then, slowly, the bottom fell out of the business. The police departments got wind that I had a felony conviction and that Matt was enrolled in treatment in lieu of conviction for his own dalliances. Several of them confronted us about this and, though they were very pleased with our work, were reluctant to do further business with us on the off-chance that someone outside of the department learned they were using fallen-from-grace consultants.

Not ones to throw in the towel and quit without a fight, we dug our heels in and attempted to broaden the scope of our business in order to entertain work outside of the state as well as outside of the US. We used our existing relationship with the Cleveland Clinic to parlay that into an opportunity. We devised a business model to take Aeromedical Transport both into the private sector and into the government sector for wealthy VIP members, dignitaries, and heads of state.

Matt and I opened conversations with an aviation company that was already doing work with the Clinic, and together we began assembling the plans to develop a company that would rescue and transport VIPs and dignitaries with logistical difficulties and medical issues or both. This had the potential to be extremely lucrative.

But the aviation company was not geared up to do what it claimed it could. That was disappointing, so the venture never got past the late planning stages. At the same time, the police department work was drying up because of the fact that their money was extremely tight and they were also questioning their involvement with us. Also, by now, Matt had finished the treatment-in-lieu program and had been re-issued his state medical license. He was, subsequently, allowed to pick up a few ER shifts and told me he wanted to return to his profession rather than go all-in with the pursuit of any new business ideas.

Fortunately for me, I had earned some new-found fame during my time at MSI and become something of a TV personality and an expert on all-things in the Spec Ops area of the military. I had just been offered a once-of-a-lifetime opportunity to join my SEAL buddy, Travis Lively, in Africa for seven weeks, in order to film a new television program for Animal Planet called *Ivory Wars*. So we closed the doors to MSI, ending yet another chapter of my entrepreneurial life. The idea still rumbles around in my brain and I still believe that it has tremendous potential, if brought before the right people.

<<<>>>

I only kept four items that were issued to me in boot camp: 1) A black wool watch cap; 2) A black wool (mock turtle neck) sweater; 3) A black Pea Coat; 4) and one blue dungaree shirt with my last name

UNDAUNTED

on it. This last item I kept in my locker on a hangar all through BUD/S to remind myself every day that I NEVER wanted to have to wear that damn thing again! I still have all of them today and they remind me of the initial moves I made and the fearless chances I took, good and bad, in order to be where I am today. Nothing worth anything in life comes easy or without a sacrifice. The reason why most people live lives of mediocrity is because they lacked the ability to step out of their comfort zones and create possibilities for themselves. Comfort zones are like cancers, they eventually eat you up from the inside and kill you! Step AWAY from the comfort zones, people!

CHAPTER 8

"This is not a costume. It does not come with a cape. To the wearer it does not convey super powers. To the bearer, it promises nothing. It does not come with a set of instructions. Those who don it have earned the right to do so through a forging process unlike any other on the face of this Earth. As iconic as the weapon it is hanging from, this uniform—and especially the symbol stitched upon it—is a staunch reminder, to our enemies, that we will always prevail. For life, liberty, and the pursuit of all who threaten it: Long live the Brotherhood and God bless America!"

—Christopher Mark Heben

There is little question in my mind; I would not have had the mental fortitude to keep trying my hand at entrepreneurship had I not experienced something even more mentally and physically stressful than anything else on earth—BUD/S training.

Navy boot camp in Great Lakes, Illinois was an interesting and indoctrinating eight weeks, but it wasn't until I was sent to Coronado, California, for 27 weeks of BUD/S training, that my mettle was to be truly tested.

BUD/S, without question, is the most holistically demanding military training program in the world. It's truly designed to separate the wheat from the chaff, the shit from the Shine-Ola. Because of its brutal and unrelenting intensity, it develops a class of warrior that is unmatched on any field of battle, even if that battlefield is one atmosphere below the earth's surface. There are a lot of Special Forces groups around the world. Some are amazing and some are downright shitty. However, 'downright shitty' is still a classification above your average grunt. That being said, the quality of the commando that is cranked out of the meat grinder that is BUD/S, is unlike any other the world has ever seen. There's a reason why we are called Jedi Knights, Spartans, or Ninjas. We kick a metric-shit-ton of ass. We do it with precision and panache, and we do it in some of the most inhospitable and hazardous environments, most notably, on, in and under water. As a nation, as a world, we were able to put men on the moon long before we could ever locate and get eyes on the *Titanic*—let alone get close to it. There is only one atmospheric change that takes place from the Earth's surface to the moon, but to the earth's surface to the *Titanic*, there are over 350! So I don't care who says what, SEALs can shoot, move, communicate and work a bag of medicine—and do it all in water if need be—and we've been doing it successfully for more than 50 years. In my opinion, that makes us the best. BUD/S will test you, in every way possible. If you cannot become what is, you will QUICKLY become what is not. More than 85 percent of those who try never become what is. They, in fact, become what is not. And that is: Not a U.S. Navy SEAL.

As I arrived at the Phil Bucklew Naval Special Warfare Center in Coronado, California, the increased level of mental and physical intensity was immediately apparent. This was the testosterone pit of America. People were literally scurrying around like ants on crack, shuffling everywhere at a double-time pace across every visible portion of the base. They weren't in a hurry, *per se*, they were just moving at three-quarter speed. It was dubbed the 'BUD/S Shuffle', and if you were caught doing anything else from point A to point Wherever, you were soon to be in deep shit and abject misery. It was easy to see that I was walking into a meat grinder—the Captain America Factory was open 24/7/365—and just like the *agoge* in ancient Sparta, or a *ludis* in ancient Rome, this was no place for the weak of heart, mind, body or soul.

All across the base you saw trainees giving their all—and then some. In between the partitioning and weaving of fences peppered with signs that read "SEAL Team Three"; "SEAL Team Five"; and "SEAL Team One" you could steal glimpses of actual SEAL Teams conducting a variety of mission-preparation procedures, as well as physical training evolutions. Dudes loaded weapons into trucks, packed up parachutes and slammed up onto the beach in Zodiac F470s. Amidst the kinetic chaos and heavy smell of salt air, hung a weighty sense of purpose yet also a calm sort of coolness that we all hoped to one day have the privilege to bask in. I hoped to God I would, at the very least, be able to obtain some of that coolness if only by some divine osmotic process brought on by sheer proximity.

At BUD/S, you're definitely in the thick of things. You're thrown in the fire and your body is treated like a slab of raw steel that continuously gets heated up and hammered, and heated up and hammered again. It's like a modern day blacksmith shop built inside of a pressure cooker: You might get melted down to nothing; you could get hammered and fractured and pounded so thin that you are no longer a viable or useful item. Or maybe, just maybe, you'll be forged into a hardened piece of steel that is then sharpened to a razor point and put into a scabbard on the belt of our nation's war kit! Anything less than the latter is an epic fail and one that over 85 percent of dudes who are sent to BUD/S have the displeasure of experiencing first hand.

When I checked in, I was wearing summer whites and black socks. In Chicago, I was only issued black socks for my uniforms—but this was San Diego, and it's always sunny in San Diego, so I figured that black socks with dress whites was what I was supposed to wear...LMAO...I missed the memo and I had a lot to learn, and I was about to get my first lesson.

I checked in at the Quarterdeck and was given a welcome packet and a room assignment, and then was pointed in the direction I needed to go. The guys manning the desk were all BUD/S students, so they were all too happy to make sure you only had enough info to get out of their faces. I was walking up the first set of steps at Building 618, to take my gear up to my assigned room on the 3rd floor of that building, when Master Chief Joe Goward stopped me dead in my tracks.

"You, going up them steps in that clown suit," he said. "Stop right there."

I looked around and realized he was talking to me.

"Yes, you, Clown Boy. I guess nobody taught you how to wear Navy Dress Whites. You don't wear no black socks with dress whites, son. Be glad I stopped your ass and not one of the younger instructors, or else you'd be in the Pacific right now swallowing salt water. Just get up them steps and go get into your Navy Boondockers and dungarees

UNDAUNTED

before you get messed up real bad. I've got plenty of time to mess with you later, unless you're feeling like quitting right now, and in that case I'll take you over to the bell. You're at BUD/S now, son, you better start looking the part."

I replied, "Roger that, Master Chief!" and hustled off to change my clothes. I avoided any punitive action, and I actually recognized his rank, so I was feeling double lucky! Now, if only I hadn't thrown out ALL of my dungarees and my Boondockers, I would have been able to comply with Master Chief Goward. You see, I had no plans to ever wear those items again because, as a SEAL, you never have to, and I fully expected make it through this course.

Still, this was not so great. Here was a SEAL Master Chief telling me in not-so-subtle terms that this place was different—everyone was the cream of the crop, the most elite of the elite, and I needed to learn what was going on and how to fit in and act like it immediately or I'd doom myself. He very well could have just rolled his eyes and figured I was a rookie trainee doomed to fail. But he didn't, he took the time to elucidate, to educate and intimidate as well as to dictate, all attributes that SEALs possess to a factor of 10. I am still thankful for his calibration to my compass. It made me further realize that I was now going to be conducting training on an entire compound filled with smart, squared-away, and headstrong athletes, and I needed to become one of them. We were trying to be the best America had to offer. Yet, again, somewhere between 85 percent and 92 percent of this group would wash out long before the 27 weeks was over. Nearly 50 percent would succumb to this attrition rate in the first two weeks alone.

I was assigned to class 214 with my boot-camp buds Travis Lively, Mike Branch and George Hunt, along with another 258 individuals—but that number wasn't going to last. On our first day they lined us up and said, "Men. Look left. Look right. Look in front of you. Look behind you. Only one out of 10 of you is going to be here on graduation day."

That can make you feel pretty humble right away. But I didn't give a rat's ass; I knew I would be one of them. I'm sure there were about 260 other dudes that were thinking the exact same thing. Hell, if they weren't, they were already doomed. They also said, "And don't be a dumbass and form a fast friendship with anyone until well after Hell Week is over. Half of you fucks won't even make it that far, and if you have any shot of making it to graduation it certainly won't be by aligning yourself with any fucking quitters!"

It was a very valid point. I would keep to myself, or try to for the most part, until after Hell Week.

BUD/S training begins with what's called Physical Training, Rest and Recuperation (PTR&R), or Fourth Phase (or Phase Four). Fourth Phase is where the newest students get acclimated to the program and also where the people who are injured during training are placed while they're rehabbing. I would be in Fourth Phase for both of those reasons before my time on the Silver Strand was over. During those first couple weeks you're under an electron microscope. The instructors are analyzing you very closely, trying to determine whether you're the type of guy they can send to work with their friends. If not, they do their best to force you to quit before you really ever get started. There's no sense even wasting their time, or the Navy's time, on some douche biscuit that is going to be a problem child in the Teams. But believe me, despite the scientifically sadistic sieve that BUD/S is, the occasional douche-berry gets picked and finds his way into the graduation basket.

If you're among the injured, and they think you're going to make it, they might say about you, "He's a put-out kinda dude, and he was clipping along nicely. Not to mention, his classmates liked him, and we liked him. On top of that, he had good leadership skills. I hope he recovers enough to make it through." Yes, the BUD/S instructors could be that observant and that commendatory, but only when talking with one another.

It's funny, but true, that when you're a new guy at BUD/S, they might consider shallow things at the onset, such as how you look. One instructor told us, "If you're stupid, you're not going to make it through this training. But if you're ugly, you're not going to make it either. God help those of you that are both ugly and stupid. You may as well pack your shit now. Nobody wants to be on a six-month deployment with a dumbass, and nobody wants to be on liberty and in a bar with some ugly, no pussy-getting dumbass. You see gents, pussy begets pussy, and

UNDAUNTED

if your ugly dumbass is too ugly and too dumb to get any pussy, no one else will BEGET-tin' any pussy either. Or, at the very least, I'll have to work twice as hard because you've turned them off by the very sight and sound of you. You see gents, we're Frogmen: We drink, fight, and fuck. But the first two get old pretty quick without the last one, and we can't have you fucking up our fuck, for fuck-sake!"

This was, perhaps, one of the most brilliant tirades I've ever heard. So much so, that every word has stuck with me over a decade and a half later!

Like it or not, this is reality—if you look at most SEALS, and not to sound strange, but, the vast majority are handsome. If they weren't in combat gear, many of them could be on the cover of an Abercrombie & Fitch catalog. This shouldn't come as too much of a surprise because there is a certain level of narcissism going on with SEALs. We approach our bodies aiming for a certain element of perfection—both mentally and physically. No matter what anyone else thinks, we always strive for that next level of perfection. This sense of reaching higher, of having the resiliency to achieve more than what seems humanly possible, is one of the unique things that separates us from others who serve in the regular armed forces. Besides, it takes a certain amount of narcissism to do what we do and to do it so well. It's not all that unlike a baller brain surgeon or cardiac surgeon, in that, it takes a certain amount and type of swagger to crack a person's chest or brain bucket open and start poking around in order to save them from some genetic or kinetic insult to the organs within. As SEALs, we also do precise 'body-work', except that we are sent to stop people from having birthdays via the surgical application of treatments and procedures that are high caliber in nature. Our procedures are guaranteed to always be fatal. So, yes there is a shared and necessary swagger, but each is acquired in polar opposite fashion. And no, I didn't just say that doctors were on a par with SEALs, only in the ego and drive part. Caveat: I know a few SEALs who have become doctors! I don't know any doctors that have become SEALs.

Also, our superiority comes from the fact that we own the water, which just so happens to be the most hostile environment on the planet. When you consider that we were able to put men on the moon long before we could even locate and dive on the *Titanic*, it becomes that much more impressive. Going from Earth's atmosphere is only one atmosphere change. Going 33-feet below the surface of the water is one atmosphere change. The *Titanic* is 12,500 feet below the surface, so you're talking over 30 atmospheres of change. The pressure is crushing once you dive below the surface—and it increases exponentially the deeper you go. Space is cold, but you don't have the crushing pressure that you do underwater. When you add all of this together, it's easy to see how, as SEALs, we think of ourselves as unstoppable.

Those first few weeks of BUD/S are designed to assault you mentally and physically. It's a meat grinder and the grinder never stops. Your SEAL instructors are tough and they don't relent. They are like technicians performing Gamma Knife Radiosurgery, and if they find something, anything, that tells them you're not up to par, you're zapped. You are done. They constantly talk about you behind closed doors, assessing you, sharing opinions about who they want, who they don't, who's got a chance to make it through, and who's destined to fail.

I went from basic, 'do as I say', survival in boot camp and learning a little about history and uniforms to going to BUD/S and realizing that I wasn't just a drone of a Navy guy anymore. Rather, I was trying to become a SEAL—a highly functioning and capable commando from a cerebral and physical standpoint. Every day during SEAL training, we were given a lesson to learn. And every day, something was guaranteed to happen: Someone was injured, dudes quit—some were medically dropped, some were dropped for safety violations or lack of performance. Regardless, they left, and a smaller group of us continued on toward our goal of graduating. The faint of heart never started and the feeble died along the way. As Master Chief Hershel Davis likes to say: Trample the weak and hurdle the dead!

Once we were acclimated—and the weakest among us ferreted out—Phase One of our training actually began, the Basic Conditioning phase. This is where our class underwent intense physical training, we learned water competency and they tested our mental tenacity. They also pounded the importance of teamwork into us, building us as teams, yet stressing the bleak reality that we better not forge personal relationships with our fellow students because odds were against the majority of us making it through together to the end. I would soon experience this firsthand.

Phase One was seven weeks of brutal running, swimming and calisthenics. Our performances were measured weekly by a four-mile timed run, a timed obstacle course, and a two-mile timed swim. They also taught us how to conduct hydrographic recon and beach survey operations. And just as we were getting used to the pounding, they cast us into Hell Week in order to more quickly separate the most resolute from the posers.

Back then, in 1997, we wore beaver tail 'shorty' wetsuits—a throwback to the old school Frogman days. It stopped at your waist and had a beaver tail, sort of like a modified flap that went from the small of your back, between your legs and over your nuts and then forward and upward to button up at your waist in the front. You wore that over dive shorts, and your legs were exposed to the 54-degree water. You wore a hood and a dive mask, dive booties and dive or surface fins. You were issued a green military web belt with a flare on one side and a knife on the other. It was one of those old Mark 1 MOD 0 K-Bar Marine-style knives. And when you stand at attention and show your knife to the instructor, it better be RAZOR sharp. At inspections, your uniform better be perfect, your boots shiny, your bunk expertly made and your room spotless or, well...there are just so many ways to get your ass kicked or to get kicked out of BUD/S. You quickly realize that you better be locked-on every hour of every day. There's just no room for error. Everything you face at BUD/S, even before Hell Week—is one full beat down after another and many repetitive kicks to the ass and balls. But, if you didn't know that going in to it, you were an idiot. And, you were probably going to quit in the first week. Well, we all hoped you did anyway because nobody likes to be around a whining, complaining, crying pussy. Nobody. I feel the same in business today!

If you do fail at something, you get one mulligan. If you fail something twice, you're sent to a SEAL instructor review board. You can only fail a Physical Evolution twice; on the third time, you're automatically done.

But if you fail even once, you're asked why you failed—it could be a run or a swim that you didn't make the time on, or it could be a safety violation, like a dull knife or a problem with your firearm, or that a swim flare was not properly oriented for a day or night water evolution. Ignorance is no excuse for the law, and failure, while an occurrence, is simply not an acceptable option.

So you have all these dynamics going on around you while you're facing a constant litany of mind and body challenges. Your room has three other guys in it. Therefore, beyond being personally squared away, you have to work together to be squared away as a room—keeping it up to snuff or all four of you suffer the consequences. It's very much an individual thing but with an underlying team responsibility at play as well.

"It's all for one and one for all...together we'll work on the big, and as individuals, the small!" That was a phrase I coined while there. It helped me to put things into the proper perspective.

In the middle of the compound is a concrete courtyard aptly called 'The Grinder'. It's where you stand when you're lining up for morning PT. It's insanely awesome in every way. It looks like a gladiatorial pit you'd see in a Roman *ludis* or a combat-skills development area of a Spartan *agoge*. On any given morning, at 0500 hours, you might easily do 1,000 push-ups, 500 pull-ups, or 1,000 flutter kicks and sit-ups during a 45-minute to one-hour workout. You better do each one of the exercises perfectly or they'll start the whole process again because some asshole in your class is slacking off or he can't count properly. Everything is done to a cadence, wherein the instructor calls out the pace and you give him the number of that current repetition. There is a very definite way it must be done, and the last thing you want to hear is, "And halt! ...Starting over for Smith over there... He can't fucking count!" This is going on in an open-air venue, wherein other students from classes ahead or behind are running and hustling around doing their own thing, as well as other SEAL instructors planning training sessions for those other students. Even the other SEALs, not running that session, can hit you on anything you are doing wrong. There is no escape and no quarter. And, as always, it's: "Put out or get out!" and/or

"Attention to fucking detail gents!" The pressure cooker is never off and it's always set to high.

Needless to say, you're constantly stressed out. Instructors can come into your room at any time—day or night. They pull you aside and take issue with anything—real or contrived—just to see how you react. There is a constant overlying feeling of duress. No one wants to get dropped from the program or punched in the face, so everyone is on their toes all the time. You think about injury. You think about failure. You think about whether the guy next to you in line is going to screw up and you'll all be held accountable for his failure. All of this is going through your mind. You're on edge all the time and never truly comfortable. Sleep is at a premium because, when you're not physically swimming, running, doing an obstacle course (O-course) or PT'ing, you're preparing for whatever it is they have in store for you tomorrow or later that evening. It's unrelenting, but it is all part of their plan. You see, they've been keeping meticulous records on everything at BUD/S since the beginning of time: Water temperature and how it affects the ability to function over time. Air temperature and how it affects the same. Body temperature based on exposure to the aforementioned elements, and how that affects performance or if a student is near hypo or hyperthermia and when to stop or hydrate based on those factors. The effective delivery of 'surf torture' evolutions is heavily based on all of these factors and figures. They also keep training records on every student as well as the overall performance of each BUD/S Class to ever go through. It is the most precise and longitudinal Lacedaemon study on human performance in the history of mankind. I am proud to say that there are records of me kept there.

Everything is designed during the initial orientation of PTR&R to prepare you for First Phase. And the first few weeks of Phase One are meant to lead you smoothly into Hell Week, which is six days or pure torture. Up until then (and after) they inflict both what they have to and also what they want to inflict upon you each day. There are lessons and there are just plain ole' fashion beat-downs issued. Sometimes the beat-downs occur for no other reason than the fact that there may be too many students still left in the class at the end of any given day. And just like the leader of any tribe, at the end of each day's training, your proctor gives you a synopsis of the day you just had and what you can expect tomorrow. Believe it or not, while they're grinding you into the ground they're still there to teach, so it's like a 'flip of the switch' and they become more of a mentor around day's end than the tormentor they'd been all day. This prepares you to flip a switch as a SEAL and go from hard-core commando to loving father and/or family man at the end of a deployment. Remember, I said that everything done to you here is done with a purpose.

In high school I had been a phenomenal sprinter—I was fast in quick bursts—but I've never been a great jogger or distance runner. I just hate it. So I struggled early on during a lot of those runs, ending up somewhere in the middle to the back of the pack. On more than one occasion, I barely was able to make the necessary time to keep moving along. But, during sand berm sprints, I was the guy whose time was used as the bar for others to beat. The instructors used to yell, "If you can beat Heben, you can go have lunch now."

I also became one hell of a swimmer and, toward the end, I was one of the four fastest guys in the entire class. It's ironic because I didn't start off that well at all and almost failed the very first timed swim. I needed 85 minutes or less, and I came in at 84 minutes and change. Had I come in less than a minute slower, I would have failed and then would have been an even bigger blip on the radar screen than I already was. You never want to be a big blip on the big screen at BUD/S. Never.

One of the things that helped me thrive during First Phase—and the remainder of my SEAL training—was my ability to make anger work for me. Too many fellow SEAL candidates got angry and their anger was a liability rather than an asset. They couldn't channel it. Not me. I learned, during my formative years, how to tap into the rage that always seemed to be boiling below my surface and turn it into something useful. Anger is an asset if you know how to use it. When the chips are down, if you can get angry about something and allow yourself to make it work for you, it's a good thing. The body's own endocrine hormones are very powerful, and how effectively you harness that surge of adrenalin and control the ensuing emotion, is what separates us from the animals. Hell, it's what separates the successful people from the failures.

If you know me, you know that I am a nice guy. I really am. But people often misinterpret that niceness for weakness. Instead, I'm more of a 'Type A-minus' dude. What does A-minus mean? It means that you don't know I'm about to introduce your teeth to my fist until my knuckles are touching your enamel. Up until that happens, we are having a jovial conversation. Well, so you think anyway. I'm more like that velvet fist in an iron glove, seemingly soft but don't let it hit ya'. Yes, I do have that Ying and Yang thing going for me. I've had it since grade school. SEAL training allowed me to harness that energy and channel it into something even more productive than I ever had before. I combined it with athleticism and mental focus and then punctuated it all with good nutrition. In this way, I was able to create something "smooth" and seamless to work within for the entire time I was at BUD/S. In SEAL training, there's an expression: "Slow is Smooth and Smooth is Fast." I've heard it bastardized and expressed a multitude of ways, but this one is the correct one. The entire time you are there, you take those words and place them into action: On your swims, when you use it to plane out and glide just below the surface, and especially on the O-course—where you definitely want to be methodical and smooth. Otherwise, you will burn out. It's almost like the tortoise and the hare: Be consistent, smooth and steady. That combination equates to speed. As a SEAL you shoot only 'as fast as you can kill'. I learned quickly that I'd rather be slower and deadly accurate than quickly dead. And this is something you can apply to your everyday life. Maybe I wasn't the best runner or swimmer in my group, but I was arguably one of the best athletes. So I got smart about it, and it ended up allowing me to begin to compete well with guys who were the prototypical 'Aquamen' in the water. Bottom line: I became what was so I never became what was not!

BUD/S, as a whole, was also more than just an endurance test. We also had to master some pretty complex concepts like Dive Physics. If you couldn't grasp Charles' Law, Boyles Law, Archimedes Principle or Gay-Lussac's law, you were not going to make it. We also learned about the nuances of old school hydrographic reconnaissance. You're all out in the ocean at 0300 hours, dropping a lead line into the water to measure the depth of the ocean floor as it comes up on the beach. With a plastic board and grease pen, you all mark and move. When done, you all head back to your room to put together a hydrographic reconnaissance chart that has to be perfect. It's all a massive uptake of information that tests your ability to think critically, perform complex mathematical equations and process information on-the-fly, as you'll have to do in the heat of combat when lives are hanging in the balance.

Further, you're learning water competency and how to perform in it better than anyone else. Pool Competency didn't come until Phase Two, but it didn't matter, you still have to love the water. The SEAL instructors teach you how to swim through underwater obstacle courses and how to tie knots underwater while holding your breath, so you can potentially blow up those obstacles if need be. You're tested on surviving in the water with your arms tied behind your back and your legs tied at the ankles. It's called 'drown-proofing', and was thought up by some brilliant Vietnam-era SEAL who was actually taken hostage and hog tied on a sampan (More on this later). You're taught how to 'save' instructors from drowning while they're wearing fins and lead weights around their waists and trying to drag you down with them. This is called 'Lifesaving'. Personally, I think the names of those two evolutions, should be switched. Neither of these water evolutions are for the uninitiated, and before you even reach Hell Week, close to 60 percent of your class has already been weeded out. It's a rude awakening.

Fortunately, I've always been comfortable in water. I can hold my breath for a long time, so I began mentally practicing for drown-proofing the moment we started preparing for the final evolution. Positive mental imagery and positive mental attitude are very powerful tools; you learn just how powerful when you are at BUD/S.

Drown-proofing is one of the three hardest evolutions, and the third leading cause of BUD/S students calling it quits. Hell Week is number one while Pool Competency Week, during Phase Two, is a close second. No matter how much they try to convince you otherwise, it is nowhere near a normal activity to have somebody tie your hands behind your back, bind your legs at the ankles, and then command you to jump into a 15-foot deep body of water and ask you to relax and survive for 30 to 45 minutes. There is nothing relaxing or comfortable about it. It's like a scene from a bad mafia movie where someone is thrown into the water with concrete shoes on—except that someone is you. And with 5 percent body fat, I didn't need concrete shoes to make my experience miserable—I sank just like a fucking rock!

Despite this, I remained calm because I'm a big believer in perfect planning leads to peak performance. Instead of worrying, I started thinking about all the elements involved in each evolution and how our training prepared us to pass the tests. With drown-proofing, first they tie your hands and let your feet remain free. Then they bind your feet and let your hands go free. Finally, they put it all together for a day of practice before the actual test. I wanted to be the most prepared person in my group, so I started practicing on my own. Yes, as crazy as that sounds, I practiced this tortuous activity on my own.

One day, I absconded with a pair of drown-proofing straps and headed off with a couple guys to a condo, on Coronado Island, that had a pool. I knew my body fat percentage wasn't going to get any higher, so in order to counter the sinking I had to find a way to become more relaxed and comfortable in the straps. I asked my dudes to tie me up, then jumped into the water over and over until I felt comfortable being bound underwater. It sounds bizarre, but it was all part of my brilliant plan. My buddies saw merit to my theory and willingly joined in.

I didn't stop there. Every night for two straight weeks I went to bed with my arms and ankles tied. Yes, I actually slept like that. Or, to be more accurate, I got a little sleep each night. My thinking was pretty straight-forward: If I could sleep like this for two weeks, I could Jedi mind trick myself into being much more comfortable when the actual test occurred. Everyone else would spend the first few minutes acclimating themselves to the straps that bound them; whereas I would already have an intimate relationship with them. This was positive mental attitude (PMA) mixed with positive mental imagery (PMI) re-enforcing with prior mechanical experience (PME)! As you are tied up and before you drift off to sleep, or something close to that, you do multiple mental rehearsals. So I laid there, rolling myself to sleep each night thinking about the activity and telling myself a success story about how I was going to jump into the water and perform flawlessly.

My buddies didn't take it as far as I did. They prepared themselves for the main event, but weren't crazy—or smart—enough to tie themselves up each night. We would watch each other in the pool and work together to make small changes in posture, movement and technique. Thank God there were no surprise night room inspections in those two weeks. That would have been awkward, to say the least. Shit, they probably would have dragged my bound-up body down to the Pacific and threw me in: "You want some extra practice Heben? Be our guest!"

All the PMI/PME/PMA paid off—I passed the test with flying colors. In fact, I felt as if I was in a controlled situation the entire test even though there is simply no relaxing way to swim as a manacled mariner! Especially when you have no body fat. For safety, instructors wear swim fins, dive masks, and snorkels, but they're not very comforting. You know they are there to pull you out of danger if needed, but you also know they aren't going to do it until your dumb ass has already drowned! They're trained to give you every last chance to pass an Evolution—even at your own expense. After all, the same courtesy was shown to them when they were BUD/S students. It is this same lineage that allows the first SEAL to have an immediate bond with the most recent SEALs—same shit, different day, different decade.

Another challenging evolution was Underwater Knot Tying. The instructors string a line across the bottom of the 15-foot deep pool. You're tasked with tying seven very specific knots underwater on a breath hold. You can do them on 7 different trips if necessary. Not wanting to be weak, I also took what some would call an unconventional approach to this event: I practiced underwater, with a blacked out mask, while lying on my back and tying the knots in an inverted fashion. My rationale was that if I could tie knots while underwater, blindfolded, AND inverted, I could do it even better and quicker under normal conditions. Again, my theory proved true: I was able to tie the required seven knots, plus three more, on one breath hold on one trip down to the line. I believe 10 knots on 1 breath hold is still a BUD/S record.

There's an old saying: All's fair in love and war. That's true. Believe it or not, one of the things the SEAL instructors want to see during BUD/S is just how devious and unfair you can be in a combat situation. When you're in some shit, there's no rulebook on how to survive and complete your mission. As long as things aren't morally reprehensible, and you're not committing war crimes, you just find a way to do it. At its core, BUD/S is really simulated combat, especially so in Hell Week—you're put in different stressful situations to see how you react. If you're caught cheating—outright cheating—you'll be confronted about it. They might beat your ass and discipline you, but if what you did was creative they might also say to themselves, "That was a pretty smart idea. I would go to war with this guy because he'll do what it takes to get us through any type of situation." Either way, the message becomes resoundingly clear: If you're caught stealing, lying or cheating, it had better be for the good of your men and you had better fess up to it immediately. One thing that is not tolerated, to any degree, is lying, cheating and stealing that is directed toward your brothers. And let's face it, the SEAL Teams are the most exclusive fraternity on the planet. BUD/S is merely a 10-month hazing process by which you gain eternal access. Well, for the most part. You still have to complete the SEAL version of Jump School and SQT (SEAL Qualification Training) before you are fully 'cleared hot' to be awarded and to wear the U.S. Navy SEAL Trident.

I apparently excelled at the lying and stealing part (we all have our strengths), so one of my ancillary jobs once I became an active Navy SEAL was to steal stuff. OK, let's just say it was to 'creatively acquire' pieces of gear that we needed anywhere, at any time, to complete our mission. I was that guy. They would say, "We don't want to know how you're getting it, just get it." I may have learned this skill early on in life when I would walk home from grade school with my brothers, but it was during my time at SEAL Team Eight that I honed it.

One morning, a senior officer pressed me on how I got the equipment and kits we all needed. I answered him with: "Sir, let's get all the dudes together in the platoon hut in 30 minutes, I'll show ya!"

After everyone assembled in our secure space, I put on a gear acquisition clinic. Let's just say that the dudes were in awe as I worked my magic on the phone and promptly had all the items they requested in that same space within a few hours.

The general consensus was, "Sweet Jesus! That was fucking awesome!"

I can't divulge how I worked my magic, but let's say having the inane ability to voice act can serve as a very powerful tool in the right situation.

Back to BUD/S: When we reached the beginning of our fifth week of training, Hell Week started. Nowadays, it's the third week. Hell Week starts Sunday and ends in the late afternoon on Friday. It is essentially six straight days of nonstop activity. What makes it even more challenging is that by the time you get to Hell Week there is a certain level of injury that's widespread among the men because of the intensity of physical activity thrust upon them. It was survival of the fittest. Those people who get severely injured and dropped or voluntarily drop out, are reassigned to the "X Division." You do not want to be a member of "X Division," because it means you're an ex-student. The SEAL motto is "The only easy day was yesterday." The X Division motto: "The only easy day is every day." If you're part of the X Division you're forced to wear a T-Shirt with that slogan on the back. Hell Week is the first real test of whether you really want to be in BUD/S and if you have what it takes to become a full-fledged Navy SEAL. Even if you make it through, you still have to survive another 32 weeks of intensive training to get your Trident. You either adapt to the terrain or you go away..... It's simple evolution really. One must evolve in order to survive the evolutions. At the end of the day, it all boils down to how bad you want to be there.

CHAPTER 9

"I challenge you to hold yourself to a higher standard."

—Christopher Mark Heben

Class 214 Hell Week began Sunday, July 12, 1997, just after the sun set. It was supposed to last until late Friday afternoon, and for many it did. Unfortunately, I would not be among the survivors who lasted to that day. A medial collateral ligament (MCL) tear in my right knee ended my best efforts to persevere late on Wednesday morning, and I was kicked back to PTR&R for medical rehabilitation.

I tore it one week earlier, during a night evolution called Rock Portage. Due to El Nino, the surf was unusually high. Normal sets are around four- to seven-foot waves, but these had now increased to between 10 and 15 feet. Rock Portage is done as both a day and a night evolution. In doing it, we learn how to safely pilot and land our boats on a rocky, hazardous, enemy coastline. We pilot the IBS (Itty Bitty Ships) or Inflatable Boat Small, a roughly 275-pound inflatable raft, through the surf and our goal was to safely land them onto the rocks in front of the Hotel del Coronado, a luxury resort one-mile north of the Naval Special Warfare Center.

Before I go into detail about the MCL hit, let me tell you a little about the Del Coronado, the Silver Strand, and the proximity of BUD/S to it. This is, perhaps, the biggest dichotomy I have ever personally been

UNDAUNTED

associated with. You are a BUD/S student and are getting the living shit kicked out of you every day. You're also being totally Jedi mind-tricked on a daily basis because as soon as you hit the public beach areas on runs and such, you routinely see bikini-clad vacationers from all over the globe. It's amazing to see how a trainee, who is suffering miserably, suddenly, visibly, magically pulls his shit together as he runs past a beach blanket filled with German supermodels and begins running like Jesse Owens taking a victory lap. It was then that I fully and completely realized just how the mind can affect the body. If you think you are defeated, you most certainly are; but I digress....

During Rock Portage, a huge wave crashed into our mal-positioned IBS and capsized it just 10 yards from the rocks. My leg got caught underneath one of the sponson tubes in the middle of the boat. When it flipped, I heard a pop and felt something rip as my body hit the water and my leg stayed in the boat. Enter the torn MCL. I knew at that moment that this was going to be problematic, but I was also headstrong enough to believe I could push through it. The MCL tear didn't present itself immediately, and I was so amped up on adrenaline that I didn't feel the injury's full impact. True to Frogman form already, I thoroughly convinced myself it was nothing, shrugged it off, and kept the injury to myself. Motrin, especially 800 mg of it, is a wonderful thing. We called it Vitamin 'M', and I would be a religious consumer of that supplement over the next 10 days. In fact, by the time Hell Week began, I was already putting full weight on my knee—running around and keeping up with my classmates. A few instructors asked if I was limping, but I firmly denied it. Admit nothing, deny everything, and make counter accusations. Well, at least I could employ the first two tenets of that SEAL principle. I wasn't about to accuse a SEAL instructor of anything.

There's a lot of chatter about Hell Week from the moment you step onto the BUD/S compound. They even tell you what's going to happen. But that doesn't soften the blow—not one bit. You catch all the 'would of, could of, should of' stories from all the X-Division bubbas. Until they were given new assignments in other Navy commands, they were the SPECWAR Centers' 'custodial commandos', for they became masters of the broom and mop. You avoided these guys at all costs because they were full of excuses, gloom and doom. I swear that the Command kept some of them around to mentally poison BUD/S students who were still 'phased up' and in the running—anything to thin the herd of BUD/S graduation hopefuls. There's nothing better than crushing a weak man's hopes and dreams, especially when you're a SEAL Instructor. The SEALs make a pact with one another not to let any shit bags make it out alive. And I'll be damned if they haven't devised the perfect system.

Hell Week is grueling. No, revise that: It's FUCKING grueling. No other week or segment of any military training is as brutal or as unrelenting at BUD/S Hell Week. There are three sets of instructors, each assuming an eight-hour shift. Many are pulled from the ranks of advanced schools of instruction attached to SPECWAR Group 1. In this way, you didn't know them and they didn't know you. This meant there was no chance for favoritism and a better chance of punishing trainees and twisting them up with more Jedi mind tricks, all designed to catch quitters. Hell Week is a pure war of attrition and the epitome of survival of the fittest. If only Darwin could have witnessed the barbarism, he would have abandoned the Galapagos and focused his study entirely on the Silver Strand and its inhabitants of SEAL wannabes, SEAL is-nows and SEAL has-beens. I say the latter with all due respect because some of the senior SEALs there were men from the books I had read. Men with names like 'Demo Dick', 'The Snake' and 'Hoss'. They hailed from places named 'Mob Six' and 'Red Cell'. How does one survive in a crucible like this? Well, that really depends on how far you are willing to sink on the evolutionary chain of man in order to assume the most basic of survival skills when needed. Conversely, how quickly can you flip that switch and become that cerebral classmate who embraces teamwork and altruism, and relies on trust over technology? Finally, you often end up asking yourself: Why am I here and why am I doing this to myself? In many a moment, those questions are the ones you end up asking yourself most. But unlike most humans, you actually learn the answers to those questions real quick.

Yet, every day the instructors ask a much different question: How bad do you want this? You have this question fired at you, relentlessly, until the answer becomes self-evident: You graduate from SEAL training. Until then, the SEAL Instructors always preface any learning evolution with: "In the rare event that you graduate from this program you will have to do this...." And you feel a huge sense of accomplishment each day, as you personally hear that statement, while you're listening to the X-Division dudes sweeping up the never-ending and ubiquitous grains of Silver Strand sand that finds its way onto the grinder via wet gear and the easterly winds sweeping up from the beach. At BUD/S, it is these little victories and mental pleasantries that keep you going.

As Master Chief Joe Goward said the day before Hell Week began: "Men, up until now we've been engaging in foreplay. But tomorrow, tomorrow we get down to the fuckin'!" True to SEAL form, the instructors look for a reason to fuck you up and kick you out of BUD/S. They represent the omnipresent un-pleasantries, the guardians of the SEAL Team gates. For them, Hell Week provides more than enough opportunities to do so—it separates those who have the will from those who will not do what it takes to remain standing. This is your second major test on the path to becoming a SEAL. The first step is simply showing up, because even if you survive Hell Week, statistically, you have only about a 50 percent chance of graduating. These are little victories, but ones that mean the world to you when you achieve them.

For five-and-a-half straight days, instructors throw an assortment of challenges at you. You get about 2.5 hours sleep, total, if you're lucky, during that week. We ran more than 200 miles and underwent physical training for more than 22 hours per day. You barely stop to eat and never stop to use the toilet. You just go. It was the ultimate test of our individual willpower as well as our ability to work together as a team. Completing Hell Week identifies and defines those of us who have the necessary make-up—resiliency, commitment and dedication—to become a SEAL. People always ask me: How did you make it through Hell Week? In truth, I counted down the number of meals. Twenty-four meals are served during Hell Week. That's an easy number to track, even when you are legally insane by Wednesday afternoon.

While you're battling physical fatigue and mental exhaustion, every eight hours the Center throws a fresh crew of SEAL instructors at you. So even while it's possible to count meals, you can't account for the psychodynamics you face. In essence, there's a fresh group of guys grinding you down three times a day. Sleep deprivation removes your ability to know what day it is, but you're still able to discern night from day and time of day because of the sun or the moon's position in the sky. BUD/S definitely pushes your faith in yourself about as far as you've ever had it pushed before. It sets the bar for your career moving forward. If you graduate, that is. You quickly realize you are either all-in or all-out.

In reality, the SEAL instructors' job is greater than simply torturing you; it's also to keep you properly motivated. You're constantly asked if you want to quit. The instructors know you're spent and under serious mental anguish, but at the same time they don't want to push anyone off the ledge and cause them to completely lose their sanity. That wouldn't be good for anyone, especially the Navy. The SPECWAR Center has roughly adhered to a strict playbook book for many years—one that consists of formulas and algorithms designed to push you to the very limit of human endurance in every aspect of the human condition. And rightly so. If you can't cut the mustard here, you will never make it in the Teams. Worse, you might get somebody killed because of a mental or physical breakdown. Shit-bags need not apply. But when they do, they don't last very long.

There are a few good things about Hell Week. There are no room or uniform inspections. Physical evolutions aren't timed. Instead, you're engaged in one long, seemingly never-ending, endurance test. You cannot fail a run, swim or obstacle course. You need only to not quit the current evolution or Hell Week ends for you right then and there—as does BUD/S.

People start dropping out pretty damn quickly. You see it almost immediately during what is called Hell Week 'Breakout', when Hell Week officially commences and the pandemonium is at an all-time high due to the screaming SEAL instructors use of machine-gun fire, artillery simulators, smoke grenades, strobe lights, and heavy-metal music. It's like a rave party inside a prison inside a rebel encampment inside a war-torn country. You seriously think you are in an alternate universe where they are re-filming the movie *Apocalypse Now*! And while all this is happening around you, you're being forced to engage in drills intended to confuse, disorient, and break up boat crews—all in an attempt to override the brain housing unit and make students realize that the foreplay is definitely over.

The artillery simulators are discharged inside of empty oil drums—which makes the sound even more deafening. It is downright frightening, especially when you have never ever heard anything other than an M-80 or H-100 go off on the Fourth of July. Machine-gun fire comes from the M-60 E3's, running blank rounds that the instructors are walking around with, firing from the hip. If you're never heard any gun fire before, this can be terrifying. Even if you're able to keep your wits about you, you still have this foreboding feeling that if you lose your boat crew integrity you will be severely punished.

This process goes on for over an hour. It spills out of the Grinder and onto the beach, where the bear crawls and surf torture begin. This process continues relentlessly until the first man or two, or 20, quits. Yes, it doesn't end until people quit.

On Sunday night, nobody stood in front of us and yelled, "OK, welcome to Hell Week!" Instead, we were pre-organized into seven-man boat crews arranged by height order, so that we were grouped with people close to our own height. The smallest guys were lumped together in what were called the Smurf Crews. I was in Boat Crew Five along with six other guys. Having seen 213 Hell Week, each of us knew a bit about what to expect, but we sure as hell didn't know when it what was going to happen. We were just instructed to be ready to move out.

Suddenly, those simulated explosions were set off all around us—artillery, grenade, machine-gun fire, flares. It was a complete shit show. And it was unbelievable. The instructors started screaming at us through bullhorns, yelling, "Get out of your rooms, assemble your boat crews and get on the Grinder!"

It was mass confusion. There was panic, pandemonium, and people freaking out everywhere. Many of the crews were completely disjointed—they were supposed to be. While you're running around trying to pull your guys together, the explosions and gunfire keep coming. Nothing lets up. Not even for a moment.

When you finally reach the Grinder—not-surprisingly without your full boat crew—the instructors throw an absolute shit-fit. They scream, "Where the fuck is the rest of your boat crew, SIR? SIR, this is combat and you can't even get your men together? SIR, take your crew and go get wet and sandy! You've got two minutes to go hit the surf and get back here, and you better have a full muster when you return!"

A lot of the abuse was directed at the Os (officers). I think they took sick pleasure in being able to berate, without repercussions, the young officers. However, no one escaped the wrath of the instructors.

So in order to avoid the possibility of further—or greater—punishment, everyone scrambles in the chaos to track down their missing guy or two, then run together down to the surf zone, leap into the water, get out, get covered in sand, reassemble as a team, and then run at top speed back to the Grinder. And by the way, you're carrying your inflatable boat on your heads. So if and when you're missing a crew member at the beginning of the punishment, you're carrying his load of the boat.

Things are just barely getting underway when it gets worse—this is Hell Week, after all. If—and when—the instructors don't like what you're doing, they send your team running back to the Grinder to immerse yourselves into a new IBS—one filled with ice water. The drill is hard but straightforward: squeeze underneath the sponson tubes, which are horizontal supports full of air that separate the boat into three compartments (fore, middle, aft), and somehow claw through, ass to front, in this frozen rubber boat. As if the Pacific wasn't cold enough, these multiple immersions in the ice IBS will make your manhood shrink and your teeth chatter. You won't drown, but you do come pretty close to freezing! It's not good to start out the week on the low end of the body core-temperature spectrum. Yes, this was the fate of my boat crew for 20 minutes straight!

If you're the boat crew leader, you're trying to shout out commands: "Boat Crew 5 is over here. Form behind me. Boat Crew 2 is over here. Form behind me." The poor officer-in-charge (OIC) of each boat crew is losing his fucking mind. And we're not far behind him, not far at all. The maddening thing is that an instructor will keep you from you boat crew on purpose, just to add to the frustration and anguish. Remember, it's all formulaic psycho-science. You can't make this shit up.

Indeed, while all this shit is going on you're just trying to comply with whatever orders are being shouted out. You're trying to do it fast. You're trying to do it right the first time. Otherwise, you're going to have to pay the price for failure. We call it 'paying the man.' The last thing you want to do is go through the ice boat—and you definitely don't want to go through it for 20 minutes. You're running down to the beach, wet and sandy, and running back, *ad nauseam*! Everyone's hoping to stay dry and warm, but that shit never happens. Cold is a threat. It's a disciplinary tool. Being wet makes you cold. And being wet and cold puts you at a severe physical and mental disadvantage. That's what the exercise is all about. Deal with it. Adapt to the terrain. Become what is or you will become what is not.

You quickly learn that getting your boat crew assembled was only a temporary success—the chaos was such that it was designed so that you would fail and be punished. You were supposed to begin Hell Week wet, cold, tired and disoriented. If you didn't, you weren't there!

Next, we hit the beach for whistle drills. When you hear the first whistle you start running. At the second whistle, you stop, belly flop, cross your legs, open your mouth, and clamp your hands over your ears. When the third whistle sounds you get on all fours and begin bear crawling across the beach over sand dunes and seaweed and other nasty types of stinky rotten ocean flora and dead fauna. I think the instructors put it all there to add to the hell of it all. Keep in mind that this is all through the sand. And you're all already wet and sandy. Instructors are still screaming at you through the bullhorns. It's all assholes and elbows. You're trying not to snag some part of your body on driftwood and rip your skin off, or plow into the man in front of you—but of course, that's happening, too. By the way, the whistle drills are meant to simulate an incoming mortar or artillery round. As such, the prone body position we assume is designed to lesson any barotraumas from a close range, less than lethal detonation of one of those devices in combat. In reality, all it did was open up our mouth for sand to be kicked in and expose our rib cages for the boot strike of a SEAL instructor. I can remember being kicked so hard in the ribs that I flipped over and landed back on all fours, minus two lungs full of air of course! LOL. Onward and upward!

Today, the SPECWAR Center calls surf torture 'surf conditioning', but it's the same nasty exercise no matter what label you attach to it. It always sucks. All on command, and as a class, you lock arms with the dude to your left and to your right and march out into the surf zone to sit down. Then, you lay down, on your backs, facing the water, and you embrace the suck and frantically search for air as the cold Pacific starts pounding you in the face—over and over. This goes on, for God knows how long, because by now you're not even sure how much time has passed since the first explosions began. And as an added bonus, it is dark and you are getting colder and colder.

The instructors yell over the bull horn, "Gentlemen, we're going to continue this evolution until we get our first quitter. Who's it gonna to be? Help out your buddies—save them from this punishment! We're not gonna stop until somebody quits. It doesn't have to be this way!"

The whole time, you're thinking to yourself, "That's not going to be me."

All the while the SEALs are shouting, "We've got a warm van behind you. We've got coffee and donuts in there. You don't have to be doing this shit right now. You still get to be in the Navy, but many of you aren't going to be SEALs. Fucking quit out now and let's end this senseless misery."

We're all lying there thinking the same thing: Somebody please fucking quit already. Somebody give in and stop the madness so that we don't die. So that I can just get a little bit warmer. So I can stop choking on seawater. So I can stop having my arms ripped out of my sockets by this huge surf.

But you're also thinking there is no way it's going to be you that quits. You tell yourself, "Fuck this, I'm not quitting. I'm in this to win."

Usually, that's right about when the first guy gives in. And normally, it's the biggest or the toughest appearing guy who quits—or that guy who, during the first few weeks, repeatedly tells you he's gonna be there when it's over. For Class 214, that was Seaman Peach.

Peach was a little cagey guy who talked a lot of mad shit to his fellow classmates. The fact that he did it with a lisp was even more remarkable. In fact, it was so remarkable that he was our official class call-out person. Peach was the dude who announced the name of the instructor before every training evolution, and it always made me chuckle to see the look on the instructor's face when he heard his named being screamed out from the darkness of the beach at 0500 hours by the guy with the speech impediment. It was priceless, and offered all of us a small piece of comedic solace. Once, he and a guy named Jeff S. went at each other. Jeff S. and I later served together at SEAL Team Eight. During the first few weeks of BUD/S, Peach and Jeff would have these verbal exchanges that were quite humorous.

Peach would yell at Jeff, "You're a pussy; a fucking pussy."

Jeff would give it right back: "Whatever, Peacher! You're never even going to make it through Hell Week."

That would get Peach's goat and he'd get right up in Jeff's face.

"Yeah, well...we'll see who's still standing when the smoke clears on Friday," he would boast. "We'll just see who's still standing on Friday when that smoke clears."

And all of this trash talk was done with that high, lisp-laden voice.

As things are wont to turn out, Peach was one of the first guys to call it quits during that first round of surf torture Sunday night.

The constant back-and-forth mind game—the instructors yelling at you, the surf pounding your face—continues until guys quit. Ole' Peachey wasn't alone. A lot of others called it quits during those first few hours. I often wonder what happened to Peach. I hope he went on to serve with distinction in some other Navy capacity.

Then surf torture ends. The punishment stops for a hot minute while instructors scoop up the quitters and let everyone else gather themselves into boat crews. Then, they march you on to the next grueling evolution. It was quite literally non-stop like this for nearly six days.

Hell Week is an endurance test; not a speed test. You could literally run a 10-minute mile instead of a sub-seven-minute mile or an O-Course in 15 minutes. As long as you don't drown or quit, nobody cares. The only thing they care about is that you persevere, push through, and endure all the bullshit they put you through. You're part of a team, and you're supposed to help your teammates when they're at their lowest level. It's combat simulation at its best: Are you able to do 10 times what your body thinks you can do? Can you Jedi mind-trick yourself into allowing your body to do it because you don't have any other choice if you want to survive? This is what Hell Week is all about. It is designed to get rid of the people who are weak of mind, body and spirit, and don't have the will to be there. It will test you and rock your soul.

After three-and-a-half days of non-stop fun, on Wednesday afternoon you're shuttled into a GP Large—a general purpose large tent—on the beach. You walk into it and there are all these M.A.S.H.-style cots laying there. Like chaffed zombies, you plod in and everyone who has made it this far is right there with you.

A booming voice says "Lay down and get some shut-eye!" Notice that I wrote 'says' and not screams. This was the SEAL instructor equivalent of a bed-time story; they don't yell at you. Because of this, it actually sounds like a lullaby. Inside, it was warm and there was no wind. That cot felt like a feather bed at the Ritz-Carlton and being in the tent felt like being in the womb again. I was literally out cold the moment my head hit the cot.

But, in what feels like 15 seconds later—which was probably, in actuality, about 30 to 45 minutes—they're screaming again through the bullhorn, "Get the fuck up! Get up! Fucking get up....MOVE! Fall out and get your boat crews assembled in formation on the beach!"

That's pretty much the only condoned sleep you're going to get. For the remainder of Hell Week, you may get one or two periods of 20 minutes here and there—but most of it is stolen sleep, or sleep that is issued to you as a reward for a put-out evolution by your boat crew. When sleep is issued, you all literally sleep on command. But when you are told to get up and put that damn boat back on your head, you feel like a fetus self-aborting: It's painful and every bit of you wants to stay in that sleepy comfort zone! It's possible to get up to three-hours sleep in those six days, but by and large, you're only getting between one-and-a-half and two-hours of sleep, total, and none of it comes in long, restful stretches.

The remainder of Hell Week is comprised of a series of hard, physical activities, similar to what you're doing throughout BUD/S, but even more evil. You and your team carry your boat on your heads for the entire week. You carry the boat and run through an obstacle course. You carry the boat on a 14-mile run. You carry it up and down the beach and into the water—over and over. You even carry the boat to the chow! During this week, you burn a metric-shit-ton of calories and this is why you go to chow hall four times a day: If you can't sleep, you gotta' eat! It's also why I counted meals in order to keep track of time.

That damn 265 to 300-lb IBS is always banging on your head—thump, bump, thump, bump—and for me, tearing the hair out of the middle of my head. That was not a lot of fun. I lost a little bit of hair because of the boat on my head during my time in 214, but a lot more was ripped out during 215. It didn't help that I was the tallest guy in my boat crew by about an inch and a half, so because I bore a bit more of the brunt of that bump and thump, during 215, I basically lost all the hair on the top of my head from my forehead back. I ended up with a 'reverse' Mohawk. The instructors started calling me "skunk." In fact, after Hell Week was over, Chief Cairns would often say to the class, "Look around you. If you see anyone with hair missing from the middle of their head it's because they didn't put out in Hell Week." He was always fucking with me.

The instructors took us to the mud flats near Tijuana as part of the test. The mud was two-feet deep in places and it, seemingly, could grab you and slam you to the ground. Still, we were ordered to bear crawl through it. It was insanely exhausting and very slow going, and we must have looked like retarded bears wallowing in dinosaur shit. We slithered into a filthy Tijuana overflow estuary, and no one was sure if it was mud or fecal matter we were now sliding through. The smell was nearly identical. Here, the instructors decided to feed us a boxed meal. It didn't matter what I pulled out of that white cardboard lunchbox, it all smelled, tasted and felt like what I imagined a Tijuana burro's asshole would smell, taste and feel like. All the while, our boats where staged close by and waiting to go back on our heads. Those fucking boats.

While they grind your ass into the ground, mud or sand, you just keep going. You don't quit for anything or anyone. You get some strength from the guy to your left and right because you know they are going through the same thing as you. You learn and understand the meaning of teamwork, unusual suffering and sacrifice—all on a wholesale scale. You make damn sure to help your teammate because you want him to make it, too. Doing so, also helps take your mind off your own pain, causing you to force yourself to push through the misery. It actually helped me hammer through some of the tougher moments of Hell Week, which prepared me for the crucible I would face when I was sent out on real-world operations and people all around were trying to kill me. You learn how to make the best of a bad situation. You learn focus and purpose and poise and, most of all: Positivity! The glass had better be half full because if it's half empty, that means that you just drank four ounces of failure and affliction. Worse, you handed that glass of infectious piss water to one of your SEAL teammates to drink. Neither of those two options is good.

Hell Week becomes the first litmus test for the rest of your SEAL career. Interestingly, there are many times when you fall back on your training and experience—when you're tired, sore, hungry, hurt, or all of the above. Hell Week is essentially baptism by fire, except this incoming fire is deadly accurate and comes from a gyroscopic, tank-mounted howitzer. But believe me when I mention this: There are many, many times as an active duty SEAL when the abject misery experienced far exceeds that of BUD/S. But because of BUD/S, you just keep going. It is said that the hardest steel is forged in the hottest fires. BUD/S is a fucking blast furnace.

On Wednesday afternoon, after that 30- to 45-minute frog nap, the instructors marched us to the Combat Training Tank (CTT), split us into teams and ordered us into the water. The CTT is really a badass acronym that means swimming pool. There, we played water polo. Picture this: We are haggard, hurting, and half-crazy; and they've just told us to go play a game. We don't know what's going to happen to us if we're on the losing team, so we start playing hardcore against each other. We're trying to score and drown the other team in the process. It was not your usual game. The instructors expect this to happen. So in order to prevent a drowning from exhaustion or determination, a few of them are in the water wearing masks and fins.

After the so-called game, we were told to get dressed and head over to Steel Pier. The dreaded Steel Pier is aptly named because of its composition and purpose. Steel Pier was exactly what it sounded like—and it was cold. We were stripped naked and told to lay down on the metal. Then we were hosed down with 55-degree water. It sucked balls—if there were any balls to be found at this point. Shrinkage is a bitch. I only wish it had also happened to my knee and not just my cock and balls.

As we were getting dressed to run over to the pier, one of the instructors noticed that my knee had swelled up to about three times its normal size. They then observed me as I ran, looking like a three-legged dog with hip dysplasia. After Steel Pier, and when they were certain I was more of a detriment to myself and my boat crew than I was of any real benefit, they bum-rushed me and handed me over to a medic. I had been sucking up the pain and hiding a limp for a few days, but it took one week from the day I injured it for the MCL tear to finally present itself in full form. And it did so in the form of a hemarthrosis—bleeding into my knee joint. As I was being led away, I kept saying, "What the fuck is going on here? Why the fuck am I not with my boat crew?'

I kept saying this over and over even as they were aspirating what turned out to be about 300 milliliters of bloody joint fluid from my right knee. I didn't give a shit if my leg had fallen off. I needed to be with my boys and I needed them to know that, and in no uncertain terms. But the truth was that I simply could not hide my injury anymore. The vitamin M had long since worn off and, unbeknownst to me, the instructors had seen me running around with the boat on my head, dragging my leg a little bit, limping here and there. But because I had been able to keep up and not fall behind, they figured I was just aching and pushing through. I would later find out that they were as impressed as they were intrigued—probably a bit more of the latter than the former. Once the knee joint filled with bloody fluid and needed aspiration, however, my supposed deception was over. SEALs notice everything. We are masters at being in the moment. It's a critical skill that keeps us alive in hostile environments, as well as enabling us to dominate in the boardroom, on the ballfield, and in the bedroom. I highly suggest that you learn how to be in the moment.

To my dismay, I was very much in the moment when they cleaned out my knee and was consequently approached by Chief Phonay. He confronted me with the facts as he said "Son, we're rolling you out of Hell Week 214."

"What? Chief, what the fuck are you talking about?" I argued. "That's fucking bullshit. You know it and I know it. I'm good to go and I'm pushing through."

"Watch your tone with me, Seaman Heben. I'm an E7; you're an E3. You don't really have much of a knee joint anymore, Seaman. It's bleeding inside and pretty beat up. You can't even run. There's no way you're going to make it two more days. You're better off rolling out to PTR&R, rehabbing it and starting over than risking further injury and then washing out completely. I know your brain is too fucked up to realize it right now, but I'm actually doing you a favor."

I thought about it for a hot second and replied, "OK Chief. Sorry for my tone. Roger that."

He was right. I couldn't even run. My knee hurt like hell! But it was totally demoralizing to be rolled out of Class 214. Try as you may, you still get attached to the guys you're going through BUD/S with, even at Week Five. But I realized I couldn't continue on like this and wouldn't be progressing forward with those same dudes. I knew that, as pissed off as I was, I would have to suck it up and focus on recovery. It sucked, but Chief Phonay was right: I shouldn't push through no matter how hard I wanted to or even if there was a slight chance that I could. If this was a real world OP, sure, but I had to get to that point first, and injuring myself further was only going to decreases my chances of achieving that goal. Mentally, I was still in the game. And that was all that they needed to hear right now. Class 215, here I come. The good news is that

I got to spend the next six weeks rehabbing my knee. The bad news was that I would have to start BUD/S all over again, from Week One, Day One. But hey, they were allowing me to stay and continue on. The glass was still half full!

I sat there on the exam table looking at the three syringes full of my bloody joint fluid and took my first relaxed sips of water from a glass that was half full.

CHAPTER 10

> "THE CLIMB WILL BE STEEP AND NOT WITHOUT RISK, BUT YOU MUST CHASE AFTER YOUR DREAMS WITH UNBRIDLED PASSION AND A RELENTLESS SPIRIT, FOR ONLY THEN WILL YOU BEGIN TO CATCH THEM!"
>
> —CHRISTOPHER MARK HEBEN

Injuries during Hell Week often spell the end of your quest to become a Navy SEAL—but there was absolutely no way I was going out like that. I was committed to nothing less than achieving my goal. I had sacrificed way too much to get here, and this temporary setback was not going to get me down. For the next five weeks I rested and rehabbed my knee in PTR&R (Fourth Phase), remaining focused on nothing less than getting the instructors to say, "Heben, you big ugly fuck, it's time to phase back up. Don't fuck up this time!" They had an amazing grasp of the English language, and I wanted to be able to talk like that to a BUD/S student one day.

At first, I gently exercised the knee—riding a stationary bike, soaking it in the whirlpool tub, moving it around a bit, and doing bodyweight leg extensions. Around that initial regimen I did whatever odd jobs the instructors ordered me to do—push a broom, drag a mop across the floor, make photocopies, clean weapons, and polish the brass bell, etc. I was willing to do whatever job came my way, but it was that whole bell-polishing thing that really got to me. You see, that fucking bell was the same bell a student had to ring if they wanted to quit training. It wasn't knock three times on the ceiling. It wasn't click your heels three times.

UNDAUNTED

It was ring the bell three times and stand at attention while saying your name and rank, and stating your desire to quit. Hell, I didn't want to be anywhere near that damn thing but, and call it morbid curiosity, I dealt with it. Much like a kid that picks up that paddle in the principal's office, you are awed by the sight and feel of it, just as long as it's never actually employed on you!

Each day, I tested my knee. I was eager to get back in the proverbial saddle. So eager, in fact, that my two hours of rehab each day turned into about eight hours. My regimen swelled to doing voluntary swim sessions with my old Class 214, as well as sessions in the Small Arms Repair shop, the Team weight room in the middle of the compound that was, yes, actually used by real SEALs. Nobody asked me who I was, so I felt extra cool about being in there without true permission. One day, SEAL Instructor Greg Farmerie came in to work out and saw me in there. He simply said, "What are you training? Let me guess, legs, back and arms?"

Boom! We did a workout together.

As I continued to maniacally rehab myself, a few of the other instructors stopped by to check on me or they would stop me on the grinder or pull me aside during a beach PT. They would say things like, "You know you are a leader here. You're just an E3, but a lot of the other students look up to you. Hurry up and get healed." In Chief Cairn's world it was simply, "You know I'll be waiting for your ass when you phase back up, Heben. It would behoove you to stay as inconsequential as possible. Nobody fucking likes a roll back, especially one that doesn't put out."

He always knew what to say in order to piss me off, and he always got thoroughly under my skin and into my dura matter. His words crossed my blood-brain barrier quicker than some FDA-rejected Alzheimer's drug accidentally designed to actually expedite dementia! I swear he must have been from Michigan and knew I was from Ohio. LOL.

What bothered me the most is that he was one of the instructors that goon-squaded me on more than one occasion. And I can think of one such time wherein all the muscles in my legs were locked up with cramps. But I refused to quit despite the fact that he asked me if I wanted to about every 10 feet.

"Fuck him," I thought. "I'll graduate just to piss him off!"

Chief Mark Madson was just the opposite. After a morning PT, he brought me into his office and sat me down. As he poured himself a cup of coffee, I took a visual inventory of everything I could. His office was like a SEAL Smithsonian dedicated to omnipresent ass-kickery. He had bullets here and grenades there. Pictures of badass guns and rocket launchers were all over his office. He even had some schematics from Soviet bloc countries. I saw platoon photos of fuzzy-faced Frogmen who looked like they ate Great White sharks while swimming the English Channel after climbing Everest. It was obvious that he had been there, done that, and had gone back for more. The fact that this man was even interested in saying anything to me was something I'll never understand. I guess we all have those mentors in our lives that we will always hold in an exalted fashion. Chief Madson was one such SEAL. There would be many more.

Chief Madson turned around and sipped on his coffee like a cowboy about to head out on a two-month cattle drive—slow, deliberate, and with an attitude that seemed to say, "If you even think about opening up your mouth right now, I'll choke slam you into next week." He must have seen my eyes darting around his office like Don Knotts on crack and having a seizure during REM sleep. After he was able to visually lock on to me, he simply stated: "Heebs, I just need you take it down about 25 percent. Do you understand me?"

Hugh? I looked like an expressionless zombie. What he was saying wasn't registering. Picking up on this, he then said, "What I mean is, just get through this course. You are a jet engine when all you need to be is diesel powered. So, downshift a few gears and coast through first phase without any injury. We already know you are capable of lift-off. Hell, I've never seen anyone do the Dirty Name like you. The men are inspired by your can-do attitude and, as instructors, we know we would probably go to war with you if we had to. So just get through. You can re-launch when you get to Second Phase. You copy that, Seaman Heben?"

UNDAUNTED

"HOO-YAH, Chief Madson!" I replied, feeling nearly 10-feet tall. That would be the first of many affirmations I would receive during BUD/S. Again, it's the little victories that can propel you forward. Don't always look for the big things when the little things can still help get you to the same goal.

That was all great. Apparently, I had already made a positive impression on the SEAL instructors. Well, most of them anyway. As a result, I wasn't one of the shit bags they wanted to see quit, fail, or get washed out due to injury. I'd been assessed as one of the guys they felt they could go to war with, and that gave me additional strength. Meanwhile, the best news about my injury was that it wouldn't take too long to heal. The medial collateral ligament is unique in that it doesn't require a surgical repair, and my tear stayed in close proximity to itself. Once I stopped causing it repeated and violent trauma, it would naturally want to re-approximate. After two weeks, it was already starting to feel much better. I wasn't ready to return to the fracas just yet, but I could feel some desire for it all coming on and it wouldn't be too long before I was ready for that, not-so-distant and horrifically horizontal horizon.

The PA-C, Jesse 'Doc' Gross, and Doctor White, a couple of full-fledged SEALs, reviewed my ongoing progress. Four weeks into the whole re-building process, and after interpreting my MRI, the two of them determined I was ready to re-phase and class up with 215.

That was the good news.

The bad news was that I still had one more week to wait for the entire six weeks of PTR&R to be over, and then I had to re-do the whole first five fucking weeks of BUD/S. It's shitty, but when you're injured during Hell Week before Wednesday evening, get rolled, and you re-class, you don't get to just jump back in when the next class starts Hell Week. Instead, you get recycled and have to prove yourself all over again. This meant another round of drown proofing, lifesaving, underwater knot tying, and 50-meter underwater swims—all of the dreaded evolutions that cause people to quit more than all the others. Had I just made it another two or three hours, I would have been rolled forward instead of back. I would have re-phased with 215 AFTER Hell Week was over!

Luckily, I had an advantage. I had already passed all of this and knew exactly what to expect. I also had time to reflect on what I could have done differently to achieve even higher scores and better times than I had the first time around. Yeah, I'm one of those guys who is constantly doing the numbers, weighing the risks and calculating the odds. Even today, my buddies call me Rain Man. But when I'm behind the trigger of a sniper rifle, they call me something else altogether. And I'll get back to that topic soon.

I knew my knee wouldn't be at full strength, but there also wouldn't be any surprises. Chance favors the prepared mind. Some wise fucker once said that, but I bet he or she wasn't a SEAL. Nonetheless, and in this case, my knowledge weighed heavily in my favor and I was going to be insanely prepared for the next go round. Also in my favor was that during my first run with Class 214 the instructors had gotten a feel for me as a person and SEAL candidate. I'd made a reasonably good impression on both fronts, and we all know that first impressions are everything. Now, if I can only figure out how to deal with Chief Cairns!

The day I reported to re-class with 215, Chief Madson pulled me aside again and re-iterated, "We know you're a diesel dude. You go and get it. Do yourself a favor and channel it down to 75 percent this time around. We also know you have an influence on the other students. With that in mind, we may be extra hard on you in order to get to them. Just get through First Phase."

Wait...WTF? Where the fuck did that other little golden nugget of information suddenly come from? Was going right back into the fire with a target on my back? This was the very thing that Chief Cairns had warned me about. I guess I shouldn't have taken that straight razor to my head in an effort to hit the reset button on my hair growth. Now I looked like an albino Chia Pet version of Vin Diesel, with 10 layers of Mop and Glo applied. Fuck me. Stand the fuck by Heebs!

In reality, I shouldn't have reacted this way. After all, a senior enlisted SEAL told me this. So it was all still very good. He wanted me to succeed. Most of the time, these guys are in your face, screaming and telling you how much you suck. This was rock-solid validation, and a great start to my time as a member of Class 215. It was only when I

UNDAUNTED

vomited a few times and stopped hyperventilating that I realized the silver lining that was contained within that dark cloud.

Conversely, I didn't really know many of the guys in my new class. All my dudes were in 214 and had continued on after Hell Week. As it turned out, that didn't matter. I really shined the second time around and was much more at ease and relaxed. Unlike the rest of my new buds, I knew I could complete every evolution successfully because I'd already done it. That knowledge—and my general bad-assery mixed with jack-assery—gave me a totally different aura of leadership, and one the new guys could rally around. They'd look at me and other roll in's and say, "Hell yes….Lead the way!"

Shortly after Class 215 began I did have one brief moment of self-reflection—the first time I put a lot of stress on the knee and it throbbed. I was alone in my brain and looked up at the sky for a moment, just a moment, and said silently, "Why are you doing this to yourself?"

But just as soon as the thought entered my head I pushed it away. I thought about everything I had gone through to get here—the eye surgery, the rehab—and what I had given up to be here—my job, girlfriend, and generally comfy life.

"Fuck this," I thought. "I'm in it to win it. The only way I'm going home is in a coffin."

To say I excelled during 215 would be an understatement. Rather, I made an impression on everyone at every step along the way.

One such impression was during the Drown Proofing evolution.

Our class proctor was, super cool, Corey Knowles. He was the head SEAL-in-charge of us. Corey was 5' 10", 230 pounds—a stocky, blonde-haired, and total cool guy swagger.

"Come on, Heben," Instructor Knowles boomed when it was my turn at the pool. "You're up. I'm drowning. Come and save me."

So Instructor Knowles feigned he was sinking and I jumped into the water to 'save' him.

"Don't worry," I said. "I've got you."

I dove in and swam towards him. As a I got close, and as we were supposed to do, I 're-assured' him: "Hey bro, I'm gonna get you home alive. No worries. I got this!" With that, I splashed water at him as a distraction while I dove under toward his feet.

Lifesaving works like this: You re-assure, then splash to distract, and dive underwater once you reach the instructor, going toward his ankles. When you reach them, you spin him around, and continue to spin him as you contour his body while ascending back toward the surface. Your goal is to position him with his face away from you, which is where you want it to be. Then, you're supposed to cross-chest carry him while you're swimming on your side doing a modified side-stroke and, all the while, bringing him back to the side of the pool.

That's all nice and good in theory, but in reality, the instructors are trying everything to drag you down to the bottom of the CTT with them—ergo the name of the evolution: LIFESAVING. I believe it should be called drown-proofing, because they're weighted down with heavy dive belts, fins and whatever else they can pile on to achieve weight and propulsion advantages. Your goal is to save them; their goal is to make it very, very difficult—if not impossible—for you to get them back to the side of the pool and complete the evolution. If they don't particularly like you, they're going to make it even more difficult. They may even drown your ass! Most of the time, however, they're just trying to harass you, intimidate you and gauge how you perform under pressure. Why? They want to know if you can truly save their life if ever they had an issue on a real world operation. They teach you three or four other rescue techniques and it's good training for what you could feasibly encounter as a SEAL: You might have to rescue a downed pilot. You could be on a ship and have regular Navy guys you'll need to save. Or maybe one of your buddies is injured or wounded, the two of you are in the water waiting for a sub or boat to come pick you up and you're the one who has to make sure he makes it. There are myriad real-life reasons why this evolution comes in handy. Think of it like lifeguard training but Navy SEAL-style. And, of course, while you're executing these techniques the instructors are doing everything they can to make you fail.

So I reached Instructor Knowles and engaged him underwater. I turned him around and controlled my way up his body. I thrust my arm out of the water and clamped it down over his chest and began to tow his heavy ass, closer and closer, toward the edge of the pool. My knee was screaming under all the new effort I had to put forth, plus, every time the inside of my knees hit one another, it was like a blowtorch was being applied to my MCL. The painful process took forever. I felt like a tiny tugboat pulling the waterlogged *Titanic* up and back to Southampton, England. And Knowles could tell I was hurting.

That's when he reared his head forward and slammed it violently backward, head-butting me in the face and breaking my nose. I heard a loud 'crack' and saw stars and flickering lights as my blood began pouring out of both nostrils and into the pool. Clinging to consciousness, I managed to tow Instructor Knowles to the side of the pool, finishing the evolution.

There was so much blood in the pool that they had to cancel the rest of the evolution and sent us to the chow hall for lunch. After a short one, they marched us over to the O course and I ran through that damn thing with my nose packed full of cotton plugs. Imagine doing one of the world's toughest obstacle courses when you can hardly breathe. I felt like a fat, mouth-breathing, COPD patient, with an upper respiratory infection. That's what my afternoon was like. And, of course, you can't fail or you get kicked out of training—and this was my second go-around. So I sucked it up, sucked as much air in as I could, and passed. In life, you are only beaten when you decide to be and even after you take your last breath, you still have a few minutes to get something done!

After the O course, we shuffled back to the CTT to pick up the evolution where we left off—or so I thought.

Lo and behold, there was Instructor Knowles in the water again. And he was grinning—from ear to ear—at me.

"OK, Heben," he says. "Get back out here. You're up."

I was thinking, "WTF?! I already did this and passed. Didn't I? This is NOT happening right now. This can't be a good thing." I could feel the anger building.

I jumped in and as I'm swimming out there I'm now totally pissed I have to do this again. So me being me, I reached Instructor Knowles and re-engaged. I dove down to his ankles, flipped him around and came to the surface. Then instead of cross-chesting him, I cross-faced him. I slammed him with my fist across the side of his upper check, lower eye, and upper nose—and heard tiny 'pop' as I did so.

At the time, I thought to myself that I was probably done, that this guy was going to kick me out, but I was also thinking, "Fuck it! He broke my nose. Turnaround is fair play."

But I didn't pause—even for one moment. Grabbing him in a cross-chest I dragged him over to the edge of the pool again. And then, having completed the evolution, I climbed out and fell back in line with the other members of my class like nothing out of the ordinary happened. Meanwhile, the rest of my class is stunned and staring at me, then at Knowles, then back at me.

Knowles regained his composure, and attended to his nose. He just treaded water and snapped him bent nose back into place! Who does that shit? And then he called the next guy into the pool. He never said a word. He just finished the entire evolution with the rest of my group. It was awesome to watch.

Three-hours later, when we had our daily debrief, the situation changed. We came into a classroom and the instructors were there to review the day, discuss lessons learned and tell us what's coming up tomorrow. When they're not trying to kill you the instructors are shepherds of goodwill, really.

While we stood in line, Instructor Knowles stared right at me.

"Heben," he said. "Come up here."

I did so, reluctantly, approaching like a dog that has been beaten a lot. Yes, I was a bit apprehensive about what might be coming.

He surprised me and smiled. "That was some good shit today, wasn't it, Heben?" he said.

Relieved, I smiled back and confidently said, "Hoo-yah, Instructor Knowles!"

And that was the only time he acknowledged publicly what transpired between us that day.

As we were dismissed for the day and leaving the classroom, he pulled me aside; "Stay for a moment," he said. Suddenly, I had visions of doing thousands of 8-count bodybuilders into the wee hours of the morning....

"That was some good shit today," he said. "But I'll tell you what. When you graduate this program, you and I are going to go at it."

Some people might have taken that as a veiled threat and been concerned. But not me. He had said the magic words, "When you graduate." That made me feel so good because the party line from every instructor's mouth was always, "In the rare event that you make it through this program...." Instructor Knowles threw it right out at me, "When you graduate...." That was just enough fairy dust for more validation. In the course of a few weeks I had two SEALs indicate that I would, in fact, make it through the program. And who was I to prove those guys wrong?

From that moment forward I was emboldened. I was trying to earn a spot in the most exclusive fraternity in the world, and assuming I didn't die in the next 20-something weeks, I was going to succeed.

Tomorrow we would be tackling the underwater knot-tying evolution. Knot tying essentially prepares you for laying down detonation cord in the field so you can blow up underwater bunkers and structures that enemy combatants put on the beach to prevent landing crafts from making shore. In wars past, they sent the prototypical, hairy-chested Frogmen in first—the naked warriors—to go blow up the obstacles. Today, it's the SEALs—and the process remains the same: You wrap satchel charges full of C4 on these barriers and tie them together with a trunk line, made of detonation cord. Then you set a timer and swim back to the ship and the charges blow up. This evolution was designed to honor old-school Frogmen training by teaching you how to tie all these different types of knots. And you have to demonstrate it underwater while all the instructors are floating above, watching and assessing your progress.

I did well the first time around—mostly because I had been practicing it in that condo pool on Coronado Island, but also because I could hold my breath underwater for an ungodly amount of time.

So when it was my turn with 215 I went to Instructor Getka, who was a real maniac, and said, "I'm going to try to do all the knots on one breathe of air."

He says, "Heben, shut the fuck up and get down there!"

I took my, perfunctory, three breaths of air and submerged.

I tied one knot.

Instructor Getka looked at it and gave me the "OK."

I tied another one.

He looked at it and again, I got an "OK."

This went on for eight more knots, as I did them all plus the first three knots over again. Keep in mind that I was still on that one initial breath hold. I felt like Aquaman on valium and a beta blocker; no worries and a heart beat as slow as a watch with a dying battery. That short-lived, feel-good moment was shattered when Instructor Getka reached over and grabbed me by the mask and, with it, pulled me up from underwater. Of course my mask was flooded and no longer on my face, it was twisted around my neck and I was still without oxygen, this time from an involuntary choke hold. But I didn't care one damn bit. I just tied 10 knots on one trip. Another small victory.

"Attention on deck," he yells. "Attention on the fucking deck!"

Everyone looked over, half expecting to see my limp lifeless body being hauled over to the side for chest compressions.

"All of you fucking meat-headed ass fucks. I just wanted to tell you that fucking Heben just did 10 fucking knots on one fucking breathe hold. He's still a pussy, but all you other fucking pussies better fucking step your fucking game the fuck up! Next pussy, enter the fucking water!"

Everyone was looking at me with combinations of awe and disgust on their faces. They were thinking, "Why the hell did you do that? Now we're all screwed!"

I don't know why I did it. It's probably because I wasn't the strongest runner but I was damn good underwater, so I decided to showcase that. I was pretty happy about how things were going. So it went onto the next evolution.

UNDAUNTED

A lot of these early phase competency exercises are individual evolutions. You're pretty much on your own, in that, no one can assist you from your class. For some of the evolutions, you aren't even permitted to observe the others. You can, sure as shit, hear them but you cannot look. You are made to turn around and face the fence at the CTT, your back to the pool. This adds to the anxiety and maximizes the mind-fuck. And it is exactly this mind-fuck that you must control if you ever expect to graduate.

There's an old saying passed around during BUD/S: "If you ain't cheating, you ain't trying." Operating under these auspices, I would crane my neck to see the pool clock and get a sense of how much time it was taking the guys to complete the 50-meter, underwater-swim evolution. Because I was timing students upon 'splash down' and up to completion of the evolution, I was able to determine the average time to completion was 48 seconds. Hell, I thought, I can hold my breath for over three minutes. When you factor in exertion-related oxygen consumption, that still left me with a metric shit ton of time to cover that distance comfortably. It also helped me to further focus cerebrally by utilizing the physics of compressed air to aid me from a physiology standpoint. Take three breaths, hold the third, jump in and be smooth on the flip, get deep as possible as soon as possible, thereby maximizing retained air and compressing it in order to use atmospheric pressure to ration its consumption. It was a solid plan for victory, and it worked. I learned and understood that I had to be aware of my surroundings in order to succeed, and I did just that. It was not my problem there was a clock on the pool deck. To this day, I feel they kept it there to see who was smart enough to actually use it. These same dive physics would help me later in Phase Two.

Finally, we reached Week Five. And I reached Hell Week. AGAIN!

First, as you know, when I was part of 214 I got a lot of my hair ripped up and my scalp torn because of the way the IBS hit me on the head. I decided I wasn't going through that again. I found an old wet suit, cut it up, and sewed it underneath the inside of my 8-point cover (hat). My theory was that I was going to have some padding on my head this time, so when the boat was hammering me there, it wouldn't be as bad. I also stashed away a few 800mg Motrin so that if my knee felt sore I could pop a few and keep moving along.

Then, I had this predilection with food.

Unlike most of the other guys in Class 215, I knew exactly what to expect and how much of a cluster fuck those first few hours on the Grinder and the beach were going to be. I was ready, which meant that my boat crew was ready, too. And despite the chaos and the confusion, we performed pretty damn well right out of the gate. Of course this made Chief Cairns all the more hateful, and myself, as well as my boat crew, would certainly bear the brunt of it. My being in the "Chain Gang" didn't help either though.

At the start of 215 Hell Week, the instructors lined us all up and they found everything any of the guys had hidden. They found my food, the Motrin, and the extra lining in my hat. They put a handful of us, the worst offenders, into what they called the "Chain Gang," which meant down the stretch we got some extra attention. Instead of a tiny break or rest when everyone else earned it, we got more bear crawls, more runs down to the surf and rolls in the sand. At one point, they made us carry a tire around our necks while we were also carrying the boat. It wasn't fun, but I wasn't the least bit deterred. I was already there, already in pain, already pissed off, and I already decided to die before I quit. Life takes on a whole new meaning and purpose when you are willing to die instead of quitting something.

As Hell Week continued, I began to feel a little more returning pain in my right knee. The pain increased and so did the swelling, but functionally and aesthetically, it was a knee again. I could extend, flex and put weight on it. It was laterally stable, but knowing it might start hurting again, I took preparatory steps while I was rehabbing and making daily visits to the BUD/S health center. I managed to squirrel away a couple 40-milligram shots of Toradol IM (intramuscular) injections and stashed them away in my room. The thought of that knee knocking me out again, was more concerning to me than the thought of getting caught with it in my room. Remember: 'if you ain't cheatin', you ain't tryin'!' I believed in that BUD/S & SEAL mantra 100 percent, and I still do today.

UNDAUNTED

I knew that on Wednesday we would have our first and only health inspection. They would run us through the medical clinic, look into our eyes and see if our brains were still intact, our blood pressure good and we were not on the verge of hypothermia or something worse, like Necrotizing Fasciitis (or for the medically challenged, flesh-eating bacteria). They let us change our socks, but first, they put this lubrication lotion on our feet. At that moment in time, when I felt those hands and that creamy application to my feet, it truly felt better than sex—certainly any sex I'd been having since I was in 10th grade, and that includes the kind you have with just yourself. In short, that quasi-foot massage was orgasmic! Then they line you up, check you out, and run you next door to the clinic to make sure you're still, somewhat sane.

After I got lubricated feet and put on a new pair of dry socks, I snuck upstairs to my room on the third floor of the building. I retrieved the syringes, took down my pants, slammed one of the shots into my left glute and injected it. Then I did the same with my right glute, and pulled my pants back on.

Unfortunately, it had taken a little longer than I thought and heard my class mustering on the beach and someone calling my name.

"Where the fuck is your boat crew, eight? Where's Heben?"

There wasn't time to walk down the steps, shuttle out the door and get in line on the beach. Besides, I didn't need them seeing me walk down the steps. That would have tipped them off that something was amiss and then me, and my boat crew, would have been hammered into oblivion. I could not bring that upon them! Instead, I jumped over the balcony and dropped onto the second floor landing. Then I jumped from the second story balcony onto the ground so I was entering the health center from a different trajectory than the bottom of the steps and right there in line.

"I'm here, Instructor Hewlett," I yelled. "Sorry I didn't sound off."

He looked at me like I was crazy—one moment I wasn't there; the next I was. My Class 214 buddies, who saw me leap the window, bounce off the landing, land on the ground and roll with this gymnastic parkour thing right into line as if I had been there the whole time, thought it was fucking great. I was just glad I pulled it off.

After Hell Week, people came up to me and kept saying, "I'll never forget that. They called your name and I saw you jump off the balcony, hit the concrete, do this monkey roll and slide into line. It was fucking hilarious and you didn't get caught."

None of the instructors ever found out what I had done. I didn't look at it as doing anything wrong—my knee was hurting and I was doing what I needed to do in order to function, help my boat crew and get us all through. It was a proactive approach, and one they most likely would not have punished me, too severely, for had they found out. I would have come clean and they would have looked at me as someone who does whatever it takes to get his team home safely.

It's been like that my entire life—making things happen for myself and others, that ensured the Greater Good. I've always wanted people to say that I get shit done, not matter how difficult or tricky.

The rest of Hell Week was relatively uneventful, except when I had to punch one of my boat crew members in the face.

Craig Imp could be a real prick. He was a whining, bitching and moaning kind of guy, and he went into this Hell Week without a tampon. He made it very clear throughout the week that he didn't want to have the boat on his head. It was a discomfort and an inconvenience for him, so he was a real asshole and wouldn't rotate out on schedule. He was always coming up with a reason he couldn't do it. Every hour or so it was someone else's turn to be the coxswain on the team. The coxswain had the privilege of not having the boat on his head while the six other guys did. He basically just pushed from behind. So instead of having the boat pounding you in the brain for a couple hours, you got the easy job.

By Wednesday afternoon, Imp decided he wasn't going to relinquish the coxswain position once he got it. Needless to say, I wasn't having any of that bullshit, not one second longer.

We were waiting to cross the street and go from where the chow hall is—the main Amphibious Base—to the Center on the other side of the highway. We were standing there, waiting for traffic to die down enough to march across the street with this boat on our heads. And Craig was just whining and bitching, crying, "I'm staying the coxswain. I'm not carrying the boat. I'm not getting back under it!"

UNDAUNTED

I was underneath the boat, holding it up over my head, and yelled, "Craig, you need to shut the fuck up! Shut the fuck up!"

And he wouldn't. He just kept complaining.

I was standing in the rear, holding onto my handle. I finally had enough. I turned around and punched Craig square in the face, knocking him on his ass. "Fuck off, bro!" I yelled. "How's that feel?"

So he's lying there, on his ass, rubbing his face and staring at me with this confused look on his face. Three instructors, who were behind us in a truck and following us during the exercise, watched the whole thing happen and started laughing. They drove up beside us right away and called out to me.

"HEBEN!" One of them wryly said. "That was a great punch. But quit assaulting your boat crew members. Help him up and get across the road. If you hit anyone again you're gonna be in big trouble."

I helped him to his feet and the traffic cleared enough that we ran the boat across the street. When we got there, one of my boat mates moved out from under the boat and handed his handles to Craig. Craig didn't even hesitate or say a word. He just took them and moved under the boat and out of the coxswain position. And that was the last time he complained during Hell Week. Attitude is infectious and it truly is everything, and a little adjustment goes a long way.

It's funny. I knew what the instructors were saying when they dressed me down but they were also looking at what happened and said, "Wow, that's cool. He doesn't take any shit and he handled business. If someone's getting out of line, Heben's a good regulator." One of them later told me.

A few years later, Craig was on a deployment in Thailand and decided he wanted to stay there and not re-enlist. So he used his government credit card to open a bar down there—spending around $20,000. I think he worked it out though and it all ended well in time. He's a super family guy now and I love the dude to this day! Once a SEAL, always a SEAL.

The last evolution during Hell Week is called "Around the World." It's an IBS paddle evolution that starts on Thursday night, around midnight, and lasts for 12 mind-numbing hours. Normally, it was all supposed to be about a 15-mile or so IBS paddle, wherein, hallucinations are the norm and students fall asleep in mid stroke. But because the waves were so freakin' high, we had to run an extra eight miles with the boats on our heads, just so we could get to a point where the surf was low enough that we could realistically get out past it all. Because of El Niño, nothing was normal. We finally found that water entry point, paddled a bit North and then East around Point Loma, toward Glorietta Bay on the East side of Coronado Island. Here, we exited and put boats on heads to run across the highway to the demo pits where we had a late breakfast. True, we ended up not paddling as far as we were supposed to, but the hallucinations were probably even worse because we ran three times as far as we normally should have and—with boats cracking down on our heads. And all the while, I'm losing more and more fucking hair. I would have rather paddled. Alas, normal is not for me. In fact, it's a setting on a dryer, and I pray that I am never labeled as such.

After breakfast we normally would have had to put boats back into the water, but because of the 12- to 15-foot surf, we were instructed to run the 2 miles to the sand PT area. It was insane. We were insane. The finish line would be in front of the BUD/S compound. They did this so that there wouldn't be some deadly insane wipeout scenes to witness, as they felt there would be serious injury or death if we attempted to beach our IBS in our current shit state of physical and mental being. The SEALs instructors always love a good laugh, especially at the expense of the students, but not if it meant purposeful injury. Well, 90 percent of the time anyway!

It was brutal, but so is combat. Everything we endured that week was supposed to simulate combat situations—the stresses of dealing with the unknown, exhaustion, extremes in temperature, limited access to food and water, following orders in the midst of it all and working together in a small group to achieve a common goal. The "Around the World" exercise accomplished this, and the out-of-control waves coupled with the, much longer than normal, run, just made it that much more realistic.

But after that ridiculously altered evolution, Hell Week would be over!

None of us realized it then, but when we put our boats down in the sand and were instructed to fall into boat crews on the Grinder, standing there, right in front of us, was the director of training. You're not sure what's going on, but your first thought is that it's nothing good. Because it never is! But, in reality, that couldn't be further from the truth.

"Gentlemen," he says. "Congratulations. Hell Week, Class 215, is secured."

Everyone got a little emotional—mostly because we hadn't slept for days and were basically zombies functioning on pure adrenaline and muscle memory, but also because we just realized we had survived Hell Week. I'm not kidding when I tell you that I had a few tears of joy streaming down my face. I think the emotion is so raw that it's impossible to contain it. Not to be too happy though, the director of training promptly informed us that we now only had a 50 percent chance of making it through BUD/S. Kick 'em in the balls, then pat 'em on the back and then promptly kick 'em in the balls again. That was Hell Week. Shit, to be completely accurate, that was BUD/S! Today, I use the same philosophy in business!

My personal, after-action, inventory report looked like this: During this second round of Hell Week, my body hit some different rough patches—especially during the initial melee and the barrel of fun that was the ice boat. Let's just say I liken this experience—and everything that followed of being wet, sandy, cold, hot, tired and confused for a week—to wearing 16-grit sandpaper as clothing and being on psychotropic drugs while crossing the Himalayas in a wet sandstorm. It's a mind and body and body chemistry altering experience. An event horizon that many don't finish, and one I'd gladly experience again, but only if I had to. I lost all the toenails on each of my feet during 215 Hell Week. I had bizarre skin abrasion rings around my waist, wrists, and neck that made me look as if my body was sewn together like some modern day Frankenstein. My crotch was rubbed raw. My inner thighs were rubbed raw. The hair was scalped off the top of my head, even more so than before, and right down the middle like some Pepe Le Pew wannabe! But wait, there's more: The bottom of my feet looked like I had scraped them across a cheese grater repeatedly. It got so bad that my Nike ACG Performance sandals, which were originally yellow and gold, became muddled with blood like what you'd see at the bottom of a ground meat Styrofoam tray at the grocery store. I could have walked onto the set of the *Walking Dead* and fit right in...without any special effects or make-up!

Seeing a lot of us like this, they gave us Friday night, Saturday and Sunday to recover—and we needed it. We were physically and mentally hammered! When Monday rolled around, training started back up again with a nice, 10-mile conditioning run. No rest for the weary. But what did we expect? We were at the hardest military training school the world has even known.

CHAPTER 11

> "FAILURE, QUITE SIMPLY, IS TAKING THE PATH OF LEAST PERSISTENCE. ONWARD AND UPWARD!"
>
> —CHRISTOPHER MARK HEBEN

After Hell Week, your class starts gelling and the relationships among your peers get deeper. Not truly a team yet, you do, however, have solid boat crew integrity. Together you've experienced a lot in a short period of time, and that feeling of teamwork the SEAL instructors have been drilling into your heads since Day One, begins to make a lot more sense. You begin to see the life-and-death consequences of the Team concept, more so than you have ever experienced in any sport you have ever played or any business or line of work you have ever been in.

Your reward for surviving Hell Week comes in many forms: You are switched to Building 618, a two-man room that's a little further north on the strand, away from the pressure cooker of the Grinder. Your shirt color changes from white to brown. There's a running joke that the brown shirts are warmer, softer and less of a target for the wrath of the SEAL Instructors, but that's not really the case. All of that is in your head. It's part of the cognitive dissonance that takes place during the process of forging a SEAL warrior. The reality is that you just survived the most physically and mentally demanding week of your life and you're walking around with a hell of a lot more swagger. Your BUD/S class has undergone its first downsizing metamorphosis and, if you thought you had a big dick before, you're now fully convinced you're a porn star. But all that swagger doesn't really amount to shit, and here's why: After completing Hell Week, one only has a 50 percent chance of graduating BUD/S. It's significant in that your chances just went from 10 to 50 percent, but rather insignificant in that you still have more than 20 weeks left and everything suddenly is faster and more challenging. It's a pressure cooker that is unrelenting and unmerciful. It has to be, because when you're on a SEAL mission and poking around at Zero Dark Thirty in some foreign land on a classified mission you can't just decide to up and quit. If that's ever the case, we'll shoot you ourselves!

The two weeks post Hell Week are known as Hydro Week 1 and Hydro Week 2 because they teach old-school Frogman shit known as Hydrographic Reconnaissance. We called it Hydro Recon for short, or 'Hydro' for super short. But, and there is always a but at BUD/S, not before they have the whole class do a 10-mile conditioning run on the Monday morning after Hell Week ended. This was absolute torture because the entire class is suffering from massive lactic-acid buildup and subsequent deposition in nearly every joint in their bodies. The run is designed to stimulate the body and force everything from our joints and into our serum and bloodstream where it would be broken down in the liver and kidneys and then pissed out.

I never felt so awful in my life. Every joint burned with pain. It was as if there was a blowtorch ignited and placed on every hinge joint and ball and socket joint I owned. I felt like I was 100-years old. You could hear every dude groaning and moaning as we lumbered through the first three to four miles. As I ran all I could think about was that I wanted to die. The wholesale aching was so bad that I actually found myself longing to be back in Hell Week! In fact, the pain was so intense that it seemed to heighten every other sensory input. I think the body does this in order to overwhelm the brain with non-painful and distracting stimuli in order to lesson the noxious signals being ram-rodded to the body's pain centers. Literally, I could smell dead fish a mile away, pick up the Chanel No. 5 on the girls from *Jersey Shore*, and hear their cute East Coast accents from the same distance. I tasted the salt in the air and the sun felt like it was my own personal tanning lamp. In a way, this assault on my senses was a welcome relief from the lactic acid that was dislodging from its orthopedic entombment and steadily coursing through my bloodstream. The Navy had this pain game business down to a fucking science. Never before did I know the body was capable of surviving so much psychodynamic and bio-physiologic battering. I can eloquently say that now, but back then I was like a BUD/S drunk, foul-mouthed sailor, running in a pack with others of a similar physical and mental disposition. Onlookers must have thought we were a pack of escaped, deranged, mental patients.

What made it all even worse was that I had lost every toenail on both feet, which made the pace exquisitely painful—no matter whether I ran fast or slow. I was a hot mess, but I learned how to focus on those things I had and not the things I didn't. I'd made it through Hell Week. I still had my toes. I had most of my hair. My boat crew was solid. I was still in BUD/S. And damn if I wasn't going to finish this run! Little victories add up to huge successes.

After the run, we leapt right into Hydrographic Reconnaissance, which forced us to be in the water for long periods of time—sometimes up to six hours per day in the bitter, blue Pacific Ocean. And this, by itself, forced another half-dozen or so guys to ring the bell and call it quits. Hell Week makes many people so hydrophobic that the mere thought of jumping back into the water for hours on end is too much to bear. To me, at least, it's amazing to think that someone grinds through Hell Week and then ends up quitting over something as simple as being out in the water.

They trained us to be Frogmen, and one of the evolutions included measuring water depths with a lead line and writing them down on a slate with a grease pen. They were mock beach-mapping sessions that mimicked the old school UDT, Scouts and Raider groups that determined water depth and mapped out potential landing-craft obstacles and land mines. This data was marked on a slate with a grease pen. Later, the data was compiled into a Hydrographic Reconnaissance chart, which was used by higher ups to determine the best time and place to land men and equipment on a beach during wartime. Today, this is all mostly

UNDAUNTED

done by satellite, but it was cool to honor the crusty old Frogmen of yesteryear and get in touch with the SEAL roots.

Beyond honoring our forefathers, these exercises rooted out the pussies who would have had mental breakdowns over getting wet again. This is important because SEAL Teams can't afford to have that happen, ever! We had many long nights drawing charts after entering the water at 0000 hours and exiting the water at 0430 hours while being told that all charts must be turned in to the Phase office by 0700 hours. This was the only time in my life that I embraced chewing tobacco—and that lasted one week. I didn't have time to mess around, so I went right to Copenhagen—and I don't mean to Denmark! It helped us stay awake. I'd only tried 'dip' once before, when I was in 9th grade and on my way to a high school track practice. I put Kodiac in my mouth and vomited five-minutes later.

Then, just when you think you can't stomach any more Copenhagen or suffer through another night of two hours of sleep, it's over, and you officially begin Dive Phase. For the next seven weeks, the Navy runs you through a series of grueling underwater evolutions that build—and hone—the underwater skills unique to Navy SEALs, thus transforming you from a 5301 UDT/SEAL Candidate into a 5320, or a Basic Combatant Swimmer. The 5320 NEC is a huge deal because it comes with Dive Pay! An extra $250.00 per month. Phase Two isn't for the faint of heart, and you need every ounce of your newly acquired swagger you can muster. People who aren't comfortable in the water, and I mean truly comfortable, struggle during Phase Two the most. At one point, during Pool Competency week, you are practically drowned. Some students, do in fact, swallow a shit ton of water and have to have all sorts of medical attention on the pool deck after their lifeless bodies are pulled from the Combat Training Tank (CTT). Those who succeed have the highest level of comfort in the water and demonstrate the ability to perform well in stressful, uncomfortable, and unforgiving environments.

During Phase Two we learned open and closed-circuit diving, and we continued to expand our competency in underwater navigation and other Frogman skill-sets we would be called upon to perform in the SEAL Teams. We were taught complex underwater navigational dives leading to placement of mock explosive charges, called limpet mines, under ships at the stern where the screws are attached. We studied how to identify and pinpoint key shipboard target zones on many types of vessels, with either total destruction or sinking in mind, or temporary immobilization as well as the placement of tracking devices. I saw more students, who survived Hell Week with me, drop out during this seven weeks of Dive Phase. Without the swagger and the psychological 'brown shirt' effects, odds are, there would have been many more quitters.

As people, we tend to buy into other peoples bullshit instead of allowing ourselves to step over it. I never understood that, fully, until I watched it happen in SEAL training. Dudes would quit based on the rumored difficulty of things instead of attempting to meet the reality of them head on and power through them. Most of the time, it was the same dudes who were always pumping the class ahead of us for information. As if, knowing exactly what is going to occur can, somehow, cause you to magically defeat the system. It was absurd at times and just laughable at others. I never wanted to know exactly what was going to happen next. In this way, I was able to take advantage of the adrenaline rush and totally immerse myself in the moment. Few people live in the moment today. It's one thing to be mentally and physically prepared, but it's another thing altogether to rob yourself of maximum adrenaline because you think you have it all planned out. It's a waste of energy because the instructors know this shit already and they are always changing everything. SEALs are some of the smartest people on the planet. Thank God for that!

Beyond the psychotically kinetic physical activities, there's a lot of academic training that takes place during Second Phase. You learn dive physics—which is a gambit of what happens to compressed air at depth as it relates to both pressure and temperature. You learn all of these critical equations. This is challenging and complex information, and on its own knocks a lot of people out of the program. Instructors will work with you if you demonstrate the mental capacity to learn this material, but if you're just a jock who met the base mental requirements, you may reach the end of the line right here.

And, as always, since day one, the runs get faster, the obstacle course times get faster, and written tests are now on the table. There's still the petty torments—of course, they have to further test your mettle, your desire, and your will, as well as drive out those people who can't take the constant pressure. We had one instructor who was working on his Master's degree at that time. He is a very cerebral guy—Instructor Frank Arnott. After night dives, he would often order us to lay on our backs on the concrete behind the Dive Phase classroom and then proceed to launch into these crazy diatribes about everything from philosophy to finance while, all the while, he would direct this garden hose on us and endlessly hose us down. So while he's doing this, and in between the diatribes, Arnott is ordering us to do flutter kicks and push-ups. This would sometimes go on for hours. It was hilarious and bizarre all at the same time. It was like Tolstoy meets Einstein meets Tony Horton. The flutter kicks and pushups were entirely necessary because you needed to keep your body core temperature up. It was October and the 50-degree nights were upon us. I know that doesn't sound cold, but try it on a windy day with just a t-shirt and shorts on while you are soaking wet.

One of the other differences once you hit Phase Two is that you see more good cop/bad cop performances from the instructors. You're under a bigger, more powerful microscope and you are still always under the gun. And now, they're changing the way you're being tested. One minute you're getting beat down by an instructor; the next you're getting praised for doing something correctly. It keeps you on your toes and ensures the stress never stops.

In the midst of all this, we underwent the dreaded Pool Competency evolutions—or 'Pool Comp' week, for short; which were, in many ways, more brutal than anything we'd faced yet. It all involved the water, and it all sucked! One of the evolutions was treading water for 15 minutes with twin 80-cubic foot high-pressure steel tanks on your back and with no fins. As if this were not bad enough, you had to keep both of your hands out of the water the whole time. Anyone caught using their hands to assist was immediately pulled from the water and failed.

Another exercise involved sharing air with a buddy during a 30-minute pool dive. Buddy breathing is an exercise in anoxia as much as it is an exercise in sharing and caring. When you are dependent upon another human to survive in a zero-oxygen environment, you learn another level of teamwork altogether. You actually learn that your air is not as important as your buddy's air, and you hope he feels the same way. It is this extreme state of empathy that solidifies the whole teamwork deal. This lesson transfers and translates into everything else you do as a SEAL, that whole state of selfless service to one another begins right there at BUD/S and, quite arguably, in that very evolution. Something about oxygen deprivation that drives home teamwork....Go figure!

The ultimate test is the final evolution, which is designed to simulate a night infiltration on an enemy coast. The conditions are supposed to be as bad as they possibly can be—high waves, rough waters, zero visibility—the whole nine yards. Basically, it simulates you having the living shit beat out of you by a breaking wave—a surf hit—and in making you come up to the surface with everything perfectly fixed and ready to creep up on the shore, it teaches you to be the master and commander of your environment. If you don't get it right, you fail the exercise. But here's the twist: Instead of a wave doing this, a number of instructors do it to you. Anything worth doing is worth overdoing. If this was a barbecue, you'd be the meat and you'd be blackened beyond recognition!

You're decked out in full, old school, SCUBA gear—an inhalation tube, exhalation tube, twin 80 tank and fins. No re-breather yet...not until you pass this evolution. Your mask is blacked out to simulate night, so you can't see anything.

Then you're told to start casually doing laps at the bottom of the pool. Yeah right, there is nothing casual about this evolution. It's like getting into your car knowing that you're going to get T-boned by a semi-tractor trailer at some point on your morning commute to work. The thought of that tractor-trailer event, however, somehow seems more pleasant than the reality of the event that is waiting for you in the water. Bruce, the Great White shark from *Jaws* had nothing on these guys! They were also apex predators and every one of us wanted to be them!

So you're swimming along when without warning—since you can't see them—the instructors descend upon you underwater and basically gang rape you. It's like Flipper and his three evil twins have an aquatic roid rage on you. They tie your hoses in knots, yank them around the valves of the tank, rip your fins off, flood your mask, slam you into the bottom of the pool, and rub you across it like you're a piece of cheese on a cheese grater. They knee you into the bottom and slam you repeatedly against the pool floor so you're completely disoriented and devoid of any air in your lungs. Your first priority in life is to identify your inhalation tube and status check that thing. All else can wait. Occasionally, a BUD/S student has an unmolested inhalation tube, and the rush of air back into your lungs makes the world a happier place, no matter what state your gear or your body is in. More often than not, however, your inhalation tube looks like a Twizzler taken out of a toddler's mouth: gnarled up and smashed.

This reality causes a panic reaction like you wouldn't believe. You are without air, and nothing else matters. Your world collapses into that one task alone, so that the only thing you care about is that hose and trying to make it work again. On an even rarer occasion, the instructors levy you with what is called the 'whammy knot', which is both good and bad. The whammy is a knot that simply cannot be undone. What they are looking for is that you attempt to undo it until you start doing the funky chicken and the lights go out in your brain like one of those old time TV sets. At which point, they pull you up and revive you. So, although you are spared the task of making everything functioning and perfect, you are put through the indignity of massive medical attention on the side of the pool. This, by the way, totally rattles everyone else who is waiting to go. Again, it is all done by design. No matter what scenario you get, it pretty much sucks major ass....and more than a few quitters are always to be found on this day. I powered through it OK. I didn't get the whammy knot and I didn't get pummeled too badly. Best of all, I didn't drown. But some of my classmates weren't so lucky....we had about a half dozen quitters that day, and many more failures.

The remainder of Combat Diving Phase is comprised of things such as becoming more proficient with the Drager LAR 5 re-breather and knowing the nuances of the rig: How to set it up and take it apart, clean it, maintain it properly and how to utilize it to its full potential. Additionally, we became moderately proficient in underwater navigation using a compass, buoyancy control, a depth gauge and timer, as well as a series of more complex dive physics lessons. You learn how to handle the mind-numbing mundanity, the abysmal blackness of night diving, and the nerve-wracking skill of being under very large ships that are fully functioning. Attaching tracking devices and limpet mines becomes second nature, as well as learning the whole "plan your dive and dive your plan" and "safe in, safe out" concepts of Combat Diving. You can never really sink a big ship with limpet mines, but you're able to disable them in the water, which allows other SEALs to move in and take the ship down from bottom-to-top or top-to-bottom. So you're learning all these applicable skills you'll, hopefully, use as a professional Frogman.

The whole time, you are also doing the typical kinetic BUD/S shit: The swims, O-courses, runs, morning PT sessions. As I said, it never stops. You get a new swim buddy assigned at this time because after Hell Week and Pool Comp, the class is pretty decimated. This is when Mike Branch, the former California Highway Patrol Officer, and I became attached at the hip. He was assigned as my swim buddy. Mike is the same dude that smoked the swim during the BUD/S screening test in boot camp, and now he was paired up with the guy that almost failed it—me. As it turned out, it was a perfect match. Despite the fact that I am 6'0" and Mike is about 5'6", we became one of the top two or three swim pairs. My first two-miler was 84 minutes. Mike and I crushed them in about 58 minutes.

About midway through the seven-week phase, our two student class leaders, both Ensigns, approached us and said they wanted us to separate as a swim pair. As it also turned out, they were also one of the top three swim pairs. We were suddenly wondering, "WTF?"

Their request got even stranger: They wanted us to pair up with two other guys—one named Dent and another named Watters, and they wanted us to purposely fail the next two-mile ocean swim with them so that Dent and Watters would be kicked out of BUD/S. Neither of those two liked Dent and Waters. They thought they should be out of the program. As Ensigns, both guys outranked Branch and me, and they wanted to make us the bad guys. Their plan was for Branch and me to purposely swim slowly, which would doom the other guys. Neither Branch nor I had failed anything yet while these guys had failed at least one swim already. So, although we wouldn't be putting ourselves in jeopardy by doing this, they would probably get the boot from BUD/S. At least that was the logic they tried to dump on us.

Branch and I looked at these two guys—the Ensigns—and immediately came to the same conclusions: 1.) It was not our job to get other students to fail out of BUD/S. 2.) We don't want to fail anything either 3.) Karma is a bitch, and in a place like this, the last thing you need is a bad dose of it!

"No way," I said. "That's some seriously bad ju-ju and I'm not doing that to anyone."

"You need to do this," one of the Ensigns said. He outranked me and was trying to put some pressure on me to do his dirty work. Dent and Watters were senior Petty Officers and the two Ensigns felt they showed very poor leadership. I didn't feel that way, and neither did Mike. They were both good men.

"Nope, sir." I said. "Fuck that. Besides, it's a terrible plan, sir. All the instructors will look at this and question why you two yahoos: 1.) Broke us up as a pair, 2.) How two, top-swimming two-milers failed a swim. 3.) Why our time was so far off our usual swims—at the same time, with different partners. So we're not fucking doing it."

Branch agreed. "No way, Sirs."

Both Ensigns spent a few more minutes pressing us before they finally realized we would not be complicit in their plan.

Dent and Waters went on to pass BUD/S and become very good SEALs. The two Ensigns had quite different fates. One would be relieved from command. He was a Bible-thumping extremist who didn't want the men in his platoon to have porn in the platoon spaces. He was preaching the Bible to them and telling them they were going to Hell, which didn't sit well with a bunch of Navy SEALs who faced death at every turn, even in training. His men eventually rebelled and, subsequently, he was railroaded out of the teams. There's a simple truth about SEALs: We know we're probably going to Hell, so we don't need someone telling us that every day and ruining our ability to appreciate the female form. The other Ensign would end up quitting BUD/S during Third Phase in favor of going to flight school. That move was something we all talked about for a long time. Hell, we still do to this day!

A few years later, I ran into Dent and Watters—separately—and told them the story about what had transpired that week in Class 215. They were shocked, but grateful neither Branch nor I were willing to be complicit in those Ensigns's plan for them. So was I!

The rest of my Combat Diving Phase was relatively uneventful. We met in front of building 618, which is where we all lived, and took a head count. Then we marched down to the Grinder and assembled as boat crews to begin our training. Other than Hell Week, SEAL training is not a 24/7 endeavor. If you start at 0500 hours, you might be done at 1600 hours that day. And then you can do whatever you want to do in sunny San Diego—chase tail, go drinking, chase tail while drinking, go surfing, hit the beach anywhere, basically you're on your own a lot, which is all part of the instructors' plan. At first, they're in your face about keeping your gear squared away, your room clean, and your shoes shiny. But as BUD/S progresses they back off a bit to see whether you're disciplined on your own. They want to see if that mentality sinks into everything you do. And if it doesn't, you find out quickly that it affects your teammates—especially your boat crew. The last thing you want to have happen is for your guys to suffer because you're not 100 percent squared away, 100 percent of the time.

Also, they want to see how you deal with your down time. As a SEAL, you might find yourself close to any number of world party spots and these guys want to see if you're the type of person they can party with in a bar, with each other, with women, whatever. They're analyzing your transformation during BUD/S—every move. It's that whole breakdown and reprogramming exercise. While it looks like they're not paying attention they're actually paying more attention—talking about you and determining whether you're the right person to keep progressing on to the next phase, or even to be considered for graduation from the Captain America Factory.

Once you pass Dive Phase, the graduation percentage rises to about 85 percent, and they begin preparing you to become a SEAL. You're given what's called a Dream Sheet. Essentially, it's a form wherein you're asked to pick your top three choices of SEAL Teams where you'd like to be assigned.

At that time, each SEAL Team had a different area of operations (AO), but today all of the teams go everywhere around the world. They changed this based on the valid concern that by having too narrowly defined and specific AOs for each SEAL team, guys weren't cross-training to operate well in myriad environments. You had guys who didn't know how to handle explosives on a building made out of concrete and rebar but who could get inside a structure made out of adobe and stone. Also, there are different ways of patrolling in jungle and urban environments, etc. The Navy fixed all that in 2000 but this was 1997 and we weren't quite there yet.

Thus, when I was going through SEAL training, the teams were pretty specialized. For example, SEAL Team Four's area of operations was South and Central America, while SEAL Team Eight had the biggest AO: North Africa, Europe and the Middle East.

East Coast teams are even numbers: Two, Four, Six, Eight, Ten, SEAL Delivery Vehicle Team Two (SDVT-2) and SEAL Team Six; West Coast teams are odd numbers: One, Three, Five, Seven, and Seal Delivery Vehicle Team One (SDVT-1), which is actually stationed out of Hawaii.

While I was in BUD/S, during 1997 and 1998, most of the real-world operations that SEALs did were done by East Coast SEAL Teams— SEAL Team Six, SEAL Team Eight, SEAL Team Two, and SEAL Team Four & SDVT-2—because it just so happened that the areas of the world that those Teams specialized in were the hot spots of the day. Being an Ohio boy with six months of winter, no sunshine and miserably cold, shitty-ass weather, I was dead-set on being a West Coast SEAL. Sunny and 75 degrees trumped Ohio weather any day of the year! Well, low and behold, I received my Dream Sheet and put SEAL Team Three at the top of my list. I chose that because its area of operations was exclusively the Middle East. Combat in Somalia had erupted a few years earlier, the First Gulf War went down, and we were always at odds with Iran and Iraq. I was thinking there was a pretty good chance that I would see combat with SEAL Team Three. What I didn't know was that Somalia had been predominantly handled by Task Force Ranger (the U.S. Army Ranger's Tier One organization) and DELTA Force as well as six SEALs from SEAL Team Six. But I put down SEAL Team Three because the Middle East made sense to me.

My second choice was SEAL Team One, which deployed around southwest Asia in places like Vietnam, the Philippines, Thailand and Singapore. I thought those were cool places to be stationed in, and I had read so much about the Vietnam War that I was enamored with it. In fact, I still am. Additionally, Abu Sayyaf was always hot and heavy in PI. Not many people know that to this day.

Lastly, I chose SEAL Team Five, which operated in Northern Asia—North and South Korea, and Eastern Russia. I figured that was a pretty tumultuous area and North Korea could explode at any given moment. I was essentially doing an oh-shit risk assessment and picking my dream Teams accordingly. But unlike most normal humans, I was purposefully trying to place myself in harm's way. You don't go through all this shit to sit around and play war. You prepare for it and become your ultimate best when your country calls for you. I know all my buddies felt the same way.

I completed my Dream Sheet, signed it and submitted it with rest of my class. Done and done!

The next morning, we reported to the Dive Phase classroom for that day's instructions and briefing from our class proctor, Instructor Pat Babolick, 'Babs' as he was called by the other SEALs. If you called him that by accident, you would spend half the morning inside the dive gear dunk tank. This was a 300-gallon trough that contained 55-degree water—not where you wanted to be sitting, motionless for a few hours. Well, Instructor Babolick comes out and yells, "Heben! Where the fuck is Heben?!"

Now there are few things that can cause you to spontaneously want to vomit, piss yourself and feel your stomach jump up into your throat, one of them is finding out you have cancer (I do not!), and the other is having your name yelled out by your SEAL Proctor.

I replied so he could get my position, and did so in my best attempt to sound unfazed: "Hoo-yah, Instructor Babolick!"

"Heben, report to Lieutenant Chaby's office immediately."

"Dammit!" I said to myself. "What is this shit?!"

I was a bit concerned about what was awaiting me. I hadn't done anything wrong, but then again, I hadn't done anything all that great either. I was aspiring to be Mr. Unknown and following the advice of Chief Madsen.

After hustling in double-time fashion, I arrived at Lieutenant Tom Chaby's office sweating like an Eskimo in a hot tub and my heart racing as fast as a meth addict on cocaine. Including Lt. Chaby, there were five instructors in the room—and they were all waiting for me. All members of East Coast SEAL Teams; two guys I'd had in First Phase, one from Third Phase and two from the current BUD/S Phase I was in.

"This is fucked up," I thought. I'm about to get hammered for God knows what from a bunch of instructors whose Phases I've already passed and from one whose Phase I haven't even seen yet. This is what it must feel like right before some scumbag from ISIS chops off your head.

Lt. Chaby motioned to me. "Heben, have a seat."

"Yes, Sir!" I said, again with false bravado.

I sat down in the only chair in the room—directly across from the Lieutenant's desk. Everyone was staring at me. Chaby pulled out a piece of paper and slid it across the table, where it stopped right in front of me....My Dream Sheet.

"What the fuck is this, Heben?" Chaby said.

"My Dream Sheet, Sir."

"I know what it is, Seaman (said with a heavy and demeaning emphasis), but WHAT THE FUCK IS THIS!? WHY do you have all West Coast teams written down?"

I thought about my answer for a moment and replied, "Well, I'm from Ohio, Sir, and I kind of wanted, well, I like it out here, Sir. San Diego's pretty awesome."

"That's a bullshit answer, Heben," he said. "Do you know that 85 percent of all of the real-world operations in the last 10 years have been done by East Coast SEAL teams?"

"Negative, Sir," I said. "I didn't know that."

"So, my question to you, Heben, is do you want to be on SEAL Team Six at some point in time?"

Who the fuck didn't? SEAL Team Six is the most exclusive team among all the SEAL Teams. A squadron from Six took out Osama bin Laden. Meanwhile, while I'm thinking this, all the other instructors are silently nodding their agreement. It was like a freaky intervention scene done Mafia-style, except that nobody was fat, smoking a cigar, wheezing while they talked, or wore an ill-fitting suit.

I replied in the affirmative. "Yes, Sir!"

Chaby continued: "Do you know that 75 percent of the men on SEAL Team Six are from East Coast Teams?"

"No, Sir," I answered. "I was not aware."

So the lieutenant smiled and said, "All right, Heben, here's what we're going to do. Hand me your Dream Sheet."

I did. And I watched that man tear it in half right in front of me. Then he took the pieces, tore them in half again, crumpled them up into a little ball and threw it over his shoulder into the garbage can behind his desk; the group nodding continued.

Chaby then reached into his desk and pulled out a new Dream Sheet. He slid it across the table to me and said, "Sign this."

I looked down. On the sheet was written "SEAL Team Eight; SEAL Team Eight; and SEAL Team Eight."

"Hoo-yah, Sir!" I replied, then signed it and handed it back to him. The nodding changed to comments of 'Fuck, yeah', 'That's what I'm talking about', and other expletive-filled approvals.

One of the other instructors walked over and handed me a SEAL Team Eight sticker.

"If I see this on your car, if I see this anywhere in your room or anywhere else, you will immediately be dropped from this program," he said. "Now, have a good day and get the fuck back to your class."

I felt like that dizzy, nauseous 15-year old kid who couldn't participate in track practice—only this time I had a two-hour, night-dive, ship attack field-training exercise (FTX) to prep for. I couldn't let Mike Branch down, and I couldn't let myself down. Hell, I couldn't let my country down!

At the time, SEAL Team Eight was the youngest Team in the Navy's elite Sea, Air and Land (SEAL) program. Its area of operations was Africa, the Middle East and Europe, so the potential to see action was pretty damn good. It was, and still is, a very dynamic SEAL Team, which is why the instructors wanted me to go there. Plus, I wanted to eventually be assigned to SEAL Team Six. If there's some sort of hostage situation anywhere in the world or a high-value target that needs to be taken out, they either send Delta or Six to get the job done. SEAL Team Eight and the other Teams have a broader mission. For a long time, Six was the exclusive team catching war criminals from the Bosnian war—a mission called Persons Indicted for War Crimes (PIFWC). SEAL Team Eight helped out, but only in a limited support role. SEAL Team Eight is considered a "white operations" team, whereas SEAL Team Six is all "black ops."

Not everyone who becomes a SEAL aspires to be assigned to SEAL Team Six. Some guys love being 'normal' SEALs. I feel strange even using the word 'normal' as a SEAL descriptor because it takes a unique breed to be a SEAL and another unique type of SEAL to reach SEAL Team Six—guys who want nothing but black ops.

I was psyched when I was assigned to SEAL Team Eight, but my goal was eventually to make it to SEAL Team Six. First, however, I had to make it the rest of the way through BUD/S, which meant entering Phase Three and surviving, among other things, Land Navigation and Land Warfare Training. Only then would I physically get my official marching orders in hand. Onward and upward!

Me, the 14-month old 'baby SEAL'

Me (right) at 14 with my brother Jon and sister Lizzy

U.S. Navy Bootcamp, RTC Great Lakes, Chicago. Seaman Recruit (ARPOC) Heben. E1. You have to start somewhere! 1996

I'll be back! The day after I was rolled out of Hell Week 214 and into Class 215 to start all over again. Never quit attitude even then!.

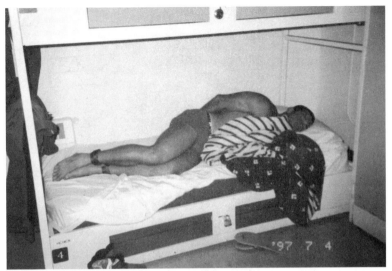

Me 'practicing' for drown proofing. Hands and feet tied up. I slept tied up like this, every night, for two weeks!

STT Land Warfare Training. SEAL Team Eight, 1998

First TRIDENT, 1998

Getting my Trident pinned on me by Captain Randy Goodman, the Commanding Officer at SEAL Team Eight, 1998

Me and former SEAL 'Gags' somewhere in Pakistan, 2004

Me and 'Moses' (my SR25). Somewhere deep in Pakistan, 2004.

Blackwater. Gearing up for another mission in Mali, Africa, 2007

'Looking for work' on the outskirts of Bahgdad, 2007

Looking for 'work' in Sudan. Summer, 2007

Anna, our amazing safe house chef and our entire kitchen staff

Southwestern Sudan. I cured this little guy of a very nasty leg infection. I came back to see him a week later. We were both happy to see one another! 2007

Battle of N'Djamena, Chad. Chadian rebels of the United Front for Democratic Change (FUC) pour into the city, 2008

Battle of N'Djamena. The bodies of two rebels who decided to fire AKs at the wrong people.

Battle of N'Djamena. French APV's during Embassy evacuation.

Battle of N'Djamena. Somebody shot this poor guy in the ass

Safehouse. Barred windows and a big kill zone, 2008

Safehouse. Burkina Faso, Africa. Pool & Gym

Me and Jessie L, on another 6-hour flight in Africa

Looking aggravated. Fulton County Jail mugshot, March 2008

Me, Maggie Mutahi Beseda and Mitch Tannen in Kenya, 2012

Me, Harry Brainch, Mitch Tannen & Maggie enjoy a few cold ones in Kenya!

She was killed by poachers with AK-47s. Her ivory was hacked off her face while she was still alive. Kenya, 2012

Chris in Kenya, dead Elephant

Travis and I recovering ivory, with my Winkler Tomahawk, so poachers can't come back and get it. A horrific task!

CHAPTER 12

> "THE EXCEPTIONAL WILL ALWAYS FACE CRITICISM FROM THE UNEXCEPTIONAL. WHILE COURAGE IS A SWITCH YOU MUST FLIP IN ORDER TO PUSH THROUGH IT, COURAGE ALONE WILL NOT SUSTAIN YOU. FOR, IN ORDER TO CONTINUOUSLY SUCCEED, YOU MUST HAVE PASSION, RESILIENCY, OPTIMISM, AND ABOVE ALL ELSE, PEOPLE SKILLS.
>
> I CHALLENGE YOU TO BE EXCEPTIONAL FOR YOUR FAMILY, YOUR FAITH, YOUR COMMUNITY, AND YOUR COUNTRY!"
>
> —CHRISTOPHER MARK HEBEN

One of the things that stuck with me from the cover of that *Popular Mechanics,* what originally drew me to the Navy SEALs, was that Heckler & Koch MP-5 the SEAL held in his hands. And yet, here we were, more than two-thirds of the way through BUD/S and my class had not trained with any live weapons. Saying that I was ready would be a colossal understatement. I was super ready. I was more excited and eager to learn about weapons than a North Korean is to make plans to defect!

But that's just how it is in BUD/S; you don't actually pick up a weapon until after you've survived Hell Week and First Phase, Pool Comp and Second Phase, and are cleared hot to head into the last phase of Navy SEAL training—Phase Three, aka Land Warfare Phase. The one awesome thing that happened before anyone touched weapons was that you were issued Woodland Camouflage BDUs or Cammies. Believe it or not, this was a huge flipping deal! Up to that point you've been wearing these *Gomer Pyle* greens, and stick out like a sore thumb. They are not rip-stop fabric, so they stayed soaked forever. And when they're wet and sandy, they weigh more than an anti-shark, chain-mail suit, minus the protection of course. But once again, it's all really part of the mind game taking place at BUD/S. If you can picture a Spartan *agoge* mixed with a Roman *ludis* dropped down onto some of the most expensive real estate on earth, that's BUD/S. No prisoners. No mercy. And it's all housed in the middle of a vacationer's dream. We finally shed our *Gomer Pyle* greens and started wearing high-speed, low-drag, combat-sexy, rip-stop woodland cammies. We all felt like underwater gangsters that day. Well, at least I did! The only other times I wore woodland camouflage before that were on Halloween or when I was playing Army with my grade-school buddies. And I bought that pair at the local Army/Navy store. Today, however, my government was issuing them to me. It could only get better from here, I thought...erroneously. Hell, I already had the sticker for SEAL Team Eight, so how bad could the next two months really be? Stand the F by, Heebs!

Well, I was still at BUD/S. And the Land Warfare Phase is actually a lot of epic shit rolled into two crazy months. The Navy saves this for those last eight weeks because at the end of this phase you are deadly proficient and the master of a few deadly skill sets. Thanks to the Navy, you are an expert marksman with a pistol, rifle and machine gun; proficient in hand-to-hand combat, grenade usage, and sentry stalking. You can deal with myriad underwater and land demolitions using shape charges and time fuses with plastic explosives. You're a reconnaissance master and capable of executing small-unit and ambush tactics, patrolling, rappelling, direct-action missions, covert infiltration and covert exfiltration. They've even taught you highly complex compass and celestial navigation. In essence, you make Jason Bourne look like someone in need of treatment for Low T! It's as though the instructors flip a switch and say, "Hell, you can underwater navigate now on a rebreather, so there's no reason why you can't start doing it on land. Oh, and by the way, here are a few grenades, some guns, a few bullets, and some explosives. Have at it."

If only the Land Warfare Phase were that cut-and-dry and casual. But know this: Everything that is cool in life comes with a price.

The last month of this phase is happening 60 miles west of San Diego, out on San Clemente Island, where the saying is: "No one can hear your scream!"

Forget about all the physical prowess you must possess to survive this experience; you have to be incredibly cerebral to pass the Land Warfare Phase. That's because of the insanely complex calculations you're required to demonstrate on a daily basis—such as determining the right radio frequencies, figuring out the maximum ranges of weapons or how to properly call in an airstrike. You learn how to cut a length of detonation cord correctly so that it detonates at 10 minutes instead of at 3½ minutes—ensuring you are at a safe distance when it goes ka-boom! They even teach you to recognize, in the blink of an eye, how much explosive to put on the side of a door or wall so that it blows just enough to get everyone through the hole instead of blowing you all up. These can be very complex mathematical equations and must often be completed under extreme duress.

That said, the first hard-core training evolution when you start Land Warfare is to hop your happy ass onto a bus with all the warm shit you think you have been issued, which doesn't amount to jack shit, and head off to Mount Laguna.

Mount Laguna is located at almost 6,000 feet above sea level in a forest of Jeffrey Pine, east of San Diego in the Laguna Mountains on the eastern edge of the Cleveland National Forest. It is here that you are force fed the ninja skills of Land Navigation. On the surface that sounds simple. We had already learned how to use a compass underwater, at night, under ships, all the while doing it in 58-degree water. You think to yourself: How much harder can it be to navigate on land? In reality, it's an extremely stressful experience. We each carried a 70-pound pack on our backs. In it, was a vintage 1965 PRC-72 radio—bigger than a breakdancers boom box with batteries the size of those 6-volt monstrosities used to give juice to an electric fence.

After classes on radio usage and Silva Ranger compass usage—and the implementation of Ranger Beads—you're handed a set of coordinates that lead to an unknown destination and ordered to start running across the uneven terrain, into the mountains, to go find that point.

Everything during land navigation is timed. And, unlike previous evolutions, it's not a team exercise. You're truly on your own.

The initial coordinates lead you to a goal—usually an old ammo can. In it, you find your next set of coordinates leading you to the next ammo can. Everyone has a different goal, different course, and different route that they're expected to take. It's somewhat funny because during your practice courses you may never see another person for hours, and then suddenly there are six of you at the last ammo can. And that's where you break for lunch after calling in as "complete" on your radios.

Back at base camp, an instructor checked everyone in. Many MREs (Meal Ready to Eat) were devoured during this training exercise. And it was cold as Hell up there, especially in February, at night. So you did what you could to keep the internal furnace stoked. The elements definitely added to the stress of the timed course, as well as the omnipresent instructor stress and that damn 70-pound pack!

At 6,000 feet up in February, there was snow on the ground. Once, it snowed over 18 inches in six hours. But the training did not stop. I missed one of the times from one ammo can to the next, and when I got back to base camp, I had to 'pay the man' for it. Never mind that I literally ran through trees the size of my wrists in order to avoid being late to that can, I still had to pay. This meant that I had to stay in the leaning rest position for an hour while instructor Guttierrez shoveled snow down my shirt and pants. The snow would melt and soak me, then he added fresh snow and the same thing would happen over and over again. I was soaked and freezing and I was more than happy to do the push-ups he demanded of me in order to generate body heat and avoid going hypothermic. This went on for just over an hour. He then asked me what the name of the dog was that belonged to the lady that I went to for massages back in Coronado. He must have seen the look of shock on my face because he laughed so hard he was doubled over with his hand on his stomach. As I mentioned before, these guys knew everything about us. As it turned out, he got massaged from this gal, too. It took me another good 15 minutes before I remembered.

"The name, Heben. What is that fucking dog's name? Tell me and you can recover!"

Dammit. I wracked my brain in an effort to remember every dog I ever knew—dismissing the ones I was sure it wasn't and internally debating the ones that it could be. The mind-numbing cold I was experiencing didn't help at all. I must have looked demented shivering in the leaning rest and talking to myself in an effort to remember the name of some damn mangy old dog.

"Odie!" I finally yelled, triumphantly, from the leaning rest position. "Her dog's name is Odie!"

True to his word, he told me to recover and go get dry. Thankfully, it was dinner time and there was a small fire going back where my classmates were. I had to relive the whole damn thing as I told them all about it. They rolled with laughter as I told them how that first shovel full of snow felt as it melted above my ass crack and sent frigid water streaming down to my nut sack. It sucked! But I enjoyed about one hour of dry time before we headed out for a night navigation event. Of course it would be a timed event, and of course it was going to be difficult. Nothing worth anything in life is ever easy! But hey, I could quit at any time.

Land Warfare Phase lasts 10 weeks. Over that time we only lost two or three guys. By this point, we had become pretty unshakable. In fact, we had the biggest BUD/S class ever to hit Third Phase, and it looked as though we were going to graduate with that same tag. After we completed Mount Laguna, we returned to the BUD/S compound for a week of weapons indoctrination. FINALLY! The weapons we handled up until now were called *shapes*: real size, shape and color, but made of rubber-coated metal. It had all the details of a real gun, but nothing was operational. They were essentially menacing looking tactical paperweights, but they prepared us for the feel of real weapons and everyone treated them as such. Muscle memory was hammered into our brains, but we were all chomping at the bit to get our hands on some legit lead lobbers! The instructors knew this, and they had it all down to a deadly science.

Our reward for reaching this point was a single day to decompress and thaw out from the Laguna Land Nav lunacy. This meant, of course, a four-mile timed run, a two-mile timed swim, and a timed obstacle course. At BUD/S, there was never any real rest, no quarter given, and no breaks to be had. After the morning madness, we all formed up

UNDAUNTED

and ran to chow. Few people realize this, but the chow hall is almost 1.5 miles away from the BUD/S training compound—at least that's the route they made us take. In this regard, you run almost nine miles a day just going back and forth to chow.

After chow, we were loaded onto two, white Navy buses and driven north to the old—and now closed—Navy Recruit Training Center shooting range across from the still active Marine Corps Recruiting Depot (MCRD). We were ushered inside and split into two groups: those who were self-proclaimed hunt/shoot/kill anything, backwoods Johnnies; and those who never had real experience with any weapons. I fell into that latter category. I had fired a shotgun a few times during some skeet and trap shooting events, and had fired a 9mm Browning hi-power into a phone book a few times at a buddy's house. I was not a weapons-savvy dude by any stretch of the imagination, especially with a handgun.

Instructor Guttierez announced: "Anyone who thinks they can shoot a weapon go over by Instructor Ryan. Anyone who has no weapons experience, stay here by me and Instructor Rihaana."

I later learned it was better to have zero experience than some. In this way, you were a clean slate and they didn't have to break you of any bad habits—especially with respect to handguns. I stayed with Guttierez and absorbed his verbal onslaught as he likened my pistol shot pattern to a shotgun blast. It was, in fact, horrible. I needed to tighten that shit up or I would never make it to the teams. After a few days of weapons training, they briefed us for the Island.

San Clemente Island is located about 60 miles from Coronado. It is the southernmost island in the Channel Island chain. A tree-less island, it is warm year-round and benefits greatly from many nutrient-rich currents and everything good about the salty ocean air. It also happens to be the first stop on the migratory route for the Great White shark because of its many, large seal rookeries. It is like a buffet-style dinning establishment for the most-efficient killing machine in the history of the modern world. The fact that we would be swimming in those waters before too long just added another level of terror and difficulty to an already formidable phase of BUD/S. Despite this, we knew training on the Island was going to be an awesome experience.

Those of us who had made it this far overcame some serious odds—both together and individually. We'd survived some of the most intense physical and mental duress any of us ever faced in our lives. It honed our bodies and our brains. Surprisingly, it also raised our spirits. And because of this, we were able to demonstrate to ourselves, to one another, and to our instructors the extraordinary commitment each of us had to becoming SEALs. This is why once you reach San Clemente Island, damn near 100 percent of your class returns. Together you graduate from BUD/S as Special Warfare Operators, but there's still a long way to go before you're able to pin on a Trident and become a full-fledged SEAL. And I had a few extra obstacles before I could even entertain such lofty ideas.

As bad luck would have it, I sustained two significant injuries during my first week at Mount Laguna. Neither was orthopedically significant, like the knee injury I'd sustained earlier, so I was convinced I could hide them and press onward. Unfortunately, I was wrong: They posed a threat to my ability to finish BUD/S, just in a different way. I tore a muscle in my pelvic floor and I incurred an inguinal hernia. As a result, my intestines were popping out through a herniation in the abdominal muscle wall in my right groin area, which feels about as bad as it sounds. Walking and running on the uneven mountain terrain with that 70-pound pack strapped to my back was the culprit. I recall the moment it happened: I took a shaky step on terrain that was about two-feet lower than I though—Bang!—pelvic muscle tear and an instant hernia.

I pushed forward and decided not to tell anyone about the injury but my bro Seth G. and my swim buddy Mike. They told me what I already knew: I had to suck it up and forge ahead. But it was terrible. I was in a metric shit ton of pain. It felt like I had a spike in my taint! You know, that area between your asshole and your nut sack. The 800 milligrams of Motrin I ate every six-to-eight hours barely touched the pain. It didn't matter. I kept saying to myself, "You're down to the last four weeks of BUD/S so you can't quit now. Suck it up buttercup and just deal with it!"

So by the time we returned to sea level, I was in dire need of a break. Even if it was just a temporary intermission, I'd be able to reduce the stress on my body. The swims were OK, but the runs and obstacles courses were absolute murder. Gravity was definitely not my friend. Somehow, I blocked out the pain and braced for the next evolution—San Clemente Island, where a 16-mile, 50-pound-ruck-sack hump awaited us. I'm a gear humping fool, so normally I'm at front of the pack on ruck stuff, but this time I was way in the back. Like, way, way, way in the back. So far back that the goon-squad truck of instructors was circling me like a school of Great Whites. You were never far from the Great White sharks when you were out on San Clemente Island—certainly not when you were in the water, and especially not when you were on land.

When we completed the ruck run, Senior Chief Richey (HMCS), pulled me aside. He was a cool instructor—bald-headed, chiseled, and tough as nails.

"We need to talk, Heben," he said.

The moment he said it, I knew this wasn't going to be one of those fun conversations.

"What's your deal, Heben?" Chief said. "Your performance on that run was terrible. You're a strong guy. You've increased your speed and endurance throughout this training. There's no way you should have been in the very back."

Chief Richey was a SEAL medic, a corpsman, so he could tell there was something wrong with me. I decided at that moment to come clean and stop hiding the injury. But I would only do so if I could strike a deal first.

"Chief, can I share something with you, in strict confidence?"

"What do you mean, Heben?"

"Well, I mean, will you promise me that if I tell you why I was so slow you'll at least give me another chance before you send me home from this class? Could you promise me that?"

He eyeballed me for a moment, rubbed his chin in that classic, 'I'm thinking' maneuver and then he slowly said, "OK, Heben. I'll make you that promise."

So I showed Chief Richey my inguinal hernia. As I coughed, my intestine popped out right in the area below my pubic bone.

Chief looked at that and went, "Uh....OK. I see. That is a big problem. How long have you been dealing with that?"

"Since Land Nav," I said through pursed lips. I had taken my last 800-milligram Ibuprofen (Motrin) about seven-hours earlier, after breakfast. "I also have a tear in my pelvic floor and I have a lot of bruising under my balls and down into my upper and inner thighs"

"What the fuck?!" he said with an expression on his face that could best be described as calculated concern. He'd never looked this way before, and it felt like I was watching someone work out a series of complex equations inside of his brain. Not waiting for him to respond, I continued, "Chief, I don't want to leave here. I don't want to be sent back to the Strand. There are about five more weeks of BUD/S, and I know I can make it through."

Snapping back into BUD/S Instructor mode from the SEAL Corpsman/medical mode, he said, "Not with times like that on your ruck runs. I understand you are hurt, but I won't be able to justify your continued presence here if you can't step it up a notch or two. I'm not saying you need to be up near the front where you were before, but just don't get gooned again!"

"I understand. Roger that, Chief!"

Chief Richey nodded. "And, you'll keep a close eye on that injury to ensure it doesn't get worse in other ways?"

"Yes, Chief," I said. I understood fully what he meant: If the intestine popped out and became trapped on the outside of the muscle-wall layer, that would be a serious problem. Your intestines begin to die as the blood supply gets strangulated or totally cut off.

"Chief, if it gets to the point where I can't manually reduce it (push it back in), I'll let you know right away." I said, "Is that a deal?"

"Yes, Heben, that's a deal. I'll let the instructors know that you're nursing a minor injury, so maybe they won't actively fuck with you as much because, obviously, you're less than five-weeks away from graduation and we know you're not a shit bag."

They never gave you any sense of feel good about how you were doing. Until you had a Trident on your chest, it didn't matter how they thought about you in any other way, you were just a turd until you had a Trident!

"Thank you, Chief." I beamed. It felt good to tell someone, outside of my fellow classmates, that I had an issue. This was certainly the right time to do it as well.

"You're welcome, Heben. I needed to know why you did so shitty on that ruck run. Now I know why. I'll get you a big bag of Motrin. Use it wisely. In others words; keep it to yourself!"

Chief Richey ended up giving me a bag with enough 800-milligram Motrin in it to help me get through to the end. After that, I sucked it up and doubled-down on my efforts, while at the same time ensuring that I didn't make my injuries any worse than they already were.

As a result, Land Warfare phase was stellar—it was non-stop explosions, small-unit tactics, ambushes, patrolling, training on how to take out sentries, how to stalk people, and how to conduct rudimentary, close-quarters combat/battle. Grenades and guns of all varieties ruled the day. We even familiarized ourselves with our adversaries' common weapons. This was non-stop commando training at its best and hairy-chested Frogman shit at its finest. We learned pieces and parts of every type of covert, clandestine, and overt warfare you could imagine. We complemented it with swims and a very difficult obstacle course. The O-course on the Island was just as challenging as the one in Coronado, but it was smaller, more intricate and more physically demanding on the upper body. But after so many weeks of training, we were all up to these new challenges. The only thing we couldn't quite adapt to was when the instructors would scream at us to exit the water because a Great White shark had been spotted. We never knew if they were fucking with us or not, but when they got on the bullhorns and said, "Everyone head into shore, the 'Man in the Gray suit' has arrived!" you never saw people making a mad swim toward the shore like that before in your life.

Our training schedule was brutal, but became pretty regular for those four weeks—a workout at 0500 hours, an ocean swim, obstacle course, and then a ruck run across the island. You still have to meet required times for certain activities, even the ones they just make up. For example, you must be able to complete the obstacle course in less than 10 minutes. My entire class did it under seven. They knew by then that we were locked in and ready, but the pressure never subsided.

Those ruck runs were brutal—even with less weight strapped onto our backs than we had in the mountains. Despite being only 45 pounds, instead of 70 pounds, we made up for the weight reduction by having to run faster—because we were doing it on more level ground.

Physical training never gets easier—even as you're closing in on graduation. There's a place out there called Frog Hill, which is this very steep ridgeline about 800-feet above sea level. You have to run up and touch this rock and then run back down. You have to do this in a certain amount of time or else you end up having to get wet and sandy, and then sit outside the chow hall to eat. You can't eat inside when you're wet and sandy. Every day before dinner, you're required to do pull-ups in full kit before being allowed in the chow hall. If you can't meet the required minimums, you're sent to go get wet and sandy. Then, again, you can't eat inside. Keep in mind that the wind whips around 24-hours-a-day, seven-days-a-week, and it's coming at you from all directions. It's so brutal that the Navy uses San Clemente as an aircraft-carrier training facility. You can often see and hear F-18s doing touch-n-goes on the nearby airfield simulating botched or otherwise-less-than-ideal carrier landings.

On the deck of a carrier, the winds can hit you from any direction as well, which made it a perfect training ground. It also conditioned us to hear F-18s overhead—something we'd get used to on our main Close Air Support (CAS) platform. Didn't I tell you that the Navy had it all figured out? So you're always being challenged with this golden carrot dangled in front of you and this stick that's ready to whack you. Everything is about performance during this phase—performance, performance, performance! After all, BUD/S breeds winners.

Something that becomes important during Phase Three are your pull-ups. If you can't do at least 18 pull-ups with your gear on, well, nothing good comes of it. You get geared up with your weapons, ammo and water, all hanging off you from your waist and shoulders, and you're straining to make every rep after 15 count. Suddenly, you are 25-pounds heavier than you were only a week ago back on the Strand. Of course, there are instructors watching and grading every rep. There is no 'kipping' or bent arms allowed, and the chin must completely go over the bar, not just become parallel with it.

"Mount the bar maggot," they say. "Show me 18, you big pussy!"

They know that if you don't make it into the chow hall there is less of a wait and more food for them. This is the first time you are actually permitted to eat with the instructors in the same area at the same time. Before the island, there was a major separation between SEAL and student. It was like the chasm between superstar and stage hand. There was no fraternizing. The fact that they now allowed it, that they encouraged it, was proof that they were preparing you for life in the teams.

The pull-up count increases every day. If you can't do 20 pull-ups by the middle of the second week you're damn near hypothermic from being ordered down to the surf zone day after day, three-times per day. When you finally get the 20 you need, they up the ante so that you then have to give them 25, then 30. Hardcore physical performance is a very big deal for Navy SEALs. Doing 30-plus pull-ups with more than 25 pounds of gear on you is a huge feat. We were so well-conditioned that when we checked into Army jump school, the Army instructors looked at us as if we were combat robots. We pretty much were.

There are other exercises out on the island. You might be cleaning or dealing with your weapons while you're standing inside a barrel of ice water—just to give you the proper motivation. You have to disassemble and reassemble weapons, then show it to an instructor to prove you've done it correctly. One time, it's an M60, the next it's a Sig 226. It's disassemble, re-assemble and function check, but you're doing it while standing in a barrel of ice water up to your stomach. Essentially it's another stress drill to ensure functioning under the rigors of extreme combat environments. Without question one is always wet and sandy, and cold and tired during BUD/S.

In the last days of BUD/S, things get faster and harder and more dangerous. Instead of tackling dive physics you're doing explosives calculations and determining net explosive weight and rate of burn for a time fuse, based on test burns. This might be an exercise where you are doing a test burn on a detonation cord and have to think, "OK, I cut 12 inches of detonation cord. It took two and a half minutes for those 12 inches of cord to burn from one end to the next. Now I need to do a charge that detonates in 15 minutes because when I place it on target I want to make sure I'm far away from a charge of that size before it blows up."

So that's the calculation you have to solve in your head: If it took two and a half minutes to burn 12 inches, how many inches do I need to cut to make it burn for 15 minutes?

And that's the magical thing about SEAL training that most people don't realize: When you leave, you're not only in insanely good physical shape, you're also very sharp mentally and capable of doing the job. Yet, even after graduation, there are still guys who don't fully make it. They reach their SEAL Team and find out they don't have the wherewithal to go into an 8' by 10' room with three other guys with automatic weapons and live ammo and accurately point shoot targets. Once you reach your SEAL Team, there is still about a 2-percent to 5-percent attrition rate because guys still can't pull it all together. It's high speed, low drag, controlled chaos, punctuated by precise timing, and topped off with a solid mixture of balls and brains. It's not for everyone and those who do make it that far, don't always stick around for one reason or another: Burnout being one of them.

One of the great things about being on San Clemente Island is that you're engaged in full-mission profile training. You're tasked with planning an operation, and then executing it. You have to do it in such a way that you accomplish the mission and get back without incurring any casualties. Sometimes, this is strictly a surveillance operation or a sniper reconnaissance mission; sometimes it's planting explosives on a target. Other times, it's planning and conducting an ambush or running a direct-action (DA) mission. In any of these scenarios, there can be multiple elements of the others mixed in. Everything that's set up is designed to feel very real. And there's a lot at stake.

All around, I was probably one of the stronger guys. Having been a college football player and an amateur, but accomplished, bodybuilder and power-lifter, I was able to run a 4.5-second forty-yard dash, had a 41-inch vertical, could bench press over 350 pounds and squat over 600 pounds. I carried a lot of that strength into SEAL training. Sometimes, it was easy to muscle through some of the evolutions—and even some of the injuries—but I also approached everything by being as heads-up and alert as possible, because you had to think through many scenarios, too.

The instructors noticed these combinations in students and they recognized the go-getters, in every phase, from the get go. Like most of the others at this point, I had both the physical strength and mental acuity, so it was only natural that they had to mess with everyone. And because I was a bigger dude, they messed with me a bit more. There is a big difference between getting fucked with because you were liked, and fucked with because you were hated. Thankfully, my instructor run-ins were because of the former and not the latter. Thus, when we were learning how to do close-quarters combat, I was chosen to be one of the entry-team members. As in, the first guy through the door! You see, on the island, we have these kill houses designed to help teach room clearing in urban combat. The tops of the kill houses were open because the instructors walk around above on catwalks and look down at us so they could grade us. They analyzed and assessed us based on how we came into the room: Did we utilize proper entry techniques, did we sweep anyone, did we shoot the targets accurately and appropriately; things like that. Remember, there was very little room for error. Ever.

One day, Warrant Officer Turcotte, a burly badass who stood about 6'3" and weighed in at 245 pounds, decided to put me through the ringer to see how I would perform. To this day I'm not sure whether it was planned to test my limits or simply for his own fucking amusement. As well as the amusement of the other instructors.

Warrant Officer Turcotte was a former college wrestler. He was an MMA-type of guy and knew that I had some MMA experience because

I'd been into that since 1992 as well as being a powerlifter, bodybuilder and college football player. Needless to say, he had this brilliant idea to test on me.

At the time, we were initially learning how to do close-quarters combat. So we had weapons but there wasn't any real ammo in the mags. We had blanks at that time. Warrant Officer Turcotte's plan was this: The first guy through the kill house would find him waiting on the other side. And he was going to physically assault whomever that guy happened to be to see how he handled the surprise.

Well, that first person into the kill house, by design, was me. Yes, it was planned that way.

My boat crew and I were all waiting outside while the instructors got up on the catwalk. You would think they were waiting for the unveiling of King Kong on that stage in New York City. The only differences were that Turcotte was Kong and I was about to be that poor bastard on that log over the canyon. They were all looking down and ready to start watching the scene unfold. They knew what was going to happen, but we didn't. So I blast through the door and go hard to the left. Another guy comes through behind me and goes to the right.

And there's Turcotte, waiting for me.

He grabbed my gun and slammed me up against a wall. I started wrestling my gun away from him as we tangled, as I twisted my M4, it broke free from his grip and I jammed him in the midsection and yanked my rifle back. He pushed it back up into my face, and I took the blow. It hurt like hell, but I didn't skip a beat with any of my movements.

With my foot I tripped him up a bit and with my M4, swung it up, around and down and butt stroked him in the top of his collarbone and then yanked it over to hit him in the side of the face. So I've now hit him three times with my weapon and gained the upper hand in the struggle—things were turning my way. But Turcotte didn't give up that easily. He's a hardcore SEAL and I'm just a lowly BUD/S student—and he's seen hundreds of guys just like me. In a millisecond, he lurched forward and I could not catch his momentum. He was latched onto my weapon with a grip like a vise this time. We ended up in another wrestling match for it, and I wasn't letting go of it. He managed to swing it up under my chin and this impact knocked me backward off my feet. I was seeing stars, but I was coming back for more and in that brief moment of separation, I was able to fire off two blank rounds at him before he clamped down on the M4 again.

Finally, the other instructors chimed-in and put a stop to it.

"All right. All right," they said. "Break it up. Break it up."

And the intense battle for my weapon was over almost as quickly as it had begun.

But those instructors saw everything they wanted to see. They saw me come into the room and face this unexpected situation. And I handled it. I didn't let my attacker take the weapon. I took the first blow and then struck back quickly and decisively. When it turned into a weapon wrestling match I didn't give an inch. I absorbed another bad blow but didn't quit, and managed to get a few rounds off. Had it been a real skirmish it would have probably ended with one of us using deadly force a lot sooner. Instead, they got to see me get smacked in the face with a rifle and me smack a SEAL instructor in the face with a rifle. They had their fun and I proved once again that I deserved to be there. My chin was split open and it felt wonderful when my sweat started to seep into the wound!

Later on that evening, we were all eating dinner in the chow hall and Warrant Officer Turcotte was in there as well. He comes up to me smiling. His ear is bloody, my chin is all cut up and bloody, and he just stands there in front of me, smiling.

Finally he says, "That was fun today, wasn't it, Heben?"

It wasn't all that fun, but I replied, "Hoo-yah, Instructor Turcotte." Internally praying to God that round two wasn't about to begin and that I might also be able to enjoy my current state of being dry! It's those little things that mean so much when your personal comfort and safety have a lot to do with the generosity of a superior being!

Then he headed toward the other instructors and sat down. From where I was sitting I could hear them laughing and talking. They were saying things like, "That was pretty awesome watching you and Heebs go at it tonight. That was cool. Heebs handled it pretty well. He didn't quit and he gave it right back to you ALMOST as good as you gave it to him."

Turcotte added, "Yeah. He was quick. I thought I knocked his ass out. Hell, I may even go to war with him if he ever manages to get a Trident pounded into his chest. I should have hammered that fucker some more!"

That was cool. I was pretty sure they had that conversation loud enough that I'd hear them, which meant they wanted me to know it had been a test, and I had passed it with flying colors. My body didn't think so though. I felt like I got trampled over by a bull in Pamplona, Spain. In many ways, I had.

This is the kind of thing the instructors are looking for—not just during the last phase of BUD/S, but during the entire length of it. They're always testing, testing your leadership, your physical prowess, your survival skills, your resiliency, and your ability to think fast on your feet. These are all tantamount to survival on operations, so they must be ascertained.

It's non-stop. Yet, sometimes, like that day, things are done for their own amusement. But there's always some sort of method to their madness. There's always some 'hidden' assessment they're making while they're doing this. And there is always something useful gained from each evolution.

I understood this pretty early on, so I started playing their game as best I could. I even began show-boating on a couple of the evolutions so that I could be that guy they talked about—in a good way, of course. For example, because I had a pretty good arm I tried to make sure I had the longest, most accurate grenade toss. So I reared back and flung that thing—giving it some serious air. Instructor Adair ended up saying, "Holy Shit! I've never seen anyone throw a grenade that far. Heebs has got an arm on him. If anyone needs to get a grenade out there and they don't have a launcher, he's your answer!"

There are a lot of ways to get booted from BUD/S training: You can fail to meet the physical requirements. You can fail the mental requirements of dive physics and explosives calculations. You can get safety violated at any point along the way. Even if you're passing the tests, if the instructors decide that you're unsafe on more than three occasions, you're done. Safety violations can be odd things. For example, you're lined up in the morning for a two-mile ocean swim. You're focused on passing the swim by meeting the mandatory time and you haven't put much thought into whether your knife is razor sharp. So the instructor decides to check on that. Suddenly, you're violated for an unsharp/unsafe knife: "Your knife's not sharp; that's a safety violation. That's number one, Heebs. Two more violations and you're gone."

But if you even breathe wrong during demolition stuff, you're automatically gone. There is no second or third chance. Plastic explosives have a way of killing a lot of people when they are mishandled.

Unfortunately, the basic fact of the matter is that if the instructors don't like you, if they deem you to be a fucking turd, they will find a way to wash you out of the program before you graduate—no matter how hard you try. They'll find a way to make you go away. It's just a matter of time. So there's no room for gross negligence or any error of any kind. There is room for fun, however, if you learn how to make your experience fun. Hell, my time at BUD/S was actually one of the periods in my life that I truly enjoyed the most!

Just as quickly as it began, Land Warfare training begins to wind down.

At a certain point, the instructors literally stop harassing you. The torment changes—it becomes more geared around having fun at your expense instead of punishing you. They know you don't need that push anymore. Also, things start to feel more professional and less like hazing. You still get the shit kicked out of you, and you're still getting punished physically, but it's no longer because they need to test your morale to become a SEAL. They are merely getting to know you more than they cared to before and the relationship becomes one of *sensei* over sadist.

Your time on the island culminates with one final physical evolution. The Monster Mash! The mash is, no doubt, the sick concoction of a drunk SEAL Instructor. It's a swim, ruck run, shooting range, obstacle course, 2nd ruck run, 2nd swim, put out evolution. It's what we call a real dick dragger. The whole event should not take more than three hours to complete. Well, "it fucking better not!" You are all told. Before you begin this event, you must first consume between one and three habanero peppers, depending on your self-stated exposure to said peppers. Put it this way: I had a hard time chocking down Taco Bell mild sauce. No matter, according to Instructor Adair: "Heben, you're a big dude, eat two!"

That bastard!

Here's what the Mash looks like: The first swim is roughly two miles in the 55- to 60-degree water, followed by an eight-mile ruck run, a gnarly obstacle course, precision shooting with M4s and Sig Sauer 226 pistols, a five-mile ruck run, and finally, another two-mile swim. When you're done, you're actually not finished until you do 50 pull-ups, 50 pushups, and a 50-foot rope climb. My Motrin wore off well before I was done, and the last 20 minutes were akin to what I would imagine it would feel like to be a woman and have a 10-pound baby crowning on you. I finished doing a bastardized version of Lamaze class meets combat breathing.

But I completed it, and Chief Richey was right there at the finish line to check me off and then discretely check me out. And with that, my training on San Clemente Island was over. Anti-climactically, they fly you back to the BUD/S Compound, where you get the rest of the day and night to relax and enjoy being back on the Silver Strand.

But you are not officially done at BUD/S until you complete one last four-mile timed run, followed by a leisurely jog through Balboa Park. Well, you can only imagine how my hernia and muscle tear were both doing after the Monster Mash out on the Island. That night, I got zero sleep. My roommate, Brett Jones, was snoring like a dying freight train and I had shooting pains radiating from my groin. Thankfully, there was no strangulation of my herniated intestines, but I felt like strangling Brett a few times. Brett and I would soon become teammates at SEAL Team Eight and do our first platoon together. Brett would later go on, as I did, to work at Blackwater. He was a tough son of a bitch. So much so that nobody really cared when in 2013 he came out of the closet and announced he was gay. Brett could be counted on when the chips were stacked against us, and that is all that ever mattered. Today, he runs a thriving security business in Huntsville, Alabama, called Riley Security. He is a great dude!

Before you reported to your team for duty, and before you were even considered for awarding of the coveted SEAL Trident, there were two additional boxes that all SEAL candidates had to successfully check: U.S. Army Airborne School (Static Line Jump School) followed by three months of SEAL Tactical Training (STT). Now, the Navy runs its own Jump School (static line and free fall are combined), and STT is now called SQT or SEAL Qualification Training. Whereas before, both events lasted a total of 15 weeks and were held at Fort Benning Georgia and East or West coast training sites (depending upon Team assignment), the entire combined event now lasts 16 weeks and was only held in San Diego. But in March 1998, I was heading to Jump School along with 42 of my soon-to-be SEAL brothers.

We all left San Diego and reported to Fort Benning, the largest U.S. Army base in Georgia and home of the Airborne and Ranger Training Brigades, as well as the 75th Ranger Regiment. The 75th Ranger Regiment is a Tier One component of US Special Operations Command (USSOCOM)/Joint Special Operations Command (JSOC) missions. Needless to say, we would be heading to a pretty kickass base with a long-standing tradition and history of kicking ass!

Over the next three weeks of parachute jump training, they taught us how to jump—day and night—out of airplanes at an altitude of 1,500 feet and not get killed in the process. In truth, the entire three weeks was an exercise in tolerance and frustration. Though it was cool to get the coveted U.S. Army Airborne pewter jump wings, most of us spent the time lamenting about how the entire course could be taught in a week or less. When we all checked into our teams, we were told to remove those "nasty wings" from our chest and promptly sign up for the next static-line jump session in order to get another five jumps in. This would qualify us for the much prettier and much cooler Navy jump wings, which are gold. Chest candy is cool, and nothing is better than a more blinging piece of chest candy, and certainly one that complements the SEAL Trident, if and when it was finally bestowed upon us.

After jump school, I was supposed to roll into STT (Seal Tactical Training). But I reported directly to SEAL Team Eight and had to wait until the next STT class started. Unfortunately, without completion of STT, I still didn't have my trident and wasn't an official SEAL. That meant I couldn't be assigned to a SEAL Platoon to begin a combat workup leading up to a combat deployment. It's one of the big drawbacks to being part of an elite squad—sometimes there aren't enough of us. So while I waited for STT to begin, I hung around the team assisting in training exercises, getting to know my new peer group as well as doing a variety of odd jobs. This last part was interesting, and what it really meant was that I was going to be wearing many hats and gaining credentials in many other fields of expertise: Mop and broom expert, paintbrush expert, red man suit expert/OPFOR or opposing force dude (munition round stopper!), bus driver, and all-around errand boy. I was still an E3 and that rank is called a 'Seaman' in the Navy. Well, as luck would have it, my name rhymes with Seaman, so I was always called to duty as such: "Screamin' Seaman Heben, report to the Master at Arms office!" I think people grabbed the 1MC (team-wide PA system) and announced it just because it was fun to say and to hear! Hell, I thought it was too! Teams-N-Shit, mostly shit!

When I finally was able to class up and go through STT with the rest of the East Coast BUD/S grads, it was pretty damn cool. It's 12 weeks of non-stop, advanced instruction. It's very much a 10-levels-up experience from the rudimentary Frogman skills and the fraternity hazing that we went through at BUD/S. Yes, it's definitely more professional in nature with respect to the demeanor and the attitude of the SEAL instructors and the tactics, techniques and procedures you learn. You are taught advanced weapons, explosives, and combat diving. It's designed to ease us into the community as well as to give us a mid to high level of mastery of craft. You learn to hone the art and skill and embrace the passion and finally feel a bit of the camaraderie that is needed to be the most lethal and capable Commando on the planet: A United States Navy SEAL.

In those days when STT was over, you had to go before a Trident Review Board in order to receive the coveted 'Budweiser' (Trident). This was the team's last chance to fuck with you before you became a legit

UNDAUNTED

SEAL. Once a Trident is awarded and a letter to that effect is sent to the Department of Defense in Washington D.C., it pretty much takes an act of Congress to take it away from you. The review board is truly a caffeine-infused tribunal of the sick and twisted; I say that with all due respect. Basically, you have to go before a panel of eight senior enlisted SEAL and senior SEAL officers, wherein, they ask you rapid-fire questions and have you, concurrently, to demonstrate certain critical skills, all while wearing some ridiculous get up that they want to see you in. In my case, I was told to get into full static-line jump gear, helmet and goggles included, and to enter the room as if I was exiting a plane on a static line insertion. It went a little something like this:

Knock on door and state your name: "Screamin' Seaman Heben reporting before the board!"

"Enter the space," came the cacophonic response from within.

I twisted the handle and jumped through the door maintaining a tight Airborne body position as I did while sounding off, "One thousand, two thousand, three thousand, four thousand!" After which I simulated the jarring effect of a successful canopy opening as well as the grabbing of my front risers. Yes, I did indeed do a full PLF in front of the semicircular table of onlookers. They were rolling in their seats with laughter, hooting and hollering like drunken hyenas bloated and happy after a successful meal on the Serengeti. They had a few candidates in before me, so this made perfect sense. They were on a roll, and I was their next cheap entertainment. Thankfully, I was wearing Pro-Tec head-gear, because, during my PLF, my head plowed into the butt-stock of an M60-E4.

"You're taking enemy fire 500 meters to your Northeast. You better get a gun put together to return fire!"

At my feet was a pile of disassembled weapons comprised of everything from that M-60 to a Sig 226. God help me if I even tried to assemble a Sig 226, for that is not a weapon that you could engage an enemy combatant at 500 meters with. I immediately dropped to the ground and low-crawled over to the first piece of the M-60 I needed, the barrel.

This was good, because it showed them that I was thinking about effective range with respect to return fire and also that I had immediately got low and started to move.

"You better get the fuck on that radio and notify someone of your position! Use the frequency of the dedicated bird: 085.081!"

This was another clue. A dedicated bird is an orbiting satellite and you would use a different radio and frequency in order to use it. Thankfully, I grabbed the right headset and programmed the right frequency.

"Heben, you need to find the best route through the valley in order to reach the nearest Forward Operating Base (FOB) at grid coordinates x1x2x3x3x4, and while you're at it, radio them on VFF frequency 189.99 to give them your approximate ETA. Move! You've got to get the platoon out of this ambush!"

That meant I had to go over to the map and plot our course, bounce over to the other radio, enter the correct frequency, and make comms. Then, "Why the hell have you not been able to put that weapon together? Your platoon does not have a machine gun on line. You're about to get overrun!"

My task load was increasing and about to get worse. I managed to get the M-60 together and 'fire' a few rounds back at the 'enemy', making sure not to point the weapon at the table of heckling, grinning and shouting SEALs.

I managed to see a few smiles among the bunch, as they were thoroughly enjoying the comedy routine I was providing for them.

"Heben, you're gonna get overrun if you don't get that compass bearing up to the point man so he can move the platoon out!"

Back to the map I went to shoot a quick bearing on my Silva Ranger

"West 272 degrees for seven clicks!" I yelled to the imaginary point man

"Heben, you've got eight minutes before your position is overrun. Pull out a Claymore mine and put a time fuse on it. Make sure the Claymore cooks off at seven minutes. Your test burn was one minute and 15-seconds per foot of detonation cord! Do it! What's the length you need? What is it?!"

UNDAUNTED

I felt like the only student in a summer school math class that was being held inside of a bull ring, and I was wearing red with my back to the bull. If I needed a seven-minute burn and one foot of cord burned at one min and 15 seconds, that would mean that I had to cut a length of cord that would be.....6 feet long....I think. The whole exercise was designed to be what we call a mud suck, or an ambush. It was designed so that you would most likely fail. But it was also designed to see how you would react to that kind of pressure. It was designed to see if you would quit. It was designed to see if you had the tenacity and the perseverance to be a SEAL.

In case you are wondering, I did make it through my board and was awarded my Trident. Just call or email Don Shipley and ask him. For a small fee, he will validate my statement. And no, dammit, I do not get a cut of that fee.

CHAPTER 13

> "I AM A GHOST, FOR I AM EVERYWHERE YET NOWHERE. I PLAY CHESS, NOT CHECKERS, THUS I AM ALWAYS TWO MOVES AHEAD OF YOU. I AM BEST FOR I WAS TAUGHT IN THE SEVEREST OF SCHOOLS BY THOSE WHOSE LESSONS WERE LEARNED IN BLOOD AND FURTHER SANCTIFIED BY THE MANY WHO CAME BEFORE THEM.
>
> TRUE TO THIS LINEAGE, I DO NOT TIRE NOR DO I EVER QUIT. THOUGH I MAY FALTER, I DO NOT FAIL. I FEEL NEITHER PAIN NOR ANGUISH AND DISCOMFORT IS MY COMFORT ZONE. RELENTLESS IN MY PURSUIT FOR PERFECTION OF CRAFT, I AM AN EXPERT AT BECOMING AN EXPERT. I ADHERE TO AN ANCIENT SET OF PRINCIPLES: THE WARRIOR CODE. THE SAME OATH THAT I SWORE TO LIVE BY, I WILL GLADLY DIE TO UPHOLD.
>
> YET, THOUGH I ACCEPT DEATH AS A HAZARD OF MY PROFESSION, I REFUSE TO GO PASSIVELY TOWARD THAT END, CHOOSING INSTEAD, TO SEND MANY OF MY ADVERSARIES THERE BEFORE ME.
>
> I AM A UNITED STATES NAVY SEAL.....BE YE WARNED!"
>
> —CHRISTOPHER MARK HEBEN

People ask me often what it's like to be a SEAL. The simple answer is that it's the most perfect physical and mental state of being. You've persevered unimaginable hardships in the toughest military training in the world, had your mettle tested, your character weighed, and you've self-ascended to a whole other plane of existence. You are privy to national secrets, entrusted with the lives of other SEALs, burdened and emboldened by the wants and needs of your nation. Our government places us on the very edges of risk, oftentimes guided only by our moral compasses. One week, we are helping to formulate U.S. foreign policy; the next week we are enforcing it with extreme prejudice. In this way, we are consuming our own product, and that moral compass plays a very big role in the way it is created and consumed.

Beyond this mechanical condition, there is a spiritual component to being a member of the teams. Your internal belief system in what you can accomplish and what you're capable of facing has forever been changed. The continuous realization and activation of this are circuitous testaments to the men, mindset, and amalgamation thereof. During the process of becoming a SEAL, a fundamental transformation takes place inside you. In order to officially become a SEAL, you've got to be willing to stare into the eyes of death and refuse to give an inch as you partake in activities, everyday, that he normally has full reign over.

Earning the Trident, the symbol of the U.S. Navy SEALs, means this and much more to me and to my fellow SEALs. By having that big, heavy, three-pronged golden Budweiser pounded into your chest, it means you've earned entry to a very prestigious club—one where only a select few carry the honor of serving under the tenets of that Warrior's Code. It's not by chance that only a few years after I left active duty in the military, King Neptune's Trident became part of my company's logo and, before long, "INVICTVS" became part of its name.

In Latin, the word *Invictus* (spelled 'INVICTVS' in Latin letters) means unconquered or undefeated. In 1875, Victorian poet, William Ernest Henley, penned his poem *Invictus*, which was published in 1888. I read the poem from time to time, and it truly reminds me of everything being a SEAL really means.

> *Out of the night that covers me,*
> *Black as the pit from pole to pole,*
> *I thank whatever gods may be*
> *For my unconquerable soul.*
>
> *In the fell clutch of circumstance*
> *I have not winced nor cried aloud.*
> *Under the bludgeoning of chance*
> *My head is bloody, but unbowed.*
>
> *Beyond this place of wrath and tears*
> *Looms but the Horror of the shade,*
> *And yet the menace of the years*
> *Find me shall find me unafraid.*

It matters not how strait the gate
How charged with punishments the scroll,
I am the master of my fate,
I am the captain of my soul.

The entire poem is powerful, and the more I read it, the more I realize it's a metaphor for my life. I've come face-to-face with a metric-shit-ton of adversity and strife. From childhood to adulthood, I've been bloodied, and I've always come through with my head up, ready for the next challenge. Unconquered means you can only be so prepared—you must be willing and able to rise up and recover after dealing with things that are beyond your control. The measure of survival and overcoming adversity is how resilient you are—how much volition do you possess for your cause and creed and for the welfare of the guy next to you? It better be a hell of a lot or else you're going to fold when the battle starts and the poop hits the props. I write 'battle' euphemistically, of course, for we all fight many types of battles. No matter what the struggle signifies or the fray you are enmeshed in is for, resilience and perseverance, combined with belief in what you are doing, become the keys to coming out ahead. You can take that shit to the bank.

There's a dirty little secret to surviving any fight, battle or scrap: All it really comes down to is this: How low on the evolutionary chain of man are you willing to descend? If you can be that Neanderthal or Cro-Magnon and pick up that fucking rock and smash a dude in his face until his brains are all over you and the ground, chances are, you're going to win any fight. Now, take that ferocity, that animalistic character that traces its lineage back over 500,000 years, and apply it to the disciplines of a Samurai or a Ninja. Suddenly, you're engaged in deception techniques. You can effectively use edged weapons and firearms. You're capable of undertaking precision shooting, working with explosives and firing anti-tank munitions. You can jump out of a plane, dive into the water, or navigate across dangerous terrain. And you're taking all of those prehistoric gut instincts, the kill or be killed instincts, and running them through a scientifically designed sieve that has been structured and fine-tuned over many decades and centuries of modern and ancient warfare and essentially becoming a very dangerous, very precision crafted and maximally effective killing machine. But one that is very cerebral, disciplined, and controlled.

When you check into BUD/S, every SEAL candidate is told to purchase a copy of Sun Tzu's *Art of War*. You better read it. All war is deception. The enemy of my enemy is my friend. Those are common expressions that mean the same thing in any language, on any continent and in any culture or creed. Everything boils down to the realization and complete understanding that you have to be physically and mentally prepared for war at all times, but also that you can only be so prepared. When the preparation is complete and everything is razor-sharp and honed to perfection, you are still susceptible to chance and Mr. Murphy (Murphy's Law). That's when you have to be a resilient bastard and deal with whatever happens. It's a matter of learning and recognizing that this is the current situation you're faced with and you will overcome it because you believe in yourself, your team, and the mission. You even accept and make friends with the possibility that you are going to get beat and hammered and bruised; you may even get killed.

One of the real secrets of success of the SEAL teams, and other groups in U.S. Special Operations Command, is that after a certain point in time working in a combat zone you willfully accept the fact that you could be killed at any given time, and you're good with that. You say to yourself, "I'm with my dudes and I'm going to go out like a warrior. And if I do go out, I'm going to take at least 100 of the enemy out before me." General George S. Patton said it best:

> *"No bastard ever won a war by dying for his country. He won it by making the other poor dumb bastard die for his country."*

You don't want to die, of course, but you accept the fact that it could happen, and this selflessness makes you a highly effective fighter. In fact, our kill ratio is unparalleled in the history of war.

Part of this ability comes from learning not to pay attention to the life-threatening situation you're faced with every day. It doesn't matter how hard-core you are, if you stop to think about your own mortality when the chips are down, it will paralyze you. It will grip you to the point where you become non-functional and non-effective. And so, you learn how to compartmentalize the dangers and instead, accept them and promptly train and de-focus yourself into disregarding them entirely—no matter the odds. That is the essence of Spec Ops—the belief that you are invincible, that, no matter what, you will remain undaunted!

There's a good lesson in there for people in the business world and those who play professional sports. You're certainly not, literally, thinking about being killed in those professions, but you are learning how to trust the volition of your team to carry your organization through whatever problems you encounter—client issues, financing, product shortfalls, customer service, logistics, personnel problems, performance issues, or anything else that happens. You learn all of these things during BUD/S when you're taught to live and die by your class and, especially, your boat crew. They hammer it into you: If you let your boat crew down that's a very bad thing. If someone isn't counting right, everyone starts over. You learn how to not let your team down. It doesn't matter what you're doing, you need team players or else somebody could get killed. And that's simply something that you can't let happen.

Another thing the Trident signifies is that your mind is in sync with your body. You've spent all this time training your body to become a honed and precision instrument, a deadly weapon, and you must have a strong mind to control it. Like *Yin* and *Yang*, they go hand-in-hand. You can't have a strong mind and weak body, or vice versa. Those who don't have this balance will never make it through BUD/S, and they will probably only make it so far in the real world. To use a very unreal but poignant example, look at Yoda from *Star Wars*. He walked around with a cane, but it was almost like a ruse. When it was time to move out, Yoda was doing flips and bouncing around, defying gravity. He was a very capable and dangerous warrior. Remember what he told Luke Skywalker when he was training him to become a Jedi Knight: "There is no try, only do!" The point is that the mind is the master of the body, and the body does what the brain tells it to do. That's why you often hear people say that BUD/S is 90 percent mental. That is utter bullshit.

UNDAUNTED

Instead, it adheres to my 90/10 rule: BUD/S is 90 percent physical, but if you are lacking that 10 percent mental toughness component, you will never make it.

Obviously, there are exceptions to the 90/10 rule. For instance, if you grow up confined to a wheelchair with something like Cerebral Palsy or another adverse neuromuscular/neuromotor condition, you still can hone a strong mind because it's the reality you were born into. I get it. But if you're in combat or a member of a Special Forces team, you can't be a brainless, out-of-shape, jiggle-bodied shit bag, and expect to do well. SEALs are ultra-fit because we know and accept the fact that when your body is firing on all cylinders, so is your mind. Believe me, the connection is undeniable, which leads me to talk more about the brain.

There's a misconception among some people that Spec Ops dudes are all brawn and no brains. That couldn't be further from the truth. Most of the SEALs and Spec Ops guys I know are higher IQ individuals—mine is 148. That's because in order to do all the things we do, in the microseconds we're forced to do them in, you have to be able to think at a high rate of speed. If you could sit on a plane next to one of us and be able to see what one of us is reading, you'd be surprised. It could be schematic for a complex piece of machinery, a complicated medical journal or an article pertaining to human neurophysiology and how to increase peak performance based on current studies in that field. I know from experience that SEALs are always on the brain uptake, always learning, whether it's how something works so it can be made better, or even a new language in order to be more effective in a theater of war. There's this inherent quest for knowledge that has to be fed all the time. A SEAL buddy of mine read Dostoyevsky or Kurt Vonnegut while we had down time. I didn't agree with his selections, but that's some lofty literature right there. I have been ripped on by other team guys for reading about ascending and descending motor tracks, and disease processes linked to a mutation in SLC18A2 that causes *dysdiadochokinesia*. In fact, I used to tape index cards to the feed tray cover of my M-60E4 so that I could study for my Anatomy & Physiology night school test on the cranial nerves between daytime fire and maneuver drills. In truth, we are eclectic and cerebral commandos. You don't get into our club by being a pussy, and you certainly don't get into it by being a dumb-ass. What is good about this overall state of smartness is the fact that we only need to be told once to do something and it gets done. Furthermore, it gets done in a way that exceeds all expectations. You have to realize that we are constantly pushing ourselves, as well as our superiors, to be better. This is because we all know that there is no room to slack, not from the lowest levels of the chain of command and not at the highest. And as a Task Unit Commander or an Assault Team Leader, with these types of men around you, this is a very good position to be in.

When you consider all these factors, it's easy to see why I placed King Neptune's Trident in my corporate logo—what it alludes to, means everything in the world to me. I have a personal and a corporate explanation for my logo. My explanation, in the corporate sense, is a bit different than my explanation as it relates to my personal life. I'll take a stab at it here with the corporate clarification first: A shield protected by an outer shield, signifying the double protection of a phalanx. 'Protect the Protectors' is one of my corporate slogans and it is manifested by the fact that I have trained many hundreds of police officers and first responders to survive deadly force encounters.

Then I've got the snake or serpent wrapped around a Trident on the face of the shield in the middle. The snake has always been known for deadly force on land while the Trident is, again, associated with a maritime disposition, or in my case, the SEAL Teams.

The teams are where my body of knowledge originates, and they serve as a launch platform for my other endeavors. The logo is a head turner. It gets attention. People look at it and immediately say that it's striking. In fact, I have nailed down more than one job after a conversation was sparked from the sight of the logo on my ball cap. "Hey buddy, what's that symbol all about?" It's unique, in that most Tridents used in other crests and logos are orientated in an upward fashion because Poseidon holds his this way. I chose to aim the prongs of my trident in a downward orientation because it's in a position to strike, ready to go, much like the Trident on our Naval Special Warfare pin (the 'Budweiser' Trident) that is imminently poised to strike laterally. The serpent wrapped around the Trident I use, however, is a bastardization of the rod of Asclepius, which is employed in medicine and has a single snake wrapped around a rod. It's also a tribute to the Gadsden Flag, which was the first flag used in the United States Navy back in 1775, when General George Washington established it as an official branch of the Continental Forces. So, it's a tribute to protection, forward projection and it honors the history of our nation, particularly our nation's Navy. It just does all this in a badass, though somewhat obscure way. Well, obscure enough that it stimulates a conversation. And that is the key to opening a lot of doors.

The personal meaning of my logo is a bit more layered. It's an amalgamation of my life as a U.S. Navy SEAL and as a former medical professional. It is the blending of the Caduceus and Asclepius from medicine with the U.S. Navy SEAL Trident, placed upon a battle-hardened, double-layered shield. It represents a precise and powerful balance, a duality of sorts. It's demonstrative of an offensive and defensive capability, the ability to harm and to heal, the power of both protection and pugilism, the adeptness to defend or to destroy. In essence, it is my personal and modern-day interpretation of *Yin* and *Yang*. I believe in the symbology so much that I actually have it inked into my skin on the inside of my right forearm. Remember: Anything worth doing is worth overdoing!

By the time I reached SEAL Team Eight, I was already a licensed EMT Paramedic with a HN, Hospital man rating. I was HN Heben, a lowly E3. Or, as I mentioned before, 'Screamin' Seaman Heben'!

After STT I was assigned to Foxtrot Platoon, where we began doing a combat work-up. We spent over a year preparing for our combat deployment. Real Frogman shit and much more advanced that STT/SQT. It seems unreal, but there are a few guys that wash out at this point. And that is what pushes the attrition rate to the 90 percent mark. It wasn't easy. Nothing worth anything in life ever is. But it sure is fulfilling. In the paragraphs and pages to follow, I will attempt to give as much of an insider's view into the teams as I can without fear of facing any verbal or physical reprisals from my teammates.

There were about 150 or so of us in SEAL Team Eight at that time. We were broken into nimble but expandable strike platoons—A through H: Alpha, Bravo, Charlie, Delta, Echo, Foxtrot, Golf and Hotel. Each platoon is comprised of 16 men and each SEAL 'Operator' has many different jobs. I was assigned, as most new guys are, to the engineering department. This meant that I was in charge of all of our Zodiac F470 boats, engines, compasses, fuel bladders, oil and gas additives, and everything else we could cram in our assigned connex boxes that would accompany us on our combat deployments. I was responsible for driving and navigating of the Zodiacs as well, so, I needed to know everything there was to know about nautical charts, celestial navigation, and compasses. Along with this duty, I was also a breacher. A breacher is a SEAL who could get into any structure via the implementation of any number of manual tools, power tools or explosives. The skill is amazing in that your knowledge base is on everything from the extremes of explosives to the precision of picking locks. Additionally, I was trained in Special Warfare Tactical Communications and Intelligence to include electronic intelligence, human intelligence, and photographic intelligence/interpretation. Lastly, I was a standby Corpsman, or if you prefer, a Combat Medic. Later in my clandestine career, I would go on to become a Dedicated Defensive Marksman, otherwise known as a sniper.

Each 16-man platoon is comprised of SEALs with similar specialties and skills. You're able to be broken into two, eight-man squads, four-man squads or even two-man sniper/reconnaissance teams. There are at least two, if not four, certified combat medics in each platoon. But that medic can also be a sniper, demolitions expert, or have some other specialized skill. And, everyone is free-fall qualified, meaning they can jump out of a plane at 30,000 feet. While everyone can use explosives and kill a man with a rifle at 700 yards, there are some dudes who want to take it to the next level—they're called breachers and snipers. They're the guys who find a way "in" when there isn't one, or kill a threat way before they have a chance to become one.

I was a breacher extraordinaire. I learned I possessed a very special talent—I was adept at getting through windows, walls, ceilings or doorways with explosives and manual tools. Tools included sledge

UNDAUNTED

hammers, Stihl quicky-saws, entry tools like Haligans or pry-bars or custom-made, super high-RPM Husquevarna chain saws. My favorite was the Broco Torch. The Broco is an oxy-acetylene cutting torch that burns at 10,000-degrees Fahrenheit. That is 6,000-degrees hotter than the melting point of any known steel on the planet, and with it, I could cut through rebar quicker than a hot knife through butter. Hell, you could breach a ship at the waterline. With these devices at my disposal, and a 'Hulk smash' mentality, there were few places I couldn't figure out how to get into, and that made me an extremely valuable member of the team.

SEALs never stop training and we never stop learning. We are sent to schools during our careers in order to learn how to be the best at anything we may encounter in times of war. We are the nation's 911 response team and we must also be prepared for anything our country orders us to do. It's a constant cycle during your time in the teams—you're training for war, you're going to war, you're recovering from war, and you're revisiting or updating the training for war. Then it starts again: You're training for war, you're going to war, and you're recovering from war. It never fucking stops. And I pray to God that it never will. The world should feel the same way, for it is the SEAL Teams and Special Forces that have kept a lot of badness from being unleashed upon the planet. Most of these stories will go untold. Thank God for this as well.

SEAL Team Eight was assigned to Africa, the Middle East, and Europe, along with all the nations and areas in and around the Mediterranean Sea. Where you go within that theater of operations depends on which assault team you're assigned to or which strike team you're on. For those of us in Foxtrot platoon, we had an initial Mediterranean deployment, a strike deployment. We were sent to Africa, and spent a lot of time in Egypt. We also traveled around the Middle East, including Israel. At the same time, our sister platoon, Hotel platoon, was stationed at Unit 2 in Stuttgart, Germany, and handled Europe. They did a lot of work in Bosnia, Kosovo, and places in Eastern Europe that I cannot mention. We could all be attached to different Naval Special Warfare Units, depending on the area nearest the next mission assignment.

For example, on more than one occasion, we were attached to Naval Special Warfare Unit 10 out of Sigonella, Sicily, while at the same time a SEAL Team Three platoon was in Bahrain and attached to Unit 3. There was always a platoon or two to be found in any area of the world where there has been a conflict, an ongoing conflict, or the potential for conflict. In fact, at any given moment there are at least 600 SEALs forward deployed around the globe. This represents roughly one-third of the force.

My platoon was a strike platoon stationed off the USS *Enterprise* (CVN-65), which served as our main aircraft-carrier support and seaward-launch platform. Here we could find hot food, a place to crash, and a place to get Intelligence updates whenever we were onboard—which wasn't often. A SEAL's job is to be forward deployed and have boots on the ground. We use ships, submarines and air assets like normal people use cab rides: They got us from point A to point Z. Many times, we would utilize all of those transportation assets in a single day. SEALs constantly interact with other Navy assets, such as helicopter squadrons and Special Boat Units. We trained with them and built a great rapport. I have worked with Special Boat Unit crews, guys who made it through Hell Week and beyond at BUD/S, but for some act of nature or God, failed to finish. It was always a great joy to work with these dudes because you knew they were badasses and that they would do whatever it took to complete the mission. Having a support mechanism like that is amazing! They are force multipliers, and that means everything in the world to us.

This was definitely an interesting time in my life. While stationed overseas you, laughably, try to maintain a schedule like you would at home—you eat and exercise. When you train you're shooting a metric-ass-ton of rounds, jumping out of planes on land or very near the F470 Zodiac boats you pushed out of the C-130s at 13,500-feet above the water. You try to set up training schedules to match what you did back in the U.S. at the team's compound. The difference is that, on occasion, you're incorporating other teams, or other NATO countries' special forces into that training with you. One prime example is a night training mission we did with Red Squadron from Naval Special Warfare

UNDAUNTED

Development Group (DEVGRU). Red Squadron had three high-speed boats (HSBs) loaded onto special aircraft capable of delivering them anywhere in the world at any time. The HSBs are made exclusively for DEVGRU and feature massive engines with laser-etched titanium screws (propellers). These boats can easily reach speed of up to 75 knots with or without a full complement of men and equipment onboard. This three-boat air insertion by Red Squadron would be done after nightfall over the eastern Mediterranean Sea. The mission was a simulated takedown of a large vessel said to be carrying weapons of mass destruction. Few people realize this, but SEALs from DEVGRU are extensively trained in all matters pertaining to nuclear weapons deployment and disarmament. They, along with highly trained, embedded, Navy Explosive Ordinance Disposal (EOD) members, are capable of dealing with any weapon of that nature, anywhere and at any time. Yes, even underwater.

SEAL Team Eight's Foxtrot Platoon, my platoon, was to augment DEVGRU by further securing the ship after the initial VBSS takedown was initiated. We were tasked with searching the vessel for weapons of mass destruction and other devices capable of being used to cause harm to U.S. assets and interests. The whole training mission went off without a hitch. The HSBs splashed down without injury and Red Squadron splashed down without injury as well, fired up the HSBs and transited until they were alongside the massive tanker. Utilizing precise yet risky techniques, they were able to transfer themselves from the HSBs onto the deck of the tanker, at which time they dynamically progressed to the bridge and stopped the tanker dead in its tracks. We followed, boarding via helicopter fast-rope insertion, then further secured the ship as planned. We assisted in the search for weapons and crew members. By 0300 hours, we were all back on board the USS *Enterprise* and enjoying a hot meal in the forward galley.

The USS *Enterprise* kept the galley open just for us that night, and we all appreciated it very much. The entire mission was successful, and further punctuated by the fact that I got to actually work as a SEAL with three of my former BUD/S instructors who were Red Squadron Assaulters. That's why BUD/S instructors make a pact to not allow any shit bags to graduate—because they, more often than not, will return to the teams to work, with dudes they trained!

One bizarre thing happened worth noting. The Red Squadron guys headed to their berthing area and Foxtrot Platoon was assigned the ancillary duty of watching all of their gear, which was laid out on the *Enterprise* in Hangar Bay Three. Being the youngest and lowest-ranking SEAL, I was assigned with the first four-hour watch duty. As luck would have it, I was about two-hours deep into my shift when a fleet (ship-assigned) Lt. Commander happened to make his way under the yellow caution tape and over to my position.

I was in the middle of all the wet gear and shaking the water out of yet of another pair of night-vision optic devices (goggles or NODs).

"Excuse me, Petty Officer!" The Lt. Commander exclaimed, with a booming voice, as he walked toward me with a certain swagger that only a fleet officer could have after being on a boat for his whole career. Picture the voice of the Skipper from *Gilligan's Island* mixed with the look of Ernest Borgnine from *McHale's Navy*. Yep, you got it, and he was headed my way. This was going to be interesting.

"Yessir! How can I be of assistance to you?" I replied with equal vigor at this 0400 hour.

"You need to tell your guys that this is *verboten* around here!" he said, as he drew a crushed Pepsi can up from his side like some Wild West gunslinger getting ready to fill me full of aluminum. "This is FOD and it will not be tolerated!"

His tone took on the tone of a 3rd-grade teacher lecturing his students when they'd done something he perceived as wrong.

Not in any mood to debate the origins of the can with this guy, and not wanting to be detained from doing what I was supposed to be doing at that moment, I decided to answer his question with a statement, followed by a question, and I needed to do it in such a way that he would know I was not to be trifled with. Using my best German accent, I calmly responded, *"Ja weiß ich dass es verboten!"* Followed immediately with: *"Sind Sie unsere Männer sind schuldig sicher?"* (Translation: "Yes, I know that is forbidden! Are you sure our men are guilty?")

The look on his face was one of shock and awe, followed by confusion. It was as if he was trying to read a street sign in Chinese while looking at a map in Japanese and listening to a radio station playing Tagalog. It was painfully clear that he had no clue what I had just said to him. He was struggling for some type of intelligent response. An officer panics when a low-to-middle ranking enlisted man says something indicative of a higher order of thinking. It goes against all they are taught in knife-and-fork school.

Not giving him a chance to even formulate a response in English, and wanting to push the ball over the goal line, I stated, "I'm sorry, sir, you used the German word *verboten* so I assumed you were fluent in that language. We can continue in English from now on."

As the color continued to drain from his face, I went on: "Sir, are you a SEAL?"

To which he responded, "No. No I am not."

Aha! This was fourth-and-goal for me, and I was going to go with the quarterback-keeper play.

"Sir, I am going to ask you to please return to the other side of this cordoned-off area. There is more than $1 million in equipment spread out here, and I'd hate to have you implicated if anything came up missing or became damaged as a result of your unauthorized presence here. Please do not confuse your rank with my authority."

With that, he did an about-face and placed himself on the other side of the caution tape. After doing so, and needing to get in one last word, he said, "Petty Officer, I will be reporting this incident to the Command Master Chief immediately."

"As you wish sir! Have a wonderful day, too!"

Apparently I, too, needed to get in the last word. That was not the first time I had an encounter like that, and it was not the last. I never did hear anything about it from either of my lieutenants, the Assistant Task Unit Commander 'DB' (with whom I graduated BUD/S), or the Task Unit Commander. We were all SEALs, and we have a wonderful habit of sticking together and having one another's backs. It's something about the whole BUD/S bonding experience, followed by combat zone camping trips, that does this to an already tightly woven group of Alpha males. Everyone has that *Three Musketeers* mentality: "All for one and one for all." Even when a SEAL does something really stupid he is still publicly backed up. But boy, does he get his ass beat behind closed doors at the team compound.

But I digress. Along with these inter-Team missions, there are also massive pre-planned exercises that the U.S. coordinates with other countries, like Operation Bright Star. Operation Bright Star is held every two years, and it's a series of Joint Training Field Exercises (JTFXs) led, predominantly, by American and Egyptian forces. The entire event takes place in and around Egypt and in Egyptian coastal waters where many allied countries get together and perform this cooperative training.

While I was in Foxtrot platoon, we were involved in the latter part of the largest Bright Star exercise in history. It included 11 nations and 70,000 military personnel—it was pretty amazing. The U.S. invited another 33 nations to observe and monitor the exercise. That year's exercise scenario was focused on a fictional hostile nation, which they called *Orangeland*.

The training went like this: Orangeland invaded Egypt and tried to take control of the Nile River. Our job, as an 11-nation coalition—was to work together and practice fighting in the air, on the land, and in the sea—trying to defend the Nile and expel Orangeland from Egypt. We even had a full-fledged amphibious assault that involved six nations.

When you're working with these other countries it makes them feel special about being part of NATO. Even when it's just the day-to-day training, instead of large-scale operations like Operation Bright Star, you're still teaching your allies things you learned when you went through BUDS, mostly rudimentary exercises. At the same time, you're gathering intelligence and data—info about what they're doing, what areas they go to, what their equipment looks like. And you're not giving away much in return. In fact, we seldom even pull out our real kit. Rather, just the bare minimum to go along with the back-to-BUD/S tactics, techniques and procedures. It's sort of like a soft porn equivalent of an intelligence gathering exercise, but with allies instead of enemies, and with Allied commandos instead of adult film stars. It was during Brightstar that I learned how to effectively say the word

UNDAUNTED

"SHARK" in Arabic. It didn't help that I kept yelling it one night at 0330 hours off the coast of Egypt as we were swimming toward one of the islands there during a night over-the-beach (OTB) insertion mission. The Egyptian Frogmen weren't too pleased, but they immediately started to swim faster. And that was what I was hoping for. There is always a way to make things happen!

During my time stationed overseas, we worked with one foreign group after another. It might be the Israelis one month, and then two- or three-months later we'd work with their polar opposites, the Egyptians. While we're working with them, we're also paying attention and finding out what's going on inside of their forces and in their country in general. There is no substitute for first-hand information from the man or woman on the ground. We gave a lot of that, human intelligence (HUMINT), up during the Clinton years, and we paid a heavy price for it in the form of 9/11.

Our deployments involved a lot of moving around. We'd be stationed in Turkey for a month, Egypt for three weeks, then Israel for a month-and-a-half and then Italy and Sicily for a few weeks. Then on a carrier of submarine or PC boat for a few days in between. We also spent time in Bahrain and in Kuwait at camps Doha and Rhino. Our typical deployments out-of-country were for a minimum of six months, sometimes even seven or eight months. And during that time we'd often train these host nations in what we called foreign internal defense (FID) missions. The FID missions were also set up many months in advance. The FIDs in Israel were very interesting because the potential always existed for them to turn into real-world mission just over the next hill in the Beqaa Valley in Lebanon or around the next turn in the West Bank or Gaza.

When you weren't working with foreign troops or engaged in FID missions, you'd participate in personal training exercises to pass the time—jumping out of planes, hopping onto boats, anything and everything to do with being a Naval commando in order to keep your skill sets sharpened. Skills like precision shooting, closed-circuit combat diving and HALO jumping are perishable skills, in that, if you do not do them with relative frequency, they begin to diminish—not something you want to happen to the nation's 911 response teams. So we find ways to employ our craft. You just cannot sit around and twiddle your thumbs on an aircraft carrier—well, you can but that hurts your chances of being constantly ready. When you're not using your gear, you're maintaining your gear and maintaining your state of supreme physical fitness. This also means that you need access to proper nutrition as well as access to fitness equipment, no matter how rudimentary. You're always training for war; and you're always engaged in some sort of combat prep activity. If not, you are planning for it. A warrior never truly sleeps, he just lies dormant until which time he is activated. The regular Navy guys say that SEAL stands for: Sleep, Eat, and Lift. This is, fortunately, very true. We don't have jobs on any Navy vessel. That is, other than to shit, shower, and obtain sustenance. And weight lifting is certainly a part of those pursuits. Additionally, we also consume a steady diet of pornography—and for the single men…actual women—when the conditions are right. Conditions are usually always right, and even in a war zone, sex finds a way.

Despite the different locales and exposure to languages and cultures and customs, the days can still become quite monotonous. Sometimes, it felt like I was stuck in the movie *Groundhog Day*. Every now and then, however, we would get an actual and planned reprieve. We would get on an helicopter, go land on an aircraft carrier in port somewhere, and hop on a ferry that would take us to shore so we could spend two or three days decompressing in and around any number of small towns anywhere in that part of the world. One of my favorites was Dubrovnik, Croatia. Here, we had a couple days of liberty and it was amazing to see both the beauty and bullet wounds that place offered. Dingač Wine was one of my favorites. For around $16, you could consume one of the best red wines on the Pelješac Peninsula in the Dalmatian region of Croatia. For a few dollars more, you could consume it while eating at the best restaurants.

It is said that 85 percent of all communication is non-verbal, and I witnessed many of my fellow SEALs conversing quite nicely with members of the opposite sex the world over. You do have to give the Navy credit, however, as they made every possible effort to give us a break in the grind of our operational schedule. But think about it, anytime you're shooting guns, jumping on and off of helicopters and riding on boats, and getting paid well for it all, it's pretty damn cool. I was getting paid to do what less than 1 percent of Americans can only dream about being able to do, so it was pretty damn inspiring!

One of the amazing things about being a member of the most select group of men on the planet, is that to own a Trident means that you're part of a very exclusive fraternity. The people you train with in BUD/S—and meet during active duty—more often than not become your extended family—even the instructors who put you through Hell during your SEAL training become steadfast and long-standing brothers.

Case in point: About a year-and-a-half after I graduated from BUD/S, my platoon rolled into Bahrain for a Maritime Interdiction Operation (MIO) surge period. We were assigned to Naval Special Warfare Unit 3. The U.S. and the British navies were conducting thousands of real MIOs every year in order to enforce embargoes, intercept contraband, prevent drug and human smuggling, and to fight piracy. They're very cool initiatives. We use eight-man Visit, Board, Search and Seizure (VBSS) teams and rigid-hull inflatable boats. Think about when you see Special Forces units approach and board ships in documentaries and that's pretty much what a MIO is in real life.

So we rolled into Bahrain for this MIO surge and I ran into Chief Richey, who had been super cool to me on San Clemente Island during Third Phase of BUD/S. It was pretty surreal but pretty damn awesome to see him. It was the first time I'd seen him since BUD/S, and he was the platoon chief for SEAL Team Three, who we were there to relieve. I saw his chrome dome from across the warehouse space where we all stored our maritime assault gear. I slowly, but confidently, walked up to him and extended my hand.

"Hey, Chief, how ya' doin'?" I asked.

He smiled. The interaction we'd had on the island back in training had reached legendary proportions among the SEAL instructor cadre. My guts were hanging out and I never quit. I never wanted to quit. But he didn't even bring it up. "Chris, I'm great. And it's good to see you working."

"Thanks Chief. I've been waiting for this moment my whole life. I am ready to go to work!" I replied with a look of utter sincerity and humility.

It was as if I was thanking the doctor that delivered me alive through my mother's birth canal when all the other doctors would have wanted to abort me. It meant that much to me. In fact, this is the first time I have ever mentioned it. I don't feel any lighter, just a bit less of a badass and more of a sentimental dude I guess. But really, that was it. I was now a member of the team—a brother SEAL—and nothing more needed to be said. That was very, very cool. Being a SEAL is being part of a multi-cellular, living, breathing and dynamic organism. It's truly a solid group of men working together in combat situations to achieve a common goal. That's what the Trident is all about.

CHAPTER 14

> "I PATROLLED WITH THESE MEN, BLED WITH THESE MEN, BROKE BREAD WITH THEM, TRAINED THEM AND LEARNED FROM THEM. AS STALWART BROTHERS, UNITED FOR A COMMON CAUSE, WE WERE ABLE TO ACCOMPLISH GREAT THINGS. WHEN IT COMES TO ITS INHABITANTS, I DON'T SEE THE WORLD IN SKIN TONES. RATHER, I VIEW IT THROUGH LENSES FACTUALLY FILTERED BY MERIT AND MAGNANIMITY OR BY MALICE AND MALFEASANCE. IT IS ONLY THROUGH THESE VERY SAME EYEPIECES, THAT MY JUDGMENTS ARE BASED AND, LIKEWISE, LEVIED IN KIND."
>
> —CHRISTOPHER MARK HEBEN

From 1998 to August 2001, I traveled the nation and the world as a U.S. Navy SEAL. We trained all over the U.S., in many different foreign countries, and on many different naval and military bases. We were primarily land-based, but were assigned to ships, subs, and other surface vessels as needed. SEALs use Navy assets like people use taxi cabs—a pretty routine day on a combat deployment may include going from HMMWV (Humvee) to helicopter to ship to submarine, and back again. We were always near or on foreign waters, and always engaged in exercises and operations with soldiers and sailors from different allied nations. Somewhere along the line, and in that frenetic process, my transformation into a finely-tuned and high-octane combat-capable machine was completed. Everything we did—24 hours a day, seven days a week—stressed our bodies and our minds, tested our patience, and strengthened our resolve.

SEALs are authorized by our nation to be problem solvers, diplomats, and warriors. When the first two options run dry, you can always count on us to close the deal by utilizing the third option. It was no surprise to us that, not too long into our overseas deployment, my Strike Platoon from SEAL Team Eight was told to roll into Naval Special

Warfare Unit 3 in Bahrain in order to relieve a SEAL Team Three platoon. They were busy, and as soon as we got there, we immediately took over hostile ship takedowns. There was no break in the action and no shortage of targets to address.

We were tasked with pouncing on foreign tankers that were coming out of one of the major waterways in Southern Iraq—the Khawr Abd Allah (KAA), after they left the port of Umm Qasr. We relied heavily on human intelligence (HUMINT) in the port and along the transit down into the Northern Arabian Gulf. Additionally, we used satellite imagery and imagery gained from commercial and military flyovers. Saddam Hussein was always trying to smuggle oil out of Iraq underneath the United Nations Security Council embargo that was levied on him after the Gulf War. It was all a part of the sanctions placed upon his regime that comprised a damn near complete financial and trade embargo. The sanctions were passed on August 6, 1990, just four days after Iraq's invasion of Kuwait, and remained in effect until we routed his ass again in May 2003.

The original purpose of the sanctions was to force Iraq to withdraw from Kuwait, pay reparations to the Kuwaiti people, and to destroy or turn over weapons of mass destruction. Our mission was to enforce the U.N.-backed oil embargo. Iraq was prohibited under the sanctions from selling oil, except when the U.S.-led United Nations coalition said they could, where we said they could, and to whom we said they could. The Iraqis, not surprisingly, weren't having any of that. As a result, we were engaged in a constant game of cat-and-mouse with Iraqi oil tankers, Pakistani oil tankers, Russian oil tankers. You name it, everyone wanted to take Saddam's oil off his hands, including us!

My strike team stalked the North Arabian Gulf (NAG) for more than a month. We pored over the Intel during the day as it pertained to the target for that night, as well as identify possible targets for upcoming missions. We prosecuted most of the missions at night. We dynamically boarded the tankers, rushed to the bridge to stop them dead in the water, secured the crews and searched the ships, and then turned them over to the British Royal Marines and U.S. Coast Guard to mop up.

We were real busy, so much so that oftentimes we'd hit two or three tankers in the course of a single night. These were real-world MIOs, not the exercises we'd been practicing for months during our pre-deployment combat work-up. We utilized all of the Vessel Board Search and Seizure (VBSS) tactics we had perfected in training, and carried them out flawlessly. We did so knowing that at any given time the consequences could become dire. When you're out there on the water in foreign territory and international waters, it's a completely different world. You're on the hook as the first—and last—line of defense from the minute the sun goes down until it comes back up again in the early morning.

During these operations we relied on helicopter-mounted Forward-Looking Infra-Red (FLIR) radar with over-the-horizon (OTH) capabilities—they were our eyes and ears. Along with a full helicopter squadron from HS5, we had a fleet of 11M Rigid Hull Inflatable Boats (RHIBS) and a 185-foot Coastal Patrol (PC) boat on station as well. The 11-meter RHIBs were manned by many guys that, for one reason or another, failed to make it through BUD/S. A lot of these same dudes were post-Hell Week when they left BUD/S training, so we knew that they were tough as nails. In fact, one of my favorite crews was made up of guys that, in my opinion, should have been SEALs—they were that good.

We went into our missions knowing we had a metric shit ton of amazing assets and support, but it wasn't always enough—we knew some ships would make it through our gauntlet. It's a big-ass area of water, and the Iraqis were determined to move their ships out and evade us. They were relentless—but so were we. They had come to the conclusion that if they sent out enough ships, a few would get through. It was simple math and the law of averages was always in play.

But once our fellow SEALs and CIA operatives—all functioning in clandestine roles—identified a ship as a target that was carrying oil or weapons, nothing was going to keep us from stopping it dead in its tracks. We waited until it hit international waters and then pounced. Everything had to be precise.

Ship hits usually went down like this: We're chilling on a loitering PC boat, waiting on a call that could come at any time. Often, it comes after midnight, 1 a.m. to 2 a.m., relaying message traffic that one of the verified tankers has been sighted entering the NAG. They provide coordinates, and we move out. As we go, everyone gets fully kitted up and ready to go, including all load-bearing gear and special tools. It's not that easy to swiftly kit up and roll out, especially on a boat that's hauling ass. Sometimes, we stay in operational gear for days at a time. Hell, I've gone without a shower for more than three weeks and slept in full gear for numerous days. It often works better that way.

In 20 to 30 minutes, we leap onto one of the smaller, 11-meter (33-foot long) RHIBs and take off from the PC, speeding swiftly through the dark water in the dark of night toward God-knows-what awaiting you on that ship. Needless to say, in all this turmoil and expediency, we still need to be able to talk with one another and the higher-ups back on the PC. So along with our inter-squad communications gear, we also wear a communications device that ties us back to the Tactical Operations Center (TOC). We're heavily armed—with H&K MP5s; small, fully automatic machine pistols, as well as H&K Mk23 .45 caliber semi-automatic pistols. On occasion, we suppressed them all in order to avoid the possibility of compromising our on-board locations in the event of close-quarters gun play in the bowels of the ships.

Beyond the firearms, we carried flash-bang grenades, night-vision optic devices, strobes, and yes, zip ties—there were always zip ties! Everyone is loaded for bear and we are all pretty much ready for whatever might happen. Anything we don't plan for, we adapt to, and immediately overcome. No, we promptly crush that shit!

To pave the way, you have a guy like me—a highly trained breacher. I was a problem solver, an entry man. So in addition to carrying all that kickass regular combat gear, I bring the special sauce. Yep, I get to haul around an oxy-acetylene torch (a BROCO Torch). Sometimes, it might be a Stihl quickie saw on anabolic steroids. Interestingly enough, I've even carried a similarly amped-up chainsaw. Several manufacturers create these hyper-robust and insanely high-functioning super machines designed to work under the most extreme conditions and operate at

RPMs that make a NASCAR engine seem like a hamster wheel. Of course, every one of these devices is either painted flat black or a mixture of flat black and some type of effective camouflage. For the MIO gigs, my tools were all black. I looked like some tactical version of that *Texas Chainsaw Massacre* dude, 'Leatherface', or better yet, some demented road-rager from a *Mad Max* movie. You get the picture: It would be horrifying to see me coming at you for any reason, let alone to stop you from doing what you were currently doing.

All this shit could often be found strapped to my back because my job was to get us into the bridge if it was locked down, welded or padlocked shut. As I said before, nothing stands in our way.

Why would some of these ships be padlocked or welded shut? Simple: It wasn't a secret that we were out there, waiting in the water. The Iraqis knew it and recognized that we would do whatever it took to try to stop them dead in the water, so they did whatever they could to prevent us from accessing the bridge. Neither of us cared. Everyone was willing to play this deadly cat-and-mouse game. The Iraqis were intent on getting their tankers past us and into Iranian coastal waters, then down through the Strait of Hormuz and into Pakistan's coastal waters. They wanted to off-load oil for their strategic partners and swap it for weapons, money, or both. If they could delay us in stopping the tanker long enough—even if we were onboard—and reach Iranian coastal waters, we would be forced to leave the ship. Why? Because the Iranians were complicit. They would arrange to have gun boats at the edge of their waters to escort the tankers in, down through the Straits, and off to Pakistan. Sure, we could have stopped them...but we didn't want to start a war with Iran. Saddam's goal was singular: Sell embargoed oil so that he could acquire money and weapons. Ours was just as clear: Stop him at any cost and maintain the embargo. Sounds fun, doesn't it?

After we left our PC, we zipped through the water on the RHIBs and then pull up alongside the large tanker. In high or rough seas and at night, the tanker crew would rarely see or detect us, so more often than not we had the element of surprise on our side. If we were compromised visually, we could only hope we were shot at so we could return fire and promptly take out any watchmen on duty.

Make no mistake, boarding the tankers was challenging—not like you see on TV or in video games. Anything could happen at any time. We used high-tensile strength, fiberglass extension poles with attached caving ladders that were six-inches wide and made of flexible steel cable with aluminum rungs laid with non-skid tape.

We used the poles to attach the caving ladders to the bigger boat, then used ladders to climb aboard the ship. Picture this crazy scene, at night and in near pitch black darkness: You're on a moving boat, pulling up alongside a massive moving boat, trying to become attached to a moving boat, via a ladder that's unrolled at the end of a telescoping hook. You hope to hook this ladder onto a rail on the side of ship and then pull the pole away, leaving only the attached ladder with which to climb from one ship to another—in the dead of night, and with very cool, very deadly, very expensive, and very heavy gear. And people wonder why you can't graduate BUD/S unless you can do 30 pull-ups with 30-plus pounds of gear on.

Complicating things is the fact that although the sea can be rocky, the wake caused by the massive tanker makes it even worse. Both vessels are moving at top speed, pitching, yawing and rolling back and forth. You are at great risk of falling off the ladder if you don't pay attention—which isn't too bad unless you then fall between the two boats. If that happens, you will be crushed to death and drown. Or, you might fall, get sucked under one of the boats, and be chopped up in the propellers. The people on the opposing boats are also armed to the teeth, and they have no hesitation when it comes to shooting us. So you might also be shot at during the process—despite the fact that we have helicopter snipers on either side of the boat to cover our movements. We usually do this on three hours of sleep, so as you might now realize there are a lot of inherent risks, and planned, as well as unforeseen, factors at work. All in all, this is truly dangerous work—not for the faint of heart or weak of mind or body.

Once we successfully boarded a boat, our task really just began. We had to reach the bridge, get inside, and then deal with the captain and crew. It was important to dominate every inch of the vessel we transited across and into. If not, we would leave ourselves open to an attack. Sometimes, we would find all types of weapons on crew members or in their rooms—from pistols to rifles, and everything in between. I think they were just as afraid of one another as they were of pirates and SEALs—especially SEALs who acted like pirates. Our mission was crystal clear: Get to the bridge as fast as possible and stop the ship as fast as possible. You never wanted it to reach Iranian coastal waters or the entire situation would turn real hostile real quick: The last thing you wanted to deal with was a group of Iranian gun boats who wanted to know what the U.S. Navy was doing in their sovereign coastal waters. This is known as an 'International Incident' and clearly not very good. Inevitably, this whole MIO/VBSS operation becomes a very fascinating cat-and-mouse game, and one where you're working against time. Even though you were in a hostile region, you still didn't want to get into firefights—you don't want to get shot or be forced to shoot anyone if you don't have to. But if you do, you are prepared to be the best at it—the fastest and most accurate. If they shoot first, they die first. It's that simple.

All these factors play out while you're laser-focused on the mission. It requires you to approach the situation with the perfect mixture of stealth, speed and violence of action—you use everything they've taught you during BUD/S, STT and during a combat workup as a Trident-wearing SEAL. It's a fact that you're relentlessly honing the tip of the spear toward perfection, even after you've been assigned to a SEAL platoon. I would make the argument that the training only gets harder and more demanding from a technical and precision standpoint when you become a SEAL. Once you have that triple-pronged Trident pounded into your chest, the bar of your life, moving forward, is perpetually set pretty damn high!

Luckily, I never got shot at during the MIOs I participated in, but the threat was always there. I did, however, have to use that BROCO PC/TACMOD1 Exothermic cutting torch to sear our way into the bridges of ships—and I was very, very good at that. No matter what you think you know about the inherent dangers of compressed oxygen set aflame, an exothermic cutting torch is like a bomb waiting to go off on your back. All it would have taken was for a ricocheted bullet to penetrate the tank and I would have exploded like a flame-thrower dude in those old black-and-white film clips from Iwo Jima! After a while, we got smart and developed a ballistic wrap to go around the oxygen tank. This only reassured me a little bit, but it made the dudes around me feel a whole lot better because they knew, before, that if I was going up I would probably be cooking a few of them up with me. Such is life in the SEAL Teams: You live and die as a close-knit group of warriors, and you are never happier and more exhilarated than when you are with them and staring death in the face and, collectively, all flipping it the bird.

One particular time, when we boarded a ship in the Northern Arabian Gulf, shit went south pretty fast. The crew spotted us as we were boarding and the captain immediately went to full engines in order to make Iranian coastal waters. We could feel the ship lurch and roll as it strained under the new torsion of the screws that began grinding through the water like a Vitamix with a nitrous button! To make matters worse, the crew already had a feeling we were going to hit them because their ship was so heavily laden with oil that it set very low in the water—so low, in fact, that we had to step DOWN onto its weather deck from the RHIB. Normally, the height to this level from the water line is around 15-feet up!

While this made it easy for us to un-ass the RHIB, it made for a very slippery topside. It was perilous footing in the mix of saltwater and crude oil that was all over the deck. They must have had an all-hands-on-deck evolution with multiple crews dumping crude into the tanks below. The loading hoses were swinging everywhere and these heavy-gauge hoses felt like lead pipes when they swung against you. They looked like octopus tentacles belonging to some demented sea creature that was trying to swallow us and the ship. We did the best we could to avoid further bone-jarring impacts from the damn things as we nearly sprinted toward the bridge. Sprinting or not, we hauled ass, moving as fast as we could with our kit on. I figured I could use a good chiropractic adjustment after this was over.

It was a pretty surreal scene. In hindsight, these hoses were, no doubt, left astray and unfettered by design in order to pummel anyone who tried to board the vessel.

Of course, the bridge hatches were welded shut—not padlocked. I went to fire up my BROCO and it wouldn't light. I yelled to my teammate DK to check the valve on top of the tank. As it turned out, the knob was nearly turned off. The only thing we can figure out was that the topside transfer hoses we had to weave and bob through must have avoided my head but brushed, repeatedly, against the valve knob, turning it nearly shut.

While DK addressed that issue, I maintained security.

I scanned the deck of the ship and the portholes leading in and out of the ship, my MP5 at the low ready. As SEALs we excel at covering one another in a dynamic combat situation. We embrace the concept of the Spartan shield phalanx, not only in our professional lives, but also in our personal lives. DK managed to get the valve back on and since I had eyes on the combat environment, and he no longer did, he fired up the torch and burned at the door. Gaining access, we then directed our energies toward becoming the assault team charging into the bridge.

As Murphy's Law dictates, the torch had set the inner walls of the bridge on fire. Not only did we have to contend with a hostile crew within, but we also had to address the fire before it got out of hand. All the while, the captain was steering the ship toward the closest sand bar in an attempt to ground the vessel. A grounded ship isn't easily moved. If the captain couldn't avoid the SEAL brotherhood, he would embrace the sandbar.

This was about as close to a full-fledged and chaotic combat situation as we had faced during the entire MIO surge. In an effort to gain the upper hand and deal out some dominating force, we split the assault team in thirds. Some of us subdued the crew, others dealt with the fire, and the last group headed to the engine room to deal with the crew and take control of the ship.

During the initial bridge breach, the captain spun around on me as I entered the space. It was dimly lit, despite the fire that was spreading through the paneling on the wall behind me. As he turned, I was unsure

UNDAUNTED

what he had in his hand. As SEALs we are taught to look at hands and faces in order to ascertain intent and the available or potential equipment possessed by that person that can be used to deliver any mal-intent. It was too dark and shadowy to see what was in his hands, but they were both clasped around a metal object and his face looked menacing.

Erring on the side of caution—and not wanting to violate our Rules of Engagement (ROE)—I chose to muzzle strike him in the face, in the area between his nose and mouth. This is called the philtrum, and any impact or pressure to this area hurts like Hell. We learned it in our 'hand-to-gland' classes as well as Close Quarters Defense (CQD) training.

The captain immediately fell to the floor like a marionette with the strings cut. I pounced on him and pinned his arms behind his back with full force from one knee as I zip-tied his wrists and transferred the weight of my other knee to the back of his neck.

This near identical process was carried out by DK, CT and Brett Jones as they secured the other crew members. HR looked for more work as he maintained a watch position while we did our thing, never worrying about anyone coming through the door behind us because of our starboard and port side snipers, SN and RM, who were perched in the doorways of the hovering HH60H Seahawks. They had suppressed SR25s ready to rain death down on any non-SEAL they saw as a potential threat to our pirate posse. That was the divine beauty of the team concept—it was all for one and one for all. We lived and died by the word "Team."

While all this was happening, the Iranians detected the activity and dispatched gunboats to the scene.

Our Task Unit Commander CK and Assistant TUC DB, both on the PC boat, saw what was happening and alerted us that the Iranians were quickly approaching. They then dispatched a few more RHIBs with heavier .50 caliber and MK19 40mm weapons systems, along with more armed helicopters from HS5. They asked the captain of the PC boat to get closer to the scene, and he was all too happy to oblige. This had all the makings of a colossal shit storm, and we were all right in the middle of it. Few things in life compare to a front-row seat for your own potential demise. But we never looked at it that way, we always believed it would be the enemy's demise, and even fewer things compare to having a front-row seat for that—except the act of delivering their demise.

We were a 16-man strike force trying to secure this ship as fast as possible while we simultaneously took up defensive positions to address the hostile gunboats that approached. We readied ourselves for a standoff. It was a crazy blur of activity. In essence, the ship was grounded on a sand bar that put it half in international waters and half in Iranian coastal waters. Luckily for us, the bridge was in the international part of the whole deal so, by default, we had control of the ship in a maritime law capacity. Or so I've been told.

This is just a taste of what we dealt with while working in the Persian Gulf trying to enforce the oil embargo. Everything there happens so quickly. The moment you touch the ship deck, your life is in danger. You're in harm's way. It should be no surprise that speed, violence of action, and aggression are the skills you need to rely on—this is what's going through your brain. You're weighing odds and risks, but you never stop—even for a moment. You merely think about what you can do to ensure the success and safety of your team. To be certain, this is what you've trained for from the beginning, and so you act.

It all goes along with the concept of perfect practice makes perfect. In any other setting except for a complex military operation or combat operation, the expression "perfect is the enemy of good" works. But in those aforementioned situations, shit needs to be perfect—so you better practice that way or you're a dead man.

But even in combat, there is always a silver lining: You've got any number of other dudes around you who are doing the same thing you are. SEALs live and die by the Holy Trinity of combat: Buddies, Weapons and Options. It's a simple concept and one of the most important. First, where are my buddies and where is the enemy right now? Can we out-flank or out-maneuver them or place them in a situation they cannot win? What is our current ability to fight? Do we have all of our weapons on-line and do we have enough ammo to weather a protracted fire event? Next, what is the current status of my physical being, my weapon or weapons? What weapons do we all have and what

UNDAUNTED

weapons does the enemy have? How can we best use what we have in order to inflict maximum damage upon the enemy right now? What are the odds and how can we swing them more in our favor? Can we call in close-air support or reinforcements if needed? Finally, what are our options for attack? And, if attacked, how can we best engage, re-group, and counter assault?

You are constantly aware of these things, no matter the situation. There is an unrelenting stream of consciousness that incorporates these questions all the time. Not to mention, you've got your eyes and ears wide open. What are those things I'm noticing and seeing? What are that person's hands doing? What does the look on that person's face mean? We are always analyzing to determine outcomes for ourselves and our guys. I made a pact with my buddies to come home, and I don't care what I have to do to do that.

There's always this sliding scale of action that takes place when you're downrange. Sometimes, other people will dictate your behavior based on what they do. Other times, it doesn't matter because your job is to basically remove somebody from the food chain. Consider this: They could just be sitting on the couch, watching TV, and you come through that doorway and you take them out because it's predetermined that that's what needs to happen. Capture/Kill orders are like that. Capture if you can, kill if you have to. Sometimes, it's just kill because nobody needs or wants to talk with this particular person or group of people. In essence, they have nothing to offer in the realm of pertinent intelligence data and will only continue to do the behaviors we are hunting them down for.

All of this goes through your brain: What am I supposed to do? What are my orders? What are the Rules of Engagement (ROEs)? It's hard to convey how much goes into an operation because it's highly complex, multi-tiered and multi-factorial. This is why SEAL training has to be so brutal. It's because of all these responsibilities and constraints you have once you're out on a mission. It's no joke because at its core, you are essentially given permission to kill another human being. It all goes back to having that moral compass and making sure it is highly calibrated. Without it, you become less of a hero and more of a villain, and nobody wants that.

I was always prepared to shoot somebody if I had to, but there was a time when a SEAL could easily go an entire deployment without firing a shot in an operation. Before 9/11, that was people's reality. There was very limited engagement from the U.S. military in theaters around the world. There was some combat activity going on in Kosovo and Bosnia, especially with the war-criminal prosecution missions, and a few anti-narco-terrorism initiatives in Central and South America, but there's wasn't much else other than a small brush fire here and there that needed attention. On average, there are 48 small wars being fought around the globe on a daily basis. How do you think all the weapons and ammunition manufacturers stay in business? It's a good thing they do, because there will always be a need to have well-armed military forces in this world. For there will always be good and evil, and that is why the U.S. military should always be the strongest in the entire world.

When I did my first deployment with SEAL Team Eight and Foxtrot platoon, our Platoon Chief TH had been active for 16 years and never even been out on a real-world combat operation. His first was one of those initial MIOs in the gulf. I asked how he could be in the SEAL Teams that long and not do any operations. He just shrugged and explained that's how it was. It was the luck of the draw sometimes. Not every pro athlete plays in a championship game. One is always ready though!

SEAL Team life was very different before the Twin Towers were brought down by terrorist shit-bags. Before that cowardly act, we were engaged in steady-but-limited operations around the world—some stuff in Central and South America and in Eastern Europe, as well as in the Philippines—and there just wasn't a glut of work for SEALs. But there was work. We called these combat operations "Conflicts Other than War." You got lucky if you were deployed somewhere where they wanted you to do a particular job.

The events of 9/11 dramatically changed everything. After that, there was so much work to do that guys were getting burned out. The operational backlog is still, to this moment, pretty substantial and has affected SEALs, DELTA, Army SF and MARSOC and AFSOC as well. Even so, it's always a great time to be a SEAL because it's what we love to do. I was fresh off of active duty when the towers and the Pentagon were hit, and was on SEAL Reserve stand-by many times. I even did some training for the potential to be activated. But this was the primary reason why I joined Blackwater—to get involved in some real and meaningful action, and not only that, but to see it all from a VERY different and even deadlier perspective: A covert and clandestine one.

Looking back, it's apparent that my time as a member of SEAL Team Eight was relatively short-lived as far as many careers of Navy SEALs go. We prepped to go overseas during the second half of 1998—right after I arrived at SEAL Team Eight. I spent most of early 1999 in combat preparation for a strike platoon deployment, and then was sent on training exercises and specific schools in the U.S. for the remainder of that year. Most of the year 2000 was spent overseas on various missions. It was definitely memorable work, with amazing guys and I enjoyed it tremendously.

But in mid-2001, after I returned home safely, I began to seriously wonder about what I wanted to do next. I had just returned from a nine-month deployment overseas. A strike platoon deployment in the Mediterranean where we were stationed aboard a carrier battle group centered around the USS *Enterprise*. We were all over the place during that deployment: Italy, Sicily, Portugal, Spain, Greece, Kosovo, Croatia, Turkey, Jordan, Egypt and Israel. During this time, I noticed a lot of leadership that was lacking—not only from a standpoint of detachment, of not being there with us (not from our immediate officers-in-charge of the platoon, but the upper guys, the management above us) but also not being aggressive in their thinking about the increasingly dangerous situation in the world.

Our platoon Officer-in-Charge (OIC) and Assistant Officer-in-Charge (AOIC) were great dudes. Their names were Lt. Jeff and Lt. Chris, respectfully. Both were Annapolis graduates and were total SEAL studs. Jeff was freakishly smart and always level headed. He could run like a deer and was also strong as hell. Chris played water polo at the Naval Academy and was 6'3" and 225 pounds. He was also a very brainy badass and could swim better without fins than most of us could while wearing fins. He was a freak. He was a bit more volatile than Jeff, but they complemented each other very well because of it. Our ATUC, Lt. Jg. DB, was a good buddy, as we pushed through BUD/S together and suffered many a beating due to the fact that we were older and bigger than the other BUD/S students. No, it was not these dudes, it was very much the guys above these guys who were unwilling to utilize us more in other combat roles. At that time, nobody wanted to order men into combat situations in fear that lives would be lost, and thus, their careers would be somehow blemished. We didn't care about their potential blemishes, we only wanted to do what we were trained to do.

I noticed that the leadership almost had this antiquated Cold War mentality. We were seeing what was happening in the world—the change and rumbling that was starting to heat up in the Middle East. A lot of us felt under utilized, and that pissed us off. Among many of my colleagues you heard a lot of subtle and not-so-subtle grumbling. We could see the handwriting on the wall, and it didn't say ,"Stay here and flourish."

As a cerebral SEAL, you're always plotting your next move—are you going to stay in or jump ship to a Special Intelligence Agency like the NSA, CIA or DIA, or hit a contract organization, or more accurately, you start thinking, "Can I do stuff even more dangerous, with more autonomy and make more money while having less operational constraints?" In the past, during one portion of our platoon work-up phase, we had engaged in a couple training exercises with this young organization called Blackwater. Blackwater was founded in 1997 by Erik Prince, a former SEAL officer at SEAL Team Eight. He left about six-months before I checked in, but I met him many times after he left, both at the team and at Blackwater. I thought it was a cool organization, and it wasn't too long before I got pulled aside for a little chat.

One of the higher-up former SEALs already working there, confided in me: "If you're ever looking to get out of the teams, there are a number of spots on this side of the fence. We'd love to have you."

It was encouraging. I knew that if I did that, I'd still be in the game, just with a different letterhead. So I filed that away in my brain for later.

Meanwhile, and before 9/11, I felt we were completely underutilized in our current role. We were capable of kicking so much ass around the world, but we were most always brought right to the brink of usage and then promptly told to stand down on the back burner—especially when President Clinton was in office. All you heard among my colleagues were complaints that our Commander-in-Chief wouldn't let us put a smack down on people that sorely needed it. For example, when the USS *Cole* was blown up on October 12, 2000, and 17 of my shipmates were killed and another 39 injured that day, guys were really ticked off that we didn't do anything substantive about it. They did not unleash us, to let us out of the yard to go bite people. SEALs are in the business of stopping people from having birthdays, and we needed to do that more often, in my humble opinion.

Had George W. Bush not been elected when he was, there probably would have been a mass exodus from the SEAL Teams. A lot of us felt this way—from the top of the Department of Defense all the way down to the new arrivals at the team—that our Democratic leaders were a bunch of pussies. They were trying to be too politically correct for their own good, and didn't fully recognize the level of danger we were facing. We saw it growing every day, but they didn't. Besides, when Americans are attacked overseas—our soldiers, our men and women in the Armed Forces—there is no politically correct thing to do. You just take action, and you do so decisively. I don't remember where I read it, or who wrote it, but I recall a very poignant passage about political correctness:

> *Political correctness forms the shackles around our ankles and wrists by which Islamists are leading us to our own demise.*

That was about 10 years ago, and it's never been truer than it is today.

So that's where I was at during the spring of 2001. I already had these inklings in my brain—I worked so hard to get here and yes, we're doing some cool things and I'm privy to interesting stuff, but what was next?

During my years of active duty as a member of SEAL Team Eight, I still wanted to serve on SEAL Team Six—the ultra-elite unit that eventually was responsible for taking out Osama Bin Laden. I thought about screening for SEAL Team SIx and tried setting that ball in motion, so I went and got pre-interviewed by the team. No one opposed my move, so I started thinking I might just stay in the Navy. The only thing was that I would have to re-enlist for a period of four more years. You always have that re-enlistment to think about, especially when you are not an officer. An officer can pull the plug on their career at any time, but an enlisted guy is in until the last day of that time period. I had some choices to make.

This all gave me a couple realistic options for my future: Stay on SEAL Team Eight, try to get onto SEAL Team Six, or get out and become a private military contractor (PMC) with Blackwater or another such group. As it turned out, I initially opted for choice "D," none of the above.

At the time, my wife Michelle was pregnant. We had gotten married during the tail end of my time in BUD/S; In fact, here's a fun fact: Travis Lively of Discovery Channel's *BUD/S Class 234* fame, was the best man at my wedding. So Michelle and I discussed the potential opportunity I had to pursue a run at SEAL Team Six.

We talked about it, and I said a few things that pretty much answered my own question: "Well, if I go into SEAL Team Six, you're never going to see me. I'm going to be gone on missions a lot of the time. In fact, knowing me, I'm probably going to die there." She didn't very much like the sound of any of that, so we discussed it more. Eventually, I decided that I wanted to get off active duty, embrace my upcoming fatherhood, and go into the SEAL Reserves. What a bad decision that turned out to be!

This was in the late summer of 2001. There was no way of looking into a crystal ball and seeing what was lurking right around the corner, two-months away.

In retrospect, I wasn't ready to get out. While was ready to be a dad, I wasn't ready to not be an active duty SEAL anymore. There was this weird hodgepodge of ideas going through my head, and I wish I would have sat down and talked to somebody and got a little more mental structure to place them upon. But my reaction to it was to just get out altogether and remove myself from everything because it was the easiest thing to do.

Nothing good ever happens by taking the easy way out! Maybe talking with someone who had a little more active-duty time under his belt and had gone through similar career-choice issues like I was would have helped me make a better decision; someone who could have laid out the differences—money may be great at an organization like Blackwater but you're not guaranteed that you are going to be doing the same hardcore combat activities, and you're definitely going to miss the camaraderie, etc.

Yes, I wish I would have sought out a mentor. Had there been someone like this in my life, I would have probably stayed in the Navy as a SEAL for many years to come. That sense of wanting to serve was still there, inside me, and I knew I was part of an elite organization, but I was thinking: What's the next step above where I am? Is there one?

I considered SEAL Team Six, but thought about whether I should do it. Did I really want to do it? Not, necessarily, could I? Although the failure rate was about 50 percent, the dudes that go there and don't make it do so because of the lack of wanting it. It's that 10-percent mental component again, the 90/10 rule I mentioned. Much better odds than BUD/S, but it is six months of an über beat down. Not quite like the BUD/S beating, but still very stressful and very demanding. The precision close quarters combat shooting and HALO jumping is second to none. But, for the first time in my life, I was thinking about someone other than myself. I was thinking about two people actually—my wife and our unborn child, my son. More thoughts crept in as well: Was it better to get out completely and go back to school? I enjoyed medicine. I wanted to be a dad. Those were things I knew I would enjoy. And since there wasn't really anyone at the team at the time who could slow down my thoughts and provide me with a more well-rounded view of my options. I made my own command decision. It still haunts me to this day!

When I finally made up my mind, Michelle was a little surprised that I was getting out. She was happy about it though. My thought process reached this conclusion: I'd love to go to SEAL Team Six, but if I did, I'd probably die there because I'm the type of person who gives every bit of that extra effort and, most likely, would put myself in many a bad situation. I told Michelle I would probably never come home. When I heard myself say that out loud to her, it became a real concern, for the very first time—not just for her, but for me as well. Hearing yourself say something out loud to another person, especially your wife, places things in perspective really quick. For sure, there was a part of me that was hard-wired for this type of work, that loved it, that craved it, but was I willing to possibly sacrifice my life for all of that and perhaps never see my son grow up? At that moment, the answer was no. So I decided I was going to go with my gut and get out—it was as simple as that. When I decide, I do!

Getting out of the Navy requires you to put in a request chit. You have to take your request to different departments and everyone has to agree with it. You have tell them why you want out. Some people you speak with give you their opinion about it—you care about what some of them offer; others not so much. It was difficult in a few cases to have those conversations. But I really wish someone during that process would have pulled me aside and given me a direct order: "You're not getting out, Heben. You're brain is infected with thoughts brought on by faulty leadership. We can fix that shit!"

That faulty leadership started with a chief who was not an effective leader. The guy below him, an E6, was not that effective either. He had been in the lead for 20-something years and was getting ready to retire, so this felt like his last hurrah. He was a good guy, and I'm sure in his earlier days he was a hellacious SEAL as well as a great leader, but he was not right for our platoon. To make matters worse, two of my platoon mates, my Assistant Officer-in-Charge (AOIC) and Officer-in-Charge (OIC), were both getting out to pursue MBA degrees and to have families. These facts made my decision even easier to stomach. The bottom line is that I think, looking back, that I talked myself into leaving and would have enjoyed serving another four or five years as a SEAL. Again, no regrets, but I still wonder!

This was near the end of July 2001. It took about a month to get everything signed, sealed, and delivered. I was on terminal leave, already home, and then off terminal leave and home for good when 9/11 happened. Everything was so fresh that I couldn't have been called up and reactivated because my papers were in transit. I was just registered with the SEAL Reserve Unit, and I did fly down to Virginia Beach in case they wanted to deploy me back overseas. At Virginia Beach, active duty SEALs were gearing up and raring to go overseas and join the action. As reservists, we were the potential bodies to fill holes and manning shortfalls. But nothing like that ever happened. I was very much out of the loop—even though I was in the SEAL Reserves.

Every day I watched the news and saw what was happening and thought to myself, "Should I re-enlist, go back active, and go to war?"

Michelle and I were living in an apartment. She was five-months pregnant. I had just enrolled in some preparatory college classes, hoping to get into a Physician's Assistant (PA) program and become, eventually, a full-time PA.

During my required Reserve training, the cycle accelerated and many of the officers asked if I wanted back in. I thought long and hard about it, but in the end I came to the conclusion that I was about to be a dad. If I left I would never see my son be born and, knowing me, never meet him. So I made the conscious decision not to re-enlist. If they called me up as a Reservist I'd surely go serve, but otherwise, I'd stand by. I would go down to Virginia Beach and go to Little Creek Amphibious Base, where I would work in any number of capacities—brush up on, and teach, Close Quarters Combat (CQC), teach new SEALs about advanced demolitions, communications, and weapons, as well as supporting SEAL squadrons doing combat work-ups. My job was making sure they had what they needed. You do support and training, and also you participate in various training activities to keep your skills sharp. You're showing people how to blow stuff up, and you're blowing stuff up, too. That's how they keep guys fresh and in the flow—wearing different hats. It's a very dynamic environment to be in, but the commitment level is low so I didn't think much of it. As I said, and as it turned out, I was mobilized for a lot of training augmentation and a few potential stand-by, fill-in spots, but I never deployed for post-9/11, active-duty SEAL. I did this in 2001 and all of 2002 and most of 2003. It wasn't until I joined Blackwater that I finally did my first post-9/11 deployment, while still in the SEAL Reserves, to Pakistan in 2003 and 2004.

After a good try, I willfully left the Navy Reserves in 2006 before my contract was up. Which is also a decision I still regret. Had I stayed active or reserves, I would be close to a military retirement at this point, and who knows, maybe I would have got sucked back into active-duty status. There's a reason why we don't wear glasses on our asses—because hindsight is always 20/20. In fact, in my world it's more like 20/12.

Always speak to someone who has more experience than you do when it comes to making life-altering decisions. It helps to utilize another brain in some situation like that. Don't be stubborn and don't think you know everything. Life is too short to ever have any regrets or doubts, or to have too many, "I wonder what have happened?" moments.

CHAPTER 15

"WHAT I TRULY HOPE WE ALL SEE IN THIS PICTURE IS A REFLECTION. WE AREN'T BORN WITH PATRIOTISM COURSING THROUGH OUR VEINS. WE BECOME TRUE PATRIOTS THROUGH EXPERIENCE. IT CAN ALSO BE LEARNED THROUGH STORIES OF GREAT HONOR, SERVICE, AND SACRIFICE. IT IS FURTHER HEIGHTENED AND FUELED BY OBSERVING AND EXPERIENCING THE JOY, PASSION, BEAUTY, COMMITMENT AND DISCIPLINE EXHIBITED IN EVENTS THAT SHOWCASE AND CELEBRATE IT. GOD BLESS THOSE WHO SERVE OUR GREAT NATION AND THE AMAZING WAYS IN WHICH THEY DO IT. MAY THEY BE A REFLECTION IN THE MIRROR OF OUR LIVES! PATRIOTISM: LEARN IT AND EARN IT! ONWARD AND UPWARD!"

—CHRISTOPHER MARK HEBEN

After I left active duty I tried to live a normal life. I felt very fortunate and privileged to have watched the birth of my son, Mason, which was one of the most amazing moments of my life. I spent more time with my wife, Michelle, and attempted to settle down for a more regular role as a husband. During my active-duty time, she and I calculated that we only spent a total of eight months with one another in four years. That is rough on any relationship. In addition to daddy time and husband time, I worked a second-shift job as I carved out yet some more time and went back to school and completed my college degree. I earned a Bachelor of Arts in Independent Studies, with a concentration in Health Sciences from Cleveland State University. And during this quest, I began to think about life after college—I thought a lot about a regular 9-to-5 job—which, after being on-point 24/7 in the teams, seemed at odds with my inherent personality. Despite these so-called mental doubts and potential challenges, I forged ahead full speed. Change has never been something I've really eschewed; rather, I've welcomed it graciously as something of an old friend.

Over the years I've come to recognize that there are six traits, actions if you will, that define those of us who possess true mental

toughness—that ability to persevere, undaunted, no matter what nasty pitches life throws your way:
1. Mentally strong people move on. They don't waste time feeling sorry for themselves.
2. Mentally strong people embrace change. They demonstrate mental toughness by welcoming challenges with open arms and excitement. They are always anticipating what's next, and take pleasure in experiencing it.
3. Mentally strong people stay happy—no matter what. When you have strength of mind, you don't waste energy worrying about or focusing on things you can't control.
4. Mentally strong people are kind, fair, and unafraid to speak up. They are comfortable in their own skin, and see the world through a different lens. Base pettiness isn't part of their make-up.
5. Mentally strong people are willing to take calculated risks. They don't leap foolishly into just anything, but they're adept at assessing the situation, analyzing the variables, and determining the best course of action—even if it involves a little bit of danger.
6. Mentally strong people celebrate other people's success. And, just as important, they don't ever resent the success of others. Instead, they praise it.

When the cadre of terrorists hit our country on 9/11, it suddenly became "go time" for an entire group of people who have been consistently defined by their mental fortitude. Life changed dramatically for everyone, and I was no exception. After the numbness of the tragedy subsided, I immediately started seeing the current situation as a missed opportunity for me to serve and get back into the breach of service to my country. I wanted to dive into the fray and make a difference for my nation, but as a non-active-duty Navy SEAL that simply wasn't going to fully happen anytime soon. I was placed on a short list for Active Duty recall, but it never fully happened passed the point of being assembled in Virginia Beach at Naval Special Warfare Group Two and further assigned to the training cell there. I felt that this was going to be my reality for at least two years, and I was unwilling to accept that. Expediency was what I needed, and I needed to expedite that expediency.

I've said it earlier, but it's worth repeating here again: I've always been a plotter, a planner, and a bit of a dreamer. It's what's kept me going strong, helped me to hone my mind to razor sharpness, and strive each day to sculpt my body into the pinnacle of physical perfection—a holistically sound and deadly capable weapon to use to achieve goals. Sometimes, things go according to plan; other times I've had to re-plot and re-envision. But when it's all said and done, I always make damn sure to leave it all on the table so as to never have any regrets. There is little doubt that a life of regret is a life wasted. It's just not the way of a warrior! Admittedly, however, it was going to be painful to watch my SEAL brothers take up the fight against this new enemy while I remained on the sidelines.

During the several months that followed, as our core military responded against the enemy with deadly force in Afghanistan, I watched as most of my SEAL brothers remained stateside or in assignments where they'd been before the attacks. There was no massive initial deployment of SEAL Teams worldwide—with the exception of SEAL Team Six, which always went where the most contested and immediate action was—unless by chance another SEAL Team just so happened to walk into a shit storm somewhere first. It wasn't until around January or February 2002 before the other SEAL Teams were rolled out in any significant way.

Right after the attacks in New York City and at the Pentagon, I was sent on a trip to Little Creek. At the time, the ink was still fresh on my retirement from active duty. As a member of the Reserves, I was subject to recall. We'd suddenly been thrust into a time of war, and I was ready, but I wasn't truly called up or activated. There, the thought of re-enlisting crossed my mind—more than once—but I had already decided to spend more time with my family and plot my future, so I held my post. People on the base were constantly on the ready. They conducted day and night free-fall jumps, day and night shooting evolutions, and for the first time in SEAL history, cut down on some of the combat diving, in favor of more steadily and arduous Urban (MOUT) and Close-Quarters Combat training (CQB/CQC).

This went on for a while. SEAL teams were deployed to places like Italy and instructed to await further orders. For the most part, those orders never came, and a good deal of the Teams ended up just sitting there, waiting. SEAL Team Six remained active—it always was—and while a few other SEAL Teams were suddenly deployed to the Middle East, they held fast as well, not engaging in much meaningful action. Nothing was changing, yet everything had changed and we all needed to adjust the way we got all of our intel and sensitive data. This needed some time to catch up to all that had transpired, and many more boots-on-the-ground were eventually needed. So I waited, and waited, and waited, and wondered what was going to happen next.

It took close to a year-and-a-half before the Bush administration and its military brass started using the SEAL teams more effectively, and it wasn't until the end of 2002 and beginning of 2003 that the military began actively sending many more SEAL Teams into war in Afghanistan and Iraq. But when they did, it was a sight to see.

That's when the flood gates opened, and by then I had become very restless. I had earned my college degree and was working on a combined Surgeon Assistant/Physician Assistant extended degree program at Cuyahoga Community College, but there was a different kind of itch that needed scratching. I needed to see more action than I had as a SEAL, if possible—this was why I had joined the Navy and become a SEAL in the first place. By now, I knew re-enlisting in the Navy was not an option. Sure, I was decorated during my time in the SEALs and had been involved with more than two dozen, real-world operations, worked in more than 10 foreign countries in Eastern Europe, the Balkans, the Middle East and Africa. Yes, I had scheduled, briefed, and conducted sensitive operations with a number of other elite military and law-enforcement agencies, branches of the U.S. government and host nation units, but I now knew in my heart that the Navy just wasn't the place where I could flourish at that point in time. I wanted back in, but not as a SEAL. I still wanted to join the fight and contribute in ways where I could make a positive difference in the world, but in ways that were generally more flexible and free thinking, yet still do it all for my country. So I did what any good former Special Ops operator would do—please allow me to explain.

For the past several years I'd kept the lines of communication open with a few good contacts I'd made at Blackwater USA. My SEAL Team had trained with them at their main installation on Puddin Ridge Road in Moyock County, NC, in the middle of the Dismal Swamp, back in 1998. They were notorious for pulling aside guys and letting them know there was a spot for them if they ever wanted to untangle themselves from the constraints of all the military red tape and join the world of private military contractors. It was a powerful and effective recruiting system—and it earned them a great reputation in the Special Ops community, as well as a good amount of operators.

Blackwater, especially, had a soft spot for SEALs, because co-founder Erik Prince was a former SEAL. He and Al Clark, a SEAL firearms instructor, had a vision to build a private company that assumed some of the roles previously played by the U.S. military. Together, they built an organization filled with like-minded people and started providing training support to military and law-enforcement organizations.

The leadership at Blackwater also had a keen, intimate understanding of the SEAL and Spec Ops mentality. Officially military-branch neutral, SEALs dominated the Blackwater landscape. If you had the acronym SEAL attached to your name, the sky was the limit there. Blackwater's shining moment arrived in October 2000, shortly after the bombing of the USS *Cole* off the coast of Yemen. In the wake of that tragedy, Erik Prince bid on a job to better prepare the Navy for incoming terrorist attacks—the type of insurgency we hadn't seen since the Japanese utilized kamikaze attacks to damage us at Pearl Harbor. Blackwater won the government contract—a major one—and because of this, Blackwater Security Company was born. Yet another, offshoot, corporation from the Blackwater mothership. Others would be: Blackwater USA, Greystone, Presidential Airways, and Total Intelligence Solutions. All of which I was privy to but am not at liberty to go into any detail about. All in all, over the next several years, they formed nine divisions and a subsidiary, Blackwater Vehicles, and trained more than

100,000 Department of Defense, State Department, Federal agencies and local and national police departments, as well as private individuals.

Positions within Blackwater (BW) were custom-made for former SEALs. Everything was based on your qualifications and what you excelled at doing. For example, upon hire you might be run through a series of shooting exercises and they'd discover you're exceptional at organizing the training of shooting. BW would carve out a role for you as a director of training and deploy you to some theater of war to assume that role teaching foreign nationals. In my case, they found out that, not only was I good at weapons and tactical planning, but I was also exceptionally good at medically oriented tasks and planning, so they made me a director of medical operations. They were good at streamlining, and they expected you to perform.

At its nuclear core, BW's modus operandi was to fast-track quality new additions to the crews because they were growing by leaps and bounds and they wanted them out in the field and contributing to the missions as soon as possible. That's why BW had it's own in-house recruiting staff, and the BW recruiters had manning slots that they needed to fill all the time. That's not to infer that anyone was rushed into harm's way. Rather, once you were a member of BW, you no longer had the constraints associated with the traditional military chain-of-command—or the antiquated timelines. Life was a lot looser in BW, a lot more independent and mission-centric. They were focused on the art of ass kicking, not ass kissing. Leaders knew that you were already Spec Ops-capable, headstrong, motivated and intelligent, so they invested a small bit of time developing you in accordance with your new position, and then set you free to do your thing. It was a straightforward process, not complicated or delusional or diluted in any way. You join. You demonstrate your expertise. And the next thing you know, if you have what it takes, you could be running a program in Iraq, Afghanistan, Africa or elsewhere. You're on your own at times, or enjoying some level of autonomous functioning. In this way, you're able to be maximally effective and without question, you make a difference. It's a good system all around. It was really cool, and limitless in its potential. It was a true meritocracy, not a system where idiots where promoted in order to move them out of the way or a system where past performance would be a prognostic indicator of future performance. You had to put out, get out, or get the hell out of the way. The Peter Principle was not in play at Blackwater.

When I approached Blackwater in late 2003, they explained that they had a couple spots available that were a good fit—including mobile security details for ambassadors overseas. Basically, that was a State Department-mandated job, and BW knew you were already accustomed to dignitary protection work because the SEALs have been augmenting that sector for the U.S. State Department and Secret Service for many years. BW's head shed explains to new sub-contractors that you can get on that detail to get started, and that you'll do this or that a couple times and protect people like John Negroponte, Jr., who at the time was Assistant Secretary of State under Condi Rice. Or they'd say, "You're going to join Richard Bremmer's detail and go to Iraq." At the time, Bremmer was the head civilian in charge of Iraq, so he needed a lot of protection. There were many attempts to take his life during his tenure. The same could be said for Hamid Karzai's protection detail. He was President of Afghanistan from 2004 to 2014, and there were numerous attempts to take his life.

Those jobs would last a few months and go up to a year—typically a deployment lasted about two to three months—and then you'd either be shifted to something else or rotate back into the previous gig. BW program directors would get a feel for your operational ability and style, and look for your next fit. They'd approach you and say, "How'd you like to go to Pakistan?" Of course, you'd say yes!

They'd offer great pay—$1,100 to $1,500 a day—and explain that you'd get to operate in the middle of nowhere—where it's dangerous and there are enemy combatants all around you. That may sound ominous, but people like me look at it and say, "That's cool, I'll know exactly where the enemy is. I'm in. When do I start?"

BW's atmosphere, as I mentioned, was much more relaxed than the SEAL Team climate. There was no traditional chain of command, per se, and the structure followed was basically outside any strict military format. In the Navy, I got out as an E-6—a mid- to high-level enlisted

UNDAUNTED

guy. I was a warrior sent out on missions with my fellow SEAL Team operators on behalf of my country. We reported up the chain to other Navy leaders, who in turn reported to other military brass, eventually all the way up to the Commander-in-Chief. It was a successful but clunky, time-tested, bureaucratic system that was quickly becoming archaic under the current models of asymmetric warfare we were engaged in. There needed to be an expediency about the way we engaged the enemy, a certain definitive proactive approach to things, not a knee-jerk reaction to the actions of international terrorism. This would eventually evolve, but at that time, BW was that solution. They were our nation's force multiplier, and one that offered that "something fresh, something new" approach that military operations desperately needed. I went from standard military protocol to being the director of medical operations and operational planning on a $200 million project. To put that in context, it's the overnight equivalent of being promoted to a Commander or Captain in the Navy and put in charge of an entire SEAL Team or an entire Naval Special Warfare Group during a time of war.

It was exactly what I was looking for.

Being a SEAL gave you a lot of weight in Blackwater because of Erik Prince, Gary Jackson and Al Clark. Few people know this; Erik was a trust-fund baby—he was a multi-millionaire the moment he came through the birth canal. He never had to work, but he did. Yet, he became a Navy SEAL Officer and valiantly served his country. Blackwater was an extension of his service to his nation, and would play a critical role in helping to transform the way it identified and addressed threats in the asymmetric battlefields of the day and well into the foreseeable future. Al and Gary were his right-hand men. Erik left the SEALs in 1997 and, with his inherited fortune, bought a huge swath of land on the North Carolina/Virginia border—about 7,000 acres of what is known as the Great Dismal Swamp. He developed a training facility complete with indoor and outdoor ranges, urban-area simulations, an artificial lake, and a self-contained driving track. Clark was put in charge of the training. He named the company "Blackwater" because of the peat-colored water in the swamp—an apt name that served the company well for several years.

I joined SEAL Team Eight in 1998, about the same year Erik officially opened his facility in earnest. Because of this, my strike platoon was one of the first to utilize BW's extensive shooting ranges and kill houses. Even early on, it was like a fucking Team Guy Disneyland. There were multi-roomed kill houses with re-configurable walls and bullet traps. There were numerous outdoor shooting ranges with electronic-target systems. There was even one range exclusively for pistol with a hellacious computer-programmed course called the 'Beast of the East'. The Beast ran you through so many targets in such a short amount of time that you really had to be good at tactical reloading (magazine changes). Sometimes, if you dropped enough rounds, you'd end up not being able to even finish. I saw this happen many times. I experienced it too...LOL!

By 2002, BW began branching out into many other operations involving operatives with top-secret clearance to do such clandestine jobs as protect the CIA headquarters, CIA operatives in safe houses and even safe houses for SEAL Teams overseas in some very sketchy areas. I spent a lot of time at one such SEAL safe house in the capital city of N'Djamena, in the African country of Chad. In less than four years, Erik and his business partners transformed Blackwater from a small- to mid-sized contractor with a couple government contracts, into the second- or third-largest private military contractor to the U.S. government.

Part of making that happen was hiring the right team and recruiting capable operatives from the Special Ops community who bought into their vision. Erik hired former Navy officers that he had served with in the SEAL Teams, as well as a number of enlisted guys who were well-connected in Washington D.C. Many of those guys were retired and had been working in the Pentagon. By the time I joined BW, their government connections were second-to-none.

Gary Jackson was one of those connected guys. He served as president of Blackwater USA, was capable of picking up the phone, making a call and saying, "How soon can we get four or five helicopters?" And then they would just appear. In fact, BW had the market cornered on MH1 Little Birds in Iraq. At one point, their helicopter assets were larger than the U.S. Army's Delta Force.

Together, the BW leadership team, and BW in general, was very formidable. They tapped into their strengths, assets, and connections to build this massive, private military contracting company. Blackstone, Blackwater USA, Blackwater Worldwide, Presidential Airways—all these companies underneath the shell of Blackwater—became powerhouses until 2007, when some questionable activities in Iraq were exposed in the public media.

I feel very fortunate—both blessed and even a tad bit cursed, BUT mostly blessed—to have been involved with Blackwater. For some people, being part of the BW family was a badge of honor; for others it was a black mark in their careers. And while BW no longer exists—Erik sold the company, stepped down several years ago, and the new owners changed the name to Academi and U.S. Training Centers (USTC)—I only consider myself a member of the former and a number of the offshoot organizations.

Blackwater set up operations in Africa, Iraq, Afghanistan and Pakistan, and formed a company called Presidential Air, which housed all of its aviation assets—large and small. Presidential Air became BW's official Joint Special Operations Aviation Detachment provider and was involved in a lot of major initiatives in the War on Terror. Especially in the early stages of the push to re-gain North Africa. The book *Blackwater: The Rise of the Mercenary Empire*, introduces one of the special pilots Blackwater recruited, Andy G. Andy was with me in Africa, and he is a special person. Guys like Andy were successful bush pilots in remote, out-of-the-way places like Alaska, where they hunted and fished. They have a crazy skill set—they could land a severely overpowered aircraft in water or on a small stretch of land in the middle of nowhere or do the same thing in the middle of somewhere and during a combat operation and at great risk for injury or death. They were the new version of *Air America*. They were total stud bush pilots, the kind you saw in the movies and thought didn't exist in real life. Those were the kinds of people that BW hired—individuals who possessed niche skills. Other amazing and very talented pilots were Aria S., Eric B, and Jessie L. Yes,

Aria is a female, and she fit right in with our crew. She and I shared a bathroom in Ouagadougou, Burkina Faso, and no, we didn't share anything else.

As soon as I joined BW in late 2003, I was immediately sent to Pakistan to serve on a remote Forward Operating Base (FOB) called Site 2. Site 2 was also known as Shamsi Airfield, which was also known as the Bhandari Airstrip. Today, it's shut down, but back then, it was a prominent Predator drone base nestled in a barren desert valley between two ridges of the Central Makran Range. As the main Predator drone launch site, we coordinated most of the overflight intelligence data we were getting, as well as the entire missile-launch capability we had with respect to Al Qaida and the Taliban in a 500-mile radius. Yes, we were also looking for Bin Laden at this time, and so it was that we had a few Predators there to go along with a massive 9,000-foot runway. It was quite literally out in the middle of nowhere. And it was about as awesome a place as there could be.

I was stationed with a group of former SEALs, a few Delta, some Green Berets and some Rangers. There was also a CIA detachment assigned to the location and we were there to not only protect the facility but to be a quick-reaction force for anything that needed to be smacked down decisively using boots on the ground. Our station chief was a salty retired SEAL Master Chief named Hershel Davis. Hershel was the A1C or Chief Private Military Contractor there and served as the direct conduit between Blackwater, the contracting agency, the sub-contractors (me), and the Central Intelligence Agency (the client). Yes, again, and as usual, the Agency was our client. We served the agency's needs—all of them. We also had a protection job and a quick-strike capability if we had actionable intelligence from the Predators. For example, say there were Taliban guys in a training camp. We would and could go and take that camp down. We were totally on the edges of nowhere and doing our own thing to help our nation's post-9/11 agenda. This was known as *The Cause*.

I had what I would consider a pretty straightforward two-month deployment there: I flew into Islamabad, got picked up at the airport, went to the U.S. Embassy and checked in. Then I boarded a smaller plane that dropped me at the strike airfield in Pakistan. Thus began my time as a covert/clandestine-capable operator for Blackwater.

Some of us were known as 'Green Badgers' because we were not official CIA direct hires. If we were, we would have been assigned to the Special Activities Division (SAD) that housed Ground Branch (GB) and Air Branch (AB). GB and AB were the respective paramilitary divisions in SAD also housed at Site 2. We were inhabited by a bit of both from time to time. Over the next several years I would be deployed to such places as Pakistan, Afghanistan, Iraq, and Africa. It was a truly amazing experience. We were an integral cog in a machine that was on a never-ending mission against al Qaeda camps and we effected the take down and removal of many high-value targets in all of these locations. When we weren't in the field, we watched it all on a TV screen from a remote Predator base in the heart of the War on Terror.

Few people have the pleasure and the pain to have served in the capacity that I did. A lot of my friends have and, in fact, they are still doing it. I did slightly over 10 total years in the U.S. Navy—all of it in the SEAL Teams after boot camp, BUD/S, and Army Jump School. A few of my friends are still on active duty, and I think about what it would be like to be with them every damn day of my life. I don't have regrets, just a hard time turning a deaf ear to the call of the wild. I can only imagine how empty my life would have been had I not joined the Navy that day in September 1996.

CHAPTER 16

> "AS A SEAL AND AS A PRIVATE MILITARY CONTRACTOR, WE WERE AFFORDED MANY TYPES OF EQUIPMENT IN ORDER TO HELP US GET THE JOB DONE. BUT AT THE END OF THE DAY, REMEMBER ONE THING: THE MACHINE DOES NOT MAKE THE MAN AND, ULTIMATELY, THE MAN HAD BETTER BE A MACHINE!"
>
> —CHRISTOPHER MARK HEBEN

When you're a member of the Special Operations community, other than honor, courage and commitment, nothing is clearly black and white. Everything you're engaged with, every mission you're on, every interaction you have, all of it blurs together into some opaque shade of gray. That's often where the misinterpretations of what we do come into play, where people who have never experienced what we experience pass judgment. That's not to say we're all saints in what we do. And those of us who have served in both the U.S. military and as a private contractor can easily relate to that—and it's why I mentioned earlier that for some, serving in Blackwater was a blessing while for others it became a curse.

I was blessed to participate in eight deployments with Blackwater. All were downright amazing, and I have nothing but great things to say about the firm and its leadership. Blackwater's structure allowed me to fully utilize my skills, as well as explore and hone others that I would go on to use in the private sector with MSI and my other ventures. The list of what I was able to accomplish with Blackwater is extensive, but here's just a small list of areas where I was involved:

- Clandestine Projects Leader

- Instructor: Small Unit Tactics
- Director of Medical Operations/Team Leader: Combined US Department of State/Blackwater contract for United States Joint Special Operations Command (JSOC)/Joint Special Operations Aviation Detachment (JSOAD).
- Firearms Instructor
- Designated Defensive Marksman (SNIPER), Counter Sniper
- Protective Security Detachment Instructor
- Heavy Weapons Instructor
- Arrivals and Departures security procedures
- DoS Communications
- Navigation & GPS Fundamentals
- I.E.D. Familiarization and Countermeasures
- Instructor: Vehicle Searches, Motorcade movement, High Threat Driving
- Operations, Vehicle Deployed Weapons Dynamics.
- DoS Close Quarters Battle
- Special Skills Instructor for Designated Defensive Marksman (DDM/SNIPER)
- DoS Protective Security Operator

It's a list that looks pretty impressive on a résumé when you're applying for private-contractor jobs, but when you're applying for a Physician Assistant job or to work in an office, none of it really translates all that well to the lay person. Nevertheless, my experience with Blackwater was second-to-none (yes, even better than some SEAL stuff), and the deployments and experiences in Pakistan, Afghanistan, Iraq, and over 15 African countries, provided me with intimate knowledge of the serious problems faced by the U.S. and the global community today.

Between Blackwater and the SEAL Teams, I have probably traveled to nearly 40 countries—and each had its own unique identity. Afghanistan and Pakistan were the two most dangerous ones where I was deployed. And Israel was amazing despite the overt, as well as the lurking shadow of, threats that always seem to be there. The bulk of Europe—Germany, Italy, France—are just as advertised. Africa, on the other hand, was very mysterious. I deem it a tinderbox just waiting to catch fire and explode. And because of this, I probably loved Africa the most.

When I was in Pakistan, there were be times when I was walking through downtown Islamabad wearing Muslim headgear or attire, looking local, and taking pictures with a hidden camera mounted in a button hole on my shirt. Danger was everywhere. If the locals knew I was an American, well, you can't imagine the potential consequences. This currently and correctly mirrors what's going on with al Qaeda and even ISIL today, without the kidnapping component. Because then, they'd most likely just shoot you dead on the street or in an alley and not think twice about it. I would have done the same thing, so it's essentially all good. The willingness to engage in violence in order to affect your own immediate survival is, in many instances, the actual key to survival. Most of the time, as I stated before, it all boils down to how low on the evolutionary chain of man one is willing to fall. Me? I'm rock bottom when I need to be. Teeth and nails. Sticks and stones. I'm coming home. You're not. In fact, I mentioned on a TV documentary, *America's Book of Secrets: Black Ops*, "I'll chew your face off!" and I meant it!

A vast majority of the time when I was out and about, anywhere in the world, I hid my American-ness by my appearance as well as by the way I spoke. Speaking in a German or French-accented English—anything was better than Americanized English. But beyond that, I can speak a fair amount of French and German; know some Arabic; some medical Urdu; some Hungarian and Spanish; and can utter a few social pleasantries in a few other tongues.

Languages have always been an area where I flourished. I'm still able to pick up a fair amount of native language when I'm in an area for a long enough time. Growing up in Cleveland Heights, Ohio, which at one time was voted America's most ethnically diverse city, probably contributed to this. For example, a family of Orthodox Jews lived right next to us when I was young, so I was exposed to Hebrew at an early age. There were numerous Hispanics in our neighborhood, so I listened as they spoke Spanish. We had a biracial couple behind us and I was friends with many blacks and Jews. All of those early experiences made my ear a little more hypersensitive to the different sounds and accents that people across differing ethnicities have in their speech. It also allowed me to pick up on cultural nuances in order to not offend or to aid in blending in—which has been a gift.

When you think about it, it's actually quite sad that most people never get outside their comfort zones. They don't travel and experience the globe. As a result, they possess a limited view of the world and are constrained by this myopia. My experiences in the Navy and Blackwater provided a much different experience that few, outside the very affluent, ever get. And despite my many travels and experiences, I am constantly awed by the world around me. Isaac Newton stated, "What we know is a drop, what we don't know is an ocean." There are so many things yet to learn and to discover in this world—I truly believe that. Never lose your sense of wonder. Never give up looking for a cure. Never stop fighting the good fight. Be in the moment. Seek the truth and spread it when you find it. Find your ocean, and then get off your ass and set sail! It's really the only way to better understand this great blue and green sphere we call Earth.

During late 2003 and early 2004, I set sail—or should I say took flight—once again for the Middle East, and later on, to Africa. It was an important time for the then-nascent War on Terror, and it would be one of many occasions when I would be rocking a grizzly beard down to the top of my chest in order to look the part and, most importantly, better blend into the background. Our missions overseas were very intense and extremely diverse: At times, we worked with the French Foreign Legion and other NATO-member forces. We were in and out of many U.S. and foreign embassies. We transported high-value individuals, like U.S. and foreign diplomats and ambassadors, CIA deputy chiefs of station, U.S. military colonels and generals, and super-brainy people working on Predator drone projects. This was at the beginning of the whole push in North Africa to stave off al Qaeda, and I feel fortunate to have been on the ground floor of something that important. I had an "official" ID to go along with my bearded face—which I still have today. It states I'm a French 'bush pilot'. No one knew my real identity, which was a good thing. When you're an overseas private military contractor on a sub-contract for the Central Intelligence Agency, NSA or the State Department, you're under this quasi-identity veil of secrecy as needed, or else you will be put even more in harm's way.

Blackwater was, indeed, very fulfilling work. Even though I was no longer a SEAL, I was still making a significant difference in the efforts to keep my country safe. We knew that if al Qaeda gained a foothold in some of these African nations that they would be able to set up more training camps, which could lead to another 9/11-type attack. Through indigenous intel channels, we also knew about Boko Haram, and were taking some action on this group as well. It was a very dynamic, interesting, and necessary job, and Blackwater put me back squarely into the action in the Middle East, Southwest Asia, and Africa. I was in charge of, and oversaw anything and everything medical in Africa, as well as some of the tactical operations we engaged in when I was in that theater of operations. I loved it. Everyone's heard of the expression, "Once a Marine, always a Marine!" Well, I would argue that a near-identical expression holds true for being a SEAL. "Once a SEAL, always a SEAL!" It's in our blood, it's infused into our DNA. It becomes you and there's no separating yourself from it.

Africa was fun, and I would wind up there again later on. But in the early stages, Pakistan, being deep in the heart of where the Taliban was started, was where all the initial BW action was happening. Shamsi Airfield was an interesting place with a colorful history that most of us knew. Pakistan owned the land. It was originally known as Bhandari Airstrip and leased by Pakistan to the United Arab Emirates in 1992. The UAE renamed it Shamsi and transformed it into a jet-capable airfield. In October 2001, shortly after 9/11, the UAE subleased it to the U.S. The U.S. assigned it to the CIA and U.S. Air Force, who further developed Shamsi into a highly workable military airfield and Black Ops site. They built two permanent and one portable hanger, both designed to house Predator drones. Shamsi then served as a forward-operation Predator drone base with strike capability in the Hindu-Kush region of Pakistan/Afghanistan. The Agency hired Blackwater to assist with the tasks it wasn't able to readily do—those outside the purview of the U.S. military mission. All of the drones were armed with missiles.

The UAE dignitary who sub-leased us the base, lived in his own separate compound about a half-mile away. His compound had a 20-foot wall all around it, and he processed and trafficked heroin from there. Every two or three weeks, there'd be these enormous 2.5- and 5-ton military trucks that passed close to our FOB going directly into his walled compound. They'd enter, presumably loaded up with raw poppy plants, and a few days later the trucks left to distribute the product to who-knows-where. It wasn't our business, not our mission, so we opted not to poke around too much. In 2014, that region of the world had a record year for heroin production. You don't have to think too hard to figure out where the majority of it ends up being sent.

The 9,000-foot runway at Shamsi provided a lot of opportunities. The military landed C-5 Galaxy aircraft there, which are the largest cargo planes in the world, and they brought replacement parts for the Predators and anything else we needed for ourselves and for the mission.

There were roughly 50 people at Shamsi when I first arrived in 2003. Pakistani troops served as the first line of defense on the outer perimeter. They weren't stationed in the camp with us. We knew that they were watching us, and we always kept an eye on them. Shamsi was a CIA station that was manned by SEALs, Delta Force, Rangers and Green Berets. It was a dynamic, forward-operation base that allowed us to reach into the Hindu-Kush region and do all types of interesting things. We were an interesting group, and we did interesting things—many of which remain classified to this day.

Despite being in the middle of nowhere, there was always an element of danger present. There was a 10-foot walled compound situated on our base, which we called the Alamo. The Alamo was our fallback plan in case we ever got attacked so severely that we couldn't stave off the attackers. If we were overwhelmed or stormed by armed locals, the last stand was to head to the Alamo, which was where all the agency guys were. The Alamo was also where our communications gear, the weapons, ammo, and sensitive satellite equipment was stored. There was a M2-A .50-caliber machine gun positioned at each corner of the building, facing out. We had Carl Gustav anti-tank missiles, M66 light anti-tank weapons (LAWs), tons of ammo, and lots of food. If we had to, we could hold off an enemy attack from the Alamo for a decent amount of time.

I, and the other Blackwater guys, lived outside the Alamo in a mini-tent city. These weren't standard Boy Scout camping tents. Rather, they were GP-Large tents, which stood for General Purpose-Large, and they were furnished simply, with cots and bookshelves. The GPs were where you slept and stored your gear, but not much else. The bookshelves were used for storage and pulled double duty serving as partitions between bunks.

I loved everything about Shamsi. It was desolate, it was dangerous and it was a decisive asset in the war on terror. It was relatively straight-forward work. After each BW deployment, I'd fly back to the U.S. and have about 30-days downtime. Then, I'd get back on a plane in Cleveland, fly to France, transfer to a plane that took me to Islamabad. I'd spend a day at the embassy in Islamabad, doing whatever the U.S. asked me to do. We were all bearded up at that time, so I looked as much like a local as I could. You have a quasi-disguise on while you're mingling with the locals, wearing a Pakistani (Pakol) hat. If your hair was blonde, you'd wear one with dark hair sewn into it. You didn't advertise your real appearance or identify. You figured you were there taking pictures and gathering information, and there was probably somebody attempting to take pictures and looking to gather information about you—so hiding who you really were, at all times, was paramount. We had no ID and no dog tags. The U.S. Embassy had my passport back in

Islamabad, and if something happened to me on an operation, I didn't exist. We were ghosts. My call sign was "Heathen." That was as close to being me as it got. Once we completed any mini-missions that the Embassy required, we boarded a small Client jet and fly to Shamsi for our "real" deployment.

The Blackwater missions had a certain rhythm to them: You prepare quickly, relax, then add updates to the plan, and then you're off. There were a lot of working parts and you were constantly greasing them. Besides the traditional special operators, we had a group of mechanics for each plane and three crews of pilots. Blackwater created a redundancy for everything—it was an extremely well-oiled machine.

Beyond our military roles, everyone had to wear multiple hats. You burn the shitters one day. The next day you're on kitchen detail. Then you're on guard detail, where you watch the perimeter. At other times, you're on standby, for anything—ready to make a move on a target that needed to be taken out. You did everything. It was pretty cool.

Just beyond the base, to the Northwest, there was a set of low-lying mountains, the Central Makran Range. On the other side was Afghanistan. It reminded me of the Khyber Pass area, with old hash roads and opium routes—the old Silk Road. It was very old and mysterious. Alexander the Great's army marched across this region. It was desolate and wide open. As far as the eye could see there was nothing but sand and smatterings of mud huts. You could sit there at night and watch shooting stars go by in the sky. You would swear they made a sound. It was that dark, remote and quiet. Mostly.

We had minimal interaction with the people who lived in the villages. We did build a water well for them at one point, which was a good thing because we earned a bit of their loyalty and respect. It also probably kept them from wanting to mount an attack against us—even though we were considered to be invading infidels.

Our first defense line comprised of those regular Pakistani Army soldiers. A second group of Special Forces guys that we helped train, formed the second ring. The tertiary ring was 400- to 500-yards outside the camp, and these were our guys. When you were assigned to watch the wire, it was an eight-hour sentry shift. You'd change locations every two hours, so that you'd hit four different spots during your shift. Your job was two-fold: Watch the perimeter and watch the Pakistanis. As much as we relied on them, we still didn't completely trust them. It was up to us to make sure nobody got past or close to the camp. Everyone's lives depended on it.

There were a few times when people were intercepted out there on the range. Keep in mind that everyone you encounter is armed, so you observe with night-vision first to ascertain if there are multiple individuals and what they are trying to plan. If it looks legit, you come out of your hiding spot with bright lights on them, your own weapons openly displayed, and you, well, have a little chat. It would go something like this:

"Who are you? What are you doing here?"

They usually responded that they were camel herders or sheep herders, and their flock got too close.

We'd ask, "Are you armed?" Of course, we already know the answer. And, interestingly enough, they always responded, "Yes."

You then base your next actions off of theirs; if their weapons are in a relaxed posture, slung on their back or carried low, you must also assess body language. You can tell people's intentions just by how they behave. Behaviors are universal, and because of that, you get to be a good judge of intent right away. Once we knew they weren't a threat we'd send them away, sternly.

Luckily, when I was stationed at Shamsi we had no hostile events occur close to the base or inside our own wire. We did, however, launch numerous, Predator-enabled, Hellfire missile strikes on al Qaeda. Unfortunately we also had a Predator drone unexpectedly go down. The CIA was ready to send us to go blow it up, but they ended up having the Air Force conduct that operation instead. They sent an F-18 or F-16 to smoke it in a bombing run to make sure it was destroyed—you never wanted the enemy to get their hands on this type of U.S. technology. It wasn't the airframe anyone really cared about, it was all the sensitive stuff inside....the guts.

For the bulk of my time in Pakistan, at Shamsi anyway, we had three drones stationed at the base. After I stopped my rotations there, they brought in two more. Each drone had the capability to fire up to four Hellfire missiles. Originally, they only had the capacity for two. The drones were controlled by Langley or a place in Arizona that was teed up for satellite-driven, remote-control flight operations. A lot of the drone pilots were former fighter pilots who were now retired. Could you imagine going from being strapped into the pilot seat of a sexy-assed, Mach 2, gravity-defying, killing machine to having merely a joystick controller tied to a monitor tied to the equivalent of a passenger bus with wings piloting a high-flying, slow-mowing, missile launch platform? It must have been surreal. Especially, when you consider that due to microprocessor technology and satellite capability there was a 1.5 to 2-second delay from joystick movement to perceived movement on the monitor. It was like telling yourself to punch someone two seconds after you already did it. In that regard, it was good that there were some very experienced pilots working those joysticks. The drones were also unique, in that, they would be launched and recovered by the control station on the ground in Shamsi, but once they launched and were safely in flight away from the airfield, the agency would take over control of them, at the aforementioned sites, via satellite. This was true, state-of-the-art, satellite-driven microprocessor technology, much like playing a very deadly video game. It's even more impressive these days, and I am not at liberty to discuss these advances, but let's just say that it makes *Star Wars* look like that old TV show *Lost in Space*.

During my last rotation at Shamsi, the agency was starting to push for the U.S. Air Force command-and-control and maintenance model for the Predators. Before that, they used the pilots with whom the agency would contract to control the Predators during take-off and landing. But as the war continued, the Air Force started to actively take greater control in the field. As a result, active-duty Air Force guys were slowly coming to the drone sites—our Forward Operations Base (FOB) of Shamsi was the first. Initially, it was four dudes, then five, then six. The last week I spent in Shamsi there were around 20 Air Force guys there. That's when the cigar, scotch, and keg party turned into a piñata party with Barney as the host. In short, it just wasn't the same place it was in the beginning. God bless the U.S. Air Force, but they were in dire need of a machismo makeover. Hence, the fact that all us Spec Ops guys punked them every chance we got!

In light of this impending hostility, the station chief reminded them about the make-up of the indigenous people on the base (us) and told them it was not a place where they needed to assert their stateside rank or authority. We were a bunch of clandestine CIA Operatives, clandestine former SEALs, Delta, SF and Rangers. The Air Force guys were told to "mind your Ps and Qs" so they didn't end up in a ditch somewhere beat to a bloody pulp or worse. These guys really didn't know what they were getting into—we were all a bunch of serious souls when we needed to be, cut-ups and clowns when we wanted to be, and overall crusty fucking badasses who were not constrained by the structure of a traditional military chain of command. In short, if you got out of line with us, we would definitely let you know and it would not fare well for you at all.

Right before I left, a group of us decided to have a little fun. For the most part, we were all pretty bearded up and, at times, could look very local when and if we needed to. In light of this fact, we played a joke on this group of Air Force guys on their first day at the FOB. A few of the Special Ops guys told them all that I was a Pakistani kick-boxing champion who was assigned to the base as a tracker and as a field guide and advisor. They told them that I would be leaving soon for the 2004 Olympics and that, although I could speak fairly good English and I was very American friendly, I was not to be engaged in conversation because I could snap at any time. My 'ill temperament' was due to the fact that an A-10, piloted by an Air Force pilot, had wiped out my entire family, as well as my dog, about two years earlier at the onset of operations right after 9/11. Oh, and I was also the deadliest sniper in the Pakistani Special Forces brigade. They told them my name was Sandesh, and I was probably the baddest motherfucker in Pakistan. As the story went, I had been assigned by the Pakistani government to work hand-in-hand with the U.S. operatives on the base but only after I had completed BUD/S, Delta Force, and British SAS selection. It was the perfect punk, and the trap was set!

UNDAUNTED

On that first day, I, Sandesh, started sweeping up in the main tent where the dinner tables were, as well as where the satellite TV was located. I moved quietly and smoothly and did my best job of imitating the body movements of a Pakistani, as well as speaking in severely broken and improper English, all infused, of course, with a very strong, albeit contrived, Pakistani accent. Or, at least, to the best of my abilities at one. Hell, I had already spent enough time there, so I knew I could definitely pull it all off.

As I swept I said, "Please budge your feet, sir. I am weeping."

These Air Force guys looked at me and must have thought to themselves, "That is one scary looking, bad-ass, but very polite Pakistani dude." And thus, the trap was officially set!

Promptly, the one young E4, timidly said: "Sweeping, n n n n-not 'weeping'".

To which I/Sandesh glared and snarled back: "Oh but, most assuredly, I am very, very much WEEPING, GODDAMMIT! I am, for certainly, both sweeping and fucking weeping! Who are you to be the fucking corrector of this person who is presently at a status of speech?!" LMAO!

I had to use all of my faculties of restraint in order to avoid busting a gut and pissing myself when I saw the look of utter concern and fear on his face when he realized that he had completely disregarded the warning he was giving to avoid any interaction with me. He gathered his MP3 player and a few sports magazines and promptly stood up and made a beeline for the exit.

"Who is another person seeking to have letters to correct impertinence of my speech ability?" I yelled. "Who?!!"

No one even dared to look at me. As I approached their feet with the broom, they moved them as if it was a cobra on the verge of striking. The whole scene gave me this perverse pleasure that I would later incorporate into other such scenarios. Many, were at the behest of my Spec Ops brethren. I'd entertain requests: "Heebs, workout in the nude today!"

"OK." Then I'd promptly do just that.

Or "Sleep with a goat in your tent for the next few days!"

Done! Sandesh was beginning to take on a life of his own, and he was gnarly.

Then there was the infamous shower-boy scene, wherein, I was 'seen' coming out of the private shower area with one of the Pakistani locals, who, coincidentally, was actually a legit plumber sent in to fix the 'broken shower pipe' in the ceiling. But hey, nobody needed to know that!

I kept up the charade for a few days, as did my fellow door kickers. It was the most fun we had had in months. But all good things must come to an end, and it was time for me to rotate back home.

On the morning of the last day, I came into the mess tent with an empty cup of coffee. I cut in front of a majority of the Air Force guys in line. No one cared about my maneuver—as long as they were not a target for my 'insta-rage'. LOL.

They said, "Good morning, Sandesh."

I nodded and then replied in PERFECT English, "What's up, you brainy-assed, rank-wearing, face-shaving, non-operating, non-swinging dick sons-a-bitches?"

They were shocked, and jaws started dropping—along with a few trays full of food. They were taken aback and, quite frankly, a few of them were pretty pissed off. My buddies were already sitting at the table and witnessed my 'coming out' party. As mad as some of them were, they soon realized that we had all messed with them. Not only could none of them kick my ass, but there wasn't a chance in hell that they could take us all on. Knowing this, they quickly slowed their roll, adjusted their trajectory, and actually took it exactly as it was: One elaborate and amazingly successful joke!

I soon explained that I was from Ohio and a former Navy SEAL. Then I quickly reminded them, in no uncertain terms, that I was no less dangerous than "Sandesh" and would physically dismantle anyone who fucked with me. It was funny. As SEALs, no matter the gravity of the moment, we always find time for some levity, and I'm glad everyone else did too. We still had a mission to accomplish, Sandesh or no Sandesh. On a sober note, I named my character after a real acquaintance of mine named Sandesh. Sandesh succumbed to AIDS a few years previous to me joining the Navy. He was a really cool dude.

All of this was happening, concurrently, while I was still attending PA school back in Parma, Ohio. I had started the PA program in June 2003. In July, I started growing out my beard, knowing I planned to spend my Christmas and New Year's (winter) break working for Blackwater overseas. While I was spending my December and January in Pakistan, my classmates were safely celebrating Christmas and New Year's, stateside, in Ohio.

The program director, Sharon Luke, made it very clear that if I missed more than a few days when school started back up in mid-January that I'd have to repeat the entire first year of PA school. That wasn't something I was willing to do. In fact, I had to sign a letter stating that I understood if I wasn't back in time that I would be forced to start Year One all over again. As you might imagine, just as soon as I landed on the FOB (Predator Drone 'Site 2'), I asked Master Chief Hershel Davis to please start working on my ride home. Transportation planes didn't land here all that often, and I needed to make sure that I was on that magic bus schedule right away.

He said, "Heathen...I understand. I don't like any of that school stuff, but I'll make sure your ass is out of here. It won't be the date later than you need to get back to your program. Shit, Son, I don't need your ugly ass mad at me. There's plenty of them haji's out there who already want me dead!" He was true to his word, and there was never any doubt on my end. We are friends to this day.

PA school was intense, filled with non-stop studying, testing and patient care exams and practical exams for 27 total months. There were four tests a week, every week. They essentially cram four years of medical school into that brief time period, much like they used to do in order to rush doctors into the field during WW2 and the Korean and Vietnam wars. There are no summer vacations or Spring breaks, just Christmas and New Year's, which I spent in a combat zone. The pace at PA School was fucking brutal, but I enjoyed it. So much so, in fact, that I willingly attended one of only three combined Physician Assistant/Surgeon Assistant schools in the country. It was a kick to the gonads, but it played to my strengths, and I could see a potential career in medicine.

At the end of my Blackwater deployment, and as Master Chief Davis promised, the plane came to pick me up from the airfield, on time, which was good. We flew to Islamabad and stopped at another unmarked Pakistani airfield that we used as a launch pad for other clandestine missions. I spent a few days in Islamabad, staying at the Marriott hotel. Yes, the same Marriott that only a few years later was blown up. During the day, I was asked to do a series of tasks at the U.S. Embassy. They debriefed me each day, and then gave me several small assignments—ancillary duties like wandering around the town, taking pictures, and gathering some intelligence, among other things. Three-days later, I whipped out my 'special' U.S. Passport and skirted security in order to board a commercial airliner for London, where I was to change planes and head back home to the U.S., flip the proverbial switch, and get back to the weekly grind of school. I went from combat zone to school zone in less than 24 hours.

I remember that January in 2004, sitting on the tarmac in Islamabad for about two damn hours while airport 'security'—I use that term loosely—went through every piece of luggage underneath the plane. Apparently, they were concerned that one of them might be a bomb. It was 110 degrees on the plane, but they still took their sweet-ass time checking each bag and ensuring the plane wasn't suddenly going to explode in the sky. I had a 1-year-old son and wife at the time, so making it home alive was certainly a top priority for me. Sitting there on a commercial flight and thinking about things like that was a drastic difference from what it was like out in the field. You don't have these thoughts in the field.

Think about it: How many times during your day-to-day operations as a SEAL at home, or downrange in a combat zone, do you have a chance to die? You jump out of planes and helicopters from extremely high altitudes, you shoot live ammunition in tiny rooms with other SEALs doing the same. You ride a Harley to and from the base, where you gear up to jump into icy water for eight hours at a time. Did I also mention that you blow shit up? Lots of shit! So yes, there are lots of opportunities for things to go wrong when you're a SEAL, and you can't think about this stuff when you're doing it or you'll be paralyzed with fear. It goes to the root of understanding that some people are born risk-takers, and are very aggressive in everything they do. You learn how to apply this intrinsic mindset so that it becomes an inherent mentality to the job you're doing. A lot of SEALs find this is the best application of their tendency to take risks and be aggressive. It allows them to become hyper-focused and extremely effective. It's a natural fit, really, and that's why I say SEALs are born, not made. BUD/s training and then the teams just helps us to see the avenue for the proper application of our drive. The Navy, and other government agencies, then issues the license for us to continue on our path of proper utilization of talent.

My path returned me to PA school on time and in one piece. A lot of people knew where I had gone and what I was doing. They didn't completely understand, but they knew I was a former SEAL and someone who did not fully enjoy life through the paragraphs and pictures of a textbook. I confided in one of my buddies, Robert Plantz, about some of the things that happened on the trip. At one time, Robert was a U.S. Navy Corpsman who ran the entire Med Clinic on the Island of Vieques in Puerto Rico. He was already an impressive clinician, and I learned a lot from him. In fact, what he lacked in understanding of the body at a cellular level, I was able to assist with. And what I lacked in a clinical sense, he was able to help with. It was a perfect scholastic pairing, and we became constant study buddies. So much so, that we attracted quite the study group. Robert was a good dude and I enjoyed the fact that he was a fellow Navy man. His father was a former SEAL, an old school UDT guy, so he doubly understood that I needed somebody to talk with about my experiences. Other people didn't know how to approach me, so I really didn't hang out with anyone all that much but Robert.

One of the things you study and practice during PA school is how to give physical exams. These were in depth and very thorough, hands-on exercises, and I was really uncomfortable when I started them. I had to explain to Robert that when and if I was touching someone it was usually because I was either maiming them, killing them, or having sex with them. He laughed, but I was serious. I had to completely retrain my brain. It was a difficult transition—going from active duty and Blackwater to school—and going on those trips for Blackwater back then included some intense situations, which made the transitions even harder. Think about having to shift gears from being a covert, clandestine commando to becoming a caring, nurturing caregiver and medical provider. It wasn't easy. If I had gone home to be a mechanic at a car shop or even a SWAT cop, it would have been so much easier. But coming home and learning about patient care, pathophysiology, cytology, histology, parasitology, pharmacology, neurophysiology, and damn near everything else ending in 'ology', that was something else. I had to move from one cerebral discipline to another one that was drastically different—it was commando to caregiver—and if I couldn't flip that switch it would be worse than not coming home at all.

We started doing patient-care rotations in June 2004, so not only was I learning schoolwork but I was also spending a crazy amount of time in a hospital doing my clinical rotations. I was interacting with real people and real patients, and I had to adjust. It usually took me a good month to reintegrate to the real world. Completely flipping the switch is never easy, but we learn how to do it by compartmentalizing. We all have boxes we put things in, and that's where we like to keep them. It's an interesting dynamic when you think about it. I had someone explain it to me once, a woman who was friends with an Army Ranger who sent me an email. I've read this note over and over again because it really strikes at the heart of what I have been dealing with for years. She wrote:

> Chris, hear me out. Read this email and if it stirs nothing in you, delete it and never think of it again.
>
> I'm not a typical woman. I'm different and I've known it all my life. Sure at the end of the day, I want a warm body next to mine with a beating heart in it that adores mine, but I won't settle for just any man. I refuse to. I want one that recognizes and owns his boxes and loves to live deep within them. It's rare. And that's why I'm a single mom, former Marine, assertive, get-shit-done kind of woman.

I've been on this journey lately thinking about men and their boxes. I started a conversation with someone, we'll call him 'Max', that is a warrior at heart (Army Ranger-turned-federal hunter, an all-American bad-ass) and I mentioned one day that I wished I had a "nothing box" like men do so that I could zone out and get some homework done. He came back with one of THE most profound paragraphs I've ever read in my life. Reading it was like jumping into Lake Michigan in February; it was shocking, breathtaking and painful, but after being calm and still in it for a minute, it turned warm, familiar and oddly comforting and soothing.

What he wrote was this, "And you are so correct... We dudes have those friggin' compartmental boxes in our head. I think God gave us those so we could keep it simple: fight, hunt, kill, love, fuck...start over..."

The naked primal truth of men summed up in five words: FIGHT, HUNT, KILL, LOVE, FUCK. Speechless.

It started this internal dialogue that I cannot shut down. It spoke to the very core of who I am as a woman. It spoke to the truth of what God created man to be. It spoke to the systematic emasculation of American men (and they aren't even whimpering about it!!!). It spoke my mother's heart of fatherless boys trying to figure this out all while being told to "be good" and "don't fight" and on and on it goes and the helplessness of me not being able to teach it to them. It spoke to a nation of wimps with only a small percentage of warrior-hearted men left. It spoke to a nation of veterans who've been trained to kill and honored for it and abandoned when returning because they can't contain that God-given fierceness (that as a nation we've fostered because it was good for "us" then) in a cage or cubicle like a good boy (or girl, but that's a whole different email).

As a woman, I have never read anything sexier or more appealing than his paragraph. A woman's need to control can be directly related to the weakness of men, and the weakness of men *related directly to a woman's need to control, vicious unending circle. Adam really fucked us in the garden by not simply asking God about that woman's claim. Eve really fucked us by usurping Adam's power. And so it's gone on that man allowed woman to control him and a woman's desire would be for her husband (including his God-given strength). And here we are.*

It also started me thinking.... What if I could create a place where warriors could train these boys without fathers to be men that embraced their God-given strength and self-learning to respect it and use it to the betterment of not only themselves, but this country and anyone whose lives they would touch? Guess whose Facebook page I stumbled cross that very day? Yours. I'd never heard of you before and one of my friends had liked a picture you posted.

As I look at where I've been in life, some of the classes that I've taken and things that I've been exposed to, all those experiences lead to me to being in this place where I believe I can, with help, make this happen. A place to train boys being raised by women to be men. By the time they're ready for the military, it's too late for most of them. I believe this strength within each of you is innate but needs to be fostered properly to be effective. The ideas are still vague, a bit amorphous, but with some time and input, I believe I can make this happen. I'm not asking for a dime, just wanting to see if it stirred any desire in you to potentially be a part of something to change boys' lives, several at a time, in hopes of teaching a new generation to be strong leaders for this country in whatever form that takes.

I'm leaving on vacation today, to head home to Michigan, but I ask that you let this fester for a minute and see what shakes out of it.

Thanks for your time, for your service and for your consideration.

After reading the email I was blown away because it sums up what life is like for those of us who live and work in the Special Ops community as warriors and warriors-for-hire. Further, it underscores the very real challenges we face going from combat to the 'real world'. Or, as I like to put it; the insulated world. It also resonated with me because I, too, feel as if there is a society looking to emasculate men at every turn and deny us the rite of our biology. Lastly, it strengthened my belief that there are truly many lost souls across the spectrum of humanity. Ones that could be easily found with a little inspiration!

As I navigated my way through school, I soon discovered that I really liked the PA stuff and working with people in a medical environment. It was, damn near, a complete 180 from what I had been doing for the last eight years. Plus, I relished being at home with my son. It was just as good for me as it was for him. It all started to make perfect sense; stay home, stay safe, stay connected and practice medicine and truly be around for my family. I was still serving in the Navy Reserves at the time, so I decided to shift gears (again) and pursue a career in medicine. I let the folks at Blackwater know that I didn't want to go on further missions for the time-being, and they were good with it, saying I could come back when I was ready and that 'I was always welcome!' In fact, when just the other day I went for dinner and drinks with Master Chief Davis and he told me that I was one of the best guys he ever had the pleasure of commanding and that if I would have stayed on with him in Pakistan, he would have pushed me as far up the chain in Blackwater as I wanted to go. That would have translated into a metric shit ton of money and the responsibility and respect that goes along with it in that type of environment. That was pretty damn cool of him to say, but at that moment, I needed to be a dad and I needed to explore the PA thing. Thus, I spent all of 2004 and 2005 finishing school, then started my career as a PA. Things were going exceptionally well until the spring of 2007, when I screwed up and was drawn back, literally by default, into the Special Ops world. Ok, I'll admit that I was ready to go back.

As a postscript, the Shamsi base was shuttered in late November, early December 2011 after the Pakistani government ordered the U.S. to vacate it in response to the Salala Incident, in which U.S.-led NATO forces attacked two Pakistani border check posts, killing 24 Pakistan Army soldiers. It took more than 30 U.S. sorties—and almost two weeks—to de-Blackwater and de-militarize that base. Basically, to once and for all, get the entirety of the equipment out.

These days, I try not to spend much time thinking about what might have happened if I'd never left Blackwater to pursue medicine and where I'd be had I continued all that flying-under-the-radar stuff. Yet, just like with my time in the Navy, I believe that everything happens for a reason. I'm still alive, and I'm focused on being the best person I can for my son, for my family, and for my businesses. You'll never be able to drive effectively forward if you're always looking in the rearview mirror!

CHAPTER 17

"As SEALs we are placed out on the very edges of risk; often, guided only by our moral compasses. One week, we're helping to establish U.S. foreign policy and the next, we're enforcing it with extreme prejudice. It is in these times of absolute autonomy and utter anonymity that we truly peer into the core of our humanity. Here, the compasses get re-calibrated from time to time."

—Christopher Mark Heben

My story began by telling you that when you're a member of the Special Operations community, nothing is clearly black and white. Everything you're engaged with, every mission you're on, every interaction you have, all of it blurs into a shade of gray. What I mean by this is that there are never any absolutes. Sometimes the job description changes mid-flow and there are what are called Targets of Opportunity (TOEs) and Rules of Engagement (ROEs). The former are always welcomed; the latter should never be established by assholes who have never been downrange in a combat zone or without direct consultation with those who currently are. Period. As Spec Ops guys and PMCs, these malleable states of existence and amorphous operations make for some pretty interesting and oftentimes frustrating episodes—not to mention, they're downright dangerous! This gray reality has followed many an ex-operator from the battlefield back to their life in normal society.

Episodes of PTSD, daily episodes of short fuses, nightmares, and waking up with a case of the cold sweats in the middle of the night are all examples of the issues and trouble that many returning members of the military have readjusting to life at home. Thankfully, I don't suffer from PTSD. The Veteran's Administration agrees with me. But that doesn't mean I don't suffer from being underwhelmed on a daily basis in the slow-moving, rusty-wheeled environments I see every day. During my entire SEAL and private military contractor career I was used to a very fast pace of doing business. We did our research, made recommendations, and promptly made shit happen. In the world of business, the common theme is paralysis by analysis. Never one to sit back and accept my fate or accept a situation that I was not enjoying, I was always one to power through a problem. No matter what the cost to my personal sanity or my financial sanctity, I attacked every problem with a ferocity that has existed in me since I was born.

Believe me, I've faced numerous struggles. Most of my problems are really no different than many other peoples. I believe the major difference, as can be seen with my Spec Ops brothers, is the willingness to persevere no matter what it takes. Being a resilient bastard is a blessing and a curse, because even when you make a mistake or do something wrong, you do it all the way. One thing's for sure, however, I own my mistakes, as do my brothers—and there are always underlying reasons for why things happen. Many times, the reasons don't always matter, only the outcome. In my case, I worked for Dr. Mungo for about a year-and-a-half before forging those prescriptions and watching everything in my life unravel faster than a noisemaker on Bourbon Street as I stood tall and faced the consequences. The most resilient members of our exclusive fraternity are, like me, undaunted. We adapt to whatever shitty hand we're dealt—or, in my case, create for themselves. Rather than take a seat like some defeated fool and wait around for the court to adjudicate my case, I did what made the most sense, and what any Frogman would do: I took positive action. I voluntarily rescinded all of my medical licenses and hospital privileges, then walked away from everything in Ohio and promptly sprinted back to a place tucked way back in the heart of the Dismal Swamp—a place called Blackwater—and said, "I'm back!"

Re-integrating to life in Blackwater was seamless; it felt like home. Sure, I was going to miss my son, but he was in good hands with my now ex-wife Michelle. Things hadn't worked out between the two of us, which was a shame. But to this day she remains a great and trusted friend, and together we are raising one hell of an amazing young man. I know in my heart that he is already better than me, and in time he will prove this to be true. As for me, and at that time, I knew how to be a SEAL and Special Operator better than I knew how to be a dad and a PA in the conventional sense, even though the medical component of the job was comparable and I had been taking care of my siblings since I was a kid. So, returning to BW was a welcome event. Before my arrest in Atlanta, I managed to crank out five deployments with Blackwater, much of it in Ouagadougou, Burkina Faso, under the auspices of the U.S. Joint Special Operations Aviation Detachment (US-JSOAD) there.

The U.S. State Department had an agreement with the Burkina Faso government. As a result, we not only had an Embassy there but also a safe house. It was located smack dab in the middle of the capital city of Ouagadougou, and served as an operations center. It was an impressive compound—three-stories high with fortified eight-foot walls surrounding it—with its own generator and a medical clinic. From there we deployed to a nearby airfield where we kept a couple of CASA C-212 Aviocars, turboprop-powered, short take-off and landing (STOL), medium transport aircraft. It was a good set-up and I was playing a leading role in that theater of operations that just so happened to span across North Africa.

Our official mission subset was that we were part of the Joint Special Operations Aviation Detachment (JSOAD), teaming with Special Forces groups and Special Ops Teams from the Army, Navy, Air Force and Marines. We also worked hand-in-hand, on occasion, with the French Foreign Legion, the French Consulate, and the local host governments from many nations that were in need of assistance combating al Qaeda in that part of the continent. Blackwater was officially contracted by the Department of Defense, with Department of State authorization and CIA connections, so more often than not there were three layers to everything we did. We were problem solvers, diplomats, and warriors, and which one of those personas you got to meet depended a whole lot on who you were and what you happened to be doing. Think of us as primarily a high-dollar, concierge solutions service. We offered VIP &

diplomatic transportation, expedient and austere medical evacuation, and other definitive solutions when called upon. In short, we were there to basically do whatever was needed—no matter what the mission or what was required. No questions asked.

Most of our day-to-day work consisted of ferrying around U.S. VIPs and foreign national military members and dignitaries. Often, we dropped off supplies to Special Forces teams in the field, picked up people in the field, and handled a variety of emergent and non-emergent medical issues as they cropped up. We operated in Chad, Mali, Central African Republic, Ghana, Mauritania, Morocco, Benin, as well as a few other nearby countries in the region that I cannot mention. We were always on standby as a quick-reaction force ready to leap on a plane and rescue U.S. Special Forces operators whenever they found themselves in trouble. Our status as private military contractors provided separation from the official military on the ground. For us, it was always a very permissible environment, no matter how non-permissible or hostile. And, because Burkina Faso was a former French colony, we were able to work closely with the French and piggyback with a lot of their pre-existing arrangements, assets and locations. This was also a blessing for my quest to pick up the French language, or I should say, to *Parlez Français*. The quickest way to be labelled an *ugly American* is to be foreign language deficient. Hell, most Americans have yet to master English!

The Burkina Faso government enjoyed its relationship with the U.S. because it gave them a strong ally in a region where destabilization was a very common occurrence. The west central region of Africa, just above the equator, had tactical and strategic value for us—al Qaeda was trying to strengthen its position in the area and garner more recruits to its radical view of Islam—and from Ouagadougou you could fly anywhere you needed to go, relatively quickly, and without worrying about entering, capable, unfriendly airspace unless you headed North toward Libya. That is, they were the only ones capable of air intercept.

This was around the time that one of my Navy SEAL brothers, Jason Redman, was shot in Iraq. I was in Chad, making daily trips in and out of one of the SEAL Team Two safe houses when it all happened. Jason was a prior enlisted SEAL before accepting a Navy Commission in 2004. He attended Ranger School in 2006 and a year later, in September 2007, he deployed to Iraq. Jason was now a SEAL Lieutenant leading a SEAL Assault Team on an operation designed to take down a senior al Qaeda leader. He and his Team encountered a large enemy force and began to take heavy automatic weapons fire. In the ensuing firefight, the SEALs were able to achieve dominance, but during the battle Jason was shot eight times, including a devastating round to the face. He nearly bled out on the battlefield. I hadn't seen him in a while, but we had served together at SEAL Team Eight a few years earlier. When I heard about the incident it was a mixed bag of emotions. It sucked because I wished I could have been there to have his back. I was in Africa, not Iraq, and taking the fight to the bad guys there. Yet, here was one of my former teammates and a brother-in-arms getting shot up and nearly killed.

I remember having this lengthy conversation with some of the SEALs from Team Two in Chad. They asked me what it was like to work for Blackwater. I said that although the money was great and the operational tempo was very high, I missed being a SEAL because of the commonality we all shared. I also mentioned that the grass was always greener on the other side, and that although we made good money we didn't have the luxury of calling an F-18 in for close-air support if needed. Also, we had to pay for a lot of our own personal equipment. As a SEAL, you get damn near everything you need to complete a deployment or a mission—with no questions asked. At BW, you got a shitty initial gear issue, unless you consider 5.11 Tactical crap good. But anything after that was coming out of your pocket. But the point I really drove home was that I no longer felt that firm Team Guy connection as a PMC, and what had just happened a few days earlier to Jason made that chasm seem even wider and deeper. It was weird, but I think they understood where I was coming from.

Despite this new-found feeling of switching gears and feeling a bit out of the true SEAL Team loop, I was able to flip the switch and adjust to my return to Blackwater. Admittedly, I had been out of the game for a couple years and instead of listening to the obnoxious and obligatory *salat* (five daily prayers said by Muslims), the smell of spent ordnance mixed with Third World filth, or the rush of the wind after leaping from airplanes, I enjoyed sitting on 10 acres at my country home with fruit trees and ponds around me, listening to nature and hunting it. But now, I was back at 'work' and I needed to return my head to swivel mode. Taking in every minute detail around me was critical because it could mean the difference between life and death for me and the team.

At the same time, because I'd been working in medicine for more than a decade—both in the military and in private life—I was sharp. That was key because administering medicine in Africa is a hell of a lot different than applying it in the U.S.—you're handing out drugs that kill worms and intestinal parasites, and you have to worry about mosquitoes that carry diseases like malaria. Not to mention, the larger wildlife that wants to kill and consume you, or consume you while it's killing you. Hell, almost every tree, bush, plant or shrub there grows some sort of spike or thorn that's capable of ripping your flesh. It's a very different and extremely hostile and dangerous place, and you better be squared away and know your shit, or people will die from some pretty nasty things.

One of the things I came to immediately appreciate while I was there was the immensity that is Africa; It's not just big, it's fucking huge! When we flew from Ouagadougou (Burkina Faso), to a French Airbase in N'Djamena (Chad), it was a six-hour plus flight. To put it into perspective, that's over two-hours longer than a flight from New York to Los Angeles. Africa is so vast that the entire United States fits neatly in an area less than one-third of its total land mass. I find it humorous and sad at the same time, but most Americans don't realize Africa is a continent and not a country. In fact, there are 54 or so of them in Africa, each with their own very distinct identity. I first caught a glimpse of its enormity when I was in Egypt and Djabouti during my time in the SEAL Teams and would later get a very intimate look at it during my time at Blackwater. It's a vastly diverse place, and there are more languages spoken in Africa than I could have ever imagined.

Collectively, I have spent nearly three years of my life on the continent of Africa, in more than 30 different countries. I think that makes me somewhat of an African American. LOL. Now, I'm not claiming to be "Trans-Racial." I simply think if you're a black person in America who's never even been to Africa, you should simply be an 'American of African descent', or better yet, just be human. After all, I'm white and I don't claim another continent along with my country as part of my ethnic identity. I'm a human American male of Scotch-Irish-Lithuanian-descent. What I'm merely trying to say is that we do ourselves a disservice as a race of humans by trying to over-categorize ourselves. It only, collectively, keeps us down! Skin color is oftentimes obvious, sometimes interpretive, and it is not, nor should it ever be, indicative of the ability or the potential of any human. We should embrace merit, not the quality or quantity of a persons melanocytes and their production, or lack thereof, of melanin.

But, getting back to Africa; I learned a great deal of French in nine months because I was immersed in areas of the continent where French was still the language of business and the social set. By hearing it, reading it, seeing it, saying it, and not being afraid to make mistakes while speaking it, I was able to fast-forward my understanding of it. In fact, while flying to and from certain operations, I could be found reading *French In Ten Minutes a Day* as well as listening to the MP3 files on an iPod.

The prescribed 10-minutes-a-day turned into about 24 hours a day real fast, especially when you account for the fact that it was in use all around me. I also met a wonderful French woman named Catherine B. and her two daughters, Maelune and Marçau, aged 17 and 13 respectively. That didn't hurt either. The four of us socialized, hung out and went to dinner whenever possible. Catherine did all the record keeping at the French embassy and was also taking lessons to gain her pilot's license. She and her daughters had been in Burkina for a few years already. And between Peace Corps encounters, fleeting pool parties and lasting relationships like the ones I maintained with Catherine and her daughters, I enjoyed many moments of normalcy amidst the craziness. These were much needed and anticipated by all involved. It was always a two-way street and one we were extremely happy and very motivated to help pave for one another. Catherine and the girls are a wonderful family and a true reflection of the beauty of the French culture and French people. We remain friends to this very day.

Indeed, learning other languages is more addictive than getting a tattoo. Hell, I even picked up some African dialects during my time overseas. Anything worth doing is worth overdoing. In that vein, I managed to continuously practice those native African languages in places where we would be stationed most often. It was the least I could do to honor the cultures and assist me and the other guys in navigating through the social scene when we were on downtime or needed to liaise with someone to achieve a particular task. Most of all, speaking other languages allows me to hide the fact that I am American. Believe it or not, this can be very helpful when overseas, and for a multitude of reasons.

Each of my Blackwater deployments during this stretch lasted for 60 days. I'd be in-country for two months then head back home for three or four weeks, then head back to Africa for another 60-day hitch. So from April 2007 to March 2008, I spent about 240 total days in Africa, and it was a nice system while it lasted.

In Africa, the compound we stayed in had a single controlled entry-point. Unlike the 'Alamo' in Pakistan, where we were surrounded by un-friendlies and had to man our own security, the U.S. Embassy in Burkina Faso had its own guard service. They hired vetted locals, who would wear official uniforms and man the gates—not just at our safe house, but at all of the other embassy employees' houses, as warranted. They would rotate, so they wouldn't be at any one post for too long, but you got to know these dudes and they were decent guys. Of course, you weren't 100 percent sure you could completely trust them, but they certainly always acted as though they were on the right side. These guys served as our first line of defense. I can't discuss the rest of the measures we had in place, but we all rested better knowing that they were in effect and definitively deadly.

Inside the walls, we had a massive generator. If electricity in the city went down, we could sustain power inside the compound for a couple weeks. We had satellite TV, and internet access—this helped us all to keep in touch with friends and family back home. There was also a pretty capable medical clinic therein where we could treat bumps, scrapes and bruises. In the case of a real emergency, we could convert it into something more akin to a field hospital or, In Dan's case, a surgical center.

There was an exercise facility with dumbbells, free weights and machine-assisted cable-style weights. In the room next to the exercise facility kept an enormous stock of water, as well as another water-purifying machine—just in case. We also had our own, in-ground, swimming pool—which all added up to helping make the place our own personal little slice of heaven in Africa.

When we first moved in, there was no greenery inside the walls of the safe house. We planted flowers and grass to give it a little oasis look and make it more of a safe haven instead of a cold and calloused looking safe house—especially by the pool. At times, at least from the inside, you'd swear you were staying at a resort hotel, especially when we had bikini-clad Peace Corps gals lounging poolside or, on occasion, hot hookers from Eastern Europe. We basically had our own little multicultural and eclectic ecosystem. By design, and for obvious reasons, we kept the outside looking shitty and uninviting.

As USSOCOM's only contracted and combat-capable African air wing, our planes were custom-made for our missions. The CASA C-212s were mid-sized planes with maximum-sized capabilities—not only from a performance standpoint, but from what they contained inside. Medically, we could treat about four patients on board comfortably, but in a pinch could squeeze in six—with just enough room for the crew. We'd staff the plane with either four or five people, depending on the mission: A pilot, co-pilot, a mechanical engineer, and a combat medic or two. If possible, one of them would also run point on tactical operations. Otherwise, we'd need a sixth man. Luckily, I was both a medic and in charge of any tactical operations, so when we were in Africa the dual role fell to me, Dan or another 18-Delta, Erik H, and we all gladly accepted it.

The dynamics of the assignment and our varied missions were always amazing. Every pilot was skilled in STOL (Short Take-Off and Landing). Some of the African airports we had to land at had less than

1,000 feet of runway, so STOL was an essential skill. We needed severely overpowered planes that could take off in a short-amount of space and carry a lot of extra supplies—you never knew what kind of shit storm you were headed into or needing to escape from. Without going into any detail about any of the sensitive items on-board, rounding out our extras was the massive fuel capacity. In addition to the oversized fuel bladders in the wings, we also carried two or three huge barrels of fuel inside on the port side area of the fuselage. These massive blue drums were filled with JP8—a highly flammable aviation fuel. From time to time, one of us had to go into the back of the plane and hand-crank a pump to deliver fresh fuel to the pods in the wings. As with the planes in Pakistan, we were completely outside the realm of FAA regulations. Additionally, we also had oxygen on board for the crew and potential patients to breathe. Combined all these ingredients and we were essentially sitting in this, massive flying 'bomb' shaped like a plane. But carrying the extra fuel on board—no matter how potentially dangerous—extended our range and ability to stay high and long in the air. When you're in combat zones and austere regions of the globe and can't easily land at airfields because you don't know if the people are friendly or not, having enough spare fuel gives you the luxury of bypassing a lot of sketchy landing areas. Flying high allows the fuel to burn slower. You get it!

It was all crazy, but in a cool way. As an Operator you make a mental note of it, and then go; "Check. Moving on. What else?"

Oh yeah, you had to remind the pilots not to smoke from time to time. They were, indeed, major risk takers just like the rest of us, but some risks were unnecessary and just downright dumb.

The home airfield we used to deploy the CASAs was a few miles away from the safe house and we'd hit the airfield pretty much every day, whether we needed to take the planes off the ground or not. They needed regular maintenance and I had to keep the batteries charged for all the diagnostic units we kept on board—EKGs, blood-pressure cuffs, suction devices, oxygen-saturation devices, etc. The high heat, up to 125 degrees, had a way of draining battery life pretty quickly. It reminded me of what they drilled into our skulls at BUD/S: Having the proper impedimenta can mean the difference between success and total mission failure. Be it the mind, the body, or the belongings: Take care of your gear and your gear will take care of you! Back-ups were a must, and we lived by yet another SEAL saying: Two is one and one is none!

Our safe house always seemed to have people coming and going as part of the weekly operations. At any one time there'd be at least 10 to 12 of us milling around. We had pilots—about four to six; three flight mechanics; at least one medical guy, if not two; and the person in charge of the house. The chief of station there was David D., and he was tireless in his pursuit of excellence. He ran a tight ship and we were more than happy to assist him with that. During my last couple deployments, our lead mechanic was a guy named Curly Bob. He was in his mid-to-late 60s, but worked like he was in his 20s. Everybody loved Curly Bob—he was wise and unshakeable and he could fix damn near anything. With his snow-white hair and slow, quick thinking yet slow and calculatingly Southern way of talking, he was like a real life version of John Wayne meets MacGyver meets Hannibal from the *The A-Team*. All that was missing was the cigar and an ability to put up with shit from a large, Mohawk-wearing dude named Mr. T.

To round it out, we had a few house assistants and groundskeepers. My favorite was definitely the young and very beautiful Anna. Anna kept up the house and cooked us food. She was in charge of making us two meals per day, and this was usually lunch and dinner. On occasion, and if she had the right ingredients, she would arrive early and fire up a tasty breakfast for early risers. She was young, gorgeous, funny, and always smiling—a total pleasure to be around. Her father was a well-to-do local who originally hailed from Ghana and had moved to Ouagadougou for business. Besides several different African dialects, Anna was fluent in both French and English. She was 21-years old, and a really good kid. She knew we were Americans, and affiliated with the military in some way, but she didn't know our missions and was never nosy about what we were doing. We paid her well and she was always very happy and very well taken care of. Because of Anna, we were able to live off the local economy even more than we would have already been doing.

Oftentimes, and depending on who was home, we would accompany her to a market or store to help her buy a couple days' worth of fresh food. It was always fun to assist her in picking out fresh food and watch her wheel and deal with all the shopkeepers. She was a natural, and her beauty was a definite asset to her ability to swing a deal. That, and the 'white gorilla' she was with a lot. And that would be me! I would always hear the locals call out to me *"Le Blanc Gorille!"* or "John Cena!"

Burkina Faso was a French colony until the mid-1960s, so there were a lot of nice French restaurants, bars and boutiques. French was and is the language of commerce and of the socialites who enjoyed all the great eateries and bars. I'd go to a French restaurant every once in a while, run into girls from the Peace Corps, and chat it up. We'd invite them over for pool parties—we were, after all, trying to lead semi-normal lives in between our missions. And, yes, we chased a little tail—after all, who didn't want to chase tail in Africa? We went to numerous embassy parties and got to know the Regional Safety Officer (RSO), Pete, at the U.S. Embassy, very well. So much so, in fact, we used to have basketball blowouts in his driveway for hours at a time!

All in all, it was an extremely dynamic environment. I like to think of it as the tactical equivalent of the United Nations of diplomatic ass-kickery mixed with the tactlessly exotic and tackily erotic tomfoolery of a foreign porn industry. Indeed, many of us were taking in new tastes, sights and sounds every day, as well as doing a very critical job for our government. And we were getting paid handsomely to do so.

Africa was definitely an interesting place. It was so different from how it is often portrayed on TV and in the news. In Burkina Faso, for example, about 80 percent of the roads are paved—it's not the barren wasteland or wild jungle people think it is. Every day was sunny because we were close to the equator. The temperature regularly rose into the high 90s. The air was filled with the omnipresent and ubiquitous smells of exotic food, burning charcoal fires, and poverty. Yes, poverty does have a smell and it isn't that great. I call it "The stale stench of humanity," and it's pervasive. It's a mix between toe jam, armpit, asshole, halitosis, and stale urine. Sometimes you catch a knockout blow of a whiff from all of these not so 'Fab 5' fragrances at once, and sometimes you get an overpowering sucker punch dose of one or two. But it is all there and in some places more than others.

There are many successful and industrious people in Africa who are very intelligent and quick on their feet. They are also eager to learn and to teach. Still, the poverty was always lurking and many people also lived in simple mud-walled homes with tin roofs. Their bathrooms were 10-feet away from their homes and smelled worse than a truck-stop shitter in a heat wave. Indeed, everywhere you went there was a strange smell, sometimes good, sometimes bad. No matter the forecasted weather at the time, it was always hot, sticky and sweaty—it was inescapable.

Mopeds and bicycles served as the people movers. They outnumber cars by about a five-to-one ratio, and there is never a shortage of incredible shit to see. It's not uncommon to see a woman on a moped with a baby strapped to her back and front with a third child in front of the handlebars while bags of groceries are hanging from both of her arms! It's like a crazy circus act that you pray doesn't spill out in front of the BMW 5 series you're driving. Speaking of BMWs, it was usually rich white foreigners or wealthy African dignitaries who you saw driving these types of cars. There was never a shortage available to purchase at a very reasonable price. I cannot prove this, but we believe most of the high-end cars in Africa were stolen from the U.S. and Europe. There's an ass for every seat, even if it's a hot seat! I never really felt like I was in physical danger during my time in Burkina Faso, and I regularly pedaled my way all over Ouaga. Maybe that was because I was always at the ready, tactically aware of my surroundings and I knew I could physically handle most anything that happened, even that dreaded five-passenger moped wreck! Truth be told, we weren't rolling around with our weapons overtly displayed, but I always had a knife or two or three on me at the very least. And, quite frankly, at all times.

Our team was in Ouagadougou with a definite sense of purpose and a critical mission. We were a very professional taxi service—toting

UNDAUNTED

around VIPs from one destination to another—and a very professional medical evacuation service. More important, we could deliver a swift ass-kicking if the situation called for it. As a group, we didn't exactly have *average* days, but we did spend our downtime planning: Where do we have to go today? Tomorrow? Three weeks from now? Four? How do we plan to re-fuel? What's the best flight route? What clearance do we need to get into this or that country? When we land somewhere, are we going to have to fight our way out or pay some crazy 'ransom' or fine in order to take back off? Life was never routine, and it was always logistics, logistics, logistics. But then, emergencies would crop up—and those were the most fun of all.

Another facet of our mission included low-level intel overpasses with cameras attached to the CASAs. In some areas, and if the need arose, we had the ability to mount a mini-gun on the back so we could rain down righteousness on identified and hardened targets—like al Qaeda training camps. And as I mentioned before: The planes had medevac capability and carried a full complement of medicine—cardiac drugs and morphine—to go with diagnostic and procedural equipment. It was an air-mobile ICU/assault-capable, low-flying war machine. We flew everywhere in it—from Casablanca, Liberia, Libya, Mali, Chad, and even the Central African Republic. We took pictures. We took names. And we made a lot of shit happen. We also prevented a lot of shit from happening. But I'm required to tell you that none of that shit ever happened. Are you mopping up what I'm spilling?

We routinely went from Burkina Faso to Chad, which was a six-hour flight. The U.S. had a strong presence in Chad. Beyond the embassy in N'Djamena, Chad's capital city, we also had access to a few Navy SEAL safe houses. There was always some SEAL platoon there, so it was great to visit my previous brothers-in-arms and see old friends. Chad was much different than Burkina Faso in that only about 50 percent of the roads were paved. Most of the time, once you got only a few miles away from the embassy areas or the Presidential palace, driving in Chad was like driving down a cheese grater with tires made out of sandstone. But we adjusted, like we always did, and made the most of it. Chad was also another place where I could continue to hone my French, and that was a very good thing.

I woke up each day in Africa hoping for the best yet prepared for the worst. Plan as you may, you never knew what was going to happen. From a medical perspective, I approached Africa using protocols called Universal Precautions. Think of it as though you assume everyone you come across has AIDS: You treat them accordingly, use gloves and masks, and don't screw around. You treat every patient as if they had the worst medical malady on the planet. You don't tell them that; you lock it in your mind. But your procedures show otherwise. You treat everyone that way so you're not really being prejudice or slanted towards or against any one person. We did the same thing in the U.S, but you thought about the possibility of exposure to AIDS and Ebola even more in Africa. When it came to operational and tactical techniques and procedures, we always assumed everyone to be sketchy, unreliable, and a potential threat. Again, you don't act that way overtly, but in the forefront of your mind (NOT THE BACK!), that's the file folder you're working with.

For every mission we launched on, we received a situational report (SITREP) first, so that we knew to a certain extent what we were flying into, who our liaisons were on the ground, and where their positions where. If there was an American counterpart already on the ground, we'd connect with him or her, and share intelligence. Africa, as I mentioned, is a funky place. There's always some conflict going on in one of the countries—whether it's over oil, timber, gold or diamonds, or some other component used in some expensive item that the rest of the world thinks it needs. It's always bloody and it's always as brutal as you can imagine. Africa is like the undocumented rape victim of the world. Yet, there's no sexual-assault nurse examiner (SANE) on every corner waiting to document it. It's insane sometimes.

Making it worse is that most of these countries have cleptocratic governments that will take money and do anything that is asked of them—even kill their own people—in order to make a swift buck. It's a very strange place. Yes, it is beautiful, but it can also be deadly when you find yourself in the wrong places at the wrong times. For us, it was often our job to put ourselves in those places and at those very times.

That's what we do, what we did, and why they paid us the big bucks. We're the opposite of the Peace Corp, in that, we aren't building schools or churches or mosques, for that matter. And, we make about 1,000 times what they do in a day. But hey, they have their role and we have ours. I'll always come to their rescue if the call comes. And it has.

When we weren't flying around from country to country, we had our typical routines—checking equipment, gear and medical equipment; performing scheduled maintenance on the planes; and gathering and sharing intelligence. There was always something to do. I can't remember too many days when we didn't have at least one plane in the air.

And then there were those times when we were deployed on very specific missions or the shit would just hit the fan. Often, we'd connect with Special Forces units that were in the area and serve as back-up or re-suppliers. We'd fly into Timbuktu and drive to this little town called Mopti. Mopti was situated in the middle of this confluence of rivers and was a surprisingly nice place. Many times, we'd land in Timbuktu and sit in the staging area with our plane, waiting for a call from the Special Forces units on the ground.

In February 2008, we flew into Timbuktu and were informed that a group of Special Forces guys needed to be resupplied in the field. They had lost a couple tires on a vehicle and were also running low on fuel. We had to do a vertical resupply, where we flew at a very low level, opened the back ramp and pushed palletized tires and other supplies out the back. The packages would drop down and land in the sand where the Special Forces guys would promptly retrieve what we'd dropped.

We did our flyby in the middle of the desert and there were two or three vehicles parked in the sand and a couple herds of camels milling about. I had recently met this girl on one of our missions to Mali during a routine transport trip for a couple of ambassadors. Her name was Angie, and she was an Army Captain from Ohio. About three-weeks earlier, Angie had been tasked with picking up our two pilots, our mechanic, and me at this Malian hotel where we were staying. The two of us hit it off—on several levels—and here I was, resupplying a Special Forces unit in the middle of Chad, the same group Angie was embedded with as the Intelligence Officer and Interpreter.

I was bummed that we weren't landing, so being the hopeless romantic that I am, I decided to write her this nice, poetically charged and prosaically flowery poem of a note. After I was sure that I had penned the literary equivalent of an African aphrodisiac, I neatly rolled it up and lowered it inside a Nalgene bottle. I then screwed it down, further taped it closed, and attached it with heavy duty, olive drab, 550-para-cord, to one of the pallets. That thing wasn't going anywhere, despite the fact that we would be jettisoning the palettes out the back of the Casa at a speed of 120 knots and from a height of about 50 feet. To further ensure delivery, I wrote her name and rank on the riggers tape on the outside of the 'package' and we shoved it out of the plane. Curly Bob and I were grinning the whole time as we watched the love note-laden pallet plummet toward the sand-covered earth.

A few minutes later, the guys retrieved the packages and were unpacking the gear when they came across the bottle for Angie. It was wild—she got a message in a bottle from me, airdropped from a plane in the middle of a scorched North African desert. Wild? Yes. Weird? Perhaps. But cool? DEFINITELY. To this day, she remembers that story very well. She also remembers the non-stop, shit storm of jokes and the barrage of male-minded wisecracks she had to endure because of it. I accomplished both of my missions: 1) Profess my affection 2) Mark my territory. Despite it all, we still laugh about it whenever it comes up during a conversation. Today, Angie is working for a certain alphabet organization on the D.C. beltway. Never one to sit still, she also has a MBA from The Ohio State University's Fisher School of Business, rides a Harley-Davidson, and hunts deer whenever she can. She is a rare breed, and I am glad to call her a friend. Always. She embodies the definition of the word Patriot and her selfless service has saved countless lives.

CHAPTER 18

> "AMERICA, WE'VE GOT YOUR SIX.... METAPHORICALLY, FIGURATIVELY, LITERALLY, EMBLEMATICALLY, SYMBOLICALLY AND CATEGORICALLY!"
>
> —CHRISTOPHER MARK HEBEN

In February 2008, Blackwater was called in to help with the emergency evacuation of the U.S. Embassy in N'Djamena, Chad's capital city. Sudanese rebels from the Union of Forces for Democracy and Development (UFDD) had crossed the border, marched across the country in three days, and then stormed N'Djamena.

For three days, the UFDD and Chadian rebels waged a full-fledged assault on the city, going toe-to-toe against a contingency of Chadian security forces, French soldiers, U.S. Navy SEALs and private military contractors. The assault was UFDD's last-minute attempt to overthrow Idriss Deby, Chad's president, before European Union peacekeepers arrived to provide security for humanitarian-relief operations amid the violence spilling over from Sudan's ongoing conflict in the Darfur region. It was a cluster-fuck of a situation, but at least the Chadian forces weren't acting alone. The French Gendarmerie National and French Foreign Legionnaires lent crucial logistical and arms support to the Chadian soldiers. The U.S. utilized a SEAL Team on the ground, and Blackwater was called in to give a helping hand with whatever tasking shortfalls were encountered as well as to provide evacuation transportation from both a ground and air standpoint. While the main forces were fending off the rebels from the Chad Presidential Palace, our mission was to work with the SEALs to hastily evacuate the U.S. Embassy.

Shortly after the call came in, the other CASA was wheels-up and en route to N'Djamena. Chad's Presidential Palace was taking heavy fire—mortar rounds—from fierce rebel attacks, and the combined friendly forces were doing their damndest to hold them off. We had only a few hours to plan our part of the mission. We developed flight routes for the evacuation, planned what load supplies we'd need, and concocted contingency plans for when the shit hit the fan, because no matter how well you plan a mission, shit happens, so you better be prepared. Just like the saying, "Two is one and one is none," we always had a primary, secondary and tertiary plan of operations, to say the least. Often, there were subplans within those three sets of plans. We would *what if* everything to death. Today, in business, I approach things the same way. It just works.

The decision to evacuate a U.S. Embassy is never an easy one—you never want to give up forward positions, well, unless you are in the Obama administration. Then it's just like putting out breath mints at the hostess stand of a restaurant and saying, "take 'em if ya want 'em!" Obama-bashing aside, the fighting in Darfur had reached critical levels and pockets of violence were popping up all over as rebel forces, seemingly, sensed the opportunity to strike. SEAL Team Two was tasked to run the U.S. Embassy evacuation. We provided support—helped with the extraction, delivered medical treatment, ground transported embassy personnel to the airport, and then helped fly them out of the country. We knew a few of the guys in Team Two already, so this was going to be a mini-homecoming of sorts.

The U.S. government didn't want the public to know we had a SEAL Team on the ground in Chad, so the French were tabbed as the operation's lead, as well as its originators. It made sense. The French government maintained a strong military presence in Chad since the mid-1960s when the country was handed back to them fully. If you traveled around the city—even during calmer times—you were likely to see Gendarmes, French military police, and even French Foreign

Legionnaires in many places. They operated out of an airbase right outside the capital city and even had their own medical facilities on post nearby. They kept a fleet of helicopters and Mirage fighter jets on the same base, which gave them the ability to fully and quickly support their troops throughout the region.

Upon arrival, BW fell back to the SEAL safe house to prep for our part of the operation and then to further ensure that location was secure when Team Two launched to fulfill their part of the operation. Along with security support, BW also helped them to get all the sensitive information out and then set off to get people out of the embassy. There was one big caveat everyone had to deal with: No one was given permission to engage the rebels in street combat—essentially, we couldn't initiate gunplay. Our mission was support-related, not to start patrolling and killing rebels. The team was basically told, "Here's a gun. Look for work. But don't shoot anyone until they shoot at you first. And, if someone fires at you, but then drops their weapon, you can't fire back unless they pick the weapon up again." It's the same old bullshit ROEs (Rules of Engagement) you hear about in Afghanistan and Iraq.

Understandably, the battle was short but insane—over the course of three days, there were high-intensity, short-duration skirmishes everywhere. French helicopters were buzzing the city and sent many air-to-ground rockets at rebel troop concentrations. Explosive impact tremors from rockets and the thump and crunch of mortars were often heard and felt amidst the cacophony of small-arms fire. Luckily, French armored-personnel carriers were on hand, and these were used to conduct large portions of the personnel evacuations from the U.S. and French embassies, as well as the U.S. housing compound and the Presidential Palace.

It was total chaos, but it was chaotically fun—if that makes any sense—and made for a very dynamic operation. Yes, there were people getting shot in the streets, so it wasn't a party by any means. At one point, there was a dude that looked a whole lot like Puff Daddy casually strolling down the street with an RPG in his hand, slung over his shoulder, like he was on his way to the local ball field with his baseball bat.

As you looked down the streets in any direction, rebels were everywhere. The Blackwater guys and the SEALs on the rooftops of the US Embassy and U.S. housing compound all had a shit-ton of trigger time across the span of their collective careers. We also had superior weaponry and optics. In no time, there were bodies all over the place. Freshly dead laid in the streets—a combination of rebels and Chadians, some soldiers in uniform and also a few townspeople who had been gunned down while they were defending their homes, or looting others' homes. Before too long, the heavily armed government forces were driving up and down the streets in technical trucks with mounted recoilless rockets and heavy machine guns—matching the firepower of the rebels. These weapons made very distinct sounds when fired and their use usually resulted in very little, if any, return fire from the rebel positions. The good guys were much better trained than the rebels, yet the rebels were everywhere. And they were shooting at everyone—those in uniform and unarmed civilians and townspeople. As a result, there was general mayhem. Those people who didn't leave and weren't gunned down in the streets started looting again—making off with whatever they could carry from whichever buildings they could breach. They even raided the homes of U.S. Embassy personnel while those people were huddled together at the embassy, in the housing compound, and at the President's Palace, waiting to be evacuated and shuttled out of the country. People stole furniture, microwaves, water-purification machines, air-conditioning units, food, and other valuables. If it could be carried off, it was. We all did what we had to do—all bets were off—and so were the safeties on our weapons.

Every one moved with a definitive purpose or sat as still as possible to get a better sense of any movement nearby or in the distance. The staccato of gunfire was multi-directional. Every once in a while a bullet ricocheted off a wall behind our positions or whizzed over one of our heads. There were bullet holes in walls, burning cars in the streets, looted homes, helicopters circling overhead, rockets and mortars impacting the ground, and the sounds of heavy weapons fire in the distance. It was a tense scene. As you might imagine, the embassy staff was pretty freaked out.

With great teamwork and clockwork-like precision, guys rolled up to the embassy and housing compound in Toyota T-100 trucks and French Armored Personnel Carriers. Everyone was loaded for bear—with extra guns and ammo. Everyone was looking for work. Officially, BW was assigned to support—in any way necessary—the extraction performed by the SEALs. They arrived first in two armored vehicles, ready to transport Americans.

The SEALs already inside the compound instructed our team where to go. The heavily fortified vehicle train pulled up to the edge of one of the thick-walled embassy gates. This was our exit point. From there, the American citizens were herded into the back of the vehicles and driven to the French military airport. Each vehicle could hold about eight or nine people, so preparations were made for several trips back and forth between the two locations and the airport. The entire scene had de-escalated at that point, but the possibility of hidden rebels remained and the team was ready to escort the armored vehicles from the embassy to the airport and back, as many times as necessary. The plan also involved leaving two trucks at the embassy to keep the gates secure and eliminate anyone who tried to come over the walls.

This was controlled chaos at its best. When you're engaged in this type of operation, you're always looking for work—that is, to discharge your weapon at a verified target who is, likewise, looking to do the same to you. It's all potentially brutal, but it's very honest work. And you're always calling out directions—keeping people moving, telling them to get down, keeping your own head low and on a swivel. Everything is loud. Everything is very precise. Your goal is to keep people's brains focused on the loudness coming from your mouth and the directions you're barking rather than let them focus on what's really going on around them. Gunfire, even If very distant, can be severely paralyzing to a civilian. We're some very unique individuals in that we actually run toward the sound of gunfire!

Everybody has a role, and it's very well coordinated. You have guys who are people movers. It's their job (with a weapon in one hand) to guide, this means shout, point and direct (read: PUSH) with the other. Then you have guys who have nothing to do with anybody. They have both hands on their weapon, looking out, scanning and providing cover, and shooting bad guys as needed. About half the guys move people; the other half take up security postures around the vehicles, using the vehicles as cover. And everybody is scanning, scanning, scanning, looking for work, looking for targets. At this critical point in time, if someone's an overt, weapon-carrying threat, and they aim it in your direction, you don't stop and ask, you just engage and knock them down.

While you're moving, you use a combination of visual and verbal communications—everyone has a headset. You're using hand and arm signals, and calling out what you see: "There's a threat (unknown) behind that wall!" And you point at the wall. There are always two forms of communications going on at any given moment. You may show the number two with your fingers, then flip your fingers upside down and show them walking. It's a very quick, yet effective, and oftentimes deadly, form of charades.

You're always moving around while you're on the ground. You switch from spot to spot and you make your way through a compound, across an open area, jumping and leapfrogging from one building to the next. You move, shift and pivot, non-stop, from Point A to Point Z. You herd everyone, like cattle, into vehicles. And then you rotate again. Remember, if you're taking hostile fire, you can fire back. If not, you just keep getting more people out of the building, into the trucks, and off to the airport.

As you might imagine, the embassy personnel were terrified, but they were also eager to be led to safety. When other people freeze up with fear, you are prepared. The standard procedure during an operation is to take control of their body, almost as if they're a hostile individual. And in many ways, they are, not only to themselves, but to you and to others. Speed is a form of cover because a frozen person is an easy target. You grab them by the back of their jeans or shirt and literally throw them up in the truck. While you're moving them in this fashion, you also push their head down. You may even need to slap somebody to keep them focused on following your lead. It's that imperative to keep them moving. And, to keep their brains engaged, you are continuously letting them know you're not the enemy and that you're helping them.

The airport was about a 10-minute drive from the embassy. There were three trips made back and forth and it took about an hour and a half to get everyone evacuated. Speed is of the essence when you're in a war zone. It's called getting people off the "X." The embassy and the housing compound were two very big Xs, so you wanted to get everyone out of there as fast as possible. There were many more bodies along the routes that we travelled that day.

The airport was a controlled funnel of activity. Via radio communication, all vehicles were constantly identified as they approached: "ETA two minutes" and "Roger that." It's constant back-and-forth communication—verbal and visual action meets recognition of what's happening—then you're through the gates and safe. You unload the passengers, get them onto planes, and then go back for the next group. Once the embassy and housing compound were evacuated, everyone moved into a holding pattern. You may need to transport people elsewhere. You may need to lend support to another operation. You may need to leave the country. You're basically in a shit storm of a situation for a few hours and then on standby for a few more, just waiting on further instructions. Blackwater even had another team on standby only a short trip away. The entire event was very touch-and-go from the minute it kicked off.

From my experience, it was just another day at the office for all involved—albeit a crazy day. SEALs are trained to prepare for anything. Pre- and post-mission rituals are the keys to success. The former, comprised of positive-mental imagery, positive-mechanical experience, and positive self-talk, sets us up to dominate. The latter, via dynamic debriefings, candid peer evaluations and the streamlining of SOPs, ensures continued domination. When it comes to any combat situation, the actions you take before and after are just as important as the ones in the combat situation itself. In closing: You can't raise that glass until you've kicked some ass—or prevented someone's ass from being kicked!

For the people involved, it was one of those experiences that they'll never forget—and not like a trip to the Grand Canyon or the Great Wall of China. In fact, let's take a look at what happened from a different perspective, that of Solomon Atayi, a Foreign Service officer assigned to the U.S. Embassy in Chad.

Solomon provided this first-hand account of the evacuation in a letter he posted on the U.S. State Department's internal blog:

> We were evacuated on Sunday afternoon and taken to the French military base. Early this morning at 3 a.m. a U.S. military base in Germany sent a military plane to come bring us to Yaoundé. We evacuated dependents and children on Saturday before the start of the war. They left at 4 a.m. and the war started around 9 a.m. The Department of Defense element came to the compound to secure it. We were all divided into two groups. One group with the Ambassador was at the embassy, and the other group was on the U.S. housing compound. We were all put in one room, and the 11 of us were right on the floor. We could hear the fight. One tank stopped right under our wall, and each time it fired, the room vibrated. We could hear bullets flying as well as the rocket-propelled grenades.
>
> The U.S. Navy SEALs were on the top of the biggest building on the compound, and they had authorization to open fire if anyone came onto the compound. The fight lasted until 5 p.m. when everything got quiet for the evening prayer. Then it started again 'til 9 p.m. On Sunday, it started over again. When they moved toward the President's Palace, the looting started. We were hearing from the local guards who stayed at our separate residences how one after the other they had to abandon each post because the house was invaded by looters.
>
> We all lost everything except our life. God was looking over us. Two houses on the compound got hit by strayed cannon fire. We were hearing those guns fire all day on Saturday and part of Sunday. When the rebels stopped the fight on Sunday to regroup, that's when the French troops came to the compound in armored trucks that looked like tanks and took us to their military base. The

French sent a helicopter to the embassy to airlift our Ambassador, the marines and others who were at the embassy.

A missile miraculously sailed straight through the Ambassador's office, piercing both walls and exploding outside, while embassy staff [members] were inside burning classified documents....

By the time fighting was done and the rebels were repelled, a total of 1,389 people had been transferred from Chad to Libreville, Gabon, via French military transports. This included 537 French nationals and 852 people from other nationalities, including 69 Americans. When the operation was chronicled it was listed as officially led by the crisis cell of the French Ministry of Foreign Affairs (Quai d'Orsay) and coordinated on the ground by the French armed forces. There was no mention of the SEAL presence, other than a few references to U.S. Special Forces providing a little support to the French. A few months later, in June 2008, the U.S. pulled out all non-essential personnel from its embassy ahead of more extensive fighting.

The naked truth of combat is that training prepares you to react. You've been in tense situations before. The possibility of things going wrong exists, but you're prepared. With the training you've gone through as a SEAL, you fully expect all types of things to go wrong. When you're entering a situation with that knowledge, you can manage your mindset very well. That way, when something happens outside what is briefed, you're not all that surprised. It's also funny that when nothing happens, that is when you are truly surprised. It's all about managing expectations. You fall back on your training all the time because all is fair in war and especially in business. In fact, I find myself falling back on a lot of that training today in the corporate combat environment. In many ways, I'd love to have a gun in my hand here, too!

In truth, not every scrap we got into involved firefights and combat. Just before I left Burkina Faso, unbeknownst to me for the last time, we got a medical emergency call. A couple of Malian soldiers had driven their vehicle over a landmine and it, as well as them, had been partially blown up. They were both alive, but were badly injured in the lower extremities from the blast. We were called in to scoop these guys off the ground, stabilize and treat their injuries, and get them to a Malian medical facility. They were in a very remote area of the country—deep in a civil/tribal war zone, with enemies around them. Thus, keeping their fellow Malian soldiers from coming to their rescue. Our ability to fly in, pick them up, and get the hell out of there was our advantage and their only option.

It was a kinetic, no-sleep-for-20-plus-hours operation. We landed the CASA 212, patted the soldiers down, and quickly loaded them onto the medical cots and strapped them down. The flight there was very bumpy and it would be the same, if not worse, on the way back. I gave them both a healthy dose of morphine and then proceeded to medically stabilize them, administer infection prophylaxis, and properly re-package them, and do it all in the air as we flew them to a hospital. It was very dynamic and extremely satisfying to do. Yet, it was very unusually taxing. Why? Well, somehow, one of their wives happened to be there and wanted to accompany her husband on the plane. I agreed, but only after she was patted down fully. I wasn't about to let a non-vetted person on our bird. Needless to say, we didn't get any sleep until we were back home at our safe house, twelve-hours later, and little did I know the utter shit show that was waiting for me one-day later with Dan's arrival from the States. Nor could I even foresee the life-changing event that was lurking for me at the Atlanta airport. In the course of about 10 days I went from having a top-secret clearance and working with Joint Special Operations Command as a private military contractor to being a captured fugitive and, soon-to-be convicted felon, handcuffed in the back of a Fulton County Sheriff's car and heading to the Fulton County Jail on a state-issued, federally executed, extradition order to be carried out by the U.S. Marshal Service.

CHAPTER 19

"I AM PRIVILEGED TO HAVE WITNESSED MAN'S DEPRAVITY OF MAN ON A WHOLESALE LEVEL. FOR ONLY IN THE INTIMACY OF SUCH BRUTALITY, CAN ONE TRULY REALIZE THE NEED FOR MEN WILLING TO STAND IN THE BREACH NO MATTER THE COST. I AM HONORED TO BE COUNTED AMONG SUCH MEN…AND TOGETHER WE SHALL HOLD THE LINE."

—CHRISTOPHER MARK HEBEN

In the early morning hours of May 2, 2011, members of SEAL Team Six, CIA operatives, and the U.S. Army Special Operations Command's 160th Special Operations Aviation Regiment (SOAR) launched Operation Neptune Spear—a balls-out raid on Osama bin Laden's compound in Abbottabad, Pakistan.

SEALs, supported by other U.S. Special Forces, and all pointed there by the CIA, stormed bin Laden's compound shortly after midnight. They cornered the al Qaeda leader and shot him multiple times in the body and face, killing him instantly. It had been nearly a decade since he'd masterminded the 9/11 attack on the United States, and now he was permanently removed from the food chain.

I learned about the mission's success that evening from a couple of my SEAL buddies who were already in the know before the story hit the national and international news outlets. It shouldn't come as a surprise that we info share after the execution of an event takes place. Sometimes it happens right away. Sometimes it happens many days, weeks or months after the fact. But the real-deal details are always shared within the confines of the brotherhood, as our community is a tight-knit—albeit fickle—fraternity that, for the most part, always keeps one another informed.

I had recently returned from handling a private-security job that involved numerous back-and-forth trips to a few not-so-friendly countries in the Middle East, Arabian Peninsula, and North Africa, including Libya. Not that my civilian passport being in the custody of the asshole judge that sentenced me in August 2008 ever had anything to do with my inability to travel internationally. I mean, what kind of self-proclaimed intellectual doesn't realize that there are three types of passports issued by the State Department—and a person can possess all three? But, alas, when I was officially taken off probation in August 2010, I had some overt catching up to do. As a result, I was already geared up for some hardcore overseas work: I had a shaggy mane of hair that trailed down past the top of my shoulders and went along nicely with the long, thick beard that reached nearly down to the top of my chest. I looked like I could have walked in off the street from any town in the Islamic world, including Islamabad or Abbottabad, Pakistan.

Much like the events that transpired in March 2008 at Jackson-Hartfield Airport in Atlanta, on May 6, 2011, my life changed yet again. Things had been strange for a couple years, and I'd suffered a series of ups and downs since my life-altering indiscretions in 2008 and the insidious fall out from it. From business to personal, it had been the life-experience equivalent of a nitrous-oxide enhanced roller-coaster ride being operated by a Vicodin-addicted narcoleptic on Adderall. Basically, for the last three years, it had been a dizzying to-and-fro, stop-and-go, yes-and-no, dictated by certain people and certain things that were, oftentimes by design, out of my control. I was beginning to regain control of my life, on my terms, and it felt pretty damn good to be back in that position.

That evening, I'd gone to bed around 2 a.m., totally wiped out from a long work day and with the knowledge that we finally terminated that asshole Osama Bin Laden.

Around 4:30 a.m., I woke up to use the bathroom and as I progressed toward the pisser, I noticed that my cell phone was lit up and that I had missed a call. I first thought, "Who the hell is calling at 4:30 in the morning? This can't be good."

But, I needed to piss, and while I was doing so, my second thought was that something must have gone wrong in the hours after the raid on the compound. Was one of my buddies injured or dead? Was there a Pakistani reprisal for our incursion into their nation? I was almost dreading finding out.

Not surprisingly, I had expected the worst—some other cluster fuck of a problem that I'd inherited and would have to soon deal with. When I picked up the phone, I saw that I'd missed a few other calls, too. One was from a number I recognized; the other three weren't. The number I recognized was that of U.S. Coast Guard Lt. Commander Rick DeChant (Ret.), a good friend and colleague. Rick had been a Commander in the U.S. Coast Guard and finished his career at the station in Cleveland, Ohio. Now he was the Executive Director of Veteran Services and Veterans Programs for Cuyahoga Community College. We'd gotten together from time to time on business and scholastic projects involving veterans.

Rick left a voice mail that said, "Hey Chris, this is Rick, sorry for the early or late call, depending on where you are in the world. But, my daughter, Nicole, works for Channel 5 in Cleveland. She called me and wanted to know if I knew any Special Forces guys they could interview about the Osama bin Laden raid. I gave her your number; I hope you're OK with that."

Actually, I was OK with it. Why? Because it all sounded pretty interesting and I would be more than happy to talk on film about the demise of the asshole that I had assisted in the hunt for over the last decade. Besides, other than playing myself as a SEAL in the second-ever Discovery Channel documentary on SEALs, which was filmed in 1998, and appearing in a few morning-show spots about my weapons training, street-survival training (care under fire) and private VIP security businesses, I had never really appeared on TV before and uttered any words about SEALs. I thought, "Hell, I'm totally comfortable speaking in public and this would be a welcome change, so why not?"

The second call was from a number I didn't recognize. As it turned out, it was from Rick's daughter, Nicole. She, too, had left me a voice mail.

"Mr. Heben," she said, "my name's Nicole DeChant. You know my father, Rick. I'm a producer at News Channel 5 and we're going to be covering the Bin Laden story today. Can you come into the station early this morning for a 6 a.m. live TV interview about the raid?"

With my beard and coif I was totally unfit for human consumption on TV. I was a cross between Jesus, Hercules, and King Leonidas. Strictly with respect to my hair, that is. I would never claim to resemble Jesus in any other way. LOL.

"Shit, I look like a terrorist. I can't go on TV like this," I thought.

But I truly liked the prospect of talking about my SEAL brothers on the raid and shining a powerful beam of light on their heroic actions, and the fact that Obama already let that story out of the cage, only made me think that I needed to say a few things from a standpoint of someone who actually loves and supports the U.S. military. Without further debate, I called her back and said, "Yes. I'm in. What time do you need me?

"We're going live on the air at 6 a.m. with the story. Can you be here by 5:45?"

I told her, "I'll be there by 5:40." I really had to get my ass in gear!

This was going to be something interesting and new. I hung up and quickly started to get my shit together. I grabbed a set of hair clippers, cut my beard down to about as low as I could get it with no attachment, and then used a razor to remove the rest. My hair was a lost cause, so I had no choice but to push it back off my face on either side of my head. Basically, I did the best I could to reduce my Middle Eastern man-belonging-to-anywhere-disguise and then tried to find something decent to wear. There was no way I was going to show up on TV looking like a member of al Qaeda, even if we were going to be talking about Osama bin Laden, Mr. al Qaeda, himself. That just wouldn't cut it. Besides, my current appearance was my out-of-the-U.S. ticket to move freely and safely about the globe. I couldn't risk going on TV like that. Time was running out and I needed to get the hell on the road. I put on dress shirt, threw on a tie, grabbed a sport coat, and raced off to the TV station. As luck would have it, and with no traffic to contend with at that time of day, I managed to get there a little early, around 5:30 am. I spent a few minutes shooting the shit with a couple producers and the 6 a.m. news personalities, and getting a better sense of what they wanted me to discuss.

At 6 a.m., we went live on the air to do a segment about the bin Laden raid, Navy SEALs, Special Forces, al Qaeda, and Pakistan. It all went very well. Like the typical, glad-handing, smoke-and-mirrors bullshit artists most of them are, the producers told me I was a natural and that they would like to have me back. To be perfectly candid, I actually enjoyed the experience and welcomed the next opportunity I would have to do so. And in truth, it was one of the easiest things I've ever done, and I can honestly say that it isn't a very difficult job to pull off.

Low and behold, just minutes after the segment ended, my phone started ringing off the hook with calls from all the other local affiliates—CBS, NBC and Fox. Things spiraled from there. Within the span of four to five hours, my interviews were picked up by the national networks and then broadcast on other affiliates in more than 50 markets across the U.S.

By day's end, I was getting calls from CNN, Fox News and MSNBC, just to name a few—all of them wanting me to do interviews and discuss, from a SEAL's perspective, what had gone down in Pakistan. Within a few more days, the requests had expanded to HLN and CNN International. This was pretty cool, and I was having a damn good time.

Most of the interviews didn't require any travel, and I was able to do them from local studios in Cleveland. But then producers started asking me to fly to CNN or Fox Studios in New York City, and I was invited to make an appearance with Jon Scott and Martha MacCallum on their Fox morning show. Next they asked me to do a segment with Judge Jeanine Pirro on the *Justice with Judge Jeanine* show in the 9 p.m. time slot. That's when I realized that this might just be something with a lot of potential to make things happen for myself as well as for my business and to be a voice for veterans and the Spec Ops community. In fact, I owe a lot to Fox News. Fox was one of the first national stations to hit me with multiple requests and offer me multiple appearances across several daytime and evening shows.

For weeks, the requests were continuous, and it didn't take long before producers started seeking me out as a military expert on TV. It was a crazy time, and it reached a point where I wasn't even able to keep a regular personal schedule because so many news outlets were calling and asking for my time. For days I went from night show to morning show to midday show, and then started the cycle all over again. This went on nonstop for weeks. I would get a call, book an appearance, then spend a couple hours figuring out what I was willing or allowed to say. I'd analyze different information that was coming in about the raid that the various producers wanted me to comment on, and try to give each interview its own unique existence. It reminded me of some of the in-the-field operational work I'd been accustomed to doing while an active-duty SEAL and, later, as a member of Blackwater: You get an influx of intel from a variety of sources, you take that information, review it, and decide what you're willing to talk about, what you could talk about, and what you want to talk about. You organize those thoughts, ask for a few talking points (if possible) practice a couple of answers for those talking points, and then apply all of that to your mouth and hope the words that come out, once you're live and in front of a camera, don't suck. It's not a conscious process, but a process nonetheless. It's more a mixture of self-control than anything else. As SEALs and PMCs, there's a lot of info we are privy to. That, and the fact that you don't want to come off looking like an asshole or you'll never get a call back. We SEALs can become assholes pretty quickly. LOL.

It turned out that I had a knack for this, and the producers kept inviting me back. They would send me news articles from Al Jazeera, the BBC, the New York Times, and other sources, and ask me to sift through it. I'd also look at other speculations coming in from unnamed sources and make informed decisions about how to approach the subject matter. I didn't care about the networks political views or the views of the intended audience. I spoke my mind, just as I continue to do today. If you don't like what I'm spilling, don't have me on your program. I'm not here to appease anyone. Nor will I ever be.

When you're involved in giving talking-head media appearances—especially as a military expert—you're faced with numerous decisions: Do you want to clarify what went down officially, or do you just want to put it in a general context? Is whatever you talk about going to potentially harm your buddies overseas if you tell the media what the real deal is or was regarding an operation? How do you best explain what they did and what all went into doing it? For example, how do you describe what goes into breaching a wall? Or, what's it like when they're going up steps to clear a hallway? These things are not easy to convey, not only from a descriptive standpoint, but especially from a security clearance angle.

All this has to be put in a broader perspective because you've got to decide what you're willing to divulge publicly. As I said: A SEAL—even a retired SEAL—is still privy to all kinds of intelligence. When you stay connected to your boys in the teams, you've got real inside information. I mentioned we're a tight-knit group, so the reality is that you have friends and former colleagues who feed you under-the-rug info and tell you the real stories. Basically, you can't give away any tactics, techniques & procedures (TTPs). If you do, at best, you're a douche bag, at worst; you're a marked man. So, you're left sifting through all this and determining what you're willing to divulge, what is going to sound good, and what's going to make you and your buddies look cool on TV. Too often, you see blathering talking heads on TV that don't offer much and don't look or sound good doing it. I had no intention of being one of those idiots. It's funny though, because every once in a while you hear from a hater who thinks what your doing can be done better or that you shouldn't be doing what you are doing at all. The world is full of haters, and I thank God for them every day because you truly know you're doing something good when you start to get attacked. In fact, the haters actually fuel me. So much so that I say: Let the haters hate!

It didn't take much time for me to decide the best course of action: I could take people right up to the edge of complete and utter divulgence without divulging anything at all. This became something of an art form that I developed and honed the more and more I appeared on news shows. I became very, very good at it, and the producers loved it. One of the amazing things that happened was when Colonel David Sutherland, then-Special Assistant to Admiral Mike Mullen, the Chairman of the Joint Chiefs of Staff (CJCOS), started calling me to chat. Colonel Sutherland called, not to warn me about what I was saying, or to review the details of what I wanted to talk about or to make sure I wouldn't say anything too divulging. Instead, he wanted to make sure I hit on a few areas that would help our cause, and support veterans causes. It was pretty cool, and it was just the angle and that veteran's voice I was looking for.

Colonel Sutherland would call and say, "Chris, what you're doing is great, and how you're saying it is even better; you make all Spec Ops sound articulate and you make them all look good. You're painting a real and a great picture for Special Operations Command, and we want you to keep doing what you're doing. You couldn't be doing it any better if we crammed words down your throat and asked you to vomit them back up!" He is a great dude. He went to college at Bowling Green State University (where I went) and was a hockey player. I used to love going to hockey games when I was there. We were both Ohio boys, both went to BGSU, and we were both in the U.S. military. That was our bond, and it stands to this day.

Colonel Sutherland also gave me tips on some veteran's initiatives he wanted me to take a hard look at and, if I felt so inclined, plug at the end of the segments. These were 501(c)3 organizations that the Department of Defense was behind. It was a good underlying mission. Hell, even Admiral Mullen, himself, passed along a couple names and initiatives.

With this underlying mission in hand, I made it very clear to the news outlets when I was going to go on, that they needed to give me "about 10 seconds" at the end of a segment in order to push something out to the public about veterans groups. To their credit, and to my great surprise, every one of them was glad to do it and no one ever pushed back, even CNN!

Sometimes, we used that time as part of the opening remarks. I would talk about organizations such as the Navy SEALs Foundation, Navy SEALs Fund, Wounded Wear, and Be a Hero-Hire a Hero. Once, while on Fox, after I plugged Be a Hero-Hire a Hero, the response from viewers was so incredible that it crashed that organization's internet servers. The CEO of Be a Hero-Hire a Hero, called me the next day to tell me that within the span of that 10-second news plug, I changed the footprint of their entire organization. His call came in as I was walking into the gym and I answered it because I thought it may have been a producer from one of the networks. When he told me the news of what I had done, I have to admit that it made me a bit teary-eyed. The thought that I had done so much good for veterans, in such a short amount of time, was truly overwhelming. It also let me know that what I was doing, and the impact my appearances were having on veteran's issues, was starting to make a difference. Today, I am heavily involved as a board advisor for a 501c3 called Suiting Warriors as well as the Triton Family Foundation.

During the days, weeks, months and years that have followed, I have appeared on a myriad of TV shows that comprised a virtual who's who of TV news networks, and other media outlets.

On FOX, I appeared on: *America Live*; *Happening Now* with Jon Scott and Martha McCallum; *America's News Headquarters*: Jon Scott & Heather Childers; and *Justice with Judge Jeanine*, and the *Judge Jeanine Pirro Show*. On CNN *Headline News*, I was invited to speak on *The Jane Velez-Mitchell Show*. At CNN, I accepted invitations to appear on *The Nancy Grace Show, Don Lemon Show,* and *CNN Newsroom*. I spoke on MSNBC's *This Morning with Thomas Roberts*; C-SPAN's *Daily News Report*; and even multiple segments on NPR Radio on *Ian & Mike's How To Do Everything* show, plus a metric shit-ton of other appearances that I can't even recall.

One of my favorite TV personalities has to be Judge Jeanine Pirro. Not only in she extremely attractive and spunky as all Hell, but she pulls absolutely no punches about anyone or anything. Her support of the 2nd Amendment, as well as her take on U.S. politics and international affairs, is always spot-on. The first time I was on her show, she called me into her makeup and hair room and asked me this question: "I heard you were against water boarding. Is that true?"

"What?" I exclaimed, in a flabbergasted tone, followed by "Judge, can I be candid and speak in plain language with you?"

"Absolutely," she replied.

"Who the fuck told you that?!!" I said, smiling and chuckling.

Just then, her producer came into the room.

"Well, she did! Chris, meet my producer, Jama."

I extended my hand and told her it was nice to meet her and that I enjoyed our emails leading up to today. Immediately following that, I exclaimed so that both Jama and the judge could hear me clearly: "To be clear here: I'm not against water boarding at all. I've been water boarded, so I know that it is a very effective tool in the war on terror. In fact, when my son is in high school and comes home late on a Friday or Saturday night, I'll probably water board HIS ass!"

After hearing this, Judge Jeanine started laughing her butt off and said, in mid-chuckle, "We are going to have a great show!" And we did.

Since then, we have had many great shows with segments on topics ranging from national and international terrorism to power-grid weaknesses. In fact, this last topic brings me to another great Judge Jeanine story: She invited me on for a segment regarding the vulnerability of the U.S. power grid, so I was flown in to New York, and was driven to Fox Studios in Manhattan. After discussing the direction of the episode, we all hopped in a Chevy Tahoe to head to where we were shooting: A street corner in Manhattan across from an electrical sub-station.

On the way to the scene, it started to rain and the temperature dropped about 20 degrees. Judge Jeanine needed some coffee and was not about to take 'no' for an answer.

After one of the producers, DJ, vetoed her request for a coffee run, like a boss, she promptly went over his head and straight to the driver.

Boom! Mission accomplished.

Coffee in hand, she was ready for the camera and so was I. The rain notwithstanding, the whole segment went off without a hitch and we were soon heading back to Fox to look at all the footage, but not before the judge had to make a pit stop at the kiosk in the lobby.

She has an affinity for gummy bears and keeps her stash replenished from the hefty supply sold there. I waited as she went to peruse the latest offerings. I turned to see her squat down to sift through the basket on the floor and, in doing so, exposed her thong to anyone that happened to be passing by in the busy lobby. Her pants had a zipper in the back, and unbeknownst to her, that zipper was unzipped almost all the way.

I had to do something about it so I immediately sprang into action and made my way over to her position in the kiosk. I placed myself within a few inches of her backside and, thus, provided cover from passersby.

She noticed me and calmly said, "What's going on, dude?"

I turned my head and promptly replied, "I got your back judge, literally. Your thong is hanging out and if you think I'm kidding, it's purple and all lacey."

"Oh dear, thanks so much", she exclaimed as she stood up and pulled the zipper up as far as it would go. "I must have forgot about that earlier."

"We'll, I'll make sure I double-check that next time!" I snickered.

"You are something else," she shot back, before a hardy laugh ensued.

The cracking up continued on the elevator and until we got off the floor to her office. Here, she intro'd me to Geraldo Rivera and John Stossel before I headed off to two other programs for that day's on-camera appearances.

The judge is one cool character, and I always enjoy my time with her. So much so, that I consistently ask her out for drinks afterwards. She has yet to accept. I will just have to keep asking. One of these days she just might say, "Yes." LOL.

Another great gal is Ashleigh Banfield from *The Legal View* on CNN. I've been on her show numerous times and have accompanied her to a few events in Manhattan as well as to her family's summer home in Ontario. I consider her a good friend. All her family is pretty great, too.

UNDAUNTED

Ashleigh is a Canadian-born, naturalized U.S. citizen. Because of this, and despite the fact that she is a fixture on CNN, she doesn't slant her show to give favor to any particular political party. She stays neutral and deals purely with the facts. As such, she really gets to the heart of the matter and, with a midday following from noon until 1 p.m., she has a fantastic and energetic engaged audience.

There's a pattern to how guest appearances work. Normally, they give you about one-day to a half-day lead time before you're on live. At least from my experiences, I would receive emails and phone calls around 7 a.m. asking if I could be on the show later that morning or in the early afternoon. Your appearance, ironically, is called your hit time. They would send a list of potential topics to discuss—from ISIS and al Qaeda to Army Sgt. Bowe Bergdahl and Benghazi—anything and everything that had a military sub-line to it, and especially one with a Spec Ops angle. Sometimes they ask that you show up at a local network affiliate; other times, as I mentioned, depending on the budget, they would fly you to New York, put you up in a hotel and get you a car service to and from the airport. You're not a paid contributor when you do this on a guest basis—it takes a lot of time before you become one of those guys. You're essentially doing this to build your brand and, possibly, use each appearance as a springboard to more lucrative initiatives in that space. You have to start somewhere!

I understood the game, and in fact, I used the opportunities to build my brand and help veterans. It worked well, and suddenly, instead of worrying about what next entrepreneurial venture I needed to enter and how I was going to build a market, I shifted my focus more on the television and the multi-media space. People who saw me, liked me. I presented a good on-air presence and exuded, what I like to call; 'restrained charisma'—traits that bode well on TV. This led to invitations to do voice-over work and appear in a series of military-themed documentaries and TV shows. Over the course of the next few months my time was in high demand and I appeared on such shows as:

- *Secrets of SEAL Team Six* (NBC Universal/Peacock Productions), which aired on the Discovery Channel, History Channel and Military Channel

- *WikiLeaks: Secrets and Lies*, which ran on UK Channel 4
- *America's Book of Secrets: Black Ops* (Prometheus Entertainment), which was broadcast on the History Channel
- *Inside Bin Laden's Lair*, which aired on the Discovery Channel

I landed a gig as the narrator's voice for Under Armour's show: *Under Armour Presents Ridge Reaper*, a hunting show that currently airs on the Outdoor Channel; and then was hired to be the co-star of Animal Planet's *Ivory Wars*, which was filmed in Kenya—which, indeed, was an amazing experience.

There was a running joke around *Secrets of SEAL Team Six* because the producers used so many scenes where I appeared. People at NBC called it the "Chris Heben Show," and I didn't argue with them. From what I understand, they had to remove about a half-dozen of my segments in order to make it less ridiculous.

Things were good from 2011 to 2013. I was spending my time between training senior Air Force officers and enlisted personnel at Fort McGuire-Dix-Lakehurst, New Jersey to get ready for Iraq and Afghan deployments and doing steady media appearances. When I wasn't doing that, I was doing quick burst gigs overseas in various Middle Eastern and African nations. Concurrently, I formed a company called INVICTVS Group and subcontracted myself to the U.S. military for further work at the base in New Jersey. It was good work. I instructed them on surviving deadly force encounters, proper patrol techniques, usage of assault rifles & pistols, and high-threat driving—essentially how to drive a vehicle in a very tactical way, which included everything from handling a disabled vehicle to coping with ambushes and IEDs. All the while, the filming continued.

During filming of *Secrets of SEAL Team Six*, NBC sent a car from Manhattan to Fort Dix to bring me back to the studios at 30 Rockefeller Plaza, 30 Rock for short. Caroline Sommers was one of the main producers. She and I had several great interviews on camera and built a good rapport off camera. Even when we weren't filming interviews, Caroline started calling me up for info. I ended up doing what amounted to telephone production work for her, offering advice on graphics, segments and other elements of the show. No wonder people joked that I had assumed the starring role and put my imprint on it. Now, if only I had received credit and compensation for those efforts. Such is life when you're a 'newbie' in that space. I've since come to realize the term *residual income*. And if you don't know what that means, I suggest you look into it ASAP.

Secrets of SEAL Team Six became a monster hit, becoming one of the most-watched Discovery Channel shows of all time. Its success helped catapult me into the limelight, and with it, massive media exposure. The UK show broadened my exposure, introducing me to an international audience. With all the time I'd spent overseas—between the Navy and Blackwater—I was as comfortable internationally as I was home in the U.S.

One of the dirty little secrets I learned about documentaries is that they are not huge money makers for the people who appear on them. You get paid a rudimentary amount, a day rate, and then receive nothing else. They fly you to the studio, conduct the interview, and then fly you home. As part of the deal, you release your rights to the show, which means you will receive no future residuals—even if the show ends up being replayed over and over, thousands of times, for many years. But there's always an upside. When the show airs, people see you. If you're savvy enough, you can translate that into other lucrative paying appearances and opportunities. For the very luckiest, somebody watches the show and probably says, "Damn, I want that guy on our show. We can build a more successful TV show with that guy."

That happened to me. National Geographic Channel called and wanted to cast me for season three of a show called *Ultimate Survival Alaska*. Unfortunately, or perhaps, fortunately, I turned down the offer. I did it based on money and connectivity. As it turned out, I would have been losing money filming the show and I would have been *incommunicado* with my son for three months. Neither of those options were acceptable. I also was given an opportunity to appear on *Survivor*: Season 31, but I turned it down as well. In my not-always-so-humble opinion, that is a stupid show, and it wouldn't have done much to enhance my brand. The key to all of this is that once you get the right show, you can parlay that into sponsorship opportunities, as well as residuals. Sponsorships and residuals are where the real money is. Besides, reality TV is mostly bullshit. You can execute and say 99.5 percent of everything perfect on a show, but they will only focus on the .5 percent that you say and do wrong. And with that, in addition to the magic of editing in post-production, they can make you look like a real douche hose. Again, smoke and mirrors are the tools of the spin-masters, and I prefer to stay out of the spin zone as much as possible. I think Bill O'Reilly would concur with me on that one.

As luck would have it, I was picked up to be the voice of Under Armor. The kickass gig at Under Armor came through a friend, Shane Walker, who is one of the creators of Showtime's hit TV show, *Gigolos*. Shane knew a guy named Eric Vaughan, who owns a company called Red Point Digital. Eric's an amazing guy; very creative, loyal, and down to earth. And his company does all the filming, editing, and writing, for *Ridge Reaper*. Through Shane, and later via Eric, I became *Ridge Reaper's* TV narrator.

While I dabbled in TV, I continued to train members of state and local police forces, as well as U.S. military personnel at Fort Dix in New Jersey. It was great to keep my skills fresh while helping to improve the skill sets of men and woman who were, undoubtedly, heading overseas to where the action was. At Fort Dix, I was dealing with senior officers and enlisted members of the U.S. Air Force. Being fellow service men and woman, there was a lot of mutual respect. They appreciated my status as a retired SEAL and Blackwater operator. Most of the men and women I trained had never been in a combat zone, so the Air Force brought me in to help them learn how to hit the ground running so that they didn't become lambs to the slaughter, once their boots touched the ground down range in Iraq and Afghanistan. It was great, and I felt like I was truly making a difference for my country yet again. Myself, several other retired SEALs, a few Rangers, and a few Marines, instructed on topics such as high-threat driving, close-quarters combat, patrolling, hand-to-hand combat, combat pistol and rifle, among other topics. One morning, we got the word that a group of nine Air Force personnel were involved in a Taliban insurgent infiltration shooting incident in Afghanistan. We were shocked to learn that at least three of the Airman that were killed were people we had put through training. It was hard to hear that and we all talked amongst ourselves in order to determine if there was any training we needed to institute in order to prevent this from happening again. In times like that, it is best to stay proactive and positive. If you don't, you begin to question what you are doing and why you are doing it.*

Because of the various TV ventures, I would often be shuttled back and forth between New York and Fort Dix. As it was happening, people kept telling me, "Wow, you have an amazing on-camera presence and you've got a good voice. This is not something that comes easy for people and you seem to handle it very well. You're like a badass version of Mike Rowe."

I was glad to hear it. Being on TV was interesting, and the media exposure helped me eke out a decent livelihood. It was just a few years after the shit had hit the fan, and in 2010, I ended up having to file for bankruptcy because none of my other businesses were providing enough steady and solid revenue for me to make ends meet. Well, let's just say that my former ends were not jiving with my current means. Needless to say, I lost my house, my car, my trucks (a 1972 Chevy C20 4x4 show truck), my Harley-Davidson, and everything else material in my life that was deemed a luxury or an excess item. For sure, it had been a huge step backward, but I never gave up. Out-and-out failure just wasn't in my nature; it never was and it will never be. Every time I fell I picked myself up. Every time I was knocked down, I shook it off and I pulled myself back up to my feet. And every time I ran into a blockade that threatened to derail my life, I faced it head-on and found a way to put myself back on the right path. That's what being undaunted is all about.

So now here I was, starting to get a little traction in this strange new space called TV, and even better yet, I'm still involved in something else I love: tactical training and security services. What could be better?

---

*http://articles.latimes.com/2011/apr/28/world/la-fg-afghan-pilot-20110428)

I'm sure it's because of this optimism and perseverance, and my ever-expanding CV/BIO, that another big break came my way. My long-time pal, Travis Lively, and I were invited to do an interview and then, subsequently, we were selected by a casting agency to star in a new Animal Planet show about elephant poaching in Africa. Travis and I first met in boot camp, and it seems that, ever since then our paths were destined to continuously be aligned. Travis was working for a massive, privately owned, aerospace manufacturer that is known for its Unmanned Aerial Vehicle (UAV), or drone, technology. This was a company that was heavily in the Special Operations industry space, as was my company. So as it turns out, we had been getting together annually for the previous three years at one of the largest conferences in that arena: Special Operations Forces, Industry Conference (SOFIC). The Animal Planet opportunity was a good way for us to truly work together again—only this time in a very different theater of operations. Dark Continent, here we come!

We shipped off to Kenya for about seven weeks and lived on a huge animal preserve. This sanctuary, called Rukinga, was our home away from home from August 30, 2012 to October 5, 2012. Our mission was to help the owner of Wildlife Works train his team of park rangers and park staff in better ways to defend themselves, as well as to chase down and fend off local poachers as well as Somali poachers who were crossing into Kenya and killing elephants strictly for their ivory tusks. This sounded like a great opportunity all the way around, and I was insanely excited to put all of my skills to the test in mitigating this risk to the worlds remaining wild elephants. The fact that the producers planned to transform the footage of our adventures into a three-part, TV documentary mini-series that would air on Animal Planet, was the icing on the cake to the very great reason we were there: To save the elephants! Travis and I signed on without hesitation.

CHAPTER 20

> "Great relationships enjoy constant communication and never ending teamwork. You give 110 percent because you know you'll get it back in kind. Remember: You're much better off with a kick-ass half than with a half-assed whole."
>
> —Christopher Mark Heben

Africa is the cradle of civilization; one of the most diverse, mysterious and amazing continents on Earth. Who isn't fascinated with the Sahara, the Nile River, the pyramids at Giza, Casablanca, the wilds of Kenya and beautiful lakes and mountains of Tanzania?

I have a deep love for Africa and it's been my privilege to have spent nearly a half-dozen deployments in Africa, traveling to over a dozen countries like Burkina Faso, Ghana, Central African Republic, Chad, Sudan, Mali, Libya, Somalia, Kenya and Egypt. There's little doubt that the cultures are different, economies varied, and the landscape breathtaking. Africa represents a wildly eclectic and often contradictory mosaic of immense wealth, abject poverty, horrible corruption, brutal honesty, luscious greenery, and desolate bush, all wrapped into one. The only constant is the children. In fact, I mention this because I know that children are the same the world over: They see everything around them with wide eyes, warm hearts, open minds and active brains unaffected by the infusions of bastardized versions of religion, views on race, notions of politics, and even gender bias.

All of this became apparent to me, initially, while I served my country on my first deployment as a SEAL and later, on multiple deployments, as a PMC. I'm from a very large Catholic family. I have eight brothers and three sisters and I'm also a father to an amazing 13-year-old boy. So the family guy and the parent in me recognized what was happening in Africa.

Amidst the poverty and plenty, the pulchritude and plain, the philanthropy and cleptocracy, the Catholicism and Wahhabism, a constant battle for our morality, for our very souls, and for our very lives, was being waged. This conundrum made me love Africa even more, and the longer I reflect on this amazing continent the more I realize that in order to ensure a better world for generations to come it is our duty to be the stewards of the children there who are born with those, aforementioned, impartial and initial integrities. We need to understand that what we stand up for and to today, and how we do it, determines our future as a planet. The likes of man, as a whole, has been a very poor purser for the planet and nowhere is this more easily seen than by our exploitation of the creatures that inhabit it with us. From whales to worms, and all creatures in between, man has found a way to turn a profit from them, and any times, to the absolute detriment of an entire species. I believe what we do today, good or bad, the children will surely look to follow. So when the opportunity arose to spend seven weeks in Kenya on a wildlife sanctuary helping ensure the future of the most powerful—yet endangered—species on the planet, I jumped at the opportunity.

My good friend, and former SEAL, Travis Lively and I were selected to train a group of rangers at Wildlife Works' Rukinga Wildlife Sanctuary in Kenya. These rangers needed to learn a different type of warfare so that they could better combat poachers as part of their efforts to tamp down upon the rampant ivory trade. Our undertakings with them would be filmed and then turned into a documentary called *Ivory Wars* for Animal Planet. Hopefully, we would shine a light on the dangerous and deadly African ivory trade and look to mitigate this ivory-poaching scourge. Yes, a war was going on and the definitive prize was ivory, while the definitive end-game victims were the African bush elephants (*Loxodonta Africana*).

From what we learned and were told, Somali cattle herders, in order to realize higher prices and to avoid the web of sanctions enforced at Somali ports, were driving their cattle down to the port of Mombasa in Kenya. There have been United Nations sanctions and embargos on Somalia with respect to weapons and charcoal for many years now. Without getting into too much detail, the import and export of charcoal and illegal weapons is a huge benefit to terrorist groups, especially to the Somali-based Al-Shabaab organization. It is estimated that Al-Shabaab has kept up to one-third of the annual revenue from the $250 million charcoal trade alone.

Cattle herders were becoming opportunistic poachers on their trek to Mombasa. After crossing into Kenya from the northeast and then traveling southwest to the Kasigau Corridor, they routinely encountered elephants on the expansive-yet-protected game reserves they traversed through. These cattle herdsmen are armed with AK-47s in order to protect the herds from predators, so they have more than enough knockdown power to drop an elephant, especially after they shoot them multiple times. When they couldn't shoot them, they would set traps and snares to catch the elephants, harvest the ivory—killing them in the process—and then transport the bounty tied to the underbellies of the cattle. Upon entering the port city of Mombasa, the herdsmen meet with ivory brokers who promptly offered them a lot of cash for their stash. The pay day is often 10 times more than they make for the cattle. A very large percentage of this goes back to Al-Shabaab in Somalia. Not surprisingly, the ivory is then smuggled out of the country to sell to eager buyers in China. It is a nasty business, cyclical, and without a lot of opposition. Conflict was brewing between Kenyan villagers and Somali poachers. We would gauge our success by seeing if we could drastically reduce—or even completely halt—this bloody trade that had already deeply stained the soil in the Rukinga Sanctuary.

We came to train the rangers on proper combat-patrol techniques for daylight and for nighttime operations. The rangers were already amazing trackers, so we simply needed to help them to be better at safely moving through the bush, especially in a fashion that would allow them to survive potentially deadly encounters with AK-47-brandishing adversaries. What began as a simple training mission quickly escalated into an odd game of cat-and-mouse—us vs. the poachers. Travis and I found ourselves actively chasing down poachers, gathering intelligence data, and conducting reconnaissance missions to do the same. When we weren't patrolling the bush in Land Rovers or kicking down doors for the rangers, we were making calls and calling in favors to bring in military-grade technology, which would then be integrated as a tool in the rangers' arsenal.

Along with the new technologies, we also taught them basic combat medicine and supplied them all with mission-critical, and man-portable, medical packs. We didn't so much improve their lives as we did to give them the ability to protect and extend their lives with an increased ability to effectively fight the poachers. But our true mission's success would be determined by whether or not we could effectively deter poachers and better prepare and equip the rangers for the lengthy fight that threatened to last well into the future. Anything worth doing is worth overdoing, and this time, both Travis and believed that the juice was definitely worth the squeeze.

Introducing technology was an easy solution. We brought about $10 million to bear on the project—synthetic aperture radar (SAR), push-to-talk triangulation devices, ground-tracker sensors, helicopters, unmanned aerial devices (UAV's), and an advanced communications-tracking device called the Wolf Hound. This was all cutting-edge technology developed by private companies and being used in Iraq and Afghanistan, but from August 2012 to October 2012 we used it to engage a different kind of enemy—ivory poachers.

While we worked for the production company, our official employer was Wildlife Works Carbon LLC. The company was founded in 1997 by Mike Korchinsky, who co-founded and built one of the leading management consulting firms in the U.S., Axiom Management. Mike is a Canadian citizen who lives in Northern California and has a love for all-things nature. In 1995, he sold his company to Cambridge Technology Partners and became financially set for the rest of his life. During a trip to Kenya in 1996, Mike learned about the nasty conflict that existed between wildlife and rural communities. He saw the endless cycle of violence, and thought there must be better ways to solve the problem. Not being one to rest on his laurels, he set to work and developed a plan.

Mike provided people in wildlife-rich areas with sustainable economic alternatives to poaching and slash-and-burn agriculture. In a nutshell, he undertook to combat the ills he saw during his first trip to Kenya, by creating jobs and opportunities, thereby giving residents true hope in the future. Mike's nonprofit organization, Wildlife Works, was built on a simple belief: To protect endangered wildlife, you must balance the needs of wildlife with the need for work for those rural communities who share the same overlapping environment.

At its baseline, it all came down to children—something that I stated earlier and had learned in my first deployment overseas. Through Mike's efforts in establishing Wildlife Works, the villagers could aspire to have a better life and to feed their children without raping the environment. Mike's organization also pioneered the REDD program, which is United Nations-backed and stands for "Reducing Emissions from Deforestation and Degradation." They essentially create jobs while protecting the environment and ecosystem.

Mike used his vast fortune to establish the Rukinga Wildlife Sanctuary on 80,000 acres of now-protected farmland in South East Kenya between Tsavo East and Tsavo West National Parks, known as the Kasigau Corridor. At the base of the sanctuary, Mike built an eco-factory to produce casual apparel, some of which is for Puma. It immediately created 100 new jobs. But he wasn't done. Mike's bigger idea was tied to combining eco-preservation with wildlife preservation, thereby changing the rules of the war we'd been facing for decades. With those barriers removed, the future would be much, much brighter. Today, Wildlife Works is the world's leading REDD I project development and management firm. Its sanctuary in Kenya is home to more than 500,000 total acres, and populated by more than 20 species of bats and more than 300 species of birds. There are also majestic creatures, Africa's 'big five': Grévy's Zebras, cheetahs, lions, giraffes and rhinos. Along with these, there are also hyena and more than 12,000 African elephants— the latter of which are always in danger of poachers out to harvest their ivory tusks. You never know what you're going to see when you're out and about in the bush and you'd better have a plan in place for damn near everything.

In 1998, Mike hired his first team of rangers. And with his left-leaning belief system, he established a no-gun policy for them but forged a partnership with the Kenya Wildlife Service (KWS), which does carry guns. So although he abhors weapons, he knew the realities his rangers would face, and together, they were able to remove more than 800 poacher snares that first year alone.

These days, there are about 120 wildlife rangers on the Rukinga Sanctuary, and Travis and I interacted with about half of them on a daily basis. Every day we all put our lives in danger together, trying to stay one-step ahead of the poachers. Right now ivory is in high demand. A kilo sells for about $4,000 on the black market. There is some really big money to be made—and made quickly—by selling ivory to the burgeoning middle-class Chinese market. To acquire this ivory, there is nearly an unlimited supply of young Somalis, and to some extent, Kenyans, willing to prey on the elephants in Kenya, as well as to take the lives of other people in their pursuit of it—including us!

And that's where we came in. On Friday, January 13th, elephant poachers opened fire on unarmed Wildlife Works Rangers who were patrolling the Kasigau Corridor project area. One ranger, Abdullahi Mohammed, was fatally shot when a round from an AK-47 struck him in the collar bone and exited his body in the armpit. He bled to death from both the subclavian artery and the axillary artery. There was nothing the rangers could do about it but watch him die. Another ranger, Ijema Funan, was severely injured when he was struck in the arm and shoulder by AK-47 fire as well. At the time of the shooting, Abdullahi and Ijema were partnering with members of the Kenya Wildlife Service (KWS) to track a group of poachers after finding a gunshot-wounded elephant in the protected project area. Though this wasn't the first time a KWS or Wildlife Works ranger had been fired upon, it was the first time that any ranger had been killed in the line of duty, and it reflected an escalation in the violence caused by the ever-increasing demand for ivory.

I met with Ijema, not long after his brush with death, and he is still haunted by the event. But more than that, he is haunted by his inability to return to the bush in order to combat this scourge of poaching that is raping his land. He is a true warrior and a great bushman, and I promised him that his story would not be forgotten.

A few days after their shooting, two of the poachers were arrested in Mackinnon Road, a small village used by poachers and other outlaws as a convenient, high-transit-area hideout. One of those men led the rangers and Kenyan Police back out into the bush to where the rifle and ammunition that was used for the assault were buried. The rifle was wrapped in a pair of trousers and buried under a bush on Taita Ranch, another spot frequented by poachers. The stakes were getting higher and higher and Mike was at his wits' end. He knew he needed to find a new way to prepare his ranger force for this sudden escalation in violence. His guys were basically bringing knives to a gunfight. Why not consider military tactics and strategy? And who better to train his team than America's elite fighting force, the United Sates Navy SEALs. Mike's idea was to bring in a couple SEALs and task them with a specific, two-fold mission: Help identify and deploy technologies that could further deter poachers and, simultaneously, train rangers to avoid any more fatal contacts.

I was extremely honored to be chosen to join this great team. Travis and I figured it would be easy to catch a bunch of backwoods poachers and stem the tide of poaching in that area. We would recover some ivory, train the Wildlife Works rangers, and star in a documentary. What could go wrong? Right? It was a sweet gig, and I was excited to be part of it.

The Wildlife Work rangers are a group of independent, private rangers led by an elephant-sized man named Eric Sagwe. Eric is about 6'7", weighs in at about 325 pounds, and would fit right in on any NFL team. He serves as the lead ranger and Wildlife Works' head of security. Eric's a great guy, and one who is genuine and committed to the cause.

Travis and I went there feeling naked, without weapons. We understood that Mike meant well, but his beliefs gave him a competitive disadvantage when it came to fighting an enemy that didn't follow conventional rules. We were supposed to teach these guys how to face down AK-47-wielding poachers. It was a challenge if there ever was one. To top it off, our successes, failures, and eventual set-backs would be permanently captured—and later broadcast—as part of a television documentary. No pressure, eh?

The Kasigau Corridor, where the Rukinga Wildlife sanctuary is located, is on protected land in East Kenya. It falls along one of the main transit routes to Mombasa, the second-largest city in Kenya, and a major international port used for trading. When people kill an elephant, they head to the port of Mombasa to sell the ivory to Asian buyers. It's an effective-yet-morbid circle of life.

So Travis and I headed to Kenya with a full production crew in tow. All of us were ready to put the experience on film and show the world what terrible things were happening and how we could make a difference. We worked with Mike and his VP of African Operations, Rob Dodson. They were all great guys, completely committed to their cause and trying to make a positive mark on the world.

Our regular on-screen team was rounded out with Maggie Mutahi Beseda, who was a Kenyan national. She served as our intelligence gatherer and helicopter pilot. Maggie spoke fluent Swahili, which served us well. At the time, she was Kenya's only female helicopter pilot. We wanted someone on the show to have a vested and personal interest in the mission, which was Maggie. She received daily reports from villagers, and then we'd go out and talk to people. She collected the word on the street. We looked into it. Travis and I thought the show would turn Maggie into a national celebrity.

Our head cameraman was an accomplished South African cinematographer named Hein de Vos, who owns a company called Killyourdarlings.com. Hein's claim to fame was that he was the head cameraman on the movie *Safe House*, which starred Ryan Reynolds and Denzel Washington. Another camera op was Kire Godal, a contributing film maker at National Geographic who is very well-known for her documentaries on lions and Masai tribes in Northern Kenya. We also had very accomplished sound guys like Mike Moller (a native Kenyan) to help capture all the dialogue as well as the varied sounds of the bush. And we had a crew of production assistants (PAs) like Harry Brainch (a bushman/guide) and Olivia Robertson. One day, I was a bit crabby and must have said something to aggravate Olivia. You see, one of Olivia's jobs was to corral Travis and me to make sure we were on time for all filming events. She was very good at it because she didn't take any shit from either one of us. It's safe to say that I probably said something stupid to her early one morning. In retribution, she shoved a two-pound ball of elephant shit in my backpack! It pissed me off at first and I said, "I'm gonna beat somebody's ass when I find out who did this!" And I meant it. As the day went on I actually had to laugh about it and I downgraded my stance to something closer to being pleasantly annoyed. This allowed Olivia the opportunity to come and tell me what she had done. I hugged it out with her and I still look back and remember the event fondly—no one had ever gifted me with a two-pound ball of elephant shit before. And no one has since! Thanks Olivia! Yes, we are friends to this day.

Eric Sagwe, the head ranger, hit the bush every day with one hand tied behind his back. The only weapon he had was an elephant gun, and that was in case one of his other rangers or support staff got charged by an elephant. Otherwise, it was a no-gun zone, which definitely fell well outside my sweet spot. I liked Eric. He was a good guy. Travis and I were going to train him and his men in day- and night-patrol tactics, hostile-event techniques and emergency procedures to keep them safer against armed poachers. I put on a series of medical classes designed to teach the rangers how to use tourniquets, pressure bandages and blood-stopper infused bandages; bandages packed with substances called hemostatic agents. I brought about 50 of these special bandages and gave them to the rangers in a kit designed to treat 92 percent of all combat inflicted injuries. Like it or not, these guys were in a combat zone.

In light of that, we taught them how to work from safer distances and how to spread out—the type of stuff we would do in the field to protect ourselves from effective enemy fire and to decrease the chances of greater injury when we were contacted. It was a very balanced combination of tactical and medical training, and at the end of each day, we had a nice sit-down dinner with Eric and the top performers from that day's training. Mwambiti and Moses were two of the top performers almost every day. Mwambiti did so well, in fact, that before I left, I gave him most of my tactical gear—including my Merrill boots. He deserved all of it and more.

The media likes to focus on the blood-diamond trade in Africa, and very little is ever said about the ongoing genocide in the Congo, but animal poaching is just as bad, if not worse. It's illegal to hunt anything in Kenya, so what we were asked to help with was a big deal. Regular animal poaching and elephant poaching go hand-in-hand. The meat poachers alert the elephant poachers to where they've seen elephants. The elephant poachers track down the herd and kill as many elephants as they can using AK-47s and, often, poisoned arrows. It's not uncommon to find severely wounded elephants who have escaped poachers limping around on the verge of septic shock and death after being shot. Ivory is at its all-time high on the black market—the average bull elephant has about a half-million dollars hanging from its face in the form of ivory. That's one Hell of a curse: Being born with only six teeth, and two of them—the very biggest—worth more than your life.

Our 24/7 chase to stop poachers was pretty intense. Every three or four days we'd come across a group of them. These guys were brazen. They didn't give a shit that we were out to stop them. They don't wear uniforms, but people know who the poachers are among them. For the right price and anonymity, villagers can be quick to give them up if someone comes looking for them. The main elephant poachers are mostly Somalis, not Kenyans. The main meat poachers are Kenyans, not Somalis. It's an interesting dynamic.

Meanwhile, all this is occurring in a breathtakingly gorgeous land with amazing topography. The country is one of immaculate and ornate vistas, and ranks among the top five in the world. There are endless stretches of ground painted with brilliant red dirt that lead up to sprinkled green lush areas with soggy watering holes. Then, there's the contrast—barren spots that come up to the edge of each oasis at the feet of numerous ridgelines and towering mountain ranges. That area of the rift is massive and ominously beautiful. I know Montana claims it, but Kenya is definitely deserving of another "Big Sky" title. Every night, you see about a half-dozen shooting stars. To quote a line from an old Incubus song: "The sky resembles a backlit canopy, with holes punched in it"

When you look up at the sky, the stars are on bold display. Together with the moon they seem to command an ancient presence, presiding over the plight of both man and beast. Better still, there are virtually no buildings or other man-made sources of illumination to interrupt the astral displays. As the cherry on top, the abundant night sounds are the *Wild Kingdom* equivalent of the New York Philharmonic.

Late one afternoon, as we were heading back from a training session with the rangers, we saw over a dozen different kinds of animals—zebras, impalas, wildebeests, hyenas, oxen, lions, giraffes, kudus, and baboons, just to name a few. It was crazy, unpredictable, and awesome, all at the same time. After all, we weren't at the zoo. In fact, we were probably on the menu. Hell, people pay upwards of $10,000 for the opportunity to experience this, and I was getting paid to do it. The only caveat, as has been the case for me over the last 16 years, is that the privilege often comes with the potential for the heftiest of price tags: MY LIFE! Nonetheless, Travis and I were excited to be here and to help make a difference in a place like this.

We knew the risks, and they were acceptable. The added beauty of it all made for the perfect assuaging of them. When you're a risk taker, there is always a certain barter to be had. We were certainly risk-takers, and this was certainly a form of fair trade. In that spirit of caring, sharing and cooperation, we set up camp in some small tents on one of the Wildlife Works campsites. The first two weeks we were there, we shared the grounds with a group of 30 or so students from the UK who were on a sabbatical. They were taking a year break from their college studies in order to do projects for the nonprofit. Projects like repairing fences and building wells.

Sometimes at night, and when the cameras were off, we sat around and shot the shit about myriad topics, from music to sports. Then, after we'd consumed our fill of Tusker beers, cheap wine, and whatever booze they could scrounge, we'd head back to our respective sleeping arrangements and collectively listen to the lurking lion's low growls and the vigilant elephants roaring responses. Yes, out in the distance, just 100 meters or less, there was a nightly battle underway, life vesus death. I often laid there thinking that the only thing between us and all of that was a two-and-a-half-foot tall, non-functioning, electric fence, and a thin piece of tent fabric. I'm not sure if it did any good or not, but to make myself feel better I would piss around my tent a few times a day and at night—marking my territory, so to speak. After all, isn't that what animals do?

The roads we traveled on each day were about 10 percent improved. The ones in the Wildlife Works Sanctuary were all dirt. Once you got into the middle of a few of the main towns, they were decently paved. The main highway to Mombasa cut through a town we called the Mackinnon Road area, the town was the first major city you'd come to in Coast Province, Kenya, on the road to Mombasa. It was always jumpin' and it was a regular hangout for poachers.

Every day we were there the sun was omnipresent and the temperatures were hot. Luckily, we arrived right after the rainy season and left right before summer began. The weather was hot, but it was still pleasantly humid without being soaking wet or steam-room soggy! It did rain from time to time, and we did have numerous hot-as-Hell days, but we appreciated the variety. No matter what the weather, our typical day consisted of waking up to review the show and mission concepts for the day: What did we want to achieve? Did we find an elephant or chase a poacher? Were we able to look for hidden weapon stashes and ivory caches?

All of these were in our plans. We would keep our ears to the ground and try to gather as much intelligence as we could by listening to all the chatter from the townspeople and Wildlife Works workers. Our intelligence would consist of things like someone saw an elephant running around wounded. We'd be dispatched with a camera crew, and sometimes a couple of rangers, and go check it out.

Shortly after our arrival, we got word about a wounded elephant that was looking emaciated and lumbering about. I was training the standby group of rangers in medical operations, so Travis took the on-duty rangers and a camera crew and hit the road. When they found the elephant, one of the local veterinarians knocked it out with a tranquilizer dart shot from a safe distance. A safe distance is considered 50 or more meters, just in case you miss. That gives you enough time to reload and shoot again before the elephant has enough to time to rush you and stomp you to the ground.

Elephants are majestic beasts, and they're enormous. They can be very cantankerous—especially when they are injured, protecting their babies, or both! They can kill you with a single trunk swipe or a foot stomp. Most of the time, however, they kill humans by simply headbutting them into the ground. Such a blow will reduce the typical male human to nothing more than a broken bag of jelly that is pushed about two feet into the ground. It's not a pleasant way to go, especially if the elephant decides to cripple your legs in this manner before bashing your head in. You really do not want to mess with elephants.

After the successful dart shot, Travis, the rangers and the vet rolled up on the unconscious elephant to inspect it. What they saw was unbelievable: The remnants of a snare made from thick electric cable was sticking out of its neck. A closer look revealed that the snare wire was deeply embedded in the elephant's neck—Travis estimated it at six-inches deep. The poor 'ellie' must have got stuck in a snare and, with its brute strength, pulled itself free from a tree or whatever the Hell the snare was moored to and ran away. The vet and rangers estimated that the elephant had been running around with this snare wrapped around its neck for many weeks. The wire as thick as telephone cable wire—at least as thick as a grown man's thumb. And it was slowly killing the animal by inhibiting its ability to breath, feed, drink water, and otherwise be hearty, healthy and happy. Because of this, the elephant was severely underweight—the vet determined it had lost about 20 percent of its body weight, more than 1,000 pounds.

It required five guys working together to finally dig the noose out from around the elephant's neck without causing it to tighten further. Travis and Eric Sagwe took turns using bolt cutters to carefully cut parts of the cable. It was a long and arduous process. Finally, they had to team up on the cutters to cut through the bulk of it. Travis was then able to put the death knell on the cable with one massive final squeeze of the bolt cutters.

Once freed, the group had to work quickly before the elephant woke up from the anesthesia. If it did, it could mean death for many of them. Luckily, this didn't happen and they successfully dressed the wound, gave it a reversal drug, and ran as fast as they could. You still just have to look the fuck out when you do this because the moment the elephant wakes up it is pissed off and can blindly charge anywhere, at any time, at anyone. It's pretty crazy.

A few days after the snare incident, the rangers, Travis and I, were out patrolling and we came across two injured elephants—a mom and a baby. Both had been shot more than once, and we would later discover that the mother had a spear tip still stuck in her—which may or may not have been poisoned. Occasionally, poison will lose its potency if left on the spear tip for too long, so it is hard to tell unless it's fresh. The vet was called in to help, and he darted the two elephants. This was actually the first time either Travis or I had seen the darting of an injured elephant. Travis had arrived right after the earlier snared elephant was already knocked out.

It was a pretty amazing experience. To see an injured elephant in the wild is extremely surreal. There are no walls to protect you from the erratic behavior of an injured, 5,000-pound pachyderm. Elephants are beautiful creatures. They are so strong they can plow right through trees in their pursuit. So the element of danger is very, very high. Seeing a darted ellie fall is akin to watching a redwood tree being felled. It doesn't happen right away, and when it does fall, it happens in super slow motion. The ground seems to brace for impact, and everything alive in the immediate area scurries away in fear for its life. The impact felt when an elephant hits the ground is not unlike that of a SoCal quake.

After the dust settles, you warily approach—all the while looking for signs of incomplete anesthetization. The vet has a second dart at the ready, just in case. I was looking for the nearest Land Rover; I wanted some steel between her and me if the time came for a hasty retreat.

Once momma and her baby were unconscious, I was asked to help treat the animals. The baby had been shot twice through the right hind leg, both entry and exit holes could be seen in the area right above the knee joint. No wonder it was limping. I helped clean the baby's wounds and sprayed some antibiotic/antiseptic aerosol formula on the limb. This topical spray is bright blue on purpose—the color aids in the identification of the wounded, in this case the elephant, so that over the following days you can monitor its recovery. The color eventually wears off, and causes no harm. We also administered an injectable antibiotic to internally stave off any impending infection. The entire process was immensely fulfilling and strangely satisfying. I was definitely doing something that was on a whole new level of cool—I was helping a baby elephant. Mommy was next!

The mom's injuries were a bit tougher. She was three times the baby's size, which meant we needed to get into a wound that was a lot deeper. It was also more difficult to look for other wounds due to her thick flesh and dense musculature. Those have a way of hiding small bullet holes—unless the bullet hits a blood vessel and the animal is visibly bleeding. Thankfully, this was the case with the mother. We could easily identify and externally treat the bullet wound to the front leg, and in the process we were able to see the entry wound caused by the spear tip. Yep, there was a spear tip stuck in her hide, and we had to get it out.

After the vet and one of the Wildlife Works guys tried a few blind and unsuccessful hemostat swipes, I knew what needed to be done. I used another hemostat, which is also known as a 'roach clip' (don't ask me why) and looks like a small pair of alligator-toothed scissors, to tackle the spear hole. Hemostats are great at controlling bleeding, and are often used in surgery. I put one into the spear hole and spread it open. Then, I used the other hemostat to clamp down on the spear tip.

I slowly extracted it from the elephant. It felt like a very real and more chaotic version of that old game of "Operation" (by Milton Bradley). The difference was that I was performing actual surgery on an elephant, and if something went wrong I wasn't going to get a red light and a glowing nose. Instead, I would probably get pounded into the dirt by a very large and angry ellie.

Once again, everything is part of that Navy SEAL risk-taker mentality—we know how to take an educated risk and transform it into a well-executed risk. But it is just a very emotional situation because there's nothing normal about seeing an elephant lying on its side unconscious. I was up close and personal, and could see, hear and feel the rise and fall of its chest cavity as it struggled to breathe. I could smell every inch of the two elephants' bodies that were caked with that omnipresent red African dirt, as well as feel the coarse hairs protruding from their thick skin. In many ways, it was like that Triceratops scene from *Jurassic Park*, except they would recover and Travis and I didn't have to fish around in a huge pile of their shit in order to find what was ailing them. Instead, we were covered in blood and bits of tissue as we made certain to kill infection and expedite healing.

Thankfully, we were able to save both elephants, reverse the tranqs, and send them on their way. It felt extremely satisfying and inherently good to help them, and it's something I'll never forget.

A few days later, we received another report about downed elephants. This time, the report indicated that there were three elephants on the ground.

"Holy shit!" I thought as we raced to respond.

We arrived as quickly as possible, but the poachers had already made off with three of the six possible tusks. All three elephants were on the ground. Two were dead and a third was in the latter stages of dying. We didn't have much choice, so we put down the gravely injured elephant and then removed the other three tusks from the dead bodies. It was gruesome and gory work. Once again, it was very emotional. I was a combination of pissed off and sad, but Travis and I volunteered to be the ones who initiated the ugly task of ivory removal.

Using a combination of a Winkler Tomahawk, a Winkler knife, and a run-of-the-mill machete, Travis and I chopped, sawed, sliced and slashed until we removed the first of the three tusks. I was amazed and horrified at how deeply we had to hack into the elephant's face to do this—which was, in itself, doubly disturbing. African elephants have six teeth. Two of them are tusks, which are worth a metric shit-ton of money. They are just like our incisors. The roots are very long and extend well into the area of the skull above where the trunk is attached. If you don't get the root and just use a hacksaw on the external part of the tusk you lose between eight and 10 inches of ivory on each side. And that part of the tusk is the thickest part. By the way, there's also a thick nerve root in the upper part of that tusk, and the size of it also has a bearing on the value of that tusk. In that, more nerve equals less tusk. Getting to the very end of that tusk is an absolutely terrible experience.

The whole gruesome scene was very fucking surreal: We had come upon this and saw the poachers' handiwork—an elephant's trunk chopped off and lying next to its dead body in a pool of its own blood, covered with hundreds of thousands of flies. I hated this.

After we were done, we transported and promptly handed over the freshly harvested ivory to the Kenyan Wildlife Service. KWS has a number of facilities where they put the ivory, and I got a chance to look inside the locked rooms and saw hundreds of tusks in storage. I later learned that once or twice a year, the KWS puts all the ivory tusks in a pile and torches them. I understand what they're doing, but don't know if I agree with it. Part of me wonders what would happen if instead they flooded the market with ivory. Maybe it would drive the price down and hurt the poachers' trade. But there's a burgeoning middle class in China right now, and their hunger for ivory is insatiable. Who knows how much is enough. The Chinese want trinkets made of ivory because it's a status symbol, unlike the Rhino horn, which many believe to have sexual performance associations—it makes you more potent; it's considered medicinal. So, with respect to Rhino horn, flooding the market may be exactly what the Chinese would love to see happen.

Nevertheless, we saved three elephants over those few days and lost three others. The score now stood at Poachers: 3; SEALs: 3. I don't like those numbers. Not one bit.

Catching the poachers was a Hell of a lot harder than we thought it would be. They were cagy bastards who stayed low in the bush and knew how to blend in. It didn't help that there were a couple towns nearby where few people would even discuss the subject of poaching. To help us overcome those obstacles, we brought in a few of our SEAL and Spec Ops brothers to lend a hand. Collectively, we all made a few calls and brought in a shit load of high-tech devices and tools. One was Synthetic Aperture Radar (SAR), which we strapped to the helicopter. Maggie flew a grid—essentially a big square around the Sanctuary—and took SAR images of everything in the grid. Then, she flew the same grid an hour later; then two-hours later; and three-hours later. Each time, she took new images. With Synthetic Aperture Radar, you take those images and analyze them. Anything that changes from the previous image becomes de-pixelated and is very readily seen. This is because when you turn up dirt, its properties change and this change is picked up through SAR (Synthetic Aperture Radar). With SAR you can find above ground metal as well as metal objects buried in the ground—up to about six-inches below. Our troops use SAR in Iraq and Afghanistan to detect roadside bombs and weapons caches. It's very, very useful technology, and when strapped to a helicopter or plane, you can patrol huge swaths of land in a short amount of time.

At one point, the radar pointed us toward a bicycle abandoned by a poacher. We started scouting the area where it was found and we were able to identify the poacher's position. Maggie, in the helicopter above us, spotted him from the air. Despite air overwatch and us giving chase on the ground, we lost him in the thick bush—it's hard to describe how native the land is because it's so pure and feral, but the Kenyan bush can be extremely thick and very unforgiving. As I said before, every plant that is rooted in the soil, grows barbs or spikes in order to defend itself from consumption. Damn near everything, plant or animal, is looking to take a chunk out of your body. Africa knows how to get its pound of flesh from a person, and few escape this land unscathed in some way, shape or form. And as you may have guessed it, though he got away, we were able to trail him to the Mackinnon Road area, where he had already established a benign presence with the locals. Benign or not, we were going to cut him out!

Travis and I posed as tourists and poked around. We were wearing special glasses equipped with HD Video cameras—high-speed 1080p 'spy spectacles,' disguised as ugly Blue Blockers. We captured the entire recon mission on film. It's not as easy as you would think, as there were many things acting against us. We were two large white guys in an area filled with scrawny black guys—so we already stood out. Another thing working against us was that we could not move our heads too much or the film would look like it was taken from the head of a bobble-headed bull rider. Even the slightest movements are exaggerated ten-fold. This means that you can only move your head around like someone wearing a cervical collar doing the robot dance to composer John Cage's "As Slow as Possible." Now that is damn slow! True to our roots, we adapted and overcame!

Another piece of technology we called in was the Wolfhound, which is a special kit used to listen in on push-to-talk radios. Without giving away too much, its capabilities stretch way beyond that, but I am not at liberty to discuss that in this book. I'm sure you understand. Even better news was that the Wolfhound came with three very capable dudes to operate each of the systems: Steve, Mike, and Brian. Steve was a SEAL, Mike was an Air Force JTAC, and Brian was an Army Intel Officer. Travis and I have known them for a very long time. In fact, Steve, Travis and me initially went through BUD/S together. Our team in Kenya was now technologically and fraternally complete!

After listening to some street chatter Steve and Mike intercepted, we were led to what we believed were Somali poachers holed up in a small compound. We planned to check it out, take pictures and record conversations—essentially get eyes and ears on the entire area for about 24 hours. We hatched a plan that Maggie and I initiated after a drive through the neighborhood the day before with me hidden in the back of the Land Cruiser and taking pictures of possible places to lay up. Being Kenyan, Maggie would not draw attention. If she did, she spoke the language and could easily divert any and all questions as to what she was doing in the area. Never underestimate the abilities of a very attractive Kenyan-born female helicopter pilot behind the wheel of a Toyota Land cruiser, driving around listening to the soundtrack from *The 101 Dalmatians* while chauffeuring around a hidden, shutter-happy SEAL in the back seat. The whole intel trip was hilariously successful, to say the least. Maggie was singing most of the songs that were playing and I provided some back-up every now and then. Perhaps, also by luck, I was able to identify the perfect place for Travis and me to gain eyes on the target area for as long as we needed. Better yet, I also identified the best insertion and extraction routes, yes, routes.....because two is one and one is none!

The entire time Maggie and I were rolling through the village, Steve and Mike were up on a ridgeline acting as over watch—listening to any chatter from the village that would alert us to the fact that we had been compromised. If that happened, Maggie and I were to immediately exit the village and suspend any attempts at surveillance for a few days. We would also know we were, without a doubt, looking in the right spot.

Later that evening, Travis and I inserted under cover of darkness and ended up surveilling the compound for a solid 24 hours. We hunkered down in this tiny little church the size of a one-car garage. Here, we stayed just outside the perimeter of the target compound and had a commanding view of all the comings and goings. Each of us wore night-vision goggles. We also set up and pointed Infra-Red (IR) illuminators at the area to light up targets so we could capture images with the night-vision cameras.

As it turned out, nothing exciting went down. But we were able to identify some potential players as well as one very strong person of interest (POI) in the poaching profession—someone we had seen on our hidden sunglass cameras. He was a known elephant and meat poacher. Needless to say, we added the compound to our immediate hit list and made plans to take it down in the very near future. When I say *very near future* I meant the next night.

Maggie, Steve and Mike extracted Travis and I precisely at 0230 hours, right at the end of Hour 24. Then they shared the details of a coordinated plan they had concocted, which would take place at 10 a.m. and involve our group and the rangers.

Once Travis and I approved and improved the mission details, we briefed big Eric and the rest of his ranger team on the mission's nuances: We were to roll up in four Land Cruisers and block all points of exit from the area. Simultaneously, a fifth vehicle, which I would drive and would contain Travis and Eric, would pull right up through the front gate—with ramming force if necessary—after a delivery boy gained entry. Steve, Mike and Brian would already be in position, maintaining a quick-reaction distance. They would use the Wolfhounds to monitor for chatter and ensure we weren't compromised. If all went according to plan, the whole operation would take less than five minutes and we would have a strong lead on the poaching cell—one that might lead to the complete shutdown of poaching in the region for some time to come. Despite our exhaustion and hunger, we were pumped and ready to roll out.

Not surprisingly, the whole operation went according to plan. Before we knew it, I was piloting the Cruiser—unopposed and at a high rate of speed—through the compound gates and right up to the door of the structure we knew was occupied by our POI. With the Cruiser barely in park, and still running, we leapt from it and sprung to the door. Well, I lumbered. Travis and Eric sprung.

Eric used his entire 6'7", 365-pound body to smash down the door. Travis and I stormed in, ready for any necessarily violence. I went first, and spotted our man—looking horrified and nearly pissing himself—on the coach in the main room. As planned, Eric flooded into the sleeping room, ensuring it was clear. We were the fucking brute squad, to be sure. Our combined bodyweight was over 800 pounds. Our POI was, maybe, 140 pounds. Travis and I snatched him up with little effort while simultaneously telling Eric to take point again and head back to the Cruiser.

We followed Eric through the shattered doorway. Our POI's feet never touched the ground as we rushed him to the Cruiser. It all must have looked quite comical with my left hand grabbing him by his neck and my right hand firmly grasping his nut sack. Yes, I had him by the sack with my right hand. Travis had a right hand on the guy's belt and his left arm wrapped around the POI's left arm in a quasi rear-arm bar.

Initially, the POI's feet were flailing around in cartoon-like fashion. But he soon realized that his movements were causing him to lose his balls and left arm to these two white gorillas who were being led by Eric, the Kenyan King Kong! He was in obvious pain. Within two minutes, the POI was tossed into the back of the Cruiser and into the custody of Moses and Mwambiti, our go-to guys. We collectively left the area in under four minutes. We were very much under the budget

UNDAUNTED

on time, and that was a good thing. You never want to go over on time, especially when you are unarmed. Yes, we had only brought knives to a potential gunfight. Knowing this, we utilized another very effective form of cover: Speed.

The POI proved useful. We were able to extract a metric shit ton of information from him—so much that we were able to parlay it into a few other successful operations that netted us both people and product. In this case: IVORY!

Travis and I spent a lot of time patrolling the sanctuary with Eric and his stellar group of Wildlife Works Rangers. We would even respond to other rangers' calls when they would come upon a poacher, a poacher's vehicle, or the remnants of a poacher's handiwork. About halfway through one of these clean-up missions, Maggie caught sight of a couple poachers in the bush, heading toward the road of a nearby town. She gave us the coordinates to Sector 11 and we immediately set an intercept course. They were very near Taita Village, and Travis and I had no intentions of letting these assholes get away.

When we finally reached Sector 11, we saw them—two men strolling casually out from the sanctuary carrying what looked to be weapons. Not caring to move slow or deliberate, we began hauling ass up to them in the Land Cruiser. The two spotted us immediately and began running, weaving in and out of the bush, and in and out of our line of sight. Travis and I got close enough, then leapt out of the Cruiser and began to sprint after them. As Murphy's Law would have it, I had a partially torn hamstring, so I wasn't able to hit full speed. Of course I tore it even more, but I still managed to stay on line with Travis. I guess my 6" stride advantage was to thank for that. Travis was really pouring it on and I could not let him down by lagging behind. It was never a good idea to lose sight of your swim buddy, and I wasn't about to start that today. Travis later told me that he knew I would be able to keep up because he was aware that I had made it through BUD/S with a torn abdominal wall and pelvic floor. Regardless, my right hamstring felt like it had a knife through it and into the back of my femur bone. A few days later, I had bruising from above my knee all the way down to my ankle.

I did the last three weeks of Africa on a bag of Motrin too! I'm like the Ibuprofen poster child....LOL!

We chased the guys into Taita Village, another small town known for harboring poachers. The guys were flying through the place and we were hauling ass right behind them. Travis and I were jumping over fences, climbing up and over walls, and trying to close the gap between us and the bad guys. Every once in a while we'd lose sight of them and have to start looking inside and behind buildings. They were slippery bastards and they obviously knew the area way better than we did. After we lost them for a third time, we decided to call in Maggie for air support and the KWS for weapons support and for additional boots on the ground for our search. If these guys were armed, there was only so much I was going to be able to do with my Winkler Tomahawk and knife.

After poking around, we found the red shirt one of the men was wearing. That meant he had changed clothes in the village—he was close. We were not sure about the other man. He was last seen wearing black pants and a white and blue shirt. Maggie and KWS indicated that there were no 'squirters' from the village, and I did not observe any suspicious movement from my assumed overwatch position in the village tower. Yeah, climbing up that tower was total bitch and I don't recommend it on a torn hamstring. But sometimes, you just have to do what you have to do.

Eventually, we caught up to one guy. We pointed him out to KWS as he was hiding in broad daylight amongst shoppers at the roadside market there. He figured if he placed a ball cap on that we would not recognize him. But his outfit gave him away. KWS brought him down and took him into custody. The other guy got away, but at least we had one of our men. KWS whisked him away for questioning and, to be certain, that guy was going to have a very painful afternoon and evening. The KWS does not play around with poachers.

This was a good day. We really felt like we made a difference. Better yet, the score was definitely moving toward a win for the home team. We needed it, so did Mike Korchinsky, so did Kenya, and so did the elephants!

All in all, making *Ivory Wars* and spending nearly two months at Wildlife Works' Rukinga Wildlife Sanctuary in Kenya was an amazing project. It was tangible. It was visceral. It was critical. And by the end of my stay, it was personal! We could see that we were making a difference. You go on an operation in the SEALs or Blackwater and don't always see the immediate results. But in this case, you saw the ball cross over the goal line each day. You called the play and you ran with that ball. Seeing these types of immediate results is very addicting and you don't always get that gift in business or in war. Needless to say, we all learned a lot from the rangers and I believe they learned a number of very important things from us. Later, Eric told me that his favorite lesson from me was: "Before you head out into the field, you need to square your shit away! You never know when or where or in what form, good advice may come, but when it does, you should heed it. Sometimes, you're only as good as your last buddy check!"

In total, we recovered four ivory tusks valued at more than a million dollars. We caught six poachers and put a complete stop to poaching in that area for the following six months after we were gone. Word got around that there were two big white dudes with helicopters and vehicles coming after you, so poachers laid low for a while and stayed away. We also caught two meat poachers, which set that group on its heels. It was this cascade effect of making a big difference in Kenya, which was very satisfying. Just as important, the world got to see what we did when *Ivory Wars* debuted on Animal Planet in November 2014. The show aired after a Yao Ming documentary, and together, both programs helped shine a light on what was happening in Kenya and introduced the world to the efforts of Yao Ming, myself and Travis, as well as Wildlife Works and all the good they are doing.

I returned home from Africa with a completely different perspective of the world. This wasn't like the military missions I'd previously been on. It was something different, something more primal, even more emotional, and certainly even more moral. I came to recognize the simple fact that if elephant poaching isn't severely mitigated, there will be no elephants left in Africa or the wild by the year 2025. The only remaining elephants will be in zoos. That was a big message I hope the shows conveyed to people. In fact, there needs to be a massive world outcry against the poaching of elephants and rhinos. And after my *Ivory Wars* efforts in Kenya, I cemented for myself, what I already knew: I could never hunt the BIG FIVE: Elephants, lions, rhinos, hippos or giraffes. And I'm a hunter! Hell, I'm not sure how I feel about elephants being held in zoos. For now, as long as they are given the ability to have family units, are respected and have the room to roam, it's not too horribly awful. All in all, making *Ivory Wars* gave me a new appreciation for elephants and the web of life associated with them and the people in that part of Kenya. Now: Don't get me started on Orcas!

CHAPTER 21

> "I WAS NEVER AFRAID OF FALLING, ONLY FAILING. BUT BEING AFRAID TO FAIL HAS NEVER STOPPED ME FROM DOING ANYTHING.....EVER!"
>
> —CHRISTOPHER MARK HEBEN

There are a few simple truths in this world: First, there will always be darkness to obscure your vision. Second, there will always be objects to block your path. It is because of these truths that at times it will feel like things are exploding all around you. In these moments, it's imperative to stay focused on your sights, yet to also stay in tune with your team and your peripheral environment. You must be aware of what's going on around you, as well as what your options are. When you are in the heat of battle, you also need to keep one more thing in mind: Make every round count.

Through it all, remember that as long as you are doing your best for your family, faith, community and country, you will prevail. We will all prevail. It's a team effort, and the better your team is the better off you'll be. I guess that's the moral of my story. Through all my travels, through all my trials and travails, and with all my ups and downs, I have remained undaunted in everything I've done in my life. And although I've surrounded myself with a pretty shit-hot support network that I know I can count on, I've also never forgotten how to count on myself. When I've fallen, I've lifted myself up. When I've faced obstacles, I've overcome them. And each time, I've come back just a little bit stronger

UNDAUNTED

than before. Mistakes are experience, and experience is wisdom. Although I have enough wisdom to fill the span of 10 people's lives, I'm also wise enough to know that I still don't know shit.

To be certain, things aren't always as sharply defined as we would like them to be. In our lives, there will be many moments when we lack clarity and struggle to find the answers to our inner-most questions. But keep true to yourself and your mission statement and you will, no doubt, return to a sharp focus. If it seems like you are taking fire from all directions, and life delivers you a brutal front kick to the chest, remember to simply take a moment to bow your head, breathe deeply, and ask for some guidance and deliverance. Then promptly strap your helmet back on, grab your weapon, get the hell up and continue pushing forward.

Indeed, I choose to own everything in my past. In this way, I truly have the power to make new choices and be a leader, not a victim. You can't drive forward when you're always looking in the rearview mirror. This isn't easy, but then again, it's not supposed to be. You will never accomplish anything in life unless you are willing to get your hands dirty, your brain bruised, and your feet wet. Don't just jump in with two feet. Instead, latch on with both hands and strive to be a winner in the game of life, not just a witness to it.

That's what I did back in 2010 when, after coming off two years of felony probation and 2.5 years of being under the control of the Ohio State Medical Board, I woke up one day and decided to stop playing the Med Boards' idiotic game. I stopped the daily call-ins, which also halted the four-times-a-month mandatory urine testing. This forced the powers-that-be to not only look at but to listen to my case a lot more closely. I hired and promptly fired my attorney, then acted as my own counsel as I cross-examined my Medical Board-appointed compliance officer and, consequently, used the state's own evidence against them.

When I was done presenting my case before the 12-member Ohio State Medical board, I had accomplished what no other person had done in the last 20 years: I successfully accomplished having myself completely removed from underneath the auspice of their supervision, a situation that usually lasted between five and seven years. I took charge of that particular facet of my life. In doing so, I regained control of my entire existence. In fact, my compliance officer, Ms. B, was delighted when I won this unanimous decision.

Shortly thereafter, I started planning how to secure reinstatement of my medical license. I soon realized, however, that it would be a financial step backwards for me as I would be relegated to a set income amount—one that was also based upon my being hired by a hospital or physicians group as a Physician Assistant with a felony forgery on my record. This was a crime, I might add, that would not be a crime today due to the fact that PAs are licensed to prescribe drugs in all 50 U.S. States.

In the end however, and by choice, I never regained my Physician Assistant Certification. I still think about that license today, but I never miss the drudgery of daily patient care. Especially now with the Affordable Care Act in effect and the further bludgeoning of the practice of medicine via the implementation of the Electronic Medical Record. I believe it's all another form of control and the ability to ration medicine and food in the future. It's data mining. Now, combine that with GMO foods, and it all reminds me of a quote by Thomas Jefferson:

> *"If people let government decide what foods they eat and what medicines they take, their bodies will soon be in as sorry a state as are the souls of those who live under tyranny."*

Yet, I stay pretty current on my medical knowledge base, as it is still very intriguing to me. In fact, I feel my grasp of Naturopathic methods along with my knowledge of Western medicine allows for the perfect balance for healthy living.

But I digress: PA or not, that didn't stop me from becoming a media personality. It didn't stop me from founding and building several thriving businesses and navigating through the ups and downs of early entrepreneurship. And it didn't stop me from finally aligning my business ventures with my passions—putting music, SEAL Team Consulting, INVICTVS Media & Television Group (IMTG), and INVICTVS Group at the center of everything I was doing. A commitment to passion and to people!

Although these ardors and devotions each have a few lanes of travel—ranging from TV & Film consulting to singing, private security, security consulting, motivational speaking and professional development—I gravitated toward these last two areas as a way to help many others as efficiently as possible. Because of this, the SEAL Team Challenge was born. And it grew from these roots of fraternity, fidelity and fervency, and is now comprised of nine critical elements that are constantly being improved and updated for on-line consumption:

- The Warrior Mindset
- Leadership
- Goal Setting
- Overcoming Adversity
- Facing Fear
- Adapt & Change
- Teamwork
- Nutrition
- Fitness

There's a common theme among these elements—being bold and confident enough to ensure you're pushing your own buttons in life in order to get you where you wish to go. In some respects, we are just like an elevator—it will either take you up or take you down. I believe mediocrity is a disease, and those who think well, perform well, and don't let themselves become infected. Instead, they do something today to move their life forward tomorrow.

My experiences—good and bad—have led me to conclude that you must live your life by a code. Here are four tenets that are part of mine:
- Be CONSISTENT and do what others aren't willing to do.
- Have CONVICTION. If you want something, get up and go get it. No one is going to hand it to you.
- Be MENTALLY TOUGH. Your mind is the biggest mountain in front of you.
- Have PASSION. If nothing burns inside you, you need to sit down and re-evaluate what you're doing with your life. But like any fire,

if you don't let that passion out, let it breath, it will starve, smolder and die inside of you.

I think that through everything I've experienced and all of my acquired wisdom, I've remained consistent. Flaws and all, I always learn something about myself and use it to make myself and others better. The SEAL Team Challenge is the latest manifestation of that mantra.

I've never been one to act like a shrinking violet and hesitate to speak up for myself. I work on my mental acuity every day—a clear mind allows you to do anything you set yourself out to accomplish. I'm very passionate about all the things I'm doing now. It may have only been a few years since I was building—and then subsequently watching the collapse of—my medical device distribution business, but my current businesses are extremely vibrant. While I haven't been able to exclusively go back to what used to be Blackwater and once again be a private military contractor, I am accepting jobs that have placed me in some key overseas positions. Additionally, through the SEAL Team Challenge, I am definitely helping others succeed in their own personal missions. And although I'm not training police officers in street survival and active shooter response, as much, I was able to train a group of rangers in Kenya how to face down poachers armed with AK-47's, and come out alive.

The trade-offs have been interesting and no less important, but just in different ways. Because of this fact, the past few years have been some of the most satisfying times of my life—and a lot of it occurred after my fall from grace. I believe that the next chapter of my life—the next book—will be very different from this. But that doesn't mean I'm to be afraid of it. You shouldn't be afraid of your next story either. Rather, I say to be afraid of stagnation!

I can already see more changes on the immediate horizon: About two years ago, one of my buddies, Mike Lemire, introduced me to a Vietnam veteran who is now a very successful business man and entrepreneur: Mike Thompson. Mr. Thompson, or 'Mr. T' for short, owns a group of auto dealerships in Northeast Ohio, so he is close to home. Mike Lemire consulted with him on a few network marketing projects and had an idea for how we could work together. For several months, he and I had been discussing creating a motivational video series that we planned to call the 'Warrior Challenge'. Mike Lemire thought if we could get Mr. T on board we could kick-start the project and take it to market even faster. We pitched him the plan.

Being the consummate businessman that he is, Mr. T had an even bigger and better idea.

"I'd like to be involved, but I don't want to be an investor," he told us. "I'd like to be a part of it. Chris, I'd also like to make you the co-spokesperson for our dealerships. I want to launch a campaign on patriotism and have you and me on TV and on the forefront in some industry-leading commercials. I'd like to cause a positive paradigm shift in the auto-sales industry!"

That sounded pretty good. I had found success on television as an expert guest and documentary co-star, so this seemed like a great platform to continue to build both my brand and our brand. As part of the plan, we changed the name of our training idea to the "SEAL Team Challenge." We formed a new company called SEAL Team Consulting and developed and marketed a line of nutritional products, and training initiatives. We developed videos and workouts that people could follow to imbue energy and new strength in their bodies and lives. I started touring across the state of Ohio, as well as the entire U.S., doing motivational speaking, public speaking, and delivering corporate presentations in boardrooms and conference centers. People were eager for me to share the lessons I had learned as a SEAL, private contractor, medical professional, and yes, even a convicted felon. My message was clear: Anyone can overcome their personal obstacles and achieve success.

My personal takeaway is that if you are continuously flocking with seagulls, you will always find yourself pecking for scraps and begging for handouts. Instead, team up with eagles and sink your talons into the heart of any situation. Refuse to be beaten down by problems. Battle back and fight for your dreams. Abandon chance and embrace preparation and perspiration. Be undeterred in what you set out to do each day. As SEALs, in order to win any situation, we're taught to be chameleons, altering everything from gear, guns and clothing to language, customs and behaviors. The instructors hammer this home: Why am I doing this? Does it make sense? Can I duplicate it under stress? Or basically: Assess. Adjust. Dominate.

I even wrote a very poignant and powerfully patriotic song, aptly titled "Patriot." The song is about the price our soldiers and their families pay for the freedoms we all enjoy. It's about sacrifice, selflessness, and the overt and covert conflicts and suffering of soldiers, sailors, airmen, Marines and Coast Guard members and their families, who bear the burden of the freedoms so many take for granted. The song reflects my thoughts about life and this country I love. Over the last year, I have been invited to sing Patriot in stadiums, at festivals, and at sporting events throughout this great nation we all call home. Who could have thought this would have been possible? But it's all part of having vision to see what you want in life, believing in the vision, and putting together the team and the battle plan to do it! In essence: Become what is or you will surely become what is not!

One of the reasons why I became a Navy SEAL is that the water has always been a safe haven for me. Not only that, it's been a source of inspiration, a sanity break, and a place of respite and renewal. Besides my wonderful family, and my fellow Clevelanders, Lake Erie is one of the things I love the most about Ohio. Maybe that's something embedded deep in my DNA—I grew up around water—that I was compelled to become a Navy SEAL. It's probably also why, that no matter how many countries I have been to or brave new frontiers I explore, I always keep coming back to my roots. I've always been that way and I suspect that I always will.

There are few better feelings in life than having fun while inspiring and motivating people. Wherever I go and whenever I share my messages of overcoming adversity, maintaining hope and never giving up, people respond. It's important to help people succeed by focusing them on getting the most out of themselves. I like to call it *self-maximization*. Anyone can have self-motivation, but without self-maximization, oftentimes, it's just flailing and failing—just as I was doing before my entry into the Navy and completion of SEAL training.

Further, it's just as important to stress the message of building and being part of a solid team. Whenever I was building a team in the field I looked for a few things, including their military accomplishments, the schools they attended, their operational experience. I want to know whether people can navigate—on land and on the water. I want guys who can shoot—and not miss their targets. There's also a communication component. You need someone who can pick up a radio and make it work. In the field, the biggest asset you have is a radio because it represents your ability to call for assistance, to call in your team of force multipliers. Or, as I like to say: Your extended family of ass-kickery. And you can't forget about resiliency—having someone who can finish something they set out to complete, no matter what shit they have to slog through. You need to understand how to follow a game plan, yet be able to recognize when it's time to change it. It's no different than building a team in the workplace—you want a group of people with skills that overlap a bit but one where each person still brings something special and unique to the table.

I'm proud to own my abject failures as well as my tremendous successes. Life demonstrates that everyone has flaws, and anyone can fall from a great height if they are not careful. It is what we do in these darkest of hours and afterwards that truly defines who we are as people. Even highly trained and disciplined individuals have flaws. They fall, and they get choke slammed in those dark hours. But, and there is always a but, what they do next truly defines them as a person and allows them to be labeled as a success or failure, a role model or miscreant, a hero or, yes, even a villain.

I'm truly bothered when I see people failing or refusing to live in the now. Whether or not it's caused by a cell phone, self-esteem, or self-centeredness, I have found that many people filter through life with their heads down. I encourage everyone to get unplugged, become uninhibited and less selfish. In other words: Get your head out of your ass and truly be in the moment. Just be there. You never know who or what you will find or who or what has found you. And you'll minimize your chances of becoming that villain and maximize your potential for becoming a hero. Self-maximization starts with self-actualization and that is preceded by the self-realization that you have to be, actually and fully, where you currently are. At the very least, it will let you know that where you currently are is not where you want to be. And that's as good a start as any.

I've learned a lot of lessons in my life. Work hard. Play hard. And don't be afraid to put in the hours to bring your dreams one step closer to reality. Ask any successful businessperson and they'll tell you that a late night at the office always signifies the start of another amazing week. The truly undaunted draw their continued strength from the many hardships they've overcome and the accomplishments they have effectuated through the stalwart application of disciplined efforts. I mentioned earlier the logo I created for my business. It's something of a metaphor for this philosophy. But it's also a euphemism for my life. Whatever difficulties any of us face on this Earth, it's important for us to press on, and carry ourselves onward and upward.

Always say goodbye to those you love, and always say goodnight. Always tell those around you what you feel—good, bad, or indifferent. In short, always know where you stand with those you care about, because you just never know if that will be the last time you see that person alive again. A person's eulogy is a very shitty place to tell that someone just how much you love them, so do it now.

In keeping with that: I love my country, and I'm proud to have served it as a U.S Navy SEAL. I had a dude come up to me in a bar not too long ago and the first thing he said to me was, "Thank you for your service. I was a Marine, but I only served for four years."

I immediately told him, "Thank you, but if I ever hear you say those other words again, I'll beat your ass!"

I went on to tell him that he did, in four years, what 99.5 percent of Americans never do: He served his nation. We need to all continue to thank those who step into the ranks of that .5 percent every year. And, as a nation, may we always be a source of light and hope for the entire planet. May we celebrate life, liberty, and the pursuit of happiness while continuing to lead in the relentless pursuit of all people across the globe who threaten that. America, indeed, is undaunted. It always has been and I pray it always will be. But if not for the continued efforts of that .5 percent, however, it won't be.

Today, my life is rich and fulfilled. I have a wonderful son, great friends, and amazing business partners. Additionally, I am in love and in lust with a beautiful lady who mirrors my passions and with that, gives me the added strength every day to be the best I can be for my family, faith, community and country. Her presence in my world can only be described as indescribable, for continued words would only be a futile attempt to lend human descriptors to an angelic and heavenly soul. Because of the strength of our bond, I'm able to further make a difference in people's lives by speaking and sharing my insight with them. I want to inspire people to do what I've done—look deep inside, see what could be, and then make adjustments in order to make that vision a reality. I'm even creating new international business alliances, including bringing the number one German manufacturer of holistic health, nutrition and cosmetic products to the U.S. and, thus, to an entirely new and deserving audience. These are very different times than they were just a few short years ago, but they're just as exciting. I wouldn't change any of it. That is what being undaunted is really about: Accepting the past, learning from it, and using it as a new baseline of self-maximization.

And then, just when you think things are looking better than they have in years and you are back in the driver's seat, you put the truck in park, get out, and take a bullet to the gut. But that is another story best saved for another time, soon.

The end....for now

About the Authors

Christopher Mark Heben is a retired U.S. Navy SEAL with more than 15 years of combined Naval Special Operations Command (NAVSOC) and Joint Special Operations Command (JSOC)/Department of State (DoS) field experience as a private military contractor (PMC). Chris was assigned to SEAL Team Eight for five years before being attached to a SEAL Reserve Unit while deploying as a PMC.

After leaving the U.S. Navy, Chris earned a Master's Degree in Physician Assistant Studies from the University of Nebraska Medical Center, graduating with high honors in Orthopedic Surgery, Sports Medicine and Emergency Medicine concentrations. He worked for Blackwater USA as a section leader in the firm's WPPS Mobile Dignitary Protection Program. Additionally, he operated within Blackwater's elite Select Activities Division. Chris was also Blackwater's Director of Medical Operations for the Joint Special Operations Aviation Detachment (JSAOD) command structures. Chris' collective field experiences as a military and paramilitary operator include operations in the Middle East, Eastern Europe, and Africa. Chris is the founder of INVICTVS Group and SEAL Team Consulting, where as a civilian consultant, he has worked with the FBI HRT Teams, and numerous state law enforcement SWAT teams on tactical and covert skill sets.

He is a well-known TV personality and has appeared on national and international TV news networks as a Special Forces subject matter expert. Chris has also appeared, starred in, or done voice-over work for several TV documentaries and series, including *Ivory Wars, Secrets of SEAL Team Six, Ridge Reaper, America's Book of Secrets: Black Ops*, and *Wikileaks; Secrets And Lies*.

Dustin S. Klein is an award-winning journalist, bestselling author of five books and the publisher of *Smart Business* magazine, a national chain of management journals for senior executives. Dustin is a former news reporter and business editor, as well as noted speaker on innovation, entrepreneurship and the art of storytelling. He has interviewed thousands of business, civic and military leaders, and helped more than a dozen entrepreneurs transform their ideas into books, including as co-author and editor of the Amazon #1 bestseller,

The Benevolent Dictator, and co-author of the Amazon bestseller, *The Unexpected*. He lives in Shaker Heights, Ohio, with his wife, Laura, and children, Sam, Cole and Mollie.